HUMAN BEHAVIOR
AND THE
ENVIRONMENT

Y0-EDZ-172

HUMAN BEHAVIOR AND THE ENVIRONMENT: Interactions between Man and His Physical World

edited by

JOHN H. SIMS
George Williams College

DUANE D. BAUMANN
Southern Illinois University

Maaroufa Press, inc.
Chicago

Maaroufa Press Geography Series
Eric Moore, Advisory Editor

Copyright © 1974 by Maaroufa Press, Inc.
All rights reserved
Library of Congress Catalog Number: 73–89450
ISBN: 0-88425-002-4
Designed by Vito De Pinto
FIRST IMPRESSION
Cover Photo by Lew Harding
Manufactured in the United States of America

IUPUI
UNIVERSITY LIBRARIES
COLUMBUS CENTER
COLUMBUS, IN 47201

TO GILBERT F. WHITE,
shepherd of an
interdisciplinary flock

The editors express their
appreciation to Nancy Simkowski
for her editorial assistance and
review and evaluation of the literature,
to Tom Nieman for his comments
on selected studies, and to Evie Righter
for her generous and knowing
attention to the endless details of
preparing a manuscript.

contents

List of Contributors

Robert L. A. Adams Department of Geography,
University of New Hampshire

Stuart Albert Graduate Center,
City University of New York

Duane D. Baumann Department of Geography,
Southern Illinois University

Ian Burton Department of Geography,
University of Toronto

James M. Dabbs, Jr. Department of Psychology,
Georgia State University

Fred Davis Junior Medical Student,
Baylor University College of Medicine

Marc Fried Laboratory of Psychosocial Studies,
Boston College

Peggy Gleicher Organization for Social and Technical Innovation,
Newton, Massachusetts

Wayne Harberson Department of Psychology,
University of Houston

A. B. Hollingshead Social Science Research Center,
University of Puerto Rico

Ray Hyman Department of Psychology,
University of Oregon

Robert W. Kates Department of Geography,
Clark University

Stanley Milgram Department of Psychology,
The City University of New York

Lewis W. Moncrief Recreation Research and Planning Unit,
Michigan State University

Robert L. Munroe Department of Anthropology,
Pitzer College

Ruth H. Munroe Department of Anthropology,
Pitzer College

Thomas F. O'Dea Department of Psychology,
University of California, Santa Barbara

Alex D. Pokorny Psychiatry and Neurology Services,
Veterans' Administration Hospital, Houston

L. H. Rogler Social Science Research Center,
University of Puerto Rico

Irving Rosow Langley Porter Institute,
San Francisco

Thomas F. Saarinen Department of Geography,
University of Arizona

W. R. Derrick Sewell Departments of Economics and Geography,
University of Victoria

John H. Sims Department of Psychology and Human
Development,
George Williams College

Daniel Stokols Program on Social Ecology,
University of California, Irvine

Yi-Fu Tuan Department of Geography,
University of Minnesota

Evon Z. Vogt Department of Psychology,
Harvard University

Lynn White, Jr. Department of History,
University of California

Introduction

MULTI-DIMENSIONAL MAN AND HIS ENVIRONMENT

by John H. Sims
and Duane D. Baumann

The student who reads this book is someone who cares about the quality of the relationship between man and his physical environment. We, the editors, also care. And these readings have been assembled and commented upon to demonstrate our conviction that if such concern is to end in more than impotent idealism, it must be informed.

Many, perhaps most environmentalists have a patch of ignorance over one eye; they focus clearly only on the latter term of the man-environment equation. In a recent lecture series at a major university entitled "Man and His Environment," thirteen presentations dealt with various aspects of the environment ranging from pesticide metabolism in soils to the effect of water pollution on the guidance system of migrating salmon; one lecturer alone spoke on man. To emphasize this point, we note the co-sponsorship of this very worthy program of public lectures by the departments of Botany, Geography, Zoology, and Agriculture. Those sciences most obviously concerned with *man's* behavior—psychology, sociology, anthropology, and political science—are conspicuous by their absence. It is certain they were not unwilling to participate; rather, they were uninvited.

Why? They simply were not seen as relevant. Why not? That question is a tougher one, and demands a somewhat roundabout answer. We begin it with a true story. One of the editors, a psychologist, was invited by a world famous scholar to attend his graduate seminar in geography to present some research he had participated in on how Great Plains wheat farmers face natural hazards such as crop-destroying drought and storms.

One of the data gathering techniques used in this study was the Thematic Apperception Test (TAT). Simply put, this is a test in which a somewhat ambiguous stimulus (in this case photographs of farmers working in fields under differing weather conditions) is presented to a subject and he is asked to tell a story about it; to tell what's going on in the picture, what led up to it, and how it will turn out. To the extent that the picture is ambiguous, the subject's story is not determined by it but by his own psychology. That is, he projects a part of himself into the story. With carefully chosen stimulus pictures and with skilled, experienced analysts, one can learn a lot about a person and how he views the world from such data.

All this was explained at the seminar and the psychologist

3

began to present his findings—how, for example, the kind of response a farmer made to a storm threatening his wheat harvest was related to his conception of God's role in the world of men; whether for instance, he believed man should suffer and endure the Almighty's incomprehensible will, or whether he was convinced that God helps those who help themselves.

Suddenly the lecturer faltered, he'd become aware of the faces of his listeners: some were smiling indulgently, others were sneering scornfully, and perhaps worst of all, some wore looks of impatient boredom. Alarmed, the psychologist stopped and invited questions. It was like going before a firing squad: what made him think the test was valid, how did he know the farmers weren't lying in their stories? Why hadn't he simply asked the farmers what he wanted to know, why this ridiculously circuitous route to find out the obvious? What did a fictional story have to do with real-life behavior?

Now, all these questions about the TAT are quite legitimate. Indeed, they are asked continuously by psychologists who work with projective tests. They also have answers—long, complicated ones based, as in any discipline, on experience with the test and knowledge of the relevant research. Furthermore, those answers are not entirely satisfactory—many problems remain unsolved with such tests, even after many years of work. An appreciative skepticism is a reasonable point of view.

But it was clear that something quite different from skepticism was at work here. The vehemence of the attack, the unwillingness to hear a reply, the abandonment of reason and logic, indeed of courtesy, made it clear that, albeit unwittingly, the research presentation had touched on something which was profoundly disturbing to them. In effect, the lecturer had committed a double sin. First and foremost, he had suggested that there were inner forces of which man was unaware and over which he had no control which played a role in determining his behavior. Second, the lecturer had compounded this, had added insult to injury, by suggesting that while these forces were unknown to the subjects, they could be made known to him.

Outrage at such suggestions is not new; there is the well-known statement made by Freud in 1917 in which he speaks of the malevolent opposition to the idea of the role of the unconscious in mental life:

> Humanity has in the course of time had to endure from the hands of science two great outrages upon its naive self-love. The first was when it realized that our earth was not the centre of the universe, but only a tiny speck in a world-system of a magnitude hardly conceivable; this is associated in our minds with the name of Copernicus, although Alexandrian doctrines taught something very similar. The second was when biological research robbed man of his peculiar privilege of having been specially created, and relegated him to a descent from the animal world, implying an ineradicable animal nature in him: this transvaluation has been accomplished in our own time upon the instigation of Charles Darwin, Wallace, and their predecessors, and not without the most violent opposition from their contemporaries. But man's craving for grandiosity is now suffering the third and most bitter blow from present-day psychological research which is endeavouring to prove to the "ego" of each one of us that he is not even master in his own house . . . *(1)*

That Freud met with such resistance in the early 20's is, of course, well-known. That currently many persons, the relatively uneducated, members of the older generations, for example, do not comprehend or use the concept of unconscious dynamic forces is also understandable. But to encounter fierce antagonism to the idea of an unconscious among the faculty and graduate students of a major university in an age in which the culture is permeated, indeed saturated with psychological-mindedness, is shocking and emphasizes the intensity of the fear evoked by the idea of not being fully in control of oneself and the consequent tenacity with which the model of man as a wholly rational animal is held.

Lest the quotation from Freud be misleading, we should add that we are not talking about a resistance to Freudian psychoanalytic theory per se, but to a more basic idea which is at the very heart of psychological thought—namely, a particular model of man. What is it? It is difficult to give it a name, perhaps the phrase "multi-motivated man" captures some of it. That is, man's behavior results from an interaction between physical and psychological givens and the social and cultural institutions which make an individual a member of a given society. Further, that while a man thus embodies biological, psychological and social forces, he is not fully aware of their operation within him.

Does this mean that psychology rejects man's rationality? Clearly not; to do so would preclude its own existence. And indeed, Freud himself can truly be seen as the last great contributor to the tradition of rationalism, for it was he who strove mightily to bring into the realm of man's understanding, the non-rational in man's mental life. But it does mean that psychology has rejected absolutely and forever the model of a wholly rational man whose behavior results solely from a logical appraisal of available knowledge.

Yet it is just this model of rational man that is encountered over and over again in work done in the man-environment area—be it research by scholars, legislation by elected officials, or action programs by alarmed citizens. We've already reported meeting it in the lecture hall; let us give another first-hand example from our own research.

Both editors have long been involved in an extensive cross-cultural study of man's response to natural hazards—tornadoes, floods, earthquakes, drought, etc., directed by three eminent (and, by the way, psychologically sophisticated) geographers (2). The first aim of the study was to find out what people actually do about a natural hazard, say a flood or a hurricane, before, during, and after its occurrence. The second aim was to explore possible "explanatory variables," that is, to attempt to identify factors which might explain the differences in hazard behavior between individuals and groups. It was in the selection of these factors, since only a few of those theoretically possible could be practically considered, that the model of man being used by the investigators was revealed.

The first of these factors was hazard *experience;* that is, for example, does it make a difference as to what one does or will do about a hurricane if one has been through a hurricane before. A second factor was the *probability* of a hazard's occurrence; that is, does it make a difference in what one will do about hurricanes if the likelihood of their occurring is high. A third factor was the extent of *economic investment;* that is, does how much one has to lose in property, say, crops or buildings, make a difference in how one perceives the threat of a hurricane.

Who can deny that these three factors appear immediately reasonable as possible explanations for differences in hazard behavior. They are however, also, all predicated on the rational model of man. That is, these choices of possible "reasons" for how man responds to a natural hazard rest on the assumption that such behavior is rational. Thus, underlying the inquiry into previous experience with a hazard is the expectation that man learns from experience and improves his adaptation to the hazard's recurrence. *This*, despite the notorious facts that before the lava cools or the flood waters fully recede, people are back on the volcano's slope and the river's edge, rebuilding. Again, it is the view of man as rational that gives rise to the expectation that he will estimate the probability of a hazard occurrence, the possible extent of its damage, arrive at a risk quotient, balance his potential loss against that of the investment required for protection, and behave accordingly. *This*, despite the fact that research has shown time after time that people have a very difficult time weighing and combining information to arrive at probabilities; that to reduce the strain of problem-solving they will resort to simplified decision strategies which lead them to ignore relevant information; that the value a man places on an event will influence its perceived probability; and that few decisions are preceded by deliberate thought but are rather habitual actions. Finally, it is the view of man as rational that leads to the expectation that how much he had to lose, or had lost, economically, will determine what he would or would not do. *This*, though people will run into a flaming house to save a photograph of a loved one while their "valuables" burn.

Are we then, saying that investigation into these areas constituted research mistakes? No. The arguments cited against them are not decisive. There is evidence that, even with the weaknesses pointed out, such factors are often at work in effecting hazard behaviors. They are certainly worth investigating. But, while they are not research errors, they are research *preferences*. With limited resources there are only so many factors that can be investigated, and for each one included you pay the price of another which is excluded. Thus, the focus on these aspects of man's rationality betrays a judgment that they are more important in understanding hazard behavior than are those factors of personality, society and culture which *limit* rational action.

The concept of man as wholly rational is closely associated with another model of man, equally naive and perhaps even more pernicious in its long-range effects on the chances of improving the relationship between man and his physical environment. The associating logic runs as follows: Since man is rational, when the error of his ecological ways is pointed out to him, he will change his behavior and stop doing that which is immediately harmful to the environment and eventually harmful to mankind. Not to do so must be interpreted as at best, willfully contrary and perverse, and at worst, as immoral and evil. Thus, mankind is divided in two—the unreasonable bad guys and the reasonable good guys.

We do not dispute the realities of selfishness and avarice as well as those of generosity and concern for others. But it is simplistic to assign such characteristics on the basis of whether or not a man behaves in a manner which *we* judge to be reasonable. And it is too easy to see the moral world in only black and white. Yet such a concept of man has become extended, like the rings in a pool caused by a tossed pebble, to encompass larger and larger groups of men and their activities. Anger at the management of a manufacturing plant for its methods of waste disposal leads to disillusionment with industry and soon all economic and technological development is condemned as inimical to man's well-being. The finger of accusation points to corporate greed. The argument is equally absurd when run the other way: all technological and economic development must be left unchecked and unhampered for it is only through increased productivity that the quality of life is enhanced. Those who oppose such unbridled exploitation are ridiculed as soft-headed do-gooders.

In the literature and action programs dealing with man and his environment, one encounters such arguments in many forms. When exaggerated as above, they are easily seen through and dismissed. But more subtle versions of them often lurk beneath the surface as unstated assumptions and seduce us into agreement. After all, we are willing victims, we *want* to cast others as villains and ourselves as heroes or as innocent bystanders. The search for scapegoats and the desire to absolve ourselves from responsibility are constants. How easy then, to prove our good intentions toward the earth by contributing to the wildlife fund, and how convenient to blame pollution on Commonwealth Edison and General Motors. But it is one thing to be for the snow leopard and the whooping crane; it is quite another to do without air conditioning or to leave the car at home and ride the bus.

If rational man and moral man are foolishly naive conceptions of human nature, we must also beware of that simplistic cynicism which, contemptuous of man's intellectual and ethical weakness, finds solutions to environmental problems only through social control. The law is indeed a force of enormous power in the regulation of man, but surely the past experience with Prohibition and the present experience with desegregation indicate the limits of legislation. To be viable, a law must correspond to some desire to obey in man: all cars must now have seat-belts, but how many of them are buckled?

The point we are making is this: man is not rational *or* arational, neither is he good *or* bad, and neither is he easily manipulated. If we are to begin to understand man's relationship with his environment, we must first begin to understand *him* in all his variety. No simple model of man will do. It is his complexity that must be acknowledged (*3*). The readings in this volume share that conviction. Written from a variety of professional perspectives—geography, psychology, psychiatry, sociology, anthropology—the authors all hold sophisticated conceptions of man. Equally important, the readings cover a wide range of environmental interactions, for any serious attempt to understand what is involved in the relationship between man and his physical world must go far beyond the currently fashionable problems of fighting pollution and saving the endangered species, however important they may be.

This book, then, has one overriding purpose—to convincingly demonstrate how intricate, complex and sometimes puzzling are the interactions between man and his environment, how varied, and how marvelous. And to argue that to move even an inch toward understanding such interactions, one must abandon the fictions of an exclusively rational or exclusively moral man, and replace such simplifications with a concept of man that while acknowledging both his reason and his morality acknowledges, at the same time, the limits upon his rational and ethical behavior which arise from his personality, his society, and his culture. In doing this, we have no wish to, Hamletlike, paralyze action with thought. Rather, it is our hope to arm the student's environmental concerns with knowledge rather than opinion, and with judgment rather than prejudice. It is our conviction that bettering man's relations with this environment demands *informed* passion.

Toward these ends we have selected the eighteen papers which constitute Parts One and Two of this book. They are organized very simply: Part One presents ten chapters which show how some particular psychological dimension is related to how a man perceives, or responds to, or modifies some particular aspect of his physical environment. For example, one chapter argues that it is the Judeo-Christian conception of man as lord of the earth that has led to the exploitation of the environment. Another examines how belief in fate, God, and luck is related to how one behaves when threatened by a tornado. A third shows how the credibility of bad weather forecasts varies with how committed one is to going to the beach.

Part Two reverses this logic with eight chapters which show how some particular aspects of the physical environment are related to man's psychological status. For example, one chapter suggests that sex differences in spatial ability are not innate but are due to differences in how boys and girls are allowed to explore their environments. Another shows how belief in water witching varies with the aridity of the region lived in. A third investigates the effect of weather conditions on suicide.

Before each chapter we present our comments concerning its significance with respect to what we have said here, emphasizing the complex and intricate factors that affect both man's utilization of and adaptation to this environment.

The papers in this book were chosen with several ends in mind. First, the paper either provides a succinct overview of a general question in the man-environment equation, or the paper presents empirical data relevant to a specific facet of man-environment interaction. Consequently, the reader can share in both the more general, overriding man-environment questions, as well as in the frequently frustrating struggle over the interpretation of the findings of a specific study.

Another criterion for selecting a paper for this book was that it be readable. Unfortunately, many scholarly papers, because of a specialized jargon can be readily understood only by the author's professional peers. Our effort was to choose papers which avoided this stylistic pitfall so that they can be read with ease by the interested student.

And finally, we include only those papers which recognize man as a creature of infinite variety—greedy and generous, rational and magic-riddled, self-centered and considerate, conscious and unaware, innocent and guilty—but never easily understood.

NOTES

1. S. Freud, *A General Introduction to Psychoanalysis* (New York: Washington Square Press, 1966), p. 296.
2. Natural Hazards Research, a program funded by the National Science Foundation in a grant to Toronto, Clark, and Colorado universities; the program is directed by Ian Burton, Robert W. Kates, and Gilbert F. White.
3. Lest we be misunderstood, we should perhaps add that we certainly claim no originality for our emphasis here. The encouraging fact of a rapidly growing literature from which the readings in this volume were chosen testifies to the increasing acknowledgment by some scholars in some fields of the necessity for a complex model of man in studying his interactions with the environment. The interested reader might see Kenneth H. Craik's recent comprehensive review for an introduction to their work. ("Environmental Psychology," *Annual Review of Psychology* 24 (1973): 403–422.) Nevertheless, it unfortunately is still true that a psychologically sophisticated perspective on man-environment relationships remains relatively rare.

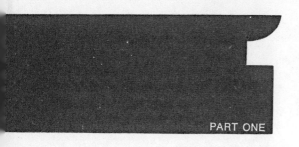

PART ONE

MAN AS MANIPULATOR OF HIS ENVIRONMENT

CHAPTER

The Historical Roots
of Our Ecologic Crisis

LYNN WHITE, JR.

Reprinted from *Science* 155
(10 March 1967): 1203–7, by permission
of the American Association for the
Advancement of Science and the author.
Copyright 1967 by the American
Association for the Advancement of
Science.
    This is the text of a lecture
delivered 26 December 1966 at the
Washington meeting of the American
Association for the Advancement of
Science.

White believes that man's relationship with the environment is importantly determined by his beliefs about his own nature, the physical world, and destiny—that is, by his religion. It is White's position that modern man's ruthless exploitation of the environment must be understood in terms of the Judeo-Christian tradition that man, created in God's image, holds dominion over all other living creatures, the lands, and the seas; all was created for man's benefit and rule. And he argues that "we shall continue to have a worsening ecologic crisis until we reject the Christian axiom that nature has no reason for existence save to serve man."

Implicit in White's logic is the idea that, compared to other religions such as those of the Orient, Christianity uniquely facilitates the indiscriminate exploitation of natural resources. But objections to this argument are obvious: currently, where is industrialism more rapacious than in non-Christian Japan; and historically, White himself cites important pre-Christian examples of human environmental modification, such as the fire-drive method of hunting used by prehistoric man. The chapters to follow by Moncrief and Tuan present such objections in detail.

Nevertheless, the essence of White's position remains viable and tantalizing. For, even if not uniquely associated with environmental exploitation, the Christian doctrine of man *over nature* can be seen as especially hospitable to, even encouraging of, such usage. And it is so in contrast to other possible religious conceptions of the proper relationship between man and the physical world. For example, the doctrine of animism, whereby *all* natural phenomena are believed to possess souls, would appear to inhibit environmental damage.

But the importance of White's paper does not rest upon the issue of whether he is right or wrong. Its general aim is achieved by making us aware of the relevance of ideology to the environmental crisis, by convincing us that the most spiritual of considerations may have the most practical of consequences.

A conversation with Aldous Huxley not infrequently put one at the receiving end of an unforgettable monologue. About a year before his lamented death he was discoursing on a favorite topic: Man's unnatural treatment of nature and its sad results. To illustrate his point he told how, during the previous summer, he had returned to a little valley in England where he had spent many happy months as a child. Once it had been composed of delightful grassy glades; now it was becoming overgrown with unsightly brush because the rabbits that formerly kept such growth under control had largely succumbed to a disease, myxomatosis, that was deliberately introduced by the local farmers to reduce the rabbits' destruction of crops. Being something of a Philistine, I could be silent no longer, even in the interests of great rhetoric. I interrupted to point out that the rabbit itself had been brought as a domestic animal to England in 1176, presumably to improve the protein diet of the peasantry.

All forms of life modify their contexts. The most spectacular and benign instance is doubtless the coral polyp. By serving its own ends, it has created a vast undersea world favorable to thousands of other kinds of animals and plants. Ever since man became a numerous species he has affected his environment notably. The hypothesis that his fire-drive method of hunting created the world's great grasslands and helped to exterminate the monster mammals of the Pleistocene from much of the globe is plausible, if not proved. For 6 millennia at least, the banks of the lower Nile have been a human artifact rather than the swampy African jungle which nature, apart from man, would have made it. The Aswan Dam, flooding 5000 square miles, is only the latest stage in a long process. In many regions terracing or irrigation, overgrazing, the cutting of forests by Romans to build ships to fight Carthaginians or by Crusaders to solve the logistics problems of their expeditions, have profoundly changed some ecologies. Observation that the French landscape falls into two basic types, the open fields of the north and the *bocage* of the south and west, inspired Marc Bloch to undertake his classic study of medieval agricultural methods. Quite unintentionally, changes in human ways often affect non-human nature. It has been noted, for example, that the advent of the automobile eliminated huge flocks of sparrows that once fed on the horse manure littering every street.

The history of ecologic change is still so rudimentary that we know little about what really happened, or what the results were. The extinction of the European aurochs as late as 1627 would seem to have been a simple case of overenthusiastic hunting. On more intricate matters it often is impossible to find solid information.

For a thousand years or more the Frisians and Hollanders have been pushing back the North Sea, and the process is culminating in our own time in the reclamation of the Zuider Zee. What, if any, species of animals, birds, fish, shore life, or plants have died out in the process? In their epic combat with Neptune have the Netherlanders overlooked ecological values in such a way that the quality of human life in the Netherlands has suffered? I cannot discover that the questions have ever been asked, much less answered.

People, then, have often been a dynamic element in their own environment, but in the present state of historical scholarship we usually do not know exactly when, where, or with what effects man-induced changes came. As we enter the last third of the twentieth century, however, concern for the problem of ecologic backlash is mounting feverishly. Natural science, conceived as the effort to understand the nature of things, had flourished in several eras and among several peoples. Similarly there had been an age-old accumulation of technological skills, sometimes growing rapidly, sometimes slowly. But it was not until about four generations ago that Western Europe and North America arranged a marriage between science and technology, a union of the theoretical and the empirical approaches to our natural environment. The emergence in widespread practice of the Baconian creed that scientific knowledge means technological power over nature can scarcely be dated before about 1850, save in the chemical industries, where it is anticipated in the eighteenth century. Its acceptance as a normal pattern of action may mark the greatest event in human history since the invention of agriculture, and perhaps in nonhuman terrestrial history as well.

Almost at once the new situation forced the crystallization of the novel concept of ecology; indeed, the word *ecology* first appeared in the English language in 1873. Today, less than a century later, the impact of our race upon the environment has so increased in force that it has changed in essence. When the first cannons were fired, in the early fourteenth century, they affected ecology by sending workers scrambling to the forests and mountains for more potash, sulfur, iron ore, and charcoal, with some resulting erosion and deforestation. Hydrogen bombs are of a different order: a war fought with them might alter the genetics of all life on this planet. By 1285 London had a smog problem arising from the burning of soft coal, but our present combustion of fossil fuels threatens to change the chemistry of the globe's atmosphere as a whole, with consequences which we are only beginning to guess. With the population explosion, the carcinoma of planless urbanism, the now geological deposits of sewage and garbage, surely no creature other than man has ever managed to foul its nest in such short order.

There are many calls to action, but specific proposals, however worthy as individual items, seem too partial, palliative, negative: ban the bomb, tear down the billboards, give the Hindus contraceptives and tell them to eat their sacred cows. The simplest solution to any suspect change is, of course, to stop it, or, better yet, to revert to a romanticized past: make those ugly gasoline stations look like Anne Hathaway's cottage or (in the Far West) like ghost-town saloons. The "wilderness area" mentality invariably advocates deep-freezing an ecology, whether San Gimignano or the High Sierra, as it was before the first Kleenex was dropped. But neither atavism nor prettification will cope with the ecologic crisis of our time.

What shall we do? No one yet knows. Unless we think about fundamentals, our specific measures may produce new backlashes more serious than those they are designed to remedy.

As a beginning we should try to clarify our thinking by looking, in some historical depth, at the presuppositions that underlie modern technology and science. Science was traditionally aristocratic, speculative, intellectual in intent; technology was lower-class, empirical, action-oriented. The quite sudden fusion of these two, towards the middle of the nineteenth century, is surely related to the slightly prior and contemporary democratic revolutions which, by reducing social barriers, tended to assert a functional unity of brain and hand. Our ecologic crisis is the product of an emerging, entirely novel, democratic culture. The issue is whether a democratized world can survive its own implications. Presumably we cannot unless we rethink our axioms.

THE WESTERN TRADITIONS OF TECHNOLOGY AND SCIENCE

One thing is so certain that it seems stupid to verbalize it: both modern technology and modern science are distinctively *Occidental*. Our technology has absorbed elements from all over the world, notably from China; yet everywhere today, whether in Japan or in Nigeria, successful technology is Western. Our science is the heir to all the sciences of the past, especially perhaps to the work of the great Islamic scientists of the Middle Ages, who so often outdid the ancient Greeks in skill and perspicacity: al-Rāzī in medicine, for example; or ibn-al-Haytham in optics; or Omar Khayyám in mathematics. Indeed, not a few works of such geniuses seem to have vanished in the original Arabic and to survive only in medieval Latin translations that helped to lay the foundations for later

Western developments. Today, around the globe, all significant science is Western in style and method, whatever the pigmentation or language of the scientists.

A second pair of facts is less well recognized because they result from quite recent historical scholarship. The leadership of the West, both in technology and in science, is far older than the so-called Scientific Revolution of the seventeenth century or the so-called Industrial Revolution of the eighteenth century. These terms are in fact outmoded and obscure the true nature of what they try to describe—significant stages in two long and separate developments. By A.D. 1000 at the latest—and perhaps, feebly, as much as 200 years earlier—the West began to apply water power to industrial processes other than milling grain. This was followed in the late twelfth century by the harnessing of wind power. From simple beginnings, but with remarkable consistency of style, the West rapidly expanded its skills in the development of power machinery, labor-saving devices, and automation. Those who doubt should contemplate that most monumental achievement in the history of automation: the weight-driven mechanical clock, which appeared in two forms in the early fourteenth century. Not in craftsmanship but in basic technological capacity, the Latin West of the later Middle Ages far outstripped its elaborate, sophisticated, and esthetically magnificent sister cultures, Byzantium and Islam. In 1444 a great Greek ecclesiastic, Bessarion, who had gone to Italy, wrote a letter to a prince in Greece. He is amazed by the superiority of Western ships, arms, textiles, glass. But above all he is astonished by the spectacle of waterwheels sawing timbers and pumping the bellows of blast furnaces. Clearly, he had seen nothing of the sort in the Near East.

By the end of the fifteenth century the technological superiority of Europe was such that its small, mutually hostile nations could spill out over all the rest of the world, conquering, looting, and colonizing. The symbol of this technological superiority is the fact that Portugal, one of the weakest states of the Occident, was able to become, and to remain for a century, mistress of the East Indies. And we must remember that the technology of Vasco da Gama and Albuquerque was built by pure empiricism, drawing remarkably little support or inspiration from science.

In the present-day vernacular understanding, modern science is supposed to have begun in 1543, when both Copernicus and Vesalius published their great works. It is no derogation of their accomplishments, however, to point out that such structures as the *Fabrica* and the *De revolutionibus* do not appear overnight. The distinctive Western tradition of science, in fact, began in the late eleventh century with a massive movement of translation of Arabic and Greek scientific works into Latin. A few notable books—Theophrastus, for example—escaped the West's avid new appetite for science, but within less than 200 years effectively the entire corpus of Greek and Muslim science was available in Latin, and was being eagerly read and criticized in the new European universities. Out of criticism arose new observation, speculation, and increasing distrust of ancient authorities. By the late thirteenth century Europe had seized global scientific leadership from the faltering hands of Islam. It would be as absurd to deny the profound originality of Newton, Galileo, or Copernicus as to deny that of the fourteenth century scholastic scientists like Buridan or Oresme on whose work they built. Before the eleventh century, science scarcely existed in the Latin West, even in Roman times. From the eleventh century onward, the scientific sector of Occidental culture has increased in a steady crescendo.

Since both our technological and our scientific movements got their start, acquired their character, and achieved world dominance in the Middle Ages, it would seem that we cannot understand their nature or their present impact upon ecology without examining fundamental medieval assumptions and developments.

MEDIEVAL VIEW OF MAN AND NATURE

Until recently, agriculture has been the chief occupation even in "advanced" societies; hence, any change in methods of tillage has much importance. Early plows, drawn by two oxen, did not normally turn the sod but merely scratched it. Thus, cross-plowing was needed and fields tended to be squarish. In the fairly light soils and semiarid climates of the Near East and Mediterranean, this worked well. But such a plow was inappropriate to the wet climate and often sticky soils of northern Europe. By the latter part of the seventh century after Christ, however, following obscure beginnings, certain northern peasants were using an entirely new kind of plow, equipped with a vertical knife to cut the line of the furrow, a horizontal share to slice under the sod, and a moldboard to turn it over. The friction of this plow with the soil was so great that it normally required not two but eight oxen. It attacked the land with such violence that cross-plowing was not needed, and fields tended to be shaped in long strips.

In the days of the scratch-plow, fields were distributed generally in units capable of supporting a single family. Subsistence farming was the presupposition. But no peasant owned eight oxen: to use the new and more efficient plow, peasants pooled their oxen to form large plow-teams, originally receiving (it would appear) plowed strips in proportion to their contribution. Thus, distribution of land was based no longer on the needs of a family but, rather, on the capacity of a power machine to till the earth. Man's relation to the soil was profoundly changed. Formerly man had been part of nature; now he was the exploiter of nature. Nowhere else in the world did farmers develop any analogous agricultural implement. Is it coincidence that modern technology, with its ruthlessness toward nature, has so largely been produced by descendants of these peasants of northern Europe?

This same exploitive attitude appears slightly before A.D. 830 in Western illustrated calendars. In older calendars the months were shown as passive personifications. The new Frankish calendars, which set the style for the Middle Ages, are very different: they show men coercing the world around them—plowing, harvesting, chopping trees, butchering pigs. Man and nature are two things, and man is master.

These novelties seem to be in harmony with larger intellectual patterns. What people do about their ecology depends on what they think about themselves in relation to things around them. Human ecology is deeply conditioned by beliefs about our nature and destiny—that is, by religion. To Western eyes this is very evident in, say, India or Ceylon. It is equally true of ourselves and of our medieval ancestors.

The victory of Christianity over paganism was the greatest psychic revolution in the history of our culture. It has become fashionable today to say that, for better or worse, we live in "the post-Christian age." Certainly the forms of our thinking and language have largely ceased to be Christian, but to my eye the substance often remains amazingly akin to that of the past. Our daily habits of action, for example, are dominated by an implicit faith in perpetual progress which was unknown either to Greco-Roman antiquity or to the Orient. It is rooted in, and is indefensible apart from, Judeo-Christian teleology. The fact that Communists share it merely helps to show what can be demonstrated on many other grounds: that Marxism, like Islam, is a Judeo-Christian heresy. We continue today to live, as we have lived for about 1700 years, very largely in a context of Christian axioms.

What did Christianity tell people about their relations with the environment?

While many of the world's mythologies provide stories of creation, Greco-Roman mythology was singularly incoherent in this respect. Like Aristotle, the intellectuals of the ancient West denied that the visible world had had a beginning. Indeed, the idea of a beginning was impossible in the framework of their cyclical notion of time. In sharp contrast, Christianity inherited from Judaism not only a concept of time as nonrepetitive and linear but also a striking story of creation. By gradual stages a loving and all-powerful God had created light and darkness, the heavenly bodies, the earth and all its plants, animals, birds, and fishes. Finally, God had created Adam and, as an afterthought, Eve to keep man from being lonely. Man named all the animals, thus establishing his dominance over them. God planned all of this explicitly for man's benefit and rule: no item in the physical creation had any purpose save to serve man's purposes. And, although man's body is made of clay, he is not simply part of nature: he is made in God's image.

Especially in its Western form, Christianity is the most anthropocentric religion the world has seen. As early as the second century both Tertullian and Saint Irenaeus of Lyons were insisting that when God shaped Adam he was foreshadowing the image of the incarnate Christ, the Second Adam. Man shares, in great measure, God's transcendence of nature. Christianity, in absolute contrast to ancient paganism and Asia's religions (except, perhaps, Zoroastrianism), not only established a dualism of man and nature but also insisted that it is God's will that man exploit nature for his proper ends.

At the level of the common people this worked out in an interesting way. In Antiquity every tree, every spring, every stream, every hill had its own *genius loci*, its guardian spirit. These spirits were accessible to men, but were very unlike men; centaurs, fauns, and mermaids show their ambivalence. Before one cut a tree, mined a mountain, or dammed a brook, it was important to placate the spirit in charge of that particular situation, and to keep it placated. By destroying pagan animism, Christianity made it possible to exploit nature in a mood of indifference to the feelings of natural objects.

It is often said that for animism the Church substituted the cult of saints. True; but the cult of saints is functionally quite different from animism. The saint is not *in* natural objects; he may have special shrines, but his citizenship is in heaven. Moreover, a saint is entirely a man; he can be approached in human terms. In addition to saints, Christianity of course also had angels and demons inherited from Judaism and perhaps, at one remove, from Zoroastrianism. But these were all as mobile as the saints themselves. The spirits *in* natural objects, which formerly had protected nature from man, evaporated. Man's effective monopoly on spirit in this world was confirmed, and the old inhibitions to the exploitation of nature crumbled.

When one speaks in such sweeping terms, a note of caution is in order. Christianity is a complex faith, and its consequences differ in differing contexts. What I have said may well apply to the medieval West, where in fact technology made spectacular advances. But the Greek East, a highly civilized realm of equal Christian devotion, seems to have produced no marked technological innovation after the late seventh century, when Greek fire was invented. The key to the contrast may perhaps be found in a difference in the tonality of piety and thought which students of comparative theology find between the Greek and the Latin Churches. The Greeks believed that sin was intellectual blindness, and that salvation was found in illumination, orthodoxy—that is, clear thinking. The Latins, on the other hand, felt that sin was moral evil, and that salvation was to be found in right conduct. Eastern theology has been intellectualist. Western theology has been voluntarist. The Greek saint contemplates; the Western saint acts. The implications of Christianity for the conquest of nature would emerge more easily in the Western atmosphere.

The Christian dogma of creation, which is found in the first clause of all the Creeds, has another meaning for our comprehension of today's ecologic crisis. By revelation, God had given man the Bible, the Book of Scripture. But since God had made nature, nature also must reveal the divine mentality. The religious study of nature for the better understanding of God was known as natural theology. In the early Church, and always in the Greek East, nature was conceived primarily as a symbolic system through which God speaks to men: the ant is a sermon to sluggards; rising flames are the symbol of the soul's aspiration. This view of nature was essentially artistic rather than scientific. While Byzantium preserved and copied great numbers of ancient Greek scientific texts, science as we conceive it could scarcely flourish in such an ambience.

However, in the Latin West by the early thirteenth century natural theology was following a very different bent. It was ceasing to be the decoding of the physical symbols of God's communication with man and was becoming the effort to understand God's mind by discovering how his creation operates. The rainbow was no longer simply a symbol of hope first sent to Noah after the Deluge: Robert Grosseteste, Friar Roger Bacon, and Theodoric of Freiberg produced startlingly sophisticated work on the optics of the rainbow, but they did it as a venture in religious understanding. From the thirteenth century onward, up to and including Leibnitz and Newton, every major scientist, in effect, explained his motivations in religious terms. Indeed, if Galileo had not been so expert an amateur theologian he would have got into far less trouble: the professionals resented his intrusion. And Newton seems to have regarded himself more as a theologian than as a scientist. It was not until the late eighteenth century that the hypothesis of God became unnecessary to many scientists.

It is often hard for the historian to judge, when men explain why they are doing what they want to do, whether they are offering real reasons or merely culturally acceptable reasons. The consistency with which scientists during the long formative centuries of Western science said that the task and the reward of the scientist was "to think God's thoughts after him" leads one to believe that this was their real motivation. If so, then modern Western science was cast in a matrix of Christian theology. The dynamism of religious devotion, shaped by the Judeo-Christian dogma of creation, gave it impetus.

AN ALTERNATIVE CHRISTIAN VIEW

We would seem to be headed toward conclusions unpalatable to many Christians. Since both *science* and *technology* are blessed words in our contemporary vocabulary, some may be happy at the notions, first, that, viewed historically, modern science is an extrapolation of natural theology and, second, that modern technology is at least partly to be explained as an Occidental, voluntarist realization of the Christian dogma of man's transcendence of, and rightful mastery over, nature. But, as we now recognize, somewhat over a century ago science and technology—hitherto quite separate activities—joined to give mankind powers which, to judge by many of the ecologic effects, are out of control. If so, Christianity bears a huge burden of guilt.

I personally doubt that disastrous ecologic backlash can be avoided simply by applying to our problems more science and more technology. Our science and technology have grown out of Christian attitudes toward man's relation to nature which are almost universally held not only by Christians and neo-Christians but also by those who fondly regard themselves as post-Christians. Despite Copernicus, all the cosmos rotates around out little globe. Despite Darwin, we are *not*, in our hearts, part of the natural process. We are superior to nature, contemptuous of it, willing to use it for our slightest whim. The newly elected Governor of California, like myself a churchman but less troubled than I, spoke for the Christian tradition when he said (as is alleged), "when you've seen one redwood tree, you've seen them all." To a Christian a tree can be no more than a physical fact. The whole concept of the sacred grove is alien to Christianity and to the ethos of the West. For nearly 2 millennia Christian missionaries have been chopping down sacred groves, which are idolatrous because they assume spirit in nature.

What we do about ecology depends on our ideas of the man-nature relationship. More science and more technology are not going to get us out of the present ecologic crisis until we find a new religion, or rethink our old one. The beatniks, who are the basic revolutionaries of our time, show a sound instinct in their affinity for Zen Buddhism, which conceives of the man-nature relationship as very nearly the mirror image of the Christian view. Zen, however, is as deeply conditioned by Asian history as Christianity is by the experience of the West, and I am dubious of its viability among us.

Possibly we should ponder the greatest radical in Christian history since Christ: Saint Francis of Assisi. The prime miracle of Saint Francis is the fact that he did not end at the stake, as many of his left-wing followers did. He was so clearly heretical that a General of the Franciscan Order, Saint Bonaventura, a great and perceptive Christian, tried to suppress the early accounts of Franciscanism. The key to an understanding of Francis is his belief in the virtue of humility—not merely for the individual but for man as a species. Francis tried to depose man from his monarchy over creation and set up a democracy for all God's creatures. With him the ant is no longer simply a homily for the lazy, flames a sign of the thrust of the soul toward union with God; now they are Brother Ant and Sister Fire, praising the Creator in their own ways as Brother Man does in his.

Later commentators have said that Francis preached to the birds as a rebuke to men who would not listen. The records do not read so: he urged the little birds to praise God, and in spiritual ecstasy they flapped their wings and chirped rejoicing. Legends of saints, especially the Irish saints, had long told of their dealings with animals but always, I believe, to show their human dominance over creatures. With Francis it is different. The land around Gubbio in the Apennines was being ravaged by a fierce wolf. Saint Francis, says the legend, talked to the wolf and persuaded him of the error of his ways. The wolf repented, died in the odor of sanctity, and was buried in consecrated ground.

What Sir Steven Ruciman calls "the Franciscan doctrine of the animal soul" was quickly stamped out. Quite possibly it was in part inspired, consciously or unconsciously, by the belief in reincarnation held by the Cathar heretics who at that time teemed in Italy and southern France, and who presumably had got it originally from India. It is significant that at just the same moment, about 1200, traces of metempsychosis are found also in western Judaism, in the Provençal *Cabbala*. But Francis held neither to transmigration of souls nor to pantheism. His view of nature and of man rested on a unique sort of pan-psychism of all things animate and inanimate, designed for the glorification of their transcendent Creator, who, in the ultimate gesture of cosmic humility, assumed flesh, lay helpless in a manger, and hung dying on a scaffold.

I am not suggesting that many contemporary Americans who are concerned about our ecologic crisis will be either able or willing to counsel with wolves or exhort birds. However, the present increasing disruption of the global environment is the product of a dynamic technology and science which were originating in the Western medieval world against which Saint Francis was rebelling in so original a way. Their growth cannot be understood historically apart from distinctive attitudes toward nature which are deeply grounded in Christian dogma. The fact that most people do not think of these attitudes as Christian is irrelevant. No new set of basic values has been accepted in our society to displace those of Christianity. Hence we shall continue to have a worsening ecologic crisis until we reject the Christian axiom that nature has no reason for existence save to serve man.

The greatest spiritual revolutionary in Western history, Saint Francis, proposed what he thought was an alternative Christian view of nature and man's relation to it: he tried to substitute the idea of the equality of all creatures, including man, for the idea of man's limitless rule of creation. He failed. Both our present science and our present technology are so tinctured with orthodox Christian arrogance toward nature that no solution for our ecologic crisis can be expected from them alone. Since ,the roots of our trouble are so largely religious, the remedy must also be essentially religious, whether we call it that or not. We must rethink and refeel our nature and destiny. The profoundly religious, but heretical, sense of the primitive Franciscans for the spiritual autonomy of all parts of nature may point a direction. I propose Francis as a patron saint for ecologists.

CHAPTER

The Cultural Basis for Our Environmental Crisis

LEWIS W. MONCRIEF

Reprinted from *Science* 170 (30 October 1970): 508–12, by permission of the American Association for the Advancement of Science and the author. Copyright 1970 by the American Association for the Advancement of Science.

The author is associate professor and director of the Recreation Research and Planning Unit and holds a joint appointment in the Department of Park and Recreation Resources Development at Michigan State University, East Lansing, Michigan 48823. This article is based on an address given at a Man and Environment Conference at Arizona State University on 16 April 1970.

Moncrief views the world as complicated; for him, what takes place between man and nature is the result of many forces, each acting upon,
and each being acted upon by others. He is impatient with those who
single out a solitary factor as the primary cause of a complex phenomenon. Thus, he dismisses White's attempt to explain environmental exploitation as resulting from the teachings of the Judeo-Christian tradition
as simplistic and indefensible on the evidence. He will admit such an
argument only as one element among many.

In this chapter Moncrief identifies what some of the other factors
might be that have contributed to the environmental crisis. Among these
are first, the increasing affluence of growing numbers of people resulting
in more production, greater use of natural resources, more consumption,
and more waste. Second, an aggressive attitude toward nature, an anachronistic leftover from our frontier heritage when nature was a series of
obstacles to be overcome—forests to be cleared, rivers to be tamed,
animals to be defended against. Third, the human tendencies to maximize self-interest and to shift the costs of production onto society.
Moncrief argues persuasively for the reality of these factors—historical,
cultural, and psychological—as contributors to the fouling of man's nest.

Though he differs as to the reasons why, Moncrief is in complete
accord with White that there is, indeed, a man-environment problem.
The title of one uses the adjective "ecologic," the other, "environmental"; but both are agreed there is a "crisis." And further, that it is de-
plorable. And finally, that misuse of the environment should cease. Perhaps we should raise a few questions about these assumptions made by
both authors.

Let us take one of Moncrief's own arguments and turn it around. If
it is the rising standard of living for increasing numbers of people that
has resulted in polluted water and air, are then pure water and clean air
worth paying the price of lowering the standard of living or, at least, of
denying improvement to the currently poor? Put another way, if strip-
mining scars the land, doesn't it also decrease the cost of energy? Another similar dilemma: both authors use the expression "exploitation of
the environment," but exploitation has two meanings—first, to employ or
utilize to the greatest possible advantage, second, to make use of self-
ishly or unethically. It is clear they use it in the latter sense. But is this a
question of fact or of value judgment? Surely it is the latter as both
authors would acknowledge. What becomes crucial then, is the question
by whom is such a judgment made. Using the example of strip-mining
again, the question becomes: who decides which is more important, the
beauty of the land or a cheaper electric bill?

One hundred years ago at almost any location in the United States, potable water was no farther away than the closest brook or stream. Today there are hardly any streams in the United States, except in a few high mountainous reaches, that can safely satisfy human thirst without chemical treatment. An oft-mentioned satisfaction in the lives of urbanites in an earlier era was a leisurely stroll in late afternoon to get a breath of fresh air in a neighborhood park or along a quiet street. Today in many of our major metropolitan areas it is difficult to find a quiet, peaceful place to take a leisurely stroll and sometimes impossible to get a breath of fresh air. These contrasts points up the dramatic changes that have occurred in the quality of our environment.

It is not my intent in this article, however, to document the existence of an environmental crisis but rather to discuss the cultural basis for such a crisis. Particular attention will be given to the institutional structures as expressions of our culture.

SOCIAL ORGANIZATION

In her book entitled *Social Institutions* (*1*), J. O. Hertzler classified all social institutions into nine functional categories: (i) economic and industrial, (ii) matrimonial and domestic, (iii) political, (iv) religious, (v) ethical, (vi) educational, (vii) communications, (viii) esthetic, and (ix) health. Institutions exist to carry on each of these functions in all cultures, regardless of their location or relative complexity. Thus, it is not surprising that one of the analytical criteria used by anthropologists in the study of various cultures is the comparison and contrast of the various social institutions as to form and relative importance (*2*).

A number of attempts have been made to explain attitudes and behavior that are commonly associated with one institutional function as the result of influence from a presumably independent institutional factor. The classic example of such an analysis is *The Protestant Ethic and the Spirit of Capitalism* by Max Weber (*3*). In this significant work Weber attributes much of the economic and industrial growth in Western Europe and North America to capitalism, which, he argued, was an economic form that developed as a result of the religious teachings of Calvin, particularly spiritual determinism.

Social scientists have been particularly active in attempting to assess the influence of religious teaching and practice and of economic motivation on other institutional forms and behavior and on each other. In this connection, L. White (*4*) suggested that the exploitative attitude that has prompted much of the environmental crisis in Western Europe and North America is a result of the teachings of the Judeo-Christian tradition, which conceives of man as superior to all other creation and of everything else as created for his use and enjoyment. He goes on to contend that the only way to reduce the ecologic crisis which we are now facing is to "reject the Christian axiom that nature has no reason for existence save to serve man." As with other ideas that appear to be new and novel, Professor White's observations have begun to be widely circulated and accepted in scholarly circles, as witness the article by religious writer E. B. Fiske in the *New York Times* earlier this year (5). In this article, note is taken of the fact that several prominent theologians and theological groups have accepted this basic premise that Judeo-Christian doctrine regarding man's relation to the rest of creation is at the root of the West's environmental crisis. I would suggest that the wide acceptance of such a simplistic explanation is at this point based more on fad than on fact.

Certainly, no fault can be found with White's statement that "Human ecology is deeply conditioned by beliefs about our nature and destiny—that is, by religion." However, to argue that it is the primary conditioner of human behavior toward the environment is much more than the data that he cites to support this proposition will bear. For example, White himself notes very early in his article that there is evidence for the idea that man has been dramatically altering his environment since antiquity. If this be true, and there is evidence that it is, then this mediates against the idea that the Judeo-Christian religion uniquely predisposes cultures within which it thrives to exploit their natural resources with indiscretion. White's own examples weaken his argument considerably. He points out that human intervention in the periodic flooding of the Nile River basin and the fire-drive method of hunting by prehistoric man have both probably wrought significant "unnatural" changes in man's environment. The absence of Judeo-Christian influence in these cases is obvious.

It seems tenable to affirm that the role played by religion in man-to-man and man-to-environment relationships is one of establishing a very broad system of allowable beliefs and behavior and of articulating and invoking a system of social and spiritual rewards for those who conform and of negative sanctions for individuals or groups who approach or cross the pale of the religiously unacceptable. In other words, it defines the ball park in which the game is played, and, by the very nature of the park, some types of games cannot be played. However, the kind of game that ultimately evolves is not itself defined by the ball park. For example, where animism is practiced, it is not likely that the believers will indiscriminately destroy objects of nature because such activity would incur the danger of spiritual and social sanctions. However, the fact that another culture does not associate spiritual beings with natural objects does not mean that such a culture will invariably ruthlessly exploit its resources. It simply means that there are fewer social and psychological constraints against such action.

In the remainder of this article, I present an alternative set of hypotheses based on cultural variables which, it seems to me, are more plausible and more defensible as an explanation of the environmental crisis that is now confronting us.

No culture has been able to completely screen out the egocentric tendencies of human beings. There also exists in all cultures a status hierarchy of positions and values, with certain groups partially or totally excluded from access to these normatively desirable goals. Historically, the differences in most cultures between the "rich" and the "poor" have been great. The many very poor have often produced the wealth for the few who controlled the means of production. There may have been no alternative where scarcity of supply and unsatiated demand were economic reality. Still, the desire for a "better life" is universal; that is, the desire for higher status positions and the achievement of culturally defined desirable goals is common to all societies.

THE EXPERIENCE IN THE WESTERN WORLD
In the West two significant revolutions that occurred in the 18th and 19th centuries completely redirected its political, social, and economic destiny (6). These two types of revolutions were unique to the West until very recently. The French revolution marked the beginnings of widespread democratization. In specific terms, this revolution involved a redistribution of the means of production and a reallocation of the natural and human resources that are an integral part of the production process. In effect new channels of social mobility were created, which theoretically made more wealth accessible to more people. Even though the revolution was partially perpetrated in the guise of overthrowing the control of presumably Christian institutions and of destroying the influence of God over the minds of men, still it would be superficial to argue that Christianity did not influence this revolution. After all, biblical teaching is one of the strongest of all pronouncements concerning human dignity and individual worth.

At about the same time but over a more extended period, another kind of revolution was taking place, primarily in England. As White points out very well, this phenomenon, which began with a number of technological innovations, eventually consummated a marriage with natural science and began to take on the character that it has retained until today (7). With this revolution the productive capacity of each worker was amplified by several times his potential prior to the revolution. It also became feasible to produce goods that were not previously producible on a commercial scale.

Later, with the integration of the democratic and the technological ideals, the increased wealth began to be distributed more equitably among the population. In addition, as the capital to land ratio increased in the production process and the demand grew for labor to work in the factories, large populations from the agrarian hinterlands began to concentrate in the emerging industrial cities. The stage was set for the development of the conditions that now exist in the Western world.

With growing affluence for an increasingly large segment of the population, there generally develops an increased demand for goods and services. The usual by-product of this affluence is waste from both the production and consumption processes. The disposal of that waste is further complicated by the high concentration of heavy waste producers in urban areas. Under these conditions the maxim that "Dilution is the solution to pollution" does not withstand the test of time, because the volume of such wastes is greater than the system can absorb and purify through natural means. With increasing population, increasing production, increasing urban concentrations, and increasing real median incomes for well over a hundred years, it is not surprising that our environment has taken a terrible beating in absorbing our filth and refuse.

THE AMERICAN SITUATION

The North American colonies of England and France were quick to pick up the technical and social innovations that were taking place in their motherlands. Thus, it is not surprising that the inclination to develop an industrial and manufacturing base is observable rather early in the colonies. A strong trend toward democratization also evidenced itself very early in the struggle for nationhood. In fact, Thistlewaite notes the significance of the concept of democracy as embodied in French thought to the framers of constitutional government in the colonies (8, pp. 33–34, 60).

From the time of the dissolution of the Roman Empire, resource ownership in the Western world was vested primarily with the monarchy or the Roman Catholic Church, which in turn bestowed control of the land resources on vassals who pledged fealty to the sovereign. Very slowly the concept of private ownership de-

veloped during the Middle Ages in Europe, until it finally developed
into the fee simple concept.

In America, however, national policy from the outset was designed to convey ownership of the land and other natural resources
into the hands of the citizenry. Thomas Jefferson was perhaps more
influential in crystallizing this philosophy in the new nation than
anyone else. It was his conviction that an agrarian society made
up of small landowners would furnish the most stable foundation
for building the nation (8, pp. 59–68). This concept has received
support up to the present and, against growing economic pressures
in recent years, through government programs that have encouraged the conventional family farm. This point is clearly relevant to
the subject of this article because it explains how the natural resources of the nation came to be controlled not by a few aristocrats
but by many citizens. It explains how decisions that ultimately de-
grade the environment are made not only by corporation boards
and city engineers but by millions of owners of our natural resources. This is democracy exemplified!

CHALLENGE OF THE FRONTIER

Perhaps the most significant interpretation of American history
has been Frederick Jackson Turner's much criticized thesis that
the western frontier was the prime force in shaping our society
(9). In his own words,

> If one would understand why we are today one nation, rather
> than a collection of isolated states, he must study this eco-
> nomic and social consolidation of the country. . . . The ef-
> fect of the Indian frontier as a consolidating agent in our
> history is important.

He further postulated that the nation experienced a series of frontier challenges that moved across the continent in waves. These included the explorers' and traders' frontier, the Indian frontier, the
cattle frontier, and three distinct agrarian frontiers. His thesis can
be extended to interpret the expansionist period of our history in
Panama, in Cuba, and in the Philippines as a need for a continued
frontier challenge.

Turner's insights furnish a starting point for suggesting a
second variable in analyzing the cultural basis of the United States'
environmental crisis. As the nation began to expand westward, the
settlers faced many obstacles, including a primitive transportation
system, hostile Indians, and the absence of physical and social security. To many frontiersmen, particularly small farmers, many of

the natural resources that are now highly valued were originally perceived more as obstacles than as assets. Forests needed to be cleared to permit farming. Marshes needed to be drained. Rivers needed to be controlled. Wildlife often represented a competitive threat in addition to being a source of food. Sod was considered a nuisance—to be burned, plowed, or otherwise destroyed to permit "desirable" use of the land.

Undoubtedly, part of this attitude was the product of perceiving these resources as inexhaustible. After all, if a section of timber was put to the torch to clear it for farming, it made little difference because there was still plenty to be had very easily. It is no coincidence that the "First Conservation Movement" began to develop about 1890. At that point settlement of the frontier was almost complete. With the passing of the frontier era of American history, it began to dawn on people that our resources were indeed exhaustible. This realization ushered in a new philosophy of our national government toward natural resources management under the guidance of Theodore Roosevelt and Gifford Pinchot. Samuel Hays (10) has characterized this movement as the appearance of a new "Gospel of Efficiency" in the management and utilization of our natural resources.

THE PRESENT AMERICAN SCENE

America is the archetype of what happens when democracy, technology, urbanization, capitalistic mission, and antagonism (or apathy) toward natural environment are blended together. The present situation is characterized by three dominant features that mediate against quick solution to this impending crisis: (i) an absence of personal moral direction concerning our treatment of our natural resources, (ii) an inability on the part of our social institutions to make adjustments to this stress, and (iii) an abiding faith in technology.

The first characteristic is the absence of personal moral direction. There is moral disparity when a corporation executive can receive a prison sentence for embezzlement but be congratulated for increasing profits by ignoring pollution abatement laws. That the absolute cost to society of the second act may be infinitely greater than the first is often not even considered.

The moral principle that we are to treat others as we would want to be treated seems as appropriate a guide as it ever has been. The rarity of such teaching and the even more uncommon instance of its being practiced help to explain how one municipality can, without scruple, dump its effluent into a stream even though it may do irreparable damage to the resource and add tremendously to the cost incurred by downstream municipalities that use the same water. Such attitudes are not restricted to any one culture. There appears to be an almost universal tendency to maximize self-interests and a widespread willingness to shift production costs to society to promote individual ends.

Undoubtedly, much of this behavior is the result of ignorance. If our accounting systems were more efficient in computing the cost of such irresponsibility both to the present generation and to those who will inherit the environment we are creating, steps would undoubtedly be taken to enforce compliance with measures designed to conserve resources and protect the environment. And perhaps if the total costs were known, we might optimistically speculate that more voluntary compliance would result.

A second characteristic of our current situation involves institutional inadequacies. It has been said that "what belongs to everyone belongs to no one." This maxim seems particularly appropriate to the problem we are discussing. So much of our environment is so apparently abundant that it is considered a free commodity. Air and water are particularly good examples. Great liberties have been permitted in the use and abuse of these resources for at least two reasons. First, these resources have typically been considered of less economic value than other natural resources except when conditions of extreme scarcity impose limiting factors. Second, the right of use is more difficult to establish for resources that are not associated with a fixed location.

Government, as the institution representing the corporate interests of all its citizens, has responded to date with dozens of legislative acts and numerous court decisions which give it authority to regulate the use of natural resources. However, the decisiveness to act has thus far been generally lacking. This indecisiveness cannot be understood without noting that the simplistic models that depict the conflict as that of a few powerful special interests versus "The People" are altogether inadequate. A very large proportion of the total citizenry is implicated in environmental degradation; the responsibility ranges from that of the board and executives of a utility company who might wish to thermally pollute a river with impunity to that of the average citizen who votes against a bond issue to improve the efficiency of a municipal sanitation system in order to keep his taxes from being raised. The magnitude of irresponsibility among individuals and institutions might be characterized as falling along a continuum from highly irresponsible to indirectly responsible. With such a broad base of interests being threatened with every change in resource policy direction, it is not surprising, although regrettable, that government has been so indecisive.

A third characteristic of the present American scene is an abiding faith in technology. It is very evident that the idea that technology can overcome almost any problem is widespread in Western society. This optimism exists in the face of strong evidence that much of man's technology, when misused, has produced harmful results, particularly in the long run. The reasoning goes something like this: "After all, we have gone to the moon. All we need to do is allocate enough money and brain power and we can solve any problem."

It is both interesting and alarming that many people view technology almost as something beyond human control. Rickover put it this way (11):

It troubles me that we are so easily pressured by purveyors of technology into permitting so-called "progress" to alter our lives without attempting to control it—as if technology were an irrepressible force of nature to which we must meekly submit.

He goes on to add:

It is important to maintain a humanistic attitude toward technology; to recognize clearly that since it is the product of human effort, technology can have no legitimate purpose but to serve man—man in general, not merely some men; future generations, not merely those who currently wish to gain advantage for themselves; man in the totality of his humanity, encompassing all his manifold interests and needs, not merely some one particular concern of his. When viewed humanistically, technology is seen not as an end in itself but a means to an end, the end being determined by man himself in accordance with the laws prevailing in his society.

In short, it is one thing to appreciate the value of technology; it is something else entirely to view it as our environmental savior —which will save us in spite of ourselves.

CONCLUSION

The forces of democracy, technology, urbanization, increasing individual wealth, and an aggressive attitude toward nature seem to be directly related to the environmental crisis now being confronted in the Western world. The Judeo-Christian tradition has probably influenced the character of each of these forces. However, to isolate religious tradition as a cultural component and to contend that it is the "historical root of our ecological crisis" is a bold affirmation for which there is little historical or scientific support.

To assert that the primary cultural condition that has created our environmental crisis is Judeo-Christian teaching avoids several hard questions. For example: Is there less tendency for those who control the resources in non-Christian cultures to live in extravagant affluence with attendant high levels of waste and inefficient consumption? If non-Judeo-Christian cultures had the same levels of economic productivity, urbanization, and high average household incomes, is there evidence to indicate that these cultures would not exploit or disregard nature as our culture does?

If our environmental crisis is a "religious problem," why are other parts of the world experiencing in various degrees the same environmental problems that we are so well acquainted with in the Western world? It is readily observable that the science and technology that developed on a large scale first in the West have been adopted elsewhere. Judeo-Christian tradition has not been adopted as a predecessor to science and technology on a comparable scale. Thus, all White can defensibly argue is that the West developed modern science and technology *first*. This says nothing about the origin or existence of a particular ethic toward our environment.

In essence, White has proposed this simple model:

I	II	III
Judeo-Christian tradition →	Science and technology →	Environmental degradation

I have suggested here that, at best, Judeo-Christian teaching has had only an indirect effect on the treatment of our environment. The model could be characterized as follows:

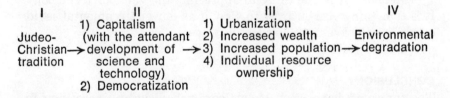

I	II	III	IV
Judeo-Christian tradition →	1) Capitalism (with the attendant development of science and technology) → 2) Democratization	1) Urbanization 2) Increased wealth → 3) Increased population 4) Individual resource ownership	Environmental → degradation

Even here, the link between Judeo-Christian tradition and the proposed dependent variables certainly have the least empirical support. One need only look at the veritable mountain of criticism of Weber's conclusions in *The Protestant Ethic and the Spirit of Capitalism* to sense the tenuous nature of this link. The second and third phases of this model are common to many parts of the world. Phase I is not.

Jean Mayer (*12*), the eminent food scientist, gave an appropriate conclusion about the cultural basis for our environmental crisis:

> It might be bad in China with 700 million poor people but 700 million rich Chinese would wreck China in no time. . . . It's the rich who wreck the environment . . . occupy much more space, consume more of each natural resource, disturb ecology more, litter the landscape . . . and create more pollution.

NOTES AND REFERENCES

1. J. O. Hertzler, *Social Institutions* (New York: McGraw-Hill, 1929), pp. 47–64.
2. L. A. White, *The Science of Culture* (New York: Farrar, Straus & Young, 1949), pp. 121–45.
3. M. Weber, *The Protestant Ethic and the Spirit of Capitalism*, translated by T. Parsons (New York: Scribner's, 1958).
4. L. White, Jr., *Science* 155 (1967): 1203.
5. E. B. Fiske, "The link between faith and ecology," *New York Times* (4 January 1970), section 4, p. 5.
6. R. A. Nisbet, *The Sociological Tradition* (New York: Basic Books, 1966), pp. 21–44. Nisbet gives here a perceptive discourse on the social and political implications of the democratic and industrial revolutions to the Western world.
7. It should be noted that a slower and less dramatic process of democratization was evident in English history at a much earlier date than the French revolution. Thus, the concept of democracy was probably a much more pervasive influence in English than in French life. However, a rich body of philosophic literature regarding the rationale for democracy resulted from the French revolution. Its counterpart in English literature is much less conspicuous. It is an interesting aside to suggest that perhaps the industrial revolution would not have been possible except for the more broad-based ownership of the means of production that resulted from the long-standing process of democratization in England.
8. F. Thistlewaite, *The Great Experiment* (London: Cambridge University Press, 1955).
9. F. J. Turner, *The Frontier in American History* (New York: Henry Holt, 1920 and 1947).
10. S. P. Hays, *Conservation and the Gospel of Efficiency* (Cambridge, Mass.: Harvard University Press, 1959).
11. H. G. Rickover, *American Forests* 75 (August, 1969): 13.
12. J. Mayer and T. G. Harris, *Psychology Today* 3 (January, 1970): 46 and 48.

CHAPTER

Discrepancies between Environmental Attitude and Behaviour:

Examples from
Europe and China

YI-FU TUAN

Reprinted from *The Canadian Geographer* 12, no. 3 (1968): 176–91, by permission of the Canadian Association of Geographers and the author.

A photograph which follows after Figure 3 and depicts a deforested and badly damaged landscape in Shan-hsi province has been deleted for this publication.

The substance of this paper was read at the University of British Columbia, 29 November 1967.

Yi-Fu Tuan is a writer whose characteristic style is to lead the reader down a rosy path at the end of which comes the prick of the thorn. For example, he contrasts the environmental ethos of the West, whereby nature is seen as subordinate to man, with that of the Orient, in which nature is felt to be in harmony with man. He illustrates this cultural difference most graphically by comparing the geometric formality of the European royal garden with that of the natural informality of the Chinese garden. Only then does he let you know that both gardens are human artifacts, that the Chinese "naturalistic" garden has been accomplished only by the relentless modification of the natural environment.

The lesson is clear: beware the sweeping generality which purports to capture a culture's range of environmental attitudes and behaviors. If it is true that China has a tradition of an adaptive attitude towards nature, of concern for the preservation of its resources, and of respect for natural beauty, it is also true that it has a long history of environmental mistreatment, of deforestation and erosion and clogged streams.

The natural environment of China, like those of Europe and America, has been transformed by man. Civilization everywhere has necessitated the exercise of human power over nature. There is no getting away from that. But, argues Tuan, it is possible that civilization, in turn, "may lead to the aesthetic appreciation of nature."

Discrepancy between stated ideal and reality is a worrisome fact of our daily experience: in the political field one learns to discriminate between an orator's fulsome profession and what he can or will, in fact, carry out. The history of environmental ideas, however, has been pursued as an academic discipline largely in detachment from the question of how—if at all—these ideas guide the course of action, or how they arise out of it. Needless to say, there are many paradigmatic views of nature, such as those of science, that have great explicatory power and may, once they are applied, affect the lives of many people; but in themselves they do not enjoin a specific course of action. In contrast, the acceptance of certain specific environmental ideas can have a definite effect on decision and on behaviour. If it is widely held, for example, that a dry and sunny climate is a great restorer of health, we may suppose that an appreciable number of people will seek out these areas for health. But what of less specific ideas? We may believe that a world-view which puts nature in subservience to man will lead to the exploitation of nature by man; and one that regards man as simply a component in nature will entail a modest view of his rights and capabilities, and so lead to the establishment of a harmonious relationship between man and his natural environment. But is this correct? And if essentially correct, how direct or tenuous is the link? These are some of the questions I wish to explore with the help of examples from Europe and China. The discrepancies are noted here; their resolution must await another occasion.

I

To the question, what is a fundamental difference between the European and the Chinese attitude towards nature, most people with any opinion at all will probably make some such reply: that the European sees nature as subordinate to him whereas the Chinese sees himself as a part of nature. Taken as a broad generalization and with a grain of salt there is much truth in this distinction; a truth illustrated with diagrammatic force when one compares the formal European garden of the seventeenth century with the Chinese naturalistic garden. The geometric contrast reflects fundamental differences in environmental evaluation. The formal European garden in the style of the Le Nôtre was designed to produce a limited number of imposing prospects. It can be appreciated to the full only at a limited number of favoured spots where the onlooker is invited by the garden's design to gaze at distant vistas.

Or, seen in another way, the European garden is a grandiose setting for man; in deference to him, nature is straitjacketed in court dress. The Chinese garden, on the other hand, is designed to produce almost constantly shifting scenes: there are no set prospects. The nature of the garden requires the perceiver to move along a winding path and to be more than visually involved with the landscape. It is not nature that is required to put on court dress in deference to man: rather, it is man who must lay aside his formalistic pretensions in order to enter nature.

This widely recognized distinction is valid and important. On the other hand, by the crude test of the total tonnage of earth removed there may not be so very much difference between the European formal and the Chinese naturalistic garden. Both are human artifacts. It is not widely known that some of the famous scenic areas of China are works of man rather than of geologic processes. The West Lake of Hang-chou, for example, was celebrated by T'ang and Sung poets and it remains to this day an adornment of China. To the casual visitor, the West Lake region may appear to be a striking illustration of how the works of man can blend modestly into the magistral context of nature. However, the pervasiveness of nature is largely an illusion induced by art. Some of the islands in the lake are man-made. Moreover, the lake itself is artificial and has to be maintained with care. In the thirteenth century, military patrols, under the command of specially appointed officials, looked after its policing and maintenance; it was forbidden, for example, to throw any rubbish into it or to plant in it lotuses or water-chestnuts. Peasants were recruited to clear and enlarge the lake, to keep it from being cluttered up by vegetation and silt (1). Hang-chou's environs, then, owe much of their calm, harmonious beauty to human art and effort. The sense of open nature in Hang-chou is enhanced by its scale: the West Lake region is a cluster of public and semi-public parks. In the much smaller compass of the private garden the illusion of pervasive nature is far more difficult to achieve: nevertheless the aim of the Chinese gardener was to achieve it with cleverly placed, water-worn limestone whose jagged outlines denoted wildness, and by means of winding footpaths that give the stroller an illusion of depth and space. In this line the Oriental's ultimate triumph is symbolized by the miniature garden, where wild nature is reduced to the scale of a dwarf landscape that can be fitted into a bowl. Complete artifice reigns: in the narrow confines of a bowl, shrubs are tortured by human skill into imitating the shape and posture of pines, the limbs of which may have been deformed by winds that swept the China Seas.

II

I have begun with a contrast and then proceeded to suggest that, from another perspective, the contrast is blurred. The publicized environmental ethos of a culture seldom covers more than a fraction of the total range of environmental behaviour. It is misleading to derive the one from the other. Simplifications that can mislead have at times been made. For example, Professor Lynn White has recently said: "What people do about their ecology depends on what they think about themselves in relation to things around them. Human ecology is deeply conditioned by beliefs about our nature and destiny—that is, by religion" (2). He goes on to say that the victory of Christianity over paganism was the greatest psychic revolution in Western culture. In his view, despite all the talk of "the post-Christian age" and despite evident changes in the forms of modern thinking, the substance often remains amazingly akin to that of the Christian past. The Western man's daily habits of action are dominated by an implicit faith in perpetual progress which was unknown either to Greco-Roman antiquity or to the Orient. It is rooted in, and is indefensible apart from, Judeo-Christian teleology. Peoples of the Western world continue to live, as they have lived for about 1700 years, very largely in a context of Christian beliefs. And what has Christianity told people about their relations with the environment? Essentially that man, as something made in God's image, is not simply a part of nature; that God has planned the universe for man's benefit and rule. According to White, Christianity is the most anthropocentric religion the world has seen. It has not only established a dualism of man and nature but has also insisted that it is God's will that man exploit nature for his proper ends (3).

To press the theme further, it is said that Christianity has destroyed antiquity's feeling for the holiness of landscapes and of natural things. The Greek religious tradition regarded the land not as an object to be exploited, or even as a visually pleasing setting, but as a true force which physically embodied the powers that ruled the world. Vincent Scully, the architectural historian, has argued that not only were certain landscapes regarded by the ancient Greeks as holy and expressive of specific gods, but also that the temples and the subsidiary buildings of their sanctuaries were so formed in themselves and so placed in the landscapes and to each other as to enhance, develop, and complement the basic meaning of the landscape (4).

Martin Heidegger, a modern philosopher whose insights have been greatly influenced by early Greek philosophy, characterized the Greek temple as disclosing the earth on which it stands. The whiteness of the temple discloses the darkness and the strength of the rock underneath; it reveals the height and blueness of the sky, the power of the storm and the vastness of the sea (5). In the Christian tradition, on the other hand, holiness was invested not in landscapes but in man-made altars, shrines, churches, and basilicas that dominated the landscapes. Constantine and Helen are said to have built basilicas over caves in the Holy Land to celebrate the triumph of Christianity over the "cave cultus" of the pagan world. In the Christian view it was not emanation from the earth but ritual that consecrated the site; man not nature bore the image of God and man's work, the hollowed edifice, symbolized the Christian cosmos. In pagan antiquity, at the level of the common people, each facet of nature had its own guardian spirit. Before one ventured to cut a tree, mine a mountain, or dam a brook, it was important to placate the spirit in charge of that particular situation, and to keep it placated. By destroying animistic beliefs, Christianity made it possible to exploit nature in a mood of indifference to the feeling of natural objects.

Much of this is now Western folklore and Lynn White is among the more recent writers to give it eloquent expression. The thesis, then, is that Christianity has introduced a fundamentally new way of evaluating the environment, and that this new evaluation has strongly affected Western man's traffic with the natural objects around him. The generalization is very useful, although one should take note of facts that appear to contradict it. As Clarence Glacken has demonstrated, in the ancient world there was no lack of interest in natural resources and their quick exploitation. Economic activities such as mining, the various ways of obtaining food, canal building, and drainage are clear proof of man's incessant restlessness in changing the earth about him (6). Glacken points out that in Sophocles' *Antigone* there are lines which remind one of the eulogies of science in the eighteenth century, and of contemporary enthusiasm for man's control over nature. At one point in the play the chorus declares how the earth has felt man's ungentle touch:

> Oh, Earth is patient, and Earth is old,
> And a mother of Gods, but he breaketh her,
> To-ing, froing, with the plough teams going,
> Tearing the soil of her, year by year (7).

The tearing of soil has led to erosion. In Plato's *Critias* there is the well-known passage in which he describes how the soils of Attica have been washed down to the sea. "And, just as happens in small islands, what now remains compared with what then existed is like the skeleton of a rich man, all the fat and soft earth have wasted away, and only the bare framework of the land being left." Plato then describes the former arable hills, fertile valleys, and forested mountains "of which there are visible signs even to this day." Mountains which today have food only for bees could, not so long ago, grow trees fit for the largest buildings. Cultivated trees provided pasturage for flocks, and the soil was well watered and the rain was "not lost to it, as now, by flowing from the bare land to the sea" (8). Plato's comments sound remarkably modern; they remind us almost of the lamentations of latter-day conservationists.

If there is evidence of man's awareness of his power to transform nature—even destructively—in the time of Sophocles and Plato, there is evidence of much greater awareness of the almost limitless capabilities of man in Hellenistic times. Agriculture and related occupations such as cattle-breeding were then the most important source of wealth in the ancient world. Land reclamation was not a haphazard affair but one based on the science of mechanics and on practical experience with canal-digging, irrigation, and swamp drainage. It was a time of faith in progress. But far more than the Greeks, the Romans have imposed their will on the natural environment (see Figure 1). And perhaps the most dramatic example of the triumph of the human will over the irregular lineaments of nature is the Roman grid method of dividing up the land. As Bradford puts it, centuriation well displayed the arbitrary but methodical qualities in Roman government. With absolute self-assurance and great technical competence, the Romans have imposed the same formal pattern of land division on the well-watered alluvium of the Po Valley as on the near-desert of Tunisia. Even today the forceful imprint of centuriation can be traced across some thousands of square miles on both sides of the central Mediterranean, and it can still stir the imagination by its scale and boldness (9).

Against this background of the vast transformations of nature in the pagan world, the inroads made in the early centuries of the Christian era were relatively modest. Christianity teaches that man had dominion over nature. St. Benedict himself had cut down the sacred grove at Monte Cassino because it was a survival of pagan worship. And the story of how monks moved into the forested wilderness, and by a combination of work and prayer, had trans-

Figure 1. The growing "second nature" in antiquity. In spite of a passive or adaptive attitude toward nature (suggested by the importance of the "environmental theory" in philosophy and by respect for the *genius loci* of natural object in folk religion), the ancient landscapes have been markedly transformed by man. Figure 1 shows how nature can even be dominated by man's engineering achievements.

Reproduced from C. Glacken, *Traces on the Rhodian Shore,* University of California Press, 1967. Originally published by the University of California Press; reprinted by permission of The Regents of the University of California.

formed them into cloistered "paradises" is a familiar one. But for
a long time man's undisputed power over nature was more a tenet
of faith than a fact of experience: to become a realized fact Europe
had to wait for the growth of human numbers, for the achievement
of greater administrative centralization and for the development
and wide application of new technological skills. Fields that were
cleared in heavy forests testified to the mediaeval farmer's great
capacity for changing his environment: it was a change, however,
that must continually be defended against the encroachments of
nature (see Figure 2). Farmsteads and arable lands multiplied
through the Middle Ages at the expense of forests and marshes, but
these man-made features lacked the permanence, the geometric order, and the prideful assertion of the human will that one can detect more readily in the Roman road system, aqueducts, and cen-
turiated landholdings. The victory of Christianity over paganism
may well have been, as Lynn White says, the greatest psychic revolution in Western culture; but for lack of real, as distinct from
theologically postulated, power the full impact of that revolution
on ecology was postponed.

Figure 2.   A fifteenth-century print showing a mediaeval scene. Foreground:
ploughing team and field; mid-ground: water mill; background: castle. Technological innovations, such as the heavy plough and the water mill, appear to have
given man a position of dominance vis-à-vis nature from about the ninth century
onward, that he lacked in the earlier Christian centuries.

III

As to China, Western humanists commonly show bias in favour of that country's Taoist and Buddhist traditions. They like to point out the virtues of the Oriental's quiescent and adaptive approach towards nature in contrast to the aggressive masculinity of Western man. Support for the quiescent view is easily found in the Taoist classics. The *Tao Tê Ching*, for example, has a rather cryptic message of seven characters (*wei wu wei, tzu wu pu chih*) which James Legge has translated as: "When there is abstinence from action, good order is universal." And Joseph Needham has recently interpreted it to mean: "Let there be no action (contrary to Nature), and there is nothing that will not be well regulated" (*10*). It is easy to see how these words might appeal to the modern man, who finds in his own environment the all-too-evident consequences of human action "contrary to nature." In another influential Taoist book of much later date (*T'ai shang kan ying p'ien*), one finds the belief that "even insects and crawling things, herbs and trees, may not be injured." These Taoist texts have been much translated into European languages; the latter, with its injunction against injuring even insects and crawling things, is believed to have had some influence on the thought of Albert Schweitzer (*11*).

Another aspect of Chinese attitude towards nature, which has found favour among some Western humanists, is embodied in the concept of *feng-shui* or geomancy. This concept has been aptly defined as "the art of adapting the residences of the living and the dead so as to co-operate and harmonize with the local currents of the cosmic breadth" (*12*). If houses and tombs are not properly located, evil effects would injure the inhabitants and the descendants of those whose bodies lay in the tombs. On the other hand, good siting would favour wealth, health, and happiness. Good siting involves, above all, taking proper note of the forms of hills and directions of watercourses since these are themselves the outcome of the moulding influences of winds and waters, that is, of *feng-shui;* but in addition one must also consider the heights and forms of buildings, the directions of roads and bridges. A general effect of the belief in *feng-shui* is to encourage a preference for natural curves —for winding paths and for structures that seem to fit into the landscape rather than to dominate it; and at the same time it promoted a distaste for straight lines and geometrical layouts. In this respect it is of interest to note the short life of China's first railway. This was built in 1876 and connected Shanghai with its port of Wu-sung. Although the venture was at first well received, the mood of the local people turned sour after a native was killed by the locomotive. The people in their hostility thought that the railway had offended the principle of *feng-shui*. On 20 October, 1877, the Chinese government closed the railway, and so a symbol of Western progress was temporarily sacrificed to the local currents of the cosmic breadth (*13*).

An adaptive attitude towards nature has ancient roots in China. It is embodied in folklore, in the philosophical-ethical precepts of Taoism, and later, Buddhism, and it draws support from practical experience: the experience that uncontrolled exploitation of timber, for example, brings hurtful results. In ancient literature one finds here and there evidence of a recognition for the need to regulate the use of resources. Even as early as the Eastern Chou period (eighth century–third century B.C.), deforestation necessitated by the expansion of agriculture and the building of cities seems to have led to an appreciation of the value of trees. In that ancient compendium of songs the *Shi Ching*, we find the sentiment expressed in lines such as these:

> On the hill were lovely trees,
> Both chestnut-trees and plum trees.
> Cruel brigands tore them up;
> But no one knew of their crime.

Trees were regarded as a blessing. As another poem put it,

> So thick grow those oaks
> That the people never look for firewood.
> Happiness to our lord!
> May the spirits always have rewards for him (*14*).

In the *Chou Li*—a work which was probably compiled in the third century B.C., but may well include earlier material—we find mentioned two classes of officials whose duties were concerned with conservation. One was the *Shan-yu*, inspector of mountains, and the other the *Lin-heng*, inspector of forests. The inspectors of mountains were charged with the care of forests in the mountains. They saw to it that certain species were preserved, and in other ways enforced conservation practices. Thus trees could only be cut by the common people at certain times; those on the south side in the middle of winter and those on the north side in the middle of summer. At other seasons the people were permitted to cut wood in times of urgent need, such as when coffins had to be made or dykes strengthened, but even then certain areas could not be touched. The inspectors of forests (in the *Lin-heng* office) had similar duties. Their authority covered the forests that lay below the mountains

(15). Another ancient literary reference to conservation practice was in the *Mencius*. The sage advised King Huai of Liang that he would not lack for wood if he allowed the people to cut trees only at the proper time (16).

Through Chinese history perspicacious officials have from time to time warned against the dire consequences of deforestation. A scholar of the late Ming dynasty reported on Shan-hsi, a province in North China: "At the beginning of the reign of Chia-ching" (1522–66), he wrote, "people vied with each other to build houses, and wood from the southern mountains were cut without a year's rest. The natives took advantage of the barren mountain surface and converted it into farms. . . . If heaven sends down a torrent, there is nothing to obstruct the flow of water. In the morning it falls on the southern mountains; in the evening, when it reaches the plains, its angry waves swell in volume and break embankments causing frequent changes in the course of the river (17).

Deforestation was deplored by the late Ming scholars not only because of its effect on stream flow and on the quality of the soil in the lowlands, but also—interestingly enough—because of their belief that the forests on mountain ridges were effective in slowing down the horse-riding barbarians. As one scholar put it, "I saw the fact that what the country relies on as strategically important is the mountain, and what the mountain relies on as a screen to prevent advance are the trees" (18). There was also recognition of the aesthetics of forested mountains. Wu-tai mountains in northern Shan-hsi, for example, were famous everywhere. But the question was asked: since they have become almost bare, what remained to keep them famous?

These brief notes suggest that there existed in China an old tradition of forest care. Officials encouraged the practice but the people engaged in it on their own initiative when it did not conflict with the urgent needs of the moment. Nearly forty years ago, the American conservationist W. C. Lowdermilk noted how thousands of acres in An-hui and Ho-non were planted with pine from local nurseries, a practice he recognized as ancient and independent of the modern forestry movement. Lowdermilk also found that the North China plain "actually exports considerable quantities of logs of *Paulownia tomentosa* to Japan and poplar (*Populus tomentosa*) to match factories. It is true that no forests are to be found in this plain, but each village has its trees, which are grown according to a system" (19).

In Communist China trees are extensively planted to control soil erosion, in answer to pressing economic needs but also for aesthetic reasons. Roadside planting, a practice dating back to the

Eastern Chou period, uses the "traditional" trees (*Populus simonii, Pinus tabulaeformis, Salix babylonica, S. matsudana, Aesculus chinensis, Ulmus parvifolia*), but in particular the poplars. Afforestation proceeds in villages, and most conspicuously, in cities, new suburbs, and industrial districts where the trees hide a great deal of the raw ugliness of new construction (*20*).

IV

Thus far I have sketched what may indeed be called the "official" line on Chinese attitude towards environment; it is widely publicized and commonly accepted. There is however another strain: the enlightened memorials to the emperor on the need for the conservation of resources are in themselves clear evidence of the follies that have already been committed. Unlike the Western man of letters the geographer is usually aware of China's frequent mistreatment of nature. He perceives that country, not through the refined sentiments of Taoist philosophy, Neo-Confucianism, and Oswald Siren, but through the bleak reports of Mallory, Lowdermilk, and Thorp. Deforestation and erosion on the one hand, the building of cities and rice terraces on the other are the common foci of his attention rather than landscape painting or poetry contests in the cool precincts of a garden. The two images of reality complement each other: in an obvious but not trite sense, civilization is the exercise of human power over nature, which in turn may lead to the aesthetic appreciation of nature. Philosophy, nature poetry, gardens, and orderly countryside are products of civilization, but so equally are the deforested mountains, the clogged streams, and, within the densely packed, walled cities, the political intrigue.

If animistic belief and Taoist nature philosophy lie at the back of an adaptive attitude towards nature, what conceptions and ideals —we may ask—have encouraged the Chinese, through their long history, to engage in gigantic transformation of environment— whether this be expressed positively in huge works of construction or negatively in deforested mountains? Several ancient beliefs and conceptions may be recognized and they, individually or together, have allowed the Chinese to express the "male" principle in human nature. Consider, for example, the fact that one of the greatest culture heroes of China was Yu, the legendary founder of the Hsia dynasty. He was famed primarily for his magnificent deeds: He "opened up the rivers of the Nine Provinces and fixed the outlets of the nine marshes"; he brought peace and order to the lands of Hsia and his achievements were of an enduring kind which benefited succeeding dynasties (21). Chinese rulers were bidden to imitate the ancient culture heroes, and one way to imitate them was to ensure order and prosperity by large-scale engineering works. Another ancient idea of importance to the "male" principle of dominance was to see in the earthly environment a model of the cosmos. The regular motions of the stars were to be translated architecturally and ritually to space and time on earth. The walled city oriented to the cardinal directions, the positioning of the twelve city gates, the location of the royal compound and the alignment of the principal axial street were given a geometric pattern that reflected the order to be found in heaven. The key concept was built on the related notions of rectilinearity, order, and rectitude. This key concept acquired architectural and social forms which were then imposed on earth, for the earth itself lacked paradigms of perfect order. Indeed the experience of mountains and waters has led to such unaggressive prescriptions as the need to observe and placate the spirits of the earth, the need for man to understand the balance of forces in nature, to contemplate this harmony and to adapt himself to it. By contrast, the observation of the stars has inspired such masculine attitudes as geometric order, hierarchy, and authoritarian control over earth and men.

The two outlooks—celestial and terrestrial, masculine and feminine—are not easy to reconcile. Events in heaven affect events on earth but not in any obvious or dependable way: abnormal floods and droughts have traditionally been taken as warnings by those who derive their power from astronomy. Tension, if not contradiction, is also revealed when these two ideas find architectural and geographical substance. The construction of Ch'ang-an in the Sui and T'ang dynasties illustrates the triumph of the cosmic principle of order and rectilinearity over the earth principle of complex harmony and natural lines (see Figure 3). Ch'ang-an was laid on new ground and on an unprecented scale. The site in the Wei Ho valley was chosen for functional reasons but also because of its great historical links: the site received the sanction of the great men and deeds in the past. Geomantic properties of the site were studied; however, unlike villages and rural roads the topographical character of the region seems to have made little impact on the city's fundamental design. Astronomers had an important role in the laying out of the city: they measured the shadow of the noon sun on successive days and observed the North Star by night in order to arrive at accurate alignments of the city walls to the four directions (22). In the course of building Ch'ang-an, which had an enclosed area of 31 square miles, villages were levelled and trees uprooted; broad straight avenues were laid out and then rows of

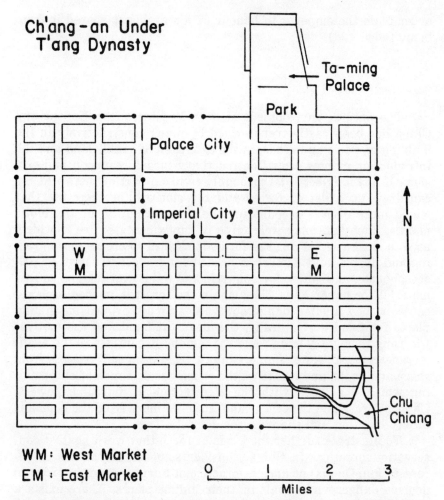

Figure 3. The cosmic paradigm in Chinese city-building as exemplified by Ch'ang-an during the T'ang dynasty. The city grid reflects the superposition of a regular cosmic pattern on the irregularities of the earth. The curves of Taoist nature are represented mainly by Chü chiang park in the southeastern corner of the city and by the gardens of the wealthy and of monasteries but the rectilinear geometry of the city streets and enclosed wards dwarfs these manifestations of terrestrial nature. The imposing, rather lifeless, north-south avenues are more than 400 feet wide.

trees planted. Thus, despite the geomantic gestures, in Ch'ang-an the superposition of man's and heaven's order on natural terrain was complete. Or rather not quite complete, if we accept the charming story of why one great old locust tree was not in line. It had been retained from the old landscape because the chief architect had sat under it as he supervised the construction, and a special order from the emperor in honour of his architect spared it from being felled (*23*).

V

The natural environment of both Mediterranean Europe and China has been vastly transformed by man: constructively in the building of cities and roads, in the extension of arable land and the introduction of new crops; destructively in deforestation and erosion. Of any long-settled, thoroughly civilized part of the world, we can draw up a list of forces and the motives for their use that would more or less account for the transformation of the biotic mantle. Such lists may well agree in fundamentals: fire is widely used to clear vegetation; the forest is cleared to create more grazing and arable land; timber is needed for the construction of palaces, houses, and ships, for domestic and industrial fuel, or as raw material for paper mills. Then again the forest is pushed back because it may shelter dangerous wild animals or provide hiding places for bandits. Naturally, the means at hand and the motives for using them vary from region to region: in contrast to the Mediterranean world, for example, China's vegetation suffered less from sheep and goats, and less from the enormous demands of shipbuilding which flourished with the Mediterranean maritime powers. China's forests, on the other hand, suffered more from the demands of city building and the need for domestic fuel.

To illustrate further the kinds of force that work against conservation practices in China, consider some of the causes of deforestation. One is the ancient practice of burning trees in order to deprive dangerous animals of their hiding places. There exists a passage in the *Mencius* of how in ancient times the luxuriant vegetation sheltered so many wild beasts that men were endangered. The great minister Shun of legendary repute ordered Yih to use fire, and "Yih set fire to, and consumed the forests and vegetation on the mountains and in the marshes, so that the birds and beasts fled away to hide themselves" (*24*). Even in the early decades of the twentieth century non-Chinese tribes in Kuang-hsi and Kueichou provinces are known to burn forests to drive away tigers and leopards; and in North China, in such long-settled areas as central Shen-hsi province, fires were ostensibly started by Chinese farmers for no other purpose. It is not always easy to establish the real reason for setting fire to forest. When asked, the farmers may say that it is to clear land for cultivation, although the extent of burning far exceeds the need for this purpose; or it is to leave fewer places in which bandits may hide; or to encourage the growth of small-sized sprouts in the burnt over area, which would then save the farmers the labour of splitting wood! (25) The last reason tends to upset any residual illusion we may have of the Chinese farmer's benign attitude towards nature. A fire can of course also be started accidentally. A risk that is special to the Chinese is the forest fire caused by the burning of paper money at the grave mounds, which, in the rugged parts of the South, are commonly located beyond the fields and at the edge of the forested hills.

Forests in North China were depleted in the past for the making of charcoal as an industrial fuel. Robert Hartwell has shown how, from the tenth century onward the expanding metallic industries had swallowed up many hundreds of thousands of tons of charcoal each year, as did the manufacture of salt, alum, bricks, tiles, and liquour (26). By the Sung dynasty (960–1279 A.D.) the demand for wood and charcoal as both household and industrial fuel had reached a level such that the timber resources of the country could no longer meet it; the result was the increasing substitution of coal for wood and charcoal.

An enormous amount of timber was needed in the construction of the old Chinese cities, probably more than that required in building Western cities of comparable size. One reason for this lies in the dependence of traditional Chinese architecture on timber as the basic structural material. Mountains may be stripped of their cover in the construction of a large palace (27). And if a large palace required much timber, a whole city would require much more, especially if it were of the size of Ch'ang-an, capital of T'ang dynasty, and Hang-chou, capital of the southern Sung dynasty. Both had populations of more than a million people. The great expansion in the size of Hang-chou in the thirteenth century led to the deforestation of the neighbouring hills for construction timber. The demand for timber was such that some farmers gave up rice cultivation for forestry (28). Cities in which houses were so largely made of wood ran the constant danger of demolition by fire; and this was especially true of the southern metropolises where the streets tended to be narrow. The necessity of rebuilding after fire put further strain on timber resources. But of even greater consequence than the accidental burning of parts of cities was the deliberate devastation of whole cities in times of upheaval, when rebels or nomadic invaders toppled a dynasty. The succeeding phase of reconstruction was normally achieved in quick time by armies of men who made ruthless inroads upon the forest.

VI

The theme we have yet to trace is the involved interplay between environmental attitude and environmental behaviour, between the philosophy identified with a people and the actions that people may undertake. Besides the more glaring contradictions of professed ideal and actual practice, there exist also the unsuspected ironies: these derive from the fact that the benign institutions of a complex society, no less than the exploitative, are not always able to foresee all the consequences of their inherent character and action. For example, Buddhism in China is at least partly responsible for the preservation of trees around temple compounds, for the islands of green in an otherwise denuded landscape; on the other hand, Buddhism introduced to China the idea of the cremation of the dead; and from the tenth to the fourteenth century the practice of cremation was sufficiently common in the southeastern coastal provinces to have had an effect on the timber resources of that area (29). The researches of E. H. Schafer provide us with another illustration of irony in Chinese life; for it would seem that the most civilized of arts was responsible for the deforestation of much of North China. The art was that of writing which required soot for the making of black ink. The soot came from burnt pine. And, as Schafer put it, "Even before T'ang times, the ancient pines of the mountains of Shan-tung had been reduced to carbon, and now the busy brushes of the vast T'ang bureaucracy were rapidly bringing baldness to the T'a-hang Mountains between Shansi and Hopei" (30).

VII

I began by noting the contrast between the European formal garden and the Chinese naturalistic garden, and then suggested that these human achievements probably required comparable amounts of nature modification. To compare artworks and construction projects on the basis of the quantitative changes made on the environment is a useful exercise in so far as we wish to emphasize the role of man as a force for change along with other geophysical forces; but it is only the beginning in the interpretation of the meaning of these works and how they reflect cultural attitudes. It seems to me valid to see the European garden as an extension of the house: in the development of the European garden some of the formality and values of the house are taken outdoors in the form of courtyards, terraces, formal parterres, and avenues, and now the smooth, carpet-like lawn. The lawn displays the house; its sloping surfaces are a pedestal for the house. The Chinese garden, on the other hand, reflects a totally different philosophy from the orthogonal rectitude of the traditional Chinese house. In stepping through a circular gate, from the rectangular courtyard into the curvilinear forms of the garden, one enters a different world. Perhaps something of the difference in attitude towards outdoor spaces is retained to the present day. Simone de Beauvoir notes how a French family picnic is often an elaborate affair involving the transportation of a considerable portion of the household goods outdoors: it is not always a harmonious event for whatever tension that may exist in the house is carried to the less organized natural environment where it is exacerbated by entanglement with flies, fishing rods, and spilled strawberry jam. In Communist China, de Beauvoir spent an afternoon (1955) in the playgrounds of the Summer Palace outside Peking. She captures the peace of the scene with an anecdote: "In the middle of the lake I see a little boat: in it a young woman is lying down peacefully asleep while two youngsters are frisking about and playing with the oars. Our boatman cups his hands. 'Hey!' he calls. 'Look out for those kids!' The woman rubs her eyes, she smiles, picks up the oars, and shows the children how they work" (*31*).

REFERENCES

1. J. Gernet, *Daily Life in China on the Eve of the Mongol Invasion, 1250–1276* (London, 1962), pp. 51–52.
2. L. White, "The Historical Roots of Our Ecologic Crisis," *Science* 155 (1967): 1205.
3. Ibid.
4. V. Scully, *The Earth, The Temple, and The Gods* (New Haven, 1962), p. 3.
5. V. Vycinas, *Earth and Gods: An Introduction to the Philosophy of Martin Heidegger* (The Hague, 1961), p. 13.
6. C. Glacken, *Traces on the Rhodian Shore* (Berkeley and Los Angeles, 1967), p. 118.
7. Sophocles, *Antigone*, translated by Gilbert Murray in Arnold Toynbee, *Greek Historical Thought* (New York, 1952), p. 128.
8. Plato, *Critias*, translated by Arnold Toynbee in *Greek Historical Thought*, pp. 146–47.
9. J. Bradford, *Ancient Landscapes* (London, 1957), p. 145.
10. J. Needham, *Science and Civilization in China*, vol. 2 (Cambridge, 1956), p. 69.
11. E. H. Shafer, "The Conservation of Nature under the T'ang Dynasty," *Journal of the Economic and Social History of the Orient* 5 (1962): 282.
12. H. Chatley, "Feng shui" in *Encyclopedia Sinica*, S. Couling, ed., (Shanghai, 1971), p. 175. See also A. March, "An Appreciation of Chinese Geomancy," *Journal of Asian Studies* 27 (1968): 253–67.
13. *Encyclopedia Sinica*, p. 470.
14. *Shi Ching*, translated by A. Waley as *The Book of Songs* (New York, 1960), pp. 138, 213.
15. *Chou Li*, translated by E. Biot as *Le Tcheou-li* (Paris, 1851), vol. 1, 371–74.
16. *Mencius*, Bk. 1, pt. 1, 3:3.
17. C. Chi, *Key Economic Areas in Chinese History* (New York, 1963), p. 22.
18. Gazetteer (1596) written by Chen Teng and translated by W. C. Lowdermilk, and D. R. Wickes, *History of Soil Use in the Wu T'ai Shan Area*, Monograph, Royal Asiatic Society, NCB, 1938, p. 8.
19. W. C. Lowdermilk, "Forestry in Denuded China," *Annals of the American Academy of Political and Social Sciences* 152 (1930): 137.
20. S. D. Richardson, *Forestry in Communist China* (Baltimore, 1966), pp. 152–53.
21. Ssu-Ma Ch'ien, *Shi Chi*, Chap. 29.
22. A. F. Wright, "Symbolism and Function: Reflections on Changan and Other Great Cities," *Journal of Asian Studies* 24 (1965): 670.
23. N. I. Wu, *Chinese and Indian Architecture* (New York, 1963), p. 38.
24. *Mencius*, Bk. 3, pt. 1. 4:7.
25. Reported by A. N. Steward and S. Y. Cheo in "Geographical and Ecological Notes on Botanical Explorations in Kwangsi Province, China," *Nanking Journal* 5 (1935): 174.
26. R. Hartwell, "A Revolution in the Chinese Iron and Coal Industries during the Northern Sung, 960–1126 A.D.," *Journal of Asian Studies* 21 (1962): 159.

27. See L. S. Yang, *Les aspects économiques des travaux publics dans la Chine impériale*, Collège de France, 1964, p. 37.
28. J. Gernet, *Daily Life in China*, p. 114.
29. A. C. Moule, *Quinsai* (Cambridge, 1957), p. 51.
30. E. H. Shafer, "The Conservation of Nature": 299–300.
31. S. De Beauvoir, *The Long March* (Cleveland, 1958), p. 77.

CHAPTER

Attitudes Toward
Slums and Public Housing
in Puerto Rico

A. B. HOLLINGSHEAD
L. H. ROGLER

Reprinted from Leonard Duhl, ed.,
The Urban Condition (New York: Basic
Books, Inc., 1963), Chapter 17, by
permission of the publisher and the
authors. Copyright © 1963 by Basic
Books, Inc., Publishers, New York.

   The research reported here is
being done by the Social Science
Research Center of The University of
Puerto Rico. It is supported, in part, by
a research grant from the National Institute of Mental Health, United States
Public Health Service.

This study by Hollingshead and Rogler provides a remarkably clear example of bungling do-gooders, the well-intentioned who are also the misguided—in this case, the Public Housing Authority of Puerto Rico.

The experience of most Americans does not prepare them for the slums of Puerto Rico, and most students will read the description of them with distaste, if not horror, and will breathe a sigh of relief to read of the clean, sanitary, privacy-providing public housing projects. How puzzling then, that the majority of those living in the slums like it, whereas the majority of those living in the public housing do not.

How can this be? The authors argue that the "good" housing, erected by a concerned government and designed according to standards established by city planners and architects, has resulted in the formation of social conditions which violate the values of the people who must live in it. For example, the rules governing the public housing units insist that an apartment be occupied by no more than a single, nuclear family. No relatives are allowed. But this restriction is directly counter to the kinship obligations of the lower-class Puerto Rican which demand that a relative by blood or marriage be fed and sheltered. Several other illustrations are given of how bureaucratic regulations conflict with the folkways of the residents, adding to their discontent. Thus, the paradox of improved housing leading to anger and unhappiness.

Lest the reader miss the moral of this study by distancing himself from the "natives," Chapter 13 by Fried and Gleicher will bring him back from the slums of exotic Puerto Rico to those of Boston.

This paper reports selected aspects of an intensive study of lower-class families who reside in a rapidly changing metropolitan area. For present purposes, we shall limit the discussion to three principal points: (1) a brief statement about the study; (2) a description of the neighborhoods where the families in our study live; and (3) some reactions of these families to the physical and human environments that enmesh their lives.

The locale of this research is the San Juan metropolitan area of Puerto Rico. Puerto Rico is of sociological interest for a number of reasons. Between 1500 and 1900, a relatively homogeneous culture developed. During the present century, selected American culture patterns have grown upon traditional Hispanic ones. Politically, this island experienced transition from a Spanish colony to a militarily-strategic possession of the United States; now it is an autonomous Commonwealth associated with the United States. Economically, it is changing from a predominantly rural, agricultural society to a highly urbanized, industrial one. Socially, it is developing classes that lie between an historic, small aristocratic segment of very rich families and the vast majority of poor people.

Today the impact of changes brought about by socio-cultural forces characteristic of our time is visible throughout the island, particularly in the metropolitan areas. New opportunities are being presented to persons in all segments of the social structure. Some aspects of the culture are changing rapidly; others are resistant to change. In different degree, all socio-economic groups are affected by the admixture of the new cultural complexes with the old ones. The impact of the new, juxtaposed with the old, has created a confused social scene.

THE STUDY DESIGN

Schizophrenia in the Lower Class
The study upon which this paper is based is focused upon schizophrenia in the lowest socio-economic class. We decided to study schizophrenia for a number of reasons. First, schizophrenia is a disabling disease. Second, in the psychiatric agencies of the Puerto Rican government, schizophrenia is the most frequently treated psychosis (1). Third, the etiology of schizophrenia is a matter of debate (2). Fourth, a number of studies have reported that schizophrenia is concentrated unduly in persons of lower socio-economic status (3). A study of schizophrenia in the lowest socio-economic class in the San Juan metropolitan area appeared to be an intellectually-challenging venture.

The Study Group

We decided to make an intensive study of families of procreation. The number had to be limited in order to collect the kinds of data we desired, but it had to be large enough to permit meaningful comparisons between groups. A minimum of forty families appeared to be necessary. Our research design required, first, that the families should fall into two categories—families with a schizophrenic spouse and families without a schizophrenic spouse; and, second, that the families should be as similar as possible in a number of other characteristics.

We established five criteria for families to be included in the study: (1) residence in the San Juan metropolitan area; (2) an age range from twenty to thirty-nine years; (3) spouses living in the same household; (4) low socio-economic status (4); (5) no contact with a psychiatric agency prior to May 1, 1958.

The Field Phase

Locating families who met our criteria was the first major field operation. We began with a list of persons who had either been referred to psychiatric clinics by a third party, or had come to the clinic themselves and solicited help. Most referrals were made by local officials in public health units, the police, physicians, and, of course, family members. As soon as the name of a disturbed person —either a referral or a solicitant—came to our attention, we visited his home to determine if he met the established criteria.

Persons who fulfilled our criteria were asked to cooperate with us. A minimal level of cooperation meant that the invited person and his, or her, spouse would submit themselves to a psychiatric examination. Each person was told, before he was taken to the psychiatrist's office, the kind of doctor he was to see, and the nature of the examination he would receive.

Each examination was made by a fully trained psychiatrist, who was himself a Puerto Rican. All examinations were made in the privacy of the psychiatrist's air-conditioned office. The psychiatric examination usually took about two hours. The spouses were given the same psychiatric examinations under the same conditions, at a different time and, usually, by a different psychiatrist. Persons who were diagnosed as schizophrenic were then asked, along with their spouses, to participate in the study.

Families with a schizophrenic spouse were matched by families drawn randomly from a pre-listed census of households taken in an earlier phase of the research. A family tentatively selected was visited by a field worker. The study was explained to the members of this family, and they were invited to participate in it. Husbands and wives were told that they would be taken to a psychiatrist and given a mental examination. We told them, also, that we would visit the home many times to gather information about the family. We believe it is worth noting that once people accepted our invitation to go to a psychiatrist, there were no refusals to participate in the study. This record we attribute to the quality and perseverance of the field staff and to the hospitality accorded to the field workers by these families. We may add that hospitality to comparative strangers is an important value in Puerto Rico.

The husband and the wife in the randomly selected families were taken separately to the office of a team psychiatrist. The psychiatrist gave the same mental-status examination used in the schizophrenic series, and under the same circumstances; that is, in private, in an air-conditioned office. If one spouse was diagnosed as suffering from an organic or functional psychosis, the family was eliminated. To be included in this study the spouses had to be diagnosed as mentally healthy, or at most showing only neurotic symptoms. The screening-in of persons suffering from schizophrenia in one group of families and the screening-out of psychotics in the other series of families was deliberate. It resulted in two groups of families with distinctly different psychiatric statuses. The two groups were equal in size; each was composed of twenty families.

These families may be viewed as a "sick" series and a "well" series. In technical terms, the sick series represented an experimental group, and the well series a control group. However, we did not perform any experiments on either the well or the sick families. We simply studied them in their homes and neighborhoods. During the twenty months of the field work, no person in the study was hospitalized for mental illness.

The Field Teams
The field team was composed of professionally trained psychiatric social workers and social scientists, who were themselves Puerto Rican. We employed both men and women. Men were needed to interview males, and women to interview females. This was essential on certain topics, such as sex history. The field workers knew the culture, the local people, and how to interview. Nevertheless, Rogler maintained vigilant supervision over their daily work. To gather the data for the eight schedules used in the study required from 110 to 125 hours of face-to-face interviewing of the members of each family. The interviews for any given family spread over four to seven months. An average of forty interviews

was necessary to complete the field work on the families with a schizophrenic member, and thirty-five with the families that did not have a schizophrenic in them. All of the interviews were conducted in Spanish.

Most of the interviews were carried out in the homes, but some were conducted in small corner coffee shops, bars, barber shops, beauty parlors, and the interviewers' cars, parks, and jails. We interviewed where we could and when we could. The field work was a give-and-take process. The male workers bought rum for some men, and some of the women field workers carried food to starving wives and children. Clothing was given to several families to cover the nakedness of children. In a few homes, interviewers sat on the floor, because this was the only place to sit. Unexpected tropical storms drenched the interviewers, and high tides caused homes over backed-up waters to sway precariously. In a number of instances, field workers walked thigh-deep in polluted water to and from humble homes on stilts. One interviewer was threatened with murder when she discovered a bootlegger surreptitiously plying his trade. Another interviewer received a friendly invitation to help castrate vicious dogs impounded by the mother of one of the wives in the schizophrenic group. With very minor and infrequent exceptions, the persons interviewed were cordial and cooperative.

AREAS OF RESIDENCE
The criterion of low socio-economic status resulted in the selection of families who live either in slums or in public housing projects known locally as *caserios*.

Slums
The slums of San Juan have been built through the efforts of individuals and their families in search of a niche, where they may meet the necessities of life and death and store their meager possessions. Slums have grown on land too swampy to support commercial buildings and on hillsides so steep they have not been attractive for other uses. Any place where people can build a shelter from the rain and the sun may become a slum. The largest slums are built on low ground on the sides of both the Martin Pena Channel and the lagoons into which it leads. These low-lying slums stretch for several miles along the sides of the lagoons and backwaters of the meandering Channel.

The pressure for a place to build is so great that many homes are built on piles over tidal waters. The farther out in the water a house is built, the longer the piles. As one moves away from the

Channel to higher ground, the piles become shorter. The houses are built on piles, even on the hillsides, to insure circulation of air, to minimize damage from termites, and to protect them from water. In the lower-lying areas, when the wind blows and the tides run high, the houses vibrate and sway. Several of our field workers reported getting seasick while interviewing in these homes. The longer the piles, the greater the amount of the movements from tidal action.

Each neighborhood within a slum has a name. One of the most delapidated and pestiferous neighborhoods is known as *Buenos Aires*—"good air." Another, surrounded by a slightly higher ground but whose center is an odoriferous pool of mud, is called "Black Ass." The most infamous slum, *La Perla*—"The Pearl"—is anchored on a steep hillside that descends to the Atlantic Ocean. The name of a slum is a sardonic indication of its inhabitant's attitude toward it.

Slums are adjacent to regularly established streets. Entrances from these streets enable the inhabitants to come and go. The "main street," or walkway, of a slum is interconnected with a network of narrow side alleys. The alleys branch into paths that end at someone's front door. In the main, the walkways meander from the entrance downhill to the edge of the lagoon, or uphill from a road. In hill slums, the walkways may be downhill from a highway.

Most walkways are simple dirt paths. Some walkways are covered with crushed rock that is dumped on the edge of the area by the city. Each householder hauls the rock to his house and spreads it on the walk, so that the walk in front of his house will not be a morass during rains. Some householders gather pieces of discarded linoleum from a dump, carry it to their home, lay it on the stones, and pound it down. Others use pieces of tar paper or discarded gunny bags to smooth the walkway. The hot tropical sun melts the linoleum and tar paper with the effect that it binds the underlying rocks into a solid mass. In low-lying slums, as the paths descend toward the water, the walkways are built out of wooden planks placed upon piles. These walkways often are washed away during storms and high waters.

The houses are not built at a uniform height above the ground or the water. Each builder sets the floor level of his house to suit his fancy and needs. The floors of homes built over the Channel and lagoons may be only a few inches above the water during high tide. When storms sweep over the area, these houses are flooded. The lack of uniformity in a house's height above the water line presents a stair-step effect from the walkways or the Channel.

Each house is built by a man who expects to live there as soon as possible, often while it is under construction. The builder is generally an unskilled worker who has a few simple tools—a hammer, a saw, and possibly a square and a plane. He selects a site, squats on it, and may assign his wife, or his child, to guard "his" property so that someone else does not claim it. He gathers pieces of wood for piles, joists, floors, walls, and rafters from a variety of sources. The incoming tide is scanned for floating lumber. Buildings being demolished are visited after, or before, regular working hours. Lumber, hardware, sheet iron, and other items are carted to the building site. New construction sites will be checked for possible materials. The watchman may be bribed to look the other way while the builder clandestinely selects something he wants. Gradually, the essential pieces are brought together and the house takes shape. The new house is likely to be very close to the next house, because of the scarcity of space and also because of the new neighbor's desire to have his house face a street, alley, path, or walkway. Frequently, not more than a foot or two separates one house from another.

These homes are rectangular in shape. The walls are made of wood, corrugated iron, opened and flattened five gallon kerosene tins, and old metal signs. The gable roofs are covered usually with corrugated iron. Apertures for the windows and doors are rough and often not trimmed. The doors and windows are made of rough boards, generally hinged to swing outward, to save inside space. The windows in adjacent houses often hit one another, unless the neighbors cooperate in opening and closing them.

When the family is at home during the day, the windows and doors are open. Otherwise, the heat is suffocating. At night the windows and doors are closed in order to keep out the night air, which is believed to be unhealthy. When the family is away, the windows are secured from the inside and the door is locked from the outside with a steel hasp and a padlock.

Practically every house has a small front porch covered with a shed roof to protect the inhabitants from the sun's piercing rays. The more elaborate ones may have a back porch. Inside the house, the living space may be divided into rooms by partitions, which may or may not extend to the roof. Only the better slum homes have ceilings. Ceilings are expensive; besides, they impede the circulation of air.

Sanitation is provided by open ditches that run from the houses to the alleys and walkways. Feces, urine, washwater, coffee grounds, and other wastes are carried in the ditches to the lagoon. Toilet facilities vary from commercial earthenware stools to a hole cut in the floor. The toilet empties into the sewage trench. A person walking by a home on occasion may see a person urinating or defecating and hear the excrement hit the waters of the trench, or the lagoon. Houses on high ground have outside latrines. The yard is usually so small that the latrine is immediately beside the house. It may block passage to the adjacent house.

The city has piped water into each slum. The water pipes are laid on top of the walks. At intervals there are public spigots beside the walkway. Some householders come to a spigot for their domestic water supply. The water is drawn into cans or jars which at one time contained kerosene, vegetables, or fruit. To avoid going to the public spigot, some householders run water lines to their houses. To do this, a hole is bored into the main. Then a copper tube is thrust into the hole and bound in place with an iron strap that encircles the main. The tube is run, in some instances, to a sink in the house and a spigot is attached. More commonly, the spigot is placed at the corner of the house. Periodically, officials from the Water Authority tear out these illicit private lines. Some homes are connected legitimately to the city's water mains.

A bathtub or a shower in the home is a rare luxury. Bathing is accomplished in a wash tub, basin, or gasoline can. Some men have built showers beside their houses. A neighborhood shower is common. It is made by tapping into the water main. A water pipe is run to a small vacant area and raised five or six feet above the ground; then a shower head is attached. A slat foot-rest is built to lay on the ground. A board wall with a door is built around the shower head; cracks from three-quarters to more than an inch wide separate one board from another.

Some homes are either legitimately or surreptitiously connected to the city's electrical system. Electricity is brought into the house on wires fastened to insulators in one or two places, so that the family can have light, a radio, and, desirably, a television set.

The slums, where most of our families live, are subject to the twice-daily flow and ebb of the tides. The incoming tide brings debris from the harbor (untreated sewage from the city, as well as the accumulation of sewage from the slums) into the network of house piles and walkways. To this accumulation is added the garbage from slum homes. Rubbish of many kinds—bottles, cans, cocoanut husks, grapefruit and orange rinds, gunny sacks, old automobile tires, rusted pieces of iron, paper boxes, newspapers, IBM cards, bones of chickens and pigs old shoes, playing cards, condoms, and so on—is thrown under the houses and along the walkways. This mulch of rubbish and garbage is soaked periodically by the sudden rains which pass over the area. The hot, tropical sun helps decompose and dry the sodden debris. It also adds to the all-pervasive stench. Gradually, the rotting debris settles into the mud. The incoming tidal flow stirs up the sediment and floods the lower-lying areas. As the tide ebbs, a malodorous scum covers the lower portions of the walkways and the ground under the houses.

Caserios

The public housing projects, *caserios,* which are planned, erected, and maintained by the Puerto Rican government, are in sharp contrast to the slums. The *caserios* embody established principles of good housing for low-income families. *Caserios* are built on solid and relatively dry land. They are surrounded by surveyed and paved streets. Each building is set apart from adjacent buildings. The foundations, walls, floors, stairs, and roofs are made of concrete. Sidewalks lead from each building to the street. The buildings are two, three, or four floors in height. High-rise buildings have not been erected.

Residential buildings in *caserios* are subdivided into one-family apartments. Each apartment has electricity, water, and sanitary facilities. The internal space is divided into a kitchen, bath, dining-living area, and one or more bedrooms. The more desirable apartments have a balcony with a wall approximately three feet high around it. In the older *caserios* windows are sometimes fitted with iron bars in order to keep thieves out of the apartments. The newer *caserios* have jalousie windows, which also provide protection and have the advantage of being easy to open and shut. The size of an assigned apartment is related to the number of persons in the family.

The construction of *caserios* to replace the slums is a major governmental objective. Although the government is building public housing as rapidly as possible, the slums are growing almost as fast as they are being replaced. This situation is traceable to the attraction that the San Juan area has for Puerto Ricans throughout the island. The vast majority of migrants to San Juan are unskilled, poorly educated, and without financial resources. The newly arrived migrant from another part of the island ordinarily drifts to the slums or a *caserio* apartment of some member of his kin group. As conditions become better for him, he moves from a room or sleeping space to a house or apartment. There is a chronic shortage of housing of any kind. Gradually, as the Housing Authority is able to carry out its program of building apartments, the worst slums are demolished. Before the debris can be hauled away, individuals in search of building materials carry off usable pieces. These raids are usually made at night or early in the morning. In this way the slums are replenished while the Housing Authority builds new apartments. Building goes on day and night—officially by day, unofficially by night.

Housing in Our Families

The families in our study are divided unequally between slums and *caserios*. Sixty-five percent live in slums, and 35 percent live in *caserios*. The families living in *caserios* pay a mean rental of $14 per month. Families in the slums pay a mean rental of $22 per month. The 40 percent of our families who own slum homes estimate their mean value as $1000. The slum dwellers are more crowded in their homes than the *caserio* dwellers are in their apartments. The *caserio* dwellers have 1.4 enclosed spaces per person in their apartments; the slum dwellers have only .9 enclosed spaces per person in their homes. The enclosed spaces in the *caserio* apartments are also larger than the enclosed spaces in slum homes. Hence, the living space per person is greater in *caserios* than in slum dwellings. By the criteria of "good" housing, *caserio* dwellers are "better" housed than the slum dwellers.

REACTIONS TO SLUMS AND CASERIOS

The third section of this paper describes some reactions of the husbands and wives in our families to their neighborhoods. The data we shall present are drawn from a series of questions we asked, which elicited information on each respondent's relations with his neighbors and his evaluation of the neighborhood where he lived. One of these questions asked the interviewee to tell us how he liked his present neighborhood. His answer is categorized on a four-point scale: "Like a lot"; "Like it a little"; "Dislike it a little"; "Dislike it a lot."

Responses to this question reveal dissimilar reactions to their neighborhoods by slum dwellers and *caserio dwellers*. Sixty-five percent of the men and women who live in slum homes like the slums, whereas 86 percent of the men and 71 percent of the women dislike *caserios*.

When the mental health of the person is taken into consideration, we find that in the *caserios* about the same proportion of sick persons and healthy persons dislike their neighborhoods. In the slums more well persons than sick persons like their neighborhoods, but the difference is not significant for either males or females.

The dislike of *caserios*, in comparison with slums, appeared in responses to other questions. These questions include relations with neighbors, persons the respondents would prefer not to have as neighbors, things the neighbors do that the husbands and wives in the study do not like, and the desire either to move to a different neighborhood or to stay in their present one. Responses to these questions show a consistent pattern of more slum dwellers than *caserio* dwellers liking their neighborhoods; this pattern is independent of the psychiatric distinction between sick and well.

The sharpest dissatisfaction with their present neighborhood, among both *caserios* and slum dwellers, is revealed in replies to the question: Do you think this is a good neighborhood in which to raise your children? This is an emotionally loaded subject to the parents in the study, because of the high hopes and aspirations they have for their children. The figures show that 38 percent of the slum-dwelling husbands think the slum is a good place to raise their children, but only 7 percent of the husbands in *caserios* believe a *caserio* is a good place to raise children. The wives are not as accepting of either slum or *caserios* conditions as the husbands. No wife in the *caserios* believes a *caserio* is a good place to raise children; only 15 percent of the wives who live in the slums think that slums are a good place to raise children.

The findings indicate that both *caserio* and slum dwellers are reacting against the physical, social, and cultural environments in which their class position has placed them. From their point of view, these environments are not conducive to the appropriate raising of children.

The Dilemma

The basic findings we have presented pose two dilemmas. First, good housing—in accord with standards established by city planners and architects, and erected by an enlightened government—may result in the formation of social conditions people do not like. Second, when we control for the neighborhood factor, families who have one or both spouses afflicted with schizophrenia react to their neighborhoods in ways that are not essentially different from families where the spouses are mentally healthy. These findings call for an explanation. Why do *caserio* dwellers dislike their neighborhood significantly more than slum dwellers do theirs?

Caserio families, as well as slum families, are clear and articulate in describing the things they do not like. Persons in the slums resent the dampness and the filth most. *Caserio* dwellers object most vociferously to the restrictions imposed upon them by the Public Housing Authority. Complaints in these groups are registered, in a sense, against nature on the one hand, and government on the other.

Caserio dwellers have escaped from the water and mud, but the government has imposed a series of irritating regulations. Most of these rules run counter to lower-class folkways. For example, the Housing Authority rents an apartment to a single, nuclear family. Relatives and boarders are not supposed to be smuggled into the apartment by the authorized tenants. This restriction runs counter to obligations entailed by the kinship system. The kin tie places a personal obligation on a man or a woman to shelter and feed a relative by blood, marriage, or custom. The kin tie is rooted in the culture of Puerto Rico. The rule of the *Caserio* Authority is imposed by governmental agents; therefore, it may be violated without a feeling of guilt. The conflict here is between a personal obligation and an impersonal rule. To turn away a relative is reprehensible; to disregard a governmental regulation is not.

The rule on tenancy is violated frequently by *caserio* residents. However, when a tenant gives shelter to relatives, he or she knows that a neighbor could report this fact to the central office. When this happens, the central Authority may force the squatters to move. The legitimate tenant usually attempts to talk the Housing Authority into assigning an apartment in the same *caserio* to the relative. If possible, the housing official complies with the tenant's request. This results in kin-group clusters in a given building, or adjacent buildings.

Rules established by the Housing Authority to promote sanitation are another source or irritation. Housing Authority rules prohibit livestock in the apartments. This rule is breached by many families. Chickens, rabbits, pigs, and goats are smuggled into the *caserios*. Their owners house them in the bathroom, or on the walled-in balcony, until a neighbor reports the violation. Then the officials force them to dispose of the animal. The squeal of a dying hog, being sacrificed unwillingly to satisfy the orders of a petty bureaucrat, is not an unusual sound in and around a *caserio*. The neighbor who reported the animal's presence is known, or suspected. Interpersonal relations between the animal's owner and the real or alleged informer are impaired seriously. The two families may also have been enemies before, with one retaliating against the other.

Financial rules are also a source of discontent in *caserios*. The Housing Authority has a definite ceiling on the amount a family who lives in a *caserio* may earn. If a family's income exceeds the established limit and this becomes known, the family is forced to move into some other type of housing. This rule means that *caserio* dwellers have incomes below the maximum, or they attempt to make the authority believe they do. Families with incomes near or above the allowable maximum know that they must conceal the amount of their income or face the prospect of moving. If the neighbors become suspicious that their income is above the maximum, a report may be made to the Housing Authority. The less successful neighbor, who is envious of the prosperous family's good fortune, to even the score, gossips to the authorities. An investigation may follow, and the family may be evicted if the report is substantiated. *Caserio* dwellers hate neighbors who report them.

Each family is required to pay the monthly rental established for it by the Housing Authority. Ability to pay is determined by the size of the family and its income. The *caserio* officials are responsible for checking on a family's income, the number of persons living in an apartment, and the maintenance of the apartment. The rule of "pay or get out," coupled with the rule of maximum earnings, eliminates those who cannot pay rent, as well as those who can afford private housing. *Caserio* dwellers, therefore, are a selected segment of the population.

In sum, *caserio* dwellers dislike the social conditions imposed upon them by the Public Housing Authority. They have been uprooted, in the main, either by the destruction of their slum homes or by their having moved directly from rural portions of the island to *caserios* in San Juan. Slum dwellers and rural migrants, who have moved to *caserios,* find it difficult to adjust to the rules imposed by the Public Housing Authority. One of the most disturbing factors in *caserio* life is the potential power that one family has over another family. This power becomes effective when a family is reported by its neighbors to the *caserio* officials for an infraction of rules. In the slums, no immediate authority intervenes between neighbors. Social controls within a slum are a product of the values and expectations of the traditional culture. Within the *caserios,* the norms and expectancies of lower-class culture clash at many points with the rules and regulations imposed by the government—rules and regulations which derive from a different social class.

The Dream House

Husbands and wives in *caserios* and slums are as clear in what they desire as they are in what they do not like. *Caserio* dwellers do not desire more and better *caserios;* they want a home of their own. Families in the slums know that they are living under the shadow of the bulldozer. Whether they own or rent their homes, it is only a matter of time until the government demolishes the slum where they live. These families, too, want a home of their own—but *not* in a *caserio.*

What kind of a home do slum and *caserio* dwellers desire? The interviewees are almost of one voice in describing the home they

want to own. The house should be located on high ground, on a lot
fifty by one hundred feet. The lot should be on a paved street with
sidewalks, so members of the family will not be maimed or killed
by trucks and automobiles. It should be near schools, stores, and a
church. There should be easy access to public transportation, doctors, and a hospital. There should be playgrounds for the children
nearby. The lot should be enclosed by a concrete wall sufficiently
high to provide privacy for the family and protection for the children.

The house should be built of concrete, with the floor covered
with glazed, ceramic tile. Corrugated iron roofs are not desired;
preferably, the roof and ceiling should be made of reinforced concrete. The kitchen and bathroom should have glazed, ceramic tile
on the walls. The interior should be divided into a kitchen, living
and dining area, a bathroom, ample closet space, and two or three
bedrooms. It should have a porch and a back patio.

These families want electricity properly installed in the home.
They want city water in their homes, with sinks in the kitchen and
in the bathroom. They also desire underground, sanitary sewers.

The neighborhood should be a quiet one. The neighbors should
be people they can respect, and the neighbors should respect them.
They want to be friendly with their neighbors, and they want their
neighbors to reciprocate.

SUMMARY AND CONCLUSION

By way of summary, we shall say again: The materials we have
presented are drawn from an intensive study of families who live
in San Juan, Puerto Rico. The families have been matched for age,
socio-economic status, marital union, and area of residence. The dif-
ferentiating criterion between families is the mental status of one
or both spouses. In one-half of the families, at least one spouse is
suffering from schizophrenia. In the other half of the families, both
spouses are mentally healthy or, at most, revealed neurotic symptoms to the examining psychiatrist. The study group, therefore, is
composed of "sick" and "well" families. The well families are controls for the sick families.

All of the families studied live either in slums or public housing projects. The families who live in apartments in the public
housing projects are housed more adequately than families who live
in the slums. They pay far less rent per month for their apartments
than the slum dwellers who rent do for their humble homes. There
is less crowding in the apartments than in the slums.

The reactions of slum families to their physical and human

environments are sharply different from the reactions of families in public housing apartments to their neighborhoods. Most slum dwellers like their neighborhoods; most dwellers in public housing dislike theirs. This finding poses a dilemma for social planners.

The slums have grown up naturally. They are overcrowded, malodorous, noisy, unsanitary, and under condemnation by "enlightened" segments of the society. Yet, their inhabitants are fonder of them than *caserio* dwellers are of their neighborhoods.

The *caserios* are a product of the planner's design. The buildings are architecturally sound, and the apartments are dry and larger than the slum homes. Modern plumbing, electricity, and other conveniences are provided. *Caserios* are organized as community centers. Yet the people in our study who live in them do not like them. They look forward to the time when they can escape both the bureaucratic apparatus of the *caserio* and the tensions between families, which this apparatus creates. The rules of the *caserios* are imposed by a bureaucracy with a different set of subcultural values and norms from those who are expected to abide by them. *Caserios* rules stem from middle-class, professional values. These values are not part of the class culture of the people who are expected to abide by them. These people are uprooted slum dwellers or rural migrants who have little understanding of the norms of the social engineers who are trying to help them and their children overcome the wretchedness of lower-class living conditions. Slum dwellers are not subject to the annoying penetration of an alien subculture. This is one of the dilemmas that confront people who must cope with ways of life that are changing rapidly.

REFERENCES

1. A study of 500 out-patients in the State Psychiatric Hospital of Puerto Rico, receiving care during the fiscal year of 1956–1957, indicated that 53 percent of the patients were schizophrenic. A study of 200 in-patients in the State Psychiatric Hospital in Puerto Rico, admitted during the fiscal year of 1956–1957, indicated that 58 percent were schizophrenic. These studies were done by the Department of Psychiatry, School of Medicine, The University of Puerto Rico. They have not been published.
2. L. Bellak and P. K. Benedict, eds., *Schizophrenia: A Review of the Syndrome* (New York: Logos Press, 1958); S. Arieti, *Interpretation of Schizophrenia* (New York: Brunner, 1955); D. D. Jackson, ed., *The Etiology of Schizophrenia* (New York: Basic Books, 1960); A. B. Hollingshead, "Some Issues in the Epidemiology of Schizophrenia," *American Sociological Review* 26 (1961): 5–13.
3. J. A. Clausen, "The Sociology of Mental Illness," in R. K. Merton, L. Broom, and L. S. Cottrell, Jr., eds., *Sociology Today, Problems and Prospects* (New York: Basic Books, 1959), pp. 485–509; R. E. L. Faris and H. W. Dunham, *Mental Disorders in Urban Areas* (Chicago: University of Chicago Press, 1939); C. W. Schroeder, "Mental Disorders in Cities," *American Journal of Sociology* 48 (1942): 40–48; R. E. Clark, "Psychoses, Income, and Occupations Prestige," *American Journal of Sociology* 54 (1949): 433–40; A. B. Hollingshead and F. C. Redlich, "Social Stratification and Psychiatric Disorders," *American Sociological Review* 18 (1953): 163–69; A. B. Hollingshead and F. C. Redlich, *Social Class and Mental Illness: A Community Study* (New York: Wiley, 1958).
4. Each family was stratified by the use of A. B. Hollingshead, *Two Factor Index of Social Position*, New Haven, Conn., privately printed, 1957.

BIBLIOGRAPHY

For other aspects of Rogler's and Hollingshead's study, see the following:

L. H. Rogler and A. B. Hollingshead, "Class and Disordered Speech in the Mentally Ill," *Journal of Health and Human Behavior* 2 (1961): 178–85.
———, "The Puerto Rican Spiritualist as a Psychiatrist," *American Journal of Sociology* 67 (1961): 17–21.
———, "Algunas Observaciones Sobre el Espiritismo y las Enfermedades Mentales Entre Puertorriquenos de Clase Baja," *Revista de Ciencias Sociales* 4 (University of Puerto Rico, 1960): 141–50.
L. H. Rogler, A. B. Hollingshead, and A. M. A. Torres, "Las Clases Sociales y la Comunicacion de Ideas de los Enfermas Mentales," *Revista de Ciencias Sociales* 3 (1959): 119–31.

There have been a large number of sociological and anthropological studies done in Puerto Rico, among which are the following:

P. K. Hatt, *Background of Human Fertility in Puerto Rico* (Princeton, N.J.: Princeton University Press, 1952).

R. Hill, J. M. Stycos, and C. W. Back, *The Family and Population Control: A Puerto Rico Experiment in Social Change* (Chapel Hill: University of North Carolina Press, 1959).

D. Landy, *Tropical Childhood, Cultural Transmission and Learning in a Rural Puerto Rican Village* (Chapel Hill: University of North Carolina Press, 1959).

S. W. Mintz, *Worker in the Cane: A Puerto Rican Life History* (New Haven, Conn.: Yale University Press, 1960).

C. C. Rogler, *Comerio, A Study of a Puerto Rican Town* (Lawrence: University of Kansas Press, 1940).

J. H. Stewart, ed., *People of Puerto Rico* (Urbana: University of Illinois Press, 1956).

J. M. Stycos, *Family and Fertility in Puerto Rico: A Study of the Lower Income Group* (New York: Columbia University Press, 1955).

M. M. Tumin and A. Feldman, *Social Class and Social Change in Puerto Rico* (Princeton, N.J.: Princeton University Press, 1961).

The Perception
of Natural Hazards
in Resource Management

IAN BURTON
ROBERT W. KATES

Reprinted from 3 *Natural Resources Journal* 432 (1964): 413–41, published by the University of New Mexico School of Law, Albuquerque, New Mexico, by permission of the publisher and the authors.
This paper has been edited for this publication and notes and art have been renumbered.

Natural hazards are defined in the following paper as ". . . those elements in the physical environment, harmful to man and caused by forces extraneous to him." Although Burton and Kates acknowledge cultural variation in the conception of what is a natural hazard, their definition may have been more appropriately stated to read "those elements in the physical environment which men *perceive* as harmful and caused by extraneous forces." An analogous situation may be smoking cigarettes: on every package is the warning that inhalation may be hazardous to one's health. Yet, smokers pay it no attention and the advice of the medical-scientific community is, for the most part, ignored. Perhaps then, it is not so strange to observe people resettling on the floodplain in the aftermath of a major flood. Who is to decide what is a hazard but man himself?

Another important theme is again illustrated in this chapter—the gap between the scientist-technician's perception of an environmental phenomenon and that of the layman. It is suggested that the expert's perception is related to his training and organizational interest. (This theme is discussed in depth in Chapter 10 by W. R. Derrick Sewell.) On the other hand, the perceptions of the resource users, the laymen, are influenced by the type of resource use. Thus, for example, the Great Plains wheat farmer perceives the occurrence of drought differently from a Corn Belt farmer.

We would like to note a possible underlying assumption by which much of the hazard-related behavior discussed in this paper is evaluated; that is, the model of rational man seems to be continually lurking in the shadows. An example is the authors' expectation of the effect of personal experience— ". . . that when personally experienced, a natural event would be more meaningful and lead to heightened perception." Is this necessary? Perhaps when a person experiences a natural event he finds it boring and meaningless. Couldn't this lead to a dulled perception?

Finally, the paper provides a wealth of ideas, grist for serious and fruitful discussions. We find that stimulating. But little can be concluded because much of what is said remains unsubstantiated; there is much speculation, but little evidence.

*"What region of the earth is not full of
our calamities?"* VIRGIL

To the Englishman on his island, earthquakes are disasters that
happen to others. It is recognized that "while the ground is liable to
open up at any moment beneath the feet of foreigners, the English
are safe because 'it can't happen here' " (*1*). Thus is described a
not uncommon attitude to natural hazards in England; its parallels
are universal.

Notwithstanding this human incapacity to imagine natural
disasters in a familiar environment, considerable disruption is frequently caused by hazards. The management of affairs is not only
affected by the impact of the calamities themselves, but also by the
degree of awareness, or perception of the hazard, that is shared by
those subject to its uncertain threat. Where disbelief in the possibility of an earthquake, a tornado, or a flood is strong, the resultant
damages from the event are likely to be greater than where awareness of the danger leads to effective precautionary action.

In this article we attempt to set down our imperfect understanding of variations in the perception of natural hazard, and to
suggest some ways in which it affects the management of resource
use. In so doing we are extending the notion that resources are best
regarded for management purposes as culturally defined variables,
by consideration of the cultural appraisal of natural hazard.

It may be argued that the uncertainties of natural hazards in
resource management are only a special case of the more general
problem of risk in any economic activity. Certainly there are many
similarities. But it is only when man seeks to wrest from nature
that which he perceives as useful to him that he is strongly challenged by the vagaries of natural phenomena acting over and above
the usual uncertainties of economic activity. In other words, the
management of resource use brings men into a closer contact with
nature (be it viewed as friendly, malevolent, or neutral) where the
extreme variations of the environment exercise a much more profound effect than in other economic activities.

I

THE DEFINITION OF NATURAL HAZARDS

For a working definition of "natural hazards" we propose the following: Natural hazards are those elements in the physical environment, harmful to man and caused by forces extraneous to him.
According to Zimmerman's view, the physical environment or na-

ture is "neutral stuff," but it is human culture which determines which elements are considered to be "resources" or "resistances" (2). Considerable cultural variation exists in the conception of natural hazards; change occurs both in time and space.

In time, our notion of specific hazards and their causal agents frequently change. Consider, for example, the insurance concept of an "act of God." To judge by the volume of litigation, this concept is under constant challenge and is constantly undergoing redefinition. The "acts of God" of today are often tomorrow's acts of criminal negligence. Such changes usually stem from a greater potential to control the environment, although the potential is frequently not made actual until after God has shown His hand.

In space a varied concept of hazard is that of drought. A recent report adequately describes the variation as follows:

> There is a clue from prevailing usage that the term 'drought' reflects the relative insecurity of mankind in the face of a natural phenomenon that he does not understand thoroughly and for which, therefore, he has not devised adequate protective measures. A Westerner does not call a rainless month a 'drought,' and a Californian does not use the term even for an entire growing season that is devoid of rain, because these are usual occurrences and the developed water economy is well bolstered against them. Similarly, a dry period lasting several years, or even several decades, would not qualify as a drought if it caused no hardship among water users (3).

This may be contrasted with the official British definition of an "absolute drought" which is "a period of at least 15 consecutive days to none of which is credited .01 inches of rain or more" (4).

Even such seemingly scientifically defined hazards as infective diseases seem to be subject to changes in interpretation, especially when applied to the assignment of the cause of death. Each decennial revision of the International Lists of Causes of Death has brought important changes to some classes of natural hazards. Thus, the change from the fifth to the sixth revision found a decrease of approximately twenty-five percent in deaths identified as caused by syphilis and its sequelae as a result of the new definition arising from ostensibly improved medical knowledge (5).

The definability of hazard is a more sophisticated form of perceiving a hazard. It is more than mere awareness and often requires high scientific knowledge, i.e., we must understand in order to define precisely. But regardless of whether we describe definitions of drought by western water users or the careful restatement of definitions by public health officials, all types of hazard are subject to wide variation in their definition—a function of the changing pace of man's knowledge and technology.

To complicate the problem further, the rise of urban-industrial societies has been coincident with a rapid increase in a type of hazard which may be described as quasi-natural. These hazards are created by man, but their harmful effects are transmitted through natural processes. Thus, man-made pollutants are carried downstream, radio-active fallout is borne by air currents, and pesticides are absorbed by plants, leaving residues in foods. The intricacies of the man-nature relationship are such that it is frequently not possible to ascribe a hazard exclusively to one class or the other (natural or quasi-natural). A case in point is the question of when fog (a natural hazard) becomes smog (quasi-natural) (6). Presumably some more or less arbitrary standard of smoke content could be developed.

In the discussion that follows, we specifically exclude quasi-natural hazards while recognizing the difficulty of distinguishing them in all cases. Our guide for exclusion is the consideration of principal causal agent.

II

A CLASSIFICATION OF NATURAL HAZARDS

Table 1 is an attempt to classify common natural hazards by their principal causal agent. It is but one of many ways that natural hazards might be ordered, but it is convenient for our purposes. The variety of academic disciplines that study aspects of these hazards is only matched by the number of governmental basic data collection agencies which amass information on these hazards. The most cohesive group is the climatic and meteorological hazards. The most diverse is the floral group which includes the doctor's concern with a minor fungal infection, the botanist's concern with a variety of plant diseases, and the hydrologist's concern with the effect of phreatophytes on the flow of water in streams and irrigation channels.

In a fundamental way, we sense a distinction between the causal agents of geophysical and biologic hazards. This distinction does not lie in their effects, for both hazards work directly and indirectly on man and are found in both large and small scales. Rather, our distinction lies in the notion of preventability, i.e., the prevention of the occurrence of the natural phenomenon of hazardous potential as opposed to mere control of hazardous effects. A

Geophysical		Biological	
CLIMATIC AND METEOROLOGICAL	GEOLOGICAL AND GEOMORPHIC	FLORAL	FAUNAL
Blizzards & Snow	Avalanches	Fungal Diseases *For example:*	Bacterial & Viral Diseases *For example:*
Droughts	Earthquakes	Athlete's foot	
	Erosion (including	Dutch elm	Influenza
Floods	soil erosion &	Wheat stem rust	Malaria
	shore and beach	Blister rust	Typhus
Fog	erosion)		Bubonic Plague
		Infestations	Venereal
Frost	Landslides	*For example:*	Disease
			Rabies
Hailstorms	Shifting Sand	Weeds	Hoof & Mouth
		Phreatophytes	Disease
Heat Waves	Tsunamis	Water hyacinth	Tobacco Mosaic
Hurricanes	Volcanic Eruptions	Hay Fever	Infestations *For example:*
Lightning Strokes & Fires		Poison Ivy	Rabbits Termites Locusts
Tornadoes			Grasshoppers
			Venomous Animal Bites

Table 1.   *Common Natural Hazards by Principal Causal Agent*

rough rule of thumb is that changes in nature are to be classed as prevention, but changes in man or his works are control.

Given this rule of thumb, it is clear that few hazards are completely preventable. Prevention has been most successful in the area of floral and faunal hazards. Some such hazards (e.g., malaria) have been virtually eliminated in the United States by preventive measures, but they are still common in other parts of the world.

At the present levels of technology, geophysical hazards cannot be prevented, while biological hazards can be prevented in most cases, subject only to economic and budgetary constraints.

We suggest that this is a basic distinction and directly related to the areal dimensions and the character and quantities of energy involved in these natural phenomena. While much encouraging work has been done, we still cannot prevent a hurricane, identify and destroy an incipient tornado, prevent the special concentration of precipitation that often induces floods, or even on a modest scale alter the pattern of winds that shift sand, or prevent the oversteepening and sub-soil saturation that induces landslides. We might again note the distinction between prevention and control: we can and do build landslide barriers to keep rock off highways, and we can and do attempt to stabilize shifting sand dunes.

Despite much loose discussion in popular journals, repeated surveys of progress in weather modification have not changed substantially from the verdict of the American Meteorological Society in 1957, which was that:

> Present knowledge of atmospheric processes offers no real basis for the belief that the weather or climate of a large portion of the country can be significantly modified by cloud seeding. It is not intended to rule out the possibility of large-scale modifications of the weather at some future time, but it is believed that, if possible at all, this will require methods that alter the large-scale atmospheric circulations, possibly through changes in the radiation balance. (7).

The non-preventability of the class of geophysical hazards has existed throughout the history of man and will apparently continue to do so for some time to come. Our training, interest, and experience has been confined to this class of hazards. Moreover, as geographers we are more comfortable when operating in the field of geophysical phenomena than biological. However, we do not know whether the tentative generalizations we propose apply only to geophysical hazards or to the whole spectrum of natural hazards. A priori speculation might suggest the hypothesis that men react to the non-preventable hazard, the true "act of God," in a special way, distinct from preventable hazards. Our observations to date incline us toward the belief that there is an orderly or systematic difference in the perception of preventable and non-preventable natural hazards.

This arises from the hiatus between popular perception of hazard and the technical-scientific perception. To many flood-plain users, floods are preventable, i.e., flood control can completely eliminate the hazard. Yet the technical expert knows that except for very small drainage areas no flood control works known can effectively prevent the flood-inducing concentration of precipitation, nor can they effectively control extremely large floods of very rare occurrence. On the other hand, in some parts of the world hoof and mouth disease is not considered preventable, although there is considerable evidence that it is preventable when there is a widespread willingness to suffer large economic losses by massive eradication of diseased cattle combined with vigorous control measures of vaccination.

The hiatus between the popular perception of hazard and the perception of the technician scientist is considered below in greater detail.

III

VARIATIONS IN PERCEPTION

. . . It is well established that men view differently the challenges and hazards of their natural environment. In this section we will consider some of the variations in view or perception of natural hazard. In so doing we will raise more questions than we shall answer; this is a reflection of the immaturity and youth of this line of research.

Our scheme will be to consider the *within group and between group* variation in perception of two well-defined groups: resource users, who are the managers of natural resources directly affected by natural hazards (including of course their own persons), (8) and technical and scientific personnel—individuals with specialized training and directly charged with study or control of natural hazards.

A. Variation in the Perception of
Natural Hazard Among Scientific Personnel

The specialized literature is replete with examples of differences in hazard perception among experts. They fail to perceive the actual nature of the hazard, its magnitude, and its location in time and space. Technical personnel differ among each other, and the use of reputable methods often provides estimates of hazards of great variance from one another.

Such variation is due in small part to differences in experience and training, vested organizational interest, and even personality. But in a profound and fundamental way, such variation is a product of human ignorance.

The epistemology of natural hazard. We have emphasized the nature of natural hazard as phenomena of nature with varying effects on man, ranging from harmless to catastrophic. To know and to fully understand these natural phenomena is to give to man the opportunity of avoiding or circumventing the hazard. To know fully, in this sense, is to be able to predict the location in time and space and the size or duration of the natural phenomenon potentially harmful to man. Despite the sophistication of modern science or our ability to state the requirements for such a knowledge system, there seems little hope that basic geophysical phenomena will

ever be fully predictable. No foreseeable system of data gathering
and sensing equipment seems likely to pinpoint the discharge of a
lightning bolt or the precise path of a tornado.

Given this inherent limitation, almost all estimation of hazard
is probabilistic in content, and these probabilities may be computed
either by counting (relative frequency) or by believing in some
underlying descriptive frequency distribution. The probability of
most hazardous events is determined by counting the observed occurrence of similar events. In so doing we are manipulating three
variables: the magnitude of the event, its occurrence in time, and
its occurrence in space.

For some hazards the spatial variable might fortunately be
fixed. Volcanic eruptions often take place at a fixed point, and rivers
in humid areas follow well-defined stream courses. For other hazards there may be broadly defined belts such as storm paths or
earthquake regions. There are no geophysical hazards that are apparently evenly or randomly distributed over the earth's surface,
but some, such as lightning, approach being ubiquitous over large
regions.

The size or magnitude of the hazard varies, and, given the
long-term human adjustment to many hazards, this can be quite
important. Blizzards are common on the Great Plains, but a pro-
tracted blizzard can bring disaster to a large region (9). On great
alluvial flood plains small hummocks provide dry sites for settlement, but such hummocks are overwhelmed by a flood event of great
magnitude.

Magnitude can be thought of as a function of time based on
the apparent truism of extreme events: if one waits long enough,
there will always be an event larger than that previously experienced. In the case of geophysical events, waiting may involve
several thousand years. Graphically, this is presented for fifty years
in Figure 1 for two common hazards.

Most harmful natural phenomena are rare events; if they
were not, we humans would probably have been decimated before
we became entrenched on this planet. Since the counting of events
is the major method of determining probabilities, rare events by
their nature are not easily counted. Equally disturbing is the possibility that by climatic change, or improved scientific knowledge,
or human interference, the class of natural events may change and
create further uncertainties in the process of observing and re-
cording.

Faced with a high degree of uncertainty, but pressed by the requirements of a technical society for judgments and decisions, sci-

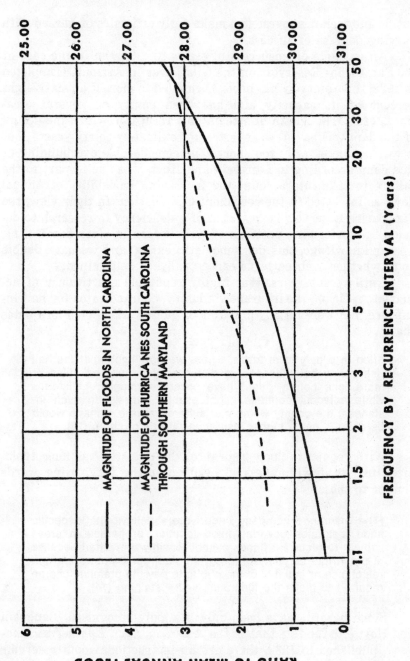

Figure 1

Source: National Hurricane Research Project Report No. 33; Floods in North Carolina; Magnitude and Frequency.

entific and technical personnel make daily estimates of hazard with varying degrees of success.

An example of unsuccessful estimating is seen in the case of the San Carlos Reservoir on the Gila River in Arizona. Completed in 1928, this reservoir has never been filled to more than sixty-eight percent of its capacity and has been empty on several occasions. (10). The length of stream flow record on which the design of the dam was based was short (approximately thirty years), but it was not necessarily too short. The considerable overbuilding of this dam, according to Langbein and Hoyt, was due in part to the failure to take into account the increasing variability of annual flows as indicated in the coefficient of variation. In their view, the San Carlos Reservoir is "a victim of a deficiency in research to develop the underlying patterns of fluctuations in river flow" (11). To our knowledge, this deficiency still exists, and we have doubts as to whether such patterns can actually be determined.

Until recent years, that highly reputable practitioner of actuarial precision, the insurance industry, charged rates for hail insurance that were largely a matter of guesswork (12). Flora notes that

> often in widely level areas, where we now know that the hail risk varies but little over a distance of a hundred miles or more, one county might have several damaging hailstorms while adjacent counties might escape entirely. In such instances, the county which had suffered severe damage would be given a much higher insurance rate than others (13).

With regard to flood insurance, the industry has long apologized for its unwillingness to even enter the fray, using words similar to these:

> [The insurance company underwriters believe that] specific flood insurance covering fixed location properties in areas subject to recurrent floods cannot feasibly be written because of the virtual certainty of loss, its catastrophic nature and the reluctance or inability of the public to pay the premium charge required to make the insurance self-sustaining (14).

Some hazards have been only belatedly recognized. Langbein and Hoyt cite the fact that in the *American Civil Engineers Handbook*, published in 1930, there are no instructions about reservoir sedimentation (15).

Public agencies charged with flood control responsibilities have had to make estimates of the long run recurrence of these phenomena. Despite a great deal of work and ingenuity, results are not overly impressive. Three highly respected methods of flood frequency analysis place the long run average return period of the largest flood of record in the Lehigh Valley as either twenty-seven, forty-five, or seventy-five years (*16*).

The disparate views and perceptions of technical and scientific personnel are a reflection of our ignorance of the chance occurrence of events, and more fundamentally of our lack of understanding of the physical forces themselves. There is little hope of eliminating this uncertainty, and the technical-scientific community follows the course of recognizing it, defining it, and finally learning to live with it.

B. Variations in the Perception of Natural Hazard Among Resource Managers

Resource users or managers do not display uniformity in their perception of natural hazard any more than do scientific and technical personnel. Not being experts, they have less knowledge or understanding of the various possible interpretations of data and are often amazed at the lack of agreement among the professionals. Their views may be expected to coincide insofar as the lay managers subscribe to the various popular myths of hazard perception (whether "it can't happen here," or "after great droughts come great rains," or "a little rain stills a great wind"). But in this age of enlightenment, perception is not easily limited to such aphorisms. Differences in perception arise both among users of the same resource and between users of different resources.

1. Perception among users of the same resource. Urban and flood-plain users display differences in the perception of flood hazard. Our own studies of urban (*17*) and agricultural (*18*) flood-plain users suggest a greater hazard sensitivity in terms of awareness on the part of agricultural land users. However, the frequency of hazard that encourages certain responses on the part of resource users is approximately equal for both urban and agricultural land users (*19*).

The limited work on flood plains in variation of perception between users suggests three explanatory factors: (1) the relation of the hazard to the dominant resource use, including in agriculture the ratio between area subject to flooding and the total size of the management unit, (2) the frequency of occurrence of floods, and (3) variations in degree of personal experience. Interestingly, there seems to be little or no significant effect in hazard perception by the few generalized indicators of level of social class or education that have been tested against hazard perception.

The first factor is essentially a reflection of an ends-means scheme of resource use. We would expect to find a heightened hazard perception in those cases, such as drought in an agricultural region or beach erosion on a waterfront cottage, where the hazard is directly related to the resource use. Where it is incidental, such as lightning or tornadoes, the perception of hazard is variant, vague, and often whimsical.

The second factor suggests that the frequency of natural events is related to the perception of hazard. Where the events in question are frequent, there is little variation among users in their perception. The same holds true where the event is infrequent, for here the failure to perceive a significant hazard is widely shared. It is in the situation of moderate frequency that one expects to find (and does find) considerable variation among resource users.

The third factor is also related to frequency. One would expect that when personally experienced a natural event would be more meaningful and lead to heightened perception. The limited evidence to date does not clearly bear this out. There is a pronounced ability to share in the common experience, and newcomers often take on the shared or dominant perception of the community. Also given a unique or cyclical interpretation of natural events, the experience of an event often tends to allay future anxiety; this is in keeping with the old adage about lightning not striking in the same place twice. Thus the effect of experience as a determinant of hazard perception is considerably blurred.

2. *Perception between different resource users.* Differences in perception are found between coastal and flood-plain land resource users in areas subject to storm damage or erosion. Unfortunately, we cannot say more about hazard perception differences between resource users. To our knowledge, they have never been carefully explored, although such study would undoubtedly throw much light on the problem of comparing the resource management policies of different groups and nations (20). Some historical comment provides suggestions for the direction that such differences might take.

In a recent article, David Lowenthal notes the changes in our attitude towards wilderness. Once viewed as awesome and tyrannical, nature in the wild is now wonderful and brings us close to the spirit of the Creator. "Our forefathers mastered a continent; today we celebrate the virtues of the vanquished foe" (21). Nature itself has become synonymous with virtue (22). This subject has been examined in some detail by Hans Huth in his study of the attitudes that led to the establishment of the conservation movement (23).

The rapid expansion of agriculture in the Great Plains during a relatively humid period by settlers from areas with different environmental experience and background is well known. Unprepared for the climatic hazards they encountered, many settlers "were predisposed to believe that the climate was becoming permanently more humid. In fact, many thought that it was the spread of cultivation that brought about an increase in rainfall" (24).

Study of other hazards suggests that there is considerable difference in the social acceptance of personal injury depending on the kind of hazard that was the causal agent. Edward Suchman notes that "a report of a few cases of polio will empty the beaches, but reports of many more deaths by automobile accidents on the roads to the beaches will have little effect." He suggests that one explanation may lie "in the greater popular acceptance of accidents as inevitable and uncontrollable" (25).

A contrast in awareness of natural hazards is exemplified by a warning sign observed in a coastal location on the island of Hawaii. Affixed to a palm tree in an area subject to *tsunamis* at the front door and the hazard of volcanic eruptions and lava flows at the back door (Mauna Loa volcano), this sign merely advises the reader: "Beware of falling coconuts!"

C. Variation in Natural Hazard Perception Between Technical-Scientific Personnel and Resource Users

It is our impression that there is considerable divergence between the perception of natural hazard of technical-scientific personnel and resource users. In the case of floods such divergence is widespread.

Although we have emphasized in the previous section the variation in probability that technical people might assign to a given flood event, these are essentially in estimation. Over the past several years we have interviewed or spoken with well over one-hundred technical people concerned with floods, and we have never met one who discounted the possibility of a flood occurring again in a valley that had been previously flooded. By contrast, out of 216 flood-plain dwellers interviewed in a variety of small urban places between 1960 and 1962, all of whom had a measurable flood hazard, some 84 categorically did not expect to be flooded in the future (26).

Another example of the disparity between the technical and resource user perception is found in the occasional experience of the rejection of plans for protective works by at least part of the resource users, even when the cost of such works directly to the users in monetary terms was nominal or non-existent. In Fairfield, Connecticut some users of waterfront property opposed the construction of a protective dike along the shore, principally on the contention that such protection "would seriously interfere with their view and result in loss of breeze" (*27*). Similarly, dune-levelling which is universally condemned by technical personnel as destructive of nature's main protection against the ravages of the sea, is widely practiced (as at West Dennis, Massachusetts) to improve the scenic view or to make room for more buildings.

Is such behavior adopted out of ignorance of the hazard; is it symptomatic of the irrationality of resource users in hazard situations; or is there some other explanation? While there are resource users who act in total ignorance of natural hazards, their number is relatively small. Nor can the difference simply be explained away in terms of irrationality. In our view, the difference arises primarily out of the evaluation of the hazard. We offer the following explanation for divergence in hazard evaluation:

1. For some resource users, the differences in perceiving a natural hazard may be a reflection of those existing among scientific and technical personnel themselves. Given the great uncertainty that surrounds the formulation of an "objective" estimate of hazard, the estimate made by a resource user may be no more divergent than that supplied by the use of a different formula or the addition of more data.

2. For some resource users we suspect the divergence in hazard perception may be as fundamental as basic attitudes towards nature. Technical-scientific estimates of hazard assume the neutrality of nature. There are resource users who perceive otherwise, conceiving of nature as malevolent or benevolent. Our language is full of metaphors and descriptions of "Mother nature," "bountiful nature," or, conversely, of "angry storms." Besides attributing motivation to nature, there is also the distinction of man's relation to nature. One recent anthropological study, using a cross-cultural approach, developed a man-nature classification comprising man over nature, man with nature, and man under nature (*28*). Each of these three divergent points of view is represented by the following statement:

> *Man Subject to Nature.* 'My people have never controlled the rain, wind, and other natural conditions, and probably never will. There have always been good years and bad years. That is the way it is, and if you are wise you will take it as it comes and do the best you can.'

> *Man With Nature.* 'My people help conditions and keep things going by working to keep in close touch with all the forces which make the rain, the snow, and other conditions. It is when we do the right things—live in the proper way—and keep all that we have—the land, the stock and the water—in good condition, that all goes along well.'

Man Over Nature. 'My people believe that it is man's job to find ways to overcome weather and other conditions just as they have overcome so many things. They believe they will one day succeed in doing this and may even overcome droughts and floods' (*29*).

Samples of respondents were selected from five different cultural groups in an area of western New Mexico, and their responses were distributed as shown in Table 2.

View of Nature Cultural Group	Man Subject to Nature	Man with Nature	Man over Nature	Number Interviewed
Spanish-Americans	71.7	10.9	17.4	23
Texans	30.0	22.5	47.5	20
Mormons	25.0	55.0	20.0	20
Zuni Indians	19.0	62.0	19.0	21
Rimrock Navaho Indians	18.2	68.2	13.6	22

Table 2. *Views of Man and Nature by Cultural Groups* (In Percentages)
Source: *Variations in Value Orientations*, Appendix 4.

The wide divergence of human views of nature, as illustrated in Table 2, is strong testimony to support our contention that variations in perception are significant and are likely to affect management policies. A society in which belief in the dominance of nature is strong, such as among the Spanish-Americans, is less likely to be conscious of the possibilities of environment control than one in which belief in the dominance of man over nature is more pronounced, as among the Texans.

The belief in technical engineering solutions of hazard is widespread in American society. This belief in the efficacy of man's control over nature is frequently encountered in studies of hazard perception. Thus, it is no longer surprising to find protective powers ascribed to flood control works far beyond their designed capacity. Notable examples are seen in those persons who consider themselves protected by dams downstream from their flood-plain location, or who are satisfied that floods will not occur in the future because a government agency has been established to study the problem (*30*).

3. How much of the divergence in hazard perception can be ascribed to fundamental views of nature is speculative. Much more of the divergence is explicable in terms of basic attitudes toward uncertainty.

We are convinced that there is a fundamental difference between the attitudes or values of technical-scientific personnel and resource users towards uncertainty. Increasingly the orientation and formal training of scientific personnel emphasizes an indeterminate and probabilistic view of the world. Common research techniques involve the use of estimates that reflect imperfect knowledge, and stress is placed on extracting the full value of partial knowledge.

We have considerable social science and psychological theory and some evidence that resource users are unwilling or unable to adopt this probabilistic view of the world and are not able to live with uncertainty in such a manner as to extract full value from partial knowledge.

Malinowsky held that every human culture possesses both sound scientific knowledege for coping with the natural environment and a set of magical practices for coping with problems that are beyond rational-empirical control (31). Festinger describes the role of the concept of "cognitive dissonance" as a motivating force, which may lead to actions or beliefs concerning the state of nature that do not accord with rational or logical expectations (32). For example, he cites the case of a severe earthquake in India in 1934, in which some people experienced the earthquake but saw no evidence of damage which was quite localized. This situation apparently led to the circulation of rumors which helped to reduce the dissonance created by the fear generated by the earthquake and the absence of signs of damage. People were left in a state of fear but no longer saw reason to be afraid. The rumors that circulated in such a situation have been described by Prasad (33) and include the following:

There will be a severe cyclone at Patna between January 18th and January 19th. [The earthquake occurred on January 15th.]

*   *   *   *

There will be a severe earthquake on the lunar eclipse day.

*   *   *   *

January 23rd will be a fatal day. Unforeseeable calamities will arise.

In our experience resource users appear to behave in ways that suggest an individual effort to dispel uncertainty. Among floodplain users and in coastal areas, the most common variant is to view floods and storms as a repetitive or even cyclical phenomenon. Thus the essential randomness that characterizes the uncertain pattern of the hazard is replaced by a determinate order in which history is seen as repeating itself at regular intervals. Some experiments in the perception of independent events and probability distributions have been conducted by psychologists. The results of such rigorous tests are interesting but are not yet at the level that affords useful generalizations about the real world (*34*). Where the hazard is made repetitive, the past becomes a guide to the approximate timing and magnitude of future hazardous events. An historical example of this is documented by Niddrie (*35*). A mild earthquake was recorded in London on February 8, 1750. A somewhat more severe earthquake occurred exactly one lunar month (twenty-eight days) later on March 8th. Predictions were made that a third and more terrible earthquake would occur on April 5th. Niddrie describes the events which followed:

> A contagious panic spreading through every district of the town required only the slightest indication that those who could afford to leave the town unobtrusively were doing so, for a wholesale evacuation to begin. The gullible who could not leave bought pills 'which were very good against the earthquake.' As Doomsday came nearer whole families moved to places of safety . . . . By April 3rd it was impossible to obtain lodgings in any neighboring town or village (*36*).

When no earthquake occurred on April 5th the prophesies changed to April 8th as though the number eight had some special connotations for earthquakes. Niddrie reports that in fact few of the gentry and well-to-do returned to London until April 9th.

Another view, which is less common, is the act of "wishing it away" by denigrating the quality of the rare natural event to the level of the commonplace, or conversely of elevating it to a unique position and ascribing its occurrence to a freak combination of circumstances incapable of repetition. Either variant has the advantage of eliminating the uncertainty which surrounds hazardous natural phenomenon.

The last alternative view that we can suggest is the completely indeterminate position that denies completely the knowability of natural phenomena. For this group, all is in the hands of God or the gods. Convinced of the utter inscrutability of Divine Providence, the resource users have no need to trouble themselves about the vagaries of an uncertain nature, for it can serve no useful purpose to do so.

These viewpoints are summarized in Table 3.

1. Divergence of values. Natural hazards are not perceived in a vacuum. They are seen as having certain effects or consequences, and it is rather the consequences that are feared than the hazard phenomenon per se. Another source of divergence in the perception of natural hazard between technical-scientific personnel and re-

Eliminate the Hazard		Eliminate the Uncertainty	
DENY OR DENI-GRATE ITS EXISTENCE	DENY OR DENI-GRATE ITS RE-CURRENCE	MAKING IT DE-TERMINATE AND KNOWABLE	TRANSFER UN-CERTAINTY TO A HIGHER POWER
"We have no floods here, only high water."	"Lightning never strikes twice in the same place."	"Seven years of great plenty . . . . After them seven years of famine."	"It's in the hands of God."
"It can't happen here."	"It's a freak of nature."	"Floods come every five years."	"The government is taking care of it."

Table 3.   *Common Responses to the Uncertainty of Natural Hazards*

source users is related to the perceived consequences of the hazard. For very good and sound reasons the set of probabilities related to the occurrence of a natural phenomenon at a given place is not the same as the set of probabilities of hazard for an individual. Given the high level of mobility in our society, the nature of the personal hazard is constantly changing, while the probabilities for a given place remain fixed (although not precisely known).

Thus, the soil erosion that concerns the technicians in Western Iowa, reported in a recent study, (*37*) is an ongoing continuous long-term hazard. The carefully calculated long-term rates of erosion, however, do not have the same meaning for farmers who averaged only nine years as individual farm managers, or where ownership itself changes hands every fourteen years on the average. Soil losses arise from a series of discrete physical events with intensive rains and high winds acting as the major erosional force. The long-term average of these erosional events may have meaning for the continued occupancy of the agriculture of this area. Hence, the technician's concern for the cumulative soil loss. But given the short average managerial period, the cumulative soil loss seems hardly worth the cost and effort involved in its control for the individual manager.

2. The case of the Modern Homesteaders. Evan Vogt's study of the "Modern Homesteader" (*38*) provides a case study that exemplifies the types of divergence that we have been describing.

Homestead, the site of Vogt's studies during 1951–1952, is in his own words "a small dry-land, bean-farming community" of 200 people in western New Mexico (*39*). It was founded in the early 1930's by families from the South Plains Region of western Texas and Oklahoma, but prior to the deep drought of 1934–1936. While spurred by low agricultural prices, Vogt felt they migrated for primarily what they perceived as a good farming opportunity, a chance to receive 640 acres for sixty-eight dollars in fees and residential and improvement investments (40).

By 1932 eighty-one families had obtained sections under what was objectively governmental encouragement to agricultural settlement in an area with an average rainfall of about twelve inches. By 1935 the official perception of the suitability of the natural environment for agriculture had changed drastically. Under the Taylor Grazing Act, (41) all the land in the area which was still in the public domain was classified for grazing, and no additional homestead applications were accepted. The official estimate had changed, but that of the local citizens had not. To this day they perceive of their submarginal farming area as one quite suitable for dry land farming. In so doing, their perception is at considerable variance with that of the governmental technicians in a variety of ways.

As we suggested before, total ignorance of natural hazards is uncommon. While drought and frost are perennial hazards (two decades have provided seven good years, seven average years, and six crop failures), these were not ignorant city folk lured to the Plains by free land. They came from agricultural families in an area of less than twenty inches average rainfall. They do, however, perceive the marginality of the area in their own fashion. So marked is the divergence of this perception that Vogt reports the following:

> But through the critical days of 'battle' with the government, which had defined their community as 'submarginal' and unsuitable for agriculture, there emerged in the Homesteaders a sense of mission in life: To demonstrate to the experts in the Departments of Agriculture and Interior that the Homestead area is farming country and that they can 'make a go of it' in this semi-arid land. They point to the fact that Pueblo Indians made a living by farming in the area long before the white man arrived. There is a general feeling that somehow the surveys and investigations made by the experts must be wrong. They insist that the Weather Bureau has falsified the rainfall figures that were submitted by the Homestead Weather station in the 1930's, and indeed they stopped maintaining a weather station because they felt that 'the figures were being used against us (42).

Vogt mentions in passing another divergence in hazard perception. Homesteaders appear alert to the high westerly wind hazard that erodes the top soil, and they strip crop and plow across the line of this prevailing wind. In so doing, they look askance at the elaborate terraces constructed by the Soil Conservation Service in the 1930's because these terraces are on the contour, and contour plowing itself inevitably results in some of the rows lying in the direct path of the westerly winds (43).

Faced with continued drought, sandstorms, and killing frosts, the "Homesteaders" exemplify much of what has been discussed in this paper. Vogt finds the predominant attitude as that of nature being something to be mastered and, arising from this, a heady optimism in the face of continued vicissitudes. He finds the strong need to eliminate uncertainty to the point of not collecting weather data as reported above, or through the widespread resort to agricultural magic, involving signs of the zodiac, planting by the moon, and water witching. It is in this last act, the use of water witching, that we find direct parallels with the behavior of flood-plain users. The geology of the Homestead area as it relates to ground water supply is one of considerable uncertainty. The geological structure generates an uncertainty as to the depth and amount of water available at a particular point. Faced with such uncertainty, there was a strong-felt need to hire the local water witch to dowse the wells. While the performance ratio of successful wells to dry holes appeared equal whether they were witched or not, Vogt gives a convincing explanation that witching provides a determinate response to uncertainty where the best that the local soil conservation geologists could provide was a generalized description of the ground water situation. Whether, as in Vogt's terms, the motive is to reduce anxiety, or in Festinger's, to reduce cognitive dissonance, or as we would put it, to eliminate uncertainty, there is the apparently strong drive to make the indeterminate determinate.

In conclusion, Vogt emphasizes

> that despite more secure economic alternatives elsewhere, most 'Homesteaders' choose to remain in the community and assume the climatic risks rather than abandon the independence of action they cherish and the leisure they enjoy for the more routinized and subordinate roles they would occupy elsewhere (44).

3. Levels of significance in hazard perception. There are men who plow up semi-arid steppes, who build villages on the flanks of volcanoes, and who lose one crop in three to floods. Are they irrational? Or, to put it another way, having looked at the variation in hazard perception and speculated on the causes of variation, what can be concluded about the rationality of hazard perception? In general, we find absent from almost every natural phenomena a standard for the objective (i.e., true) probability of an event's occurrence. Even if such existed, we are not sure that man can assimilate such probabilities sufficiently to be motivated to act upon them. If decisions are made in a prohibilistic framework, what level of probability is sufficient for action? In the terms of statistics, what level of significance is appropriate? What amount of hazard or error is tolerable? Science is of little help here, since levels of statistical significance are chosen at ninety-five percent or ninety-nine percent primarily by convention.

Despite the impressive growth of game theory, the growing literature of decision-strategies, and some psychological experimentation with perceived probabilities, the artificiality of the game or laboratory seems to provide at best only limited insights into this complex phenomenon. On the other hand, the derivation of empirical observations, i.e., estimates of the perceived frequency of events or perceived probabilities at which decisions are actually made, provides almost insuperable research difficulties.

In the last analysis, we seem destined to judge the rationality of man's actions vis-à-vis natural hazard out of a mixture of hindsight and prejudice. For the successful gambler in the game against nature there are but a few lonely voices crying that the odds will overtake him. The unsuccessful is clearly judged as foolhardy, ignorant, or irrational. Our prejudice expresses itself in our attitudes towards uncertainty, our preferences for certain types of risk, and how we feel about the objects of resource management.

CONCLUSION

There is a wide variation in the day-to-day management practices of resource users, even within culturally homogeneous groups. We believe that the variations in hazard perception reported in this article are an important explanatory variable. Unfortunately, careful studies of variation in resource management practices are few and far between. Some of the recent studies of innovation (45) and the study of farm practices in western Iowa, already cited, (46) approach what we have in mind. To our knowledge there have been no studies which adequately describe variations in management practice and rigorously attempt to assess the role of differing perception.

We can say that there is good reason to believe that variations in perception of hazard among resource managers tends to diminish over time. Those who are unwilling or unable to make necessary adjustments in a hazardous situation are eliminated, either because disaster overtakes them or because they voluntarily depart. Those who remain tend to share in a uniformity of outlook.

Long-term occupancy of high hazard areas is never really stable, even where it has persisted over time. A catastrophe, a long run of bad years, a rising level of aspiration marked by the unwillingness to pay the high costs of survival—each provides stimulants to change. The "Modern Homesteaders," while determined to stay put and exhibiting a high degree of uniformity in their assessment of the environment and its hazards, may yet yield to a combination of an extended run of drought and frost and the lure of a more affluent society. Long-term occupancy, while potentially unstable, is still marked by a tenacity to persist, reinforced, we think, by the uniformity of hazard perception that develops over time. Thus all of the homesteaders who took jobs elsewhere in the bad drought of 1950 returned to the community. More dramatic is the return of the residents of Tristan da Cunha to their volcanic island home.

We have no evidence of a similar growth in accord between resource users and scientific-technical personnel. Clearly, variations in perception may profoundly affect the chances of success of a new management proposal developed by the experts. Such new programs are constantly being devised, but assessments of past programs are seldom found. George Macinko's review of the Columbia Basin project is a recent welcome exception (47). Rarely do such studies review programs in terms of divergence of perception. L. Schuyler Fonaroff's article on differences in view between the Navajo and the Indian Service is another exception which proves the rule (48).

While lacking many detailed statements of this divergence, we can nevertheless state the implication of our findings to date. The divergence in perception implies limits on the ability of resource managers to absorb certain types of technical advice regardless of how well written or explained. Thus, to expect farmers to maintain conservation practices for long periods of time may be wishful thinking if such practices do not accord with the farmer's view of his resource and the hazards to which it is exposed. Similarly, to expect radical changes in the pattern of human adjustments to floods simply by providing detailed and precise flood hazard information is unduly optimistic. Yet another example is seen in the upper Trinity River area in Texas (49). To expect farmers to convert flood-plain land from pasture to cotton or other high value cash crops simply because flood frequency is reduced is to assume that he shares the perception of the Soil Conservation Service. Nor is it a strong argument to claim that such changes in land use were indicated as possible to the farmers themselves, if the question was put to them in terms of the technologist's evaluation of the problem. Good predictions of the future choices of resource managers are likely to be based on an understanding of their perception and the ways in which it differs from that of the technologists.

It seems likely that the hiatus between technical and managerial perception is nowhere greater than in the underdeveloped countries (50). There is good reason, therefore, for further research into this topic and for attempts to harmonize the discrepancies in technical programs wherever possible.

While the study of natural hazard perception provides clues to the ways in which men manage uncertain natural environments, it also helps to provide a background to understanding our national resource policy. Despite the self-image of the conservation movement as a conscious and rational attempt to develop policies to meet long term needs, more of the major commitments of public policy in the field of resource management have arisen out of crises generated by catastrophic natural hazards (albeit at times aided and abetted by human improvidence) than out of a need to curb man's misuse and abuse of his natural environment. Some years ago this was recognized by White: "National catastrophes have led to insistent demands for national action, and the timing of the legislative process has been set by the tempo of destructive floods" (51). It has also been documented in some detail by Henry Hart (52). The Soil Erosion Service of the Department of Agriculture was established as an emergency in 1933 following the severe drought and subsequent dust bowl early in the decade. The Service became a permanent agency called the Soil Conservation Service in 1935 (53).

Just as flood control legislation has followed hard upon the heels of major flood disasters, so the present high degree of interest in coastal protection, development, and preservation has been in part stimulated by recent severe storms on the east coast (54). Such a fundamental public policy as the provision of water supply for urban areas was created partly in response to needs for controlling such natural hazards as typhus and cholera and the danger of fire, as well as for meeting urban water demands (55). Agricultural and forestry research programs were fostered as much by insect infestations and plant diseases as by the long-range goals of increased production.

Unusual events in nature have long been associated with a state of crisis in human affairs. The decline of such superstitions and the continued growth of the control over nature will not necessarily be accompanied by a reduction of the role of crisis in resource policy. Natural hazards are likely to continue to play a significant role, although their occurrence as well as their effects may be increasingly difficult to separate from man-induced hazards of the quasi-natural variety. The smog of Donora may replace the Johnstown flood in our lexicon of major hazards, and *The Grapes of Wrath* may yield pride of place to *The Silent Spring* in the literature of the effects of environmental hazard, but there will continue to be a pattern of response to crisis in human relations to an uncertain environment. Under these circumstances, understandings of the variations of perception such as we have attempted here are likely to remain significant.

NOTES

1. Niddrie, *When the Earth Shook* (1962), p. 36.
2. Zimmermann, *World Resources and Industries* (1951); see also Zimmermann's diagram, id., p. 13.
3. Thomas, "The Meteorological Phenomenon of Drought in the Southwest, 1942–1956," at A8, United States Geological Survey Prof. Paper No. 372-A, 1962.
4. Meteorological Office, United Kingdom Air Ministry, British Rainfall, 1958 (1963), p. 10. This definition was introduced in British rainfall research in 1887.
5. DHEW, Public Health Service, I Vital Statistics of the United States, 1950, at 31 (Interpretation of Cause-of Death Statistics"), 169 ("Mortality by Cause of Death") (1954).
6. Glossary of Meteorology 516 (Huschke, ed., 1959) defines "smog" as follows: A natural fog contaminated by industrial pollutants; a mixture of smoke and fog. This term coined in 1905 by Des Voeux has experienced a recent rapid rise in acceptance but so far it has not been given precise definition.
7. Senate Select Committee on National Water Resources, 86th Congress, 2nd Session, "Weather Modification 3," Committee Print No. 22, 1960; see also Batton and Kassander, "Randomized Seeding of Orographic Cumulus," University of Chicago Meteorology Department Technical Bulletin No. 12, 1958; Greenfield, "A New Rational Approach to Weather-Control Research," Rand Corp. Memo. No. RM-3205-NSF, 1962.
8. A definition of "resource manager," as we use the term, is found in White, "The Choice of Use in Resource Management," 1 *Natural Resources Journal* (1961): 23, 24.
9. Calef, "The Winter of 1948–49 in the Great Plains," *Annals* of the Association of American Geographers 40 (1950): 267.
10. Langbein and Hoyt, *Water Facts for the Nation's Future* (1959), p. 229.
11. Id., p. 230.
12. Flora, *Hailstorms of the United States* (1956), p. 56.
13. Ibid.
14. American Insurance Association, *Studies of Floods and Flood Damage* (1956), p. 3.
15. Langbein and Hoyt, *Water Facts for the Nation's Future*, p. 232.
16. "Delaware River Basin, New York, New Jersey, Pennsylvania, and Delaware," H.R. Doc. No. 522, 87th Congress, 2nd Session, VI, Plate 42, 1962.
17. Kates, *Hazard and Choice Perception in Flood Plain Management*, Department of Geography Research Paper No. 78 (Chicago: University of Chicago Press, 1962).
18. Burton, *Types of Agricultural Occupance of Flood Plains in the United States*, Department of Geography Research Paper No. 75 (Chicago: University of Chicago Press, 1962).
19. Kates, "Perceptual Regions and Regional Perception in Flood Plain Management," Papers of the Regional Science Association, 1963. (Ed. note: A volume number has not been assigned to this set of papers.)
20. For one such attempt, see Jarrett, ed., *Comparisons in Resources Management* (1961).

21. Lowenthal, "Not Every Prospect Pleases—What Is Our Criterion for Scenic Beauty?" *Landscape* 12 (Winter, 1962–1963): 19.

22. ———, "Nature and the American Creed of Virtue," *Landscape* 9 (Winter, 1959–1960): 24.

23. Huth, *Nature and the American* (1957).

24. Thornthwaite, "Climate and Settlement in the Great Plains, Climate and Man," *USDA Yearbook* (1941), pp. 177, 184.

25. Suchman, "A Conceptual Analysis of the Accident Phenomenon," Association for Aid of Crippled Children, Behavioral Approaches to Accident Research (1961), p. 40.

26. Kates, "Perceptual Regions and Regional Perception in Flood Plain Management."

27. "An Interim Hurricane Survey of Fairfield, Connecticut," H.R. Doc. No. 600, 87th Congress, 2nd Session (1962), p. 14.

28. Kluckholm and Strodtbeck, *Variations in Value Orientations* (1961).

29. Id., pp. 86–87.

30. Such a response was given to Burton during recent field work in Belleville, Ontario. There, two respondents considered that the establishment of the Moira Valley Conservation Authority meant that no more floods would occur.

31. Malinowsky, "Magic, Science, and Religion," in Needham, ed., *Science, Religion and Reality* (1925).

32. Festinger, "The Motivating Effect of Cognitive Dissonance," in Lindzey, ed., *Assessment of Human Motives;* Festinger, *A Theory of Cognitive Dissonance* (1947).

33. Prasad, "A Comparative Study of Rumors and Reports in Earthquakes," *British Journal of Psychology* 41 (1950): 129.

34. Hake and Hyman, "Perception of the Stratified Structure of a Random Series of Binary Symbols," *Journal of Experimental Psychology* 45 (1953): 64; Cohen and Hansel, "The Idea of a Distribution," *British Journal of Psychology* 46 (1955): 111; Cohen and Hansel, "The Idea of Independence," *British Journal of Psychology* 46 (1955): 178; Hyman and Jenkin, "Involvement and Set as Determinants of Behavioral Stereotypy," *Psychological Rep.* 2 (1956): 131.

35. Niddrie, *When the Earth Shook* (1962), pp. 20–34.

36. Id., pp. 29–30.

37. Held, Blase, and Timmons, *Soil Erosion and Some Means for Its Control* (Iowa State Univ. Agri. and Home Econ. Experiment Sta. Special Rep. No. 29, 1962).

38. Vogt, *Modern Homesteaders* (1955).

39. Id., p. 1.

40. Id., pp. 17–18.

41. 48 Stat. 1269 (1934), as amended, 43 U.S.C. §§315–315r (1958).

42. Vogt, *Modern Homesteaders* (1955), p. 68.

43. Id., p. 70.

44. Id., p. 176.

45. See the bibliography in Lionberger, *Adoption of New Ideas and Practices* (1960).

46. Held, Blase, and Timmons, *Soil Erosion and Some Means for Its Control.*

47. Macinko, "The Columbia Basin Project, Expectations, Realizations, Implications," *Geography Review* 53 (1963): 185.

48. Fonaroff, "Conservation and Stock Reduction on the Navajo Tribal Range," *Geography Review* 53 (1963): 200.

49. Burton, *Types of Agricultural Occupance of Flood Plains in the United States*, Department of Geography Research Paper No. 75 (Chicago: University of Chicago Press, 1962).

50. The results of a recent effort to improve communication between technical experts and resource managers are reported in Central Treaty Organization, Traveling Seminar for Increased Agricultural Production, Region Tour, 1962.

51. White, *Human Adjustments to Floods*, Department of Geography Research Paper No. 29 (Chicago: University of Chicago Press, 1945), p. 24.

52. Hart, "Crises, Community, and Consent in Water Politics," *Law and Contemporary Problems* 22 (1957): 510.

53. Buie, "Ill Fared the Land," *USDA Yearbook* (1962), p. 155.

54. Burton and Kates, The Flood Plain and the Sea Shore: A Comparative Analysis of Hazard Zone Occupance, Unpublished manuscript, 1963, scheduled for publication in July, 1964 issue of *Geographical Review*.

55. Blake, *Water for the Cities* (1956).

CHAPTER

The Tornado Threat:
Coping Styles of the
North and South

JOHN H. SIMS
DUANE D. BAUMANN

Reprinted from *Science* 176 (30 June
1972): 1386–92, by permission of the
American Association for the
Advancement of Science and the
authors. Copyright 1972 by the American
Association for the Advancement of
Science.

   This study was supported by
Natural Hazards Research, a program
funded by the National Science Foundation in a grant to Toronto, Clark,
and Colorado universities; the program
is directed by I. Burton, R. Kates, and
G. White. Earlier drafts of this article
were delivered at the annual convention of the Association of American
Geographers, Boston, April 1971, and
at the International Geographical
Union Seminar on Natural Hazards,
Budapest, 1971.

The tornado, one of the most feared and awesome of all storms, accounts for an average of 116 deaths each year in the United States. The incidence of tornado fatalities is significantly higher in the South than any other region of the country, as shown in Figure 1. Why? The authors reviewed the literature for clues that might explain this puzzling phenomenon. They found that all of the hypothesized reasons were related to factors *external* to man; the assumption being that man is rational and, if fatalities are higher in the South, then either the tornadoes are more fierce, the population more dense, the warning system less adequate, or the housing less resistant. But analysis showed that none of these possible explanations could account for the high rate of tornado deaths in the South. Conspicuously absent were explanations that suggested that the answer might lie not in the physical environment, but *within* man himself.

Sims and Baumann explore this unknown psychological territory and suggest that one reason for the higher tornado death rate in the South may lie in the personality characteristics of the Southerner. According to the data, unlike the residents of Illinois, Alabamians were more inclined to believe that God or fate or luck controlled their lives, and they were less confident of their abilities to effect the outcome of things. When a tornado threatened, rather than take preventive action, ". . . they awaited the fated onslaught, watchful but passive."

A question arises as to whether these observed psychological differences between people living in Alabama and Illinois are reflective of cultural differences. And, if so, another question would be directed toward their historical roots.

Fortunately for the majority of Americans, their most vivid image of a tornado derives from their memory of the dark twister weaving across the plains of Kansas in the film *The Wizard of Oz*. But unfortunately for those living in certain areas of the North and South, the awesome force of the tornado is a very real presence (*1*). In these locations, the announcement of the tornado watch or the tornado warning are familiar spring messages (*2*). The kind of response made to these messages may determine the extent of physical injury an individual suffers or, indeed, whether he lives or dies. This article is concerned with the differences in human response to the threat of tornadoes and with the psychology affecting the nature of those differences, in order to attempt an explanation of a puzzling phenomenon—the disproportionately higher frequency of tornado-caused deaths in the South.

We begin with this fact: the number of tornado-caused deaths in the South is strikingly higher than it is in the remainder of the nation. This is best documented by Linehan (*3, 4*): "Compared with all others, Region I [the South] is characterized in superlatives. In every tornado-death attribute selected, Region I outranks each of the other three, usually by a very wide margin. . . . Region I has nearly 12 deaths per 1000 square miles, more than three times the comparable figure for the next ranking region; its 23 deaths per 100,000 inhabitants is over five times greater." What makes this phenomenon perplexing is the difficulty encountered in explaining it. The most ready explanation for this concentration of deaths is that the South experiences more tornadoes or has a higher population density, or both. In effect, it is suggested that the highest potential for casualties is in the South.

Yet when Sadowski's geographic distribution of casualty potentials is compared to the geographic distribution of actual tornado deaths, the two patterns fail to coincide (*5*). On the contrary, whereas the highest incidence of tornado-death days (*6*) is in the South (see Figure 1), the casualty potential from tornadoes is found to be higest in a zone running from Dallas, through Topeka and Chicago, to Detroit (see Figure 2).

For a more precise expression of this contradiction, we derived, for each county, the tornado death index (TDI), a measure of the agreement between potential and actual tornado casualties:

$$\text{TDI} = \frac{D/A}{(T/A)\,(P/A)} \times 100$$

where D is the number of tornado deaths in the county from 1953 to 1964 (*7*); A is the county area in square miles (1 square mile

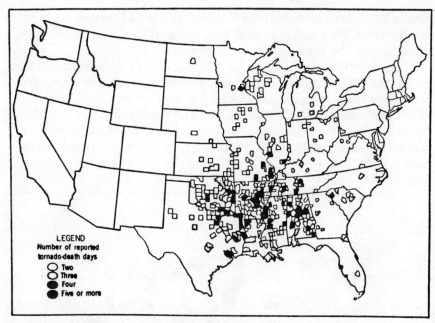

Figure 1. *Tornado-Death Days, By County, 1916 to 1953*

Source: Modified from Linehan (*3*, p. 45).

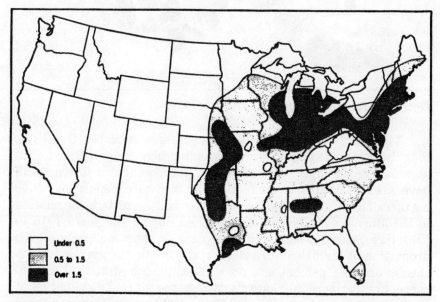

Figure 2. *Potential Casualties from Tornadoes* (Per Square Mile), *1916 to 1961*

Source: Modified from Sadowski (*5*).

equals 2.6 square kilometers) ; T is the number of tornadoes in the county from 1953 to 1964; and P is the population of the county, according to the 1960 census.

These ratios are shown in Figure 3—the larger the black circle, the closer the number of actual deaths approaches the number of potential tornado casualties for a given county. Again the disproportionately higher rate of tornado deaths that characterizes the South is illustrated, a phenomenon that differences in casualty potential (number of storms and density of population) cannot explain.

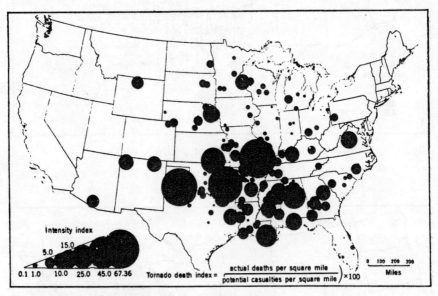

Figure 3.   *Tornado Death Index, 1953 to 1964*

There are a number of other hypotheses available. One holds that the South may experience a greater percentage of its tornadoes during the night—the argument assumes that a tornado will have a more devastating effect on an unaware population. Five northern states were compared with five southern states in relation to the diurnal distribution of tornadoes during the years 1916 to 1961 (see Table 1). Although these data do show a slightly higher proportion of nighttime tornadoes in the South, the average difference is only 3.1 percent and does not approach statistical significance. Furthermore, in Skaggs's data on the diurnal distribution of tornadoes throughout the United States (*8*), we find no pronounced incidence of nocturnal tornadoes in the South.

More specifically, although Indiana and Louisiana have vir-

State	Nocturnal tornadoes (%)
North	
Illinois	27.2
Indiana	34.4
Iowa	26.8
Missouri	35.3
Ohio	29.3
Average	30.6
South	
Alabama	36.7
Arkansas	37.0
Georgia	30.3
Louisiana	34.2
Mississippi	30.6
Average	33.7

Table 1. *Percent of Nocturnal Tornadoes* (8 p.m. to 7 a.m.), *1916 to 1961*
Source: U.S. Weather Bureau, Silver Spring, Maryland.

tually the same percentage of nocturnal tornadoes (see Table 1), Louisiana has a much higher incidence of deaths (see Figure 1) and does so despite the fact that Indiana has a casualty potential several times greater (see Figure 2).

A second hypothesis features another characteristic of the tornado—its strength. Perhaps the South has more violent storms. The most accurate available measure of a tornado's ferocity is the length of its path. The National Weather Service keeps such records, reporting measurements that vary from the designation "short" (a touchdown of a few hundred yards or less), to explicit lengths ranging from less than a mile to hundreds of miles (1 mile equals 1.6 kilometers). To explore this hypothesis, we compared these data on ferocity for the tornadoes that occurred in Alabama and Illinois in the decade 1959 to 1968 (*9*).

During those years Alabama experienced 143 tornadoes. Of these, 32 percent were labeled "short," and explicit lengths were given for 68 percent. The average length for this latter group alone is 12 miles. If we add in the "short" tornadoes, estimating the length of each at a tenth of a mile, the average length of path decreases to 8.2 miles. The analogous figures for Illinois follow: the state experienced 219 tornadoes, of which 26 percent were labeled "short"; explicit lengths were given for 74 percent; the average length for this latter group is 12.6 miles; adding the "short" tornadoes decreases the average length of path to 9.3 miles.

Clearly, by this measure, tornadoes are not more violent in the South: Alabama had more short tornadoes, fewer long ones, and, no matter how it is figured, the average length of path of the Alabama tornado was shorter than that of the Illinois tornado. Not only does Alabama experience fewer tornadoes, the evidence suggests they are of lesser violence.

Another set of hypotheses shifts the focus from variations in the characteristics of tornadoes to variations in the human environment. A frequently mentioned example stresses the kind and quality of housing in the South. It is well established that housing in the South is less substantially constructed (10). The question is, Is it therefore more vulnerable to tornado damage and thus more dangerous? Flora is convinced that it is (11): "the high death rate from tornadoes in the Deep South is undoubtedly due to a large extent to the fact that it is not necessary to construct buildings as sturdily there as in cold northern states." On the other hand, Bigler's analysis of tornado damage argues that the issue is not so clear-cut (12).

> In studying damage to structures, two general modes of collapse, one typical for frame houses, and the other for masonry structures, could be distinguished. Masonry buildings responded to the internal force caused by the pressure reduction outside of the building, which pushed the walls outward and allowed the roof to fall in, while frame houses with more ventilation and therefore more possibility for equalization of pressures, showed rather the struggle to resist the sheer driving force of the wind. In the latter, the roofs were ripped off by wind motions, and the walls blown over and strewn along the tornado path. Masonry walls, exhibiting more rigidity, acted as a unit and were pushed over at once, *while frame construction could give and was therefore not so frequently seriously damaged* [italics added].

This argument quite reasonably allows for the possibility that the greater frequency of substandard houses in the South results in their sustaining less damage from tornadoes than do the more solidly constructed houses in the North.

A similar point is demonstrated most forcefully by Fujita in a paper on tornado "suction spots," those areas in which the wind forces and pressure drop are most concentrated. He presents a photograph of three adjacent structures, all of which were in the direct path of a tornado (13):

> . . . three buildings with increasing structural strength; a wooden shack, a frame house, and a block church. After the passage of the tornado, the damage to these three structures was exactly opposite to what would be expected from constructural strength. The block church was 90% destroyed, the frame house had damage to the roof and broken windows,

while the wooden shack that could have been easily destroyed by 100 mph winds was nearly free of visible damage.

At the very least, these arguments make it clear that no easy
generalization relating housing type to tornado casualties is possible. The problem must await further evidence.

Finally, there is the question of possible differences in the
quality of warning systems; the nature and coverage of tornado
alert systems may be inferior in the South, compared to other areas
in the United States with equal or higher potential tornado casualties. However, prior to 1952, no community had the benefit of the
nationwide warning system; yet then, as now, the South recorded
the greatest frequency of tornado-caused deaths (3). And, since
1953, the forecast information from the Severe Local Storm Center
in Kansas City has been available to all communities (14).

Of course, the efficacy of a warning system is not only a function of the quality of its emission. To be effective, a warning must
be heeded. It is this consideration that draws the search for explanatory variables away from factors external to man, toward
man himself—that is, to man's perception of, and response to, the
tornado threat. For example, in a study of the warning system in
Indiana, Brouilette accounts for the increasingly poorer and slower
response to forecasts as follows (15).

> Tornado forecasts are rather frequent in Indiana and each
> concerns a very large area, in the order of 20,000 to 30,000
> square miles. The chance that funnels will develop over any
> given area is extremely small and the probability that a dam-
> aging tornado will strike is even more remote. It would be
> extremely difficult to get the general public to stop whatever
> they are doing when a tornado forecast is announced and to
> take precautionary measures . . . the Weather Bureau and
> other tornado-warning disseminators too often assume a sim-
> ple stimulus-response type of communication to be adequate.
> This fails to take into account the effect of a person's past
> experience on his interpretation of the alert.

Of course, it is not only past experience that affects an individual's interpretation of a forecast. Adams has shown that, because most people want to think of themselves as being safe, any
ambiguity in their environment will be interpreted as evidence for
the best (16). On the other hand, according to Hudson, anxiety-
high persons will perceive events in the environment as confirming
their anxiety (17).

These examples illustrate the general and well-established fact
that man's confrontation with his physical environment is influ-

enced not only by the facts of that environment, but by his ideas and feelings about it, and that these, in turn, are influenced by his personality and culture. Could it be, then, that such factors might be involved in accounting, at least in part, for the disproportionately higher incidence of tornado deaths in the South?

For purposes of our study, this large general question was reduced to a small, specific scale. A brief sentence completion test of 15 stems was designed for two purposes: first, to identify the various ways people cope with the threat of a tornado; and second, to get a measure of a single psychological dimension—the extent to which an individual feels he controls his own life, generally referred to in psychology as "internal versus external locus of control."

It was our judgment that the sense of being autonomous versus the sense of being directed by outside forces was an aspect of personality that promised to be particularly relevant to the question of how responses to tornado threat vary by geographic area. On the one hand, internal versus external control has been found to be related to general coping style. Studies report that "internals" exhibit more initiative in their attempts both to achieve goals and to control their environments, whereas "externals" appear to be more anxious, less able to respond constructively to frustration, and less concerned with achievement than with the fear of failure (18). On the other hand, internal versus external control has also been found to be related to variation in sociocultural groups. Graves (19), for example, found differences among Ute Indians, children of Spanish-American heritage, and whites in the same community, and a number of studies have found consistent differences among groups drawn from various socioeconomic levels (20). Thus, the psychological dimension of internal versus external control seemed germane to both aspects of our question—variation in response to tornado threat and variation in cultural group, represented here by Northerners and Southerners.

The sentence completion test was administered to a total of 57 respondents, 33 from four counties in Illinois, 24 from four counties in Alabama. All are white females, between the ages of 31 and 60, with at least an elementary school education, and from households with incomes ranging between $5,000 and $10,000 (21). Within each state, the four counties were selected for comparability in respect to past occurrences of tornadoes, potential casualties, and occurrence of tornado-caused deaths.

We used Sadowski's method to calculate the potential casualties per square mile, using county data from 1916 to 1961. The tornado casualty potential for the counties in Alabama is 0.30 per square mile, for those in Illinois, 0.59. The tornado death index for the counties in Alabama is 0.06 per square mile, for those in Illinois, 0.03. Thus, although the area in Illinois has a higher potential, the area in Alabama shows a higher tornado-death rate (compare Alabama and Illinois in Figures 2 and 3).

Of the 15 sentence stems used, statistically significant differences between Illinoisan and Alabamian respondents were found in the completions to eight (22). Three of these deal directly with the issue of internal-external locus of control; they will be considered first. The other five completions deal with behaviors specifically related to the tornado experience, although they too are implicitly germane to the question of autonomy.

The first stem to be discussed is "As far as my own life is concerned, God . . ." (see Table 2). Although about a quarter of the responses of both groups are idiosyncratic, the majority can be grouped into two major categories: there are those who see God as playing an active, participatory role in their lives; and, there are those who see God as a benevolent, protective presence who wards off harm or evil and makes one feel secure, but who does not "interfere" with one's life. This latter conception of God is congruous with a sense of autonomy, of self-direction, of controlling one's own life. The former conception of God, on the other hand, explicitly acknowledges a force other than self that is actively involved in determining the direction of one's life.

The Illinoisans divide themselves about equally (36 percent and 30 percent, respectively) between these "controlling" and "noninterfering" images, whereas 59 percent of the respondents from Alabama identify God as an active agent and only 8 percent identify Him as a benevolent but definitely background figure. These data suggest that Southerners place more weight than Northerners on a force external to themselves—God—as a causal agent in their lives. They consequently feel themselves to have relatively less power in the determination of their own futures.

In their completions to the next stem shown in Table 2, "I believe that luck . . . ," five times as many Alabamians (29 percent) as Illinoisans (6 percent) identify luck as a major force in their lives. On the other hand, more Illinoisans see luck as playing either a minor role or none at all. These differences in attitude toward luck are in agreement with the previous distinction. Formerly, it was the Southerners who saw God as an external force participating actively in their lives. Here, another external force—luck—is similarly acknowledged. Again then, there is the consequent lessening of self-sovereignty, of control of one's own future.

The next data in Table 2 complete this argument. There, in

Sentence stem and response	Respondents (%)	
	Illinois (N = 33)	Alabama (N = 24)
As far as my own life is concerned, God . . .		
Is active in it: for example, "controls it"	36.0	59.0
Is a protective presence: for example, "watches over me"	30.0	8.0
Other	25.0	25.0
No answer	9.0	8.0
Total	100.0	100.0
I believe that luck . . .		
Is of major importance: for example, "is very important to me"	6.0	29.0
Is of minor importance: for example, "plays only a small part in my life"	27.3	17.0
Doesn't exist: for example, "there's no such thing"	21.2	8.0
Other	36.4	42.0
No answer	9.1	4.0
Total	100.0	100.0
Getting ahead in the world results from . . .		
Religious-moral power: for example "doing good works," "God willing it"	9.0	46.0
Work: for example, "hard work"	67.0	29.0
Other	12.0	12.0
No answer	12.0	13.0
Total	100.0	100.0

Table 2. *Sentence Completions Measuring Internal-External Locus of Control*

their completions to the stem "Getting ahead in the world results from . . . ," the Alabamians again emphasize their belief in a future controlled by an external force; 46 percent see success as coming either directly from God, or indirectly from God via moral behavior. Less than a third of the Alabamians see success as resulting from their own efforts. In direct contrast are the respondents from Illinois, two-thirds of whom are believers in the Protestant Ethic —success results from hard work, one form of the more abstract conviction that one's future results from what one does himself.

This stem, touching as it does upon the issue of achievement, calls attention to what might be called the other side of the coin of autonomy—namely, a belief in one's efficacy. Belief in one's ability to control the future requires confidence that what one does will have an effect, will make a difference, will bring about a chosen end. The Illinoisans' emphasis on work reveals not only a belief system in which self can make choices, but in which self can successfully manipulate reality to effect those choices.

Three of the five stems dealing with aspects of the tornado experience focus on conditions before a tornado strikes. They are (i) "During the time when a tornado watch is out, I . . ."; (ii)

"The best way of identifying 'tornado weather' is . . ."; and (iii) "The job done by the weather bureau in forecasting tornadoes . . . ."

In their completions to the first of these stems, "During the time when a tornado watch is out, I . . . ," Illinoisan and Alabamian respondents differ in several important respects (see Table 3). First, they differ regarding the preferred mode of informing themselves on how a possible crisis is progressing. Alabamians favor the method of using one's own senses—they "watch the sky" or "look at the clouds." In direct contrast, Illinoisans keep themselves informed of the impending crisis by way of the media—they "listen to the radio" or "watch on TV."

At least two factors may be involved in these different preferences. First, it is not just metaphorical to speak of the mass media as extensions of one's eyes and ears. It is a characteristic of modern man's psychology that technology is incorporated as a part of self: like information obtained from reading, information acquired from the communications media is standard equipment for coping with reality. To watch the sky rather than listen to the radio, rather than tune in to the social system of information, can be considered psychologically anachronistic.

A second factor that may be at work here is the differing attitudes toward technology and authority, as manifested in the mass media's communicating the dicta of the weather bureau (National Weather Service). That is, implicit in their reliance on radio and television is the Illinoisans' trust in technological expertise, in the authority of science, and, indeed, in man's organized, social power to confront and cope with (if not conquer) nature. But each Alabamian is on his own and faces the whirlwind alone with his God.

This same stem, "During the time when a tornado watch is out, I . . . ," yields minor, but consistent, difference between the two groups: respondents from Illinois, with about five times the frequency of those from Alabama, take specific actions during a tornado watch—for example, seeking shelter, taking precautions, or alerting others. Such efforts are congruent with that sense of efficacy we have already pointed out.

The second stem (see Table 3) that deals with pre-tornado conditions is "The best way of identifying 'tornado weather' is . . . ." Again, we see the acceptance of technology almost exclusively in the Illinoisans: 42 percent of them, as against 4 percent of the respondents from Alabama, either identify the effectiveness of the media (for example, listening to the radio), or touch upon variables that figure in scientific explanations of tornadoes (for example, changes in barometric pressure). On the other hand, the

Sentence stem and response	Respondents (%)	
	Illinois (N = 33)	Alabama (N = 24)
During the time when a tornado watch is out, I . . .		
Am attentive to weather conditions: for example, "watch the sky"	9.1	29.0
Am attentive to news media: for example, "watch the news on TV"	24.2	0.0
Take action: for example, "alert others"	18.2	4.0
Other	21.2	17.0
No answer	27.3	50.0
Total	100.0	100.0
The best way of identifying "tornado weather" is . . .		
Using technology: for example, "listening to the radio," "the barometer"	42.4	4.0
Using one's own senses: for example, "the shape of the clouds"	9.1	33.0
Other	30.3	25.0
No answer	18.2	38.0
Total	100.0	100.0
The job done by the weather bureau in forecasting tornadoes . . .		
Is first-rate: for example, "excellent"	46.0	12.5
Is good: for example, "OK"	24.0	41.7
Is fair: for example, "not too bad"	21.0	16.7
Other	6.0	12.5
No answer	3.0	16.6
Total	100.0	100.0
The survivors of a tornado . . .		
Require assistance: for example, "need to be helped"	24.3	8.0
Experience negative emotions: for example, "feel terrible"	3.0	21.0
Are fortunate: for example, "are lucky, it could have so easily been them"	36.4	25.0
Other	12.1	12.5
No answer	12.1	12.5
Total	100.0	100.0
A community's response to the disaster of a tornado . . .		
Is to give assistance: for example, "is to help the needy"	55.0	79.0
Is seen as psychological: for example, "brings people closer together," "it brings out the curious"	21.0	0.0
Other	9.0	13.0
No answer	15.0	8.0
Total	100.0	100.0

Table 3. *Sentence Completions Measuring Responses to the Tornado Experience**

* In Table 3, under the fourth sentence stem (The survivors of a tornado . . .), the following category of completion and percentages of responses were mistakenly omitted:

RESPONSE	RESPONDENTS %	
	ILLINOIS	ALABAMA
Experience positive emotions: for example, "are happy to be alive"	12.1	21.0

Alabamians again speak primarily in terms of what their own eyes can see (for example, darkness of the clouds).

The next stem of this set is "The job done by the weather bureau in forecasting tornadoes . . ." (see Table 3). Two-thirds of the Illinoisans rate the weather bureau as "good" or better; in contrast, only half of the respondents from Alabama do so. Further, almost four times as many Illinoisans as Alabamians evaluate the weather bureau as first-rate. The trust in expertise (technology fused with authority) felt by those from Illinois is again clearly far greater than that felt by those from Alabama.

The final two stems deal with a different situation—the aftermath of a tornado (see Table 3). The first of these is "The sur-. vivors of a tornado . . . ." The completions to this stem by the respondents from Alabama are preponderantly affective. They stress either negative emotions (portraying the survivors as distraught or grief-stricken) or positive emotions (portraying the survivors as grateful and happy to be alive). In contrast, most Illinoisans are either coping-oriented and emphasize the survivors' need for aid, or, interestingly, portray the survivors as "lucky"; that is, they see survival as a matter of chance and not as a matter of fate or of God's will, a very different definition of luck from that of the Alabamians (23).

The second stem focusing on what happens following a tornado is "A community's response to the disaster of a tornado . . ." (see Table 3). This presents a situation that is less temporally immediate and that shifts from an individual to a social perspective. Here the majority of both groups define the community's response as one of helping those in need. What differentiates the two groups is a response category unique to the Illinoisans—20 percent of them are sufficiently removed from the shock experience to give responses that comment objectively on psychological phenomena (such as noting that disaster unites people or that it brings out the curious).

We have argued that the completions to the three sentence stems presented in Table 2 reveal Illinoisans to be more autonomous, more prone to see themselves as responsible for directing their own lives, and more confident in their own efficaciousness. On the other hand, Alabamians are seen to be more heteronomous, feeling themselves to be moved by external forces—fate, luck, and, particularly, God. They are consequently less confident in themselves as causal agents, less convinced of their ability to engage in effective action.

Another series of sentence completions, presented in Table 3, dealt with aspects of the tornado experience. These also revealed consistent differences between the two groups. First, Illinoisans were, at the most general level, more action-oriented, while Alabamians were more passive. Second, Illinoisans displayed more objectivity, more rationality in reacting to a tornado disaster. Finally, and most important, the respondents from Illinois were characterized by an acceptance of technology and authority—they use the expertise of professionals in forecasting and communications when confronting the possibility of a tornado. Alabamians do not. They ignore these functions of the social system; for them, the encounter is between individual man and Nature.

Juxtaposing these two sets of findings, we find them reasonably congruous. Persons like the respondents from Illinois, who believe they direct their own lives, who believe that what they do affects their futures, go about confronting the possibility of a tornado in characteristic style. They use their heads and the technology of their society, and they take action. In the aftermath of a tornado, they would indeed see those who had escaped as "lucky" (in the sense of random, not destined), go about helping the needy, and occasionally pause to observe themselves and their fellowmen as fascinating creatures.

Persons like the respondents from Alabama, who believe that God (or fate or luck) controls their lives, who have less confidence in their own ability to have an impact on reality, to effect change, also confront a tornado in a manner that is consistent with their attitudes. They place less trust in man's communal knowledge and control systems; they await the fated onslaught, watchful but passive. In the tornado's aftermath, they feel with the victims (there but for the grace of God . . .) and then recover to perform good works.

Although admittedly based upon only a small sampling of behavior of a small number of respondents, these findings and interpretations may be relevant to the disproportionately higher death rate from tornadoes in the South. Fatalism, passivity, and perhaps most important, lack of trust in and inattention to society's organized systems of warning constitute a weak defense against the terrible strike of the tornado.

In so concluding, we are not, of course, arguing that the psychological dimension of internal-external locus of control is the sole, or even the primary, determinant of the tornado death rate. Almost certainly that phenomenon is a result of multivarious forces in combination, of which the sense of locus of control is but one. Other psychological dimensions should be explored, and certain of the traditionally considered factors, such as quality of housing and storm violence, need to be reexamined with more and better data (24).

Our point is, rather, to emphasize the obvious, but so often neglected (or avoided), relation of man himself to the problems of natural hazards. The data and argument presented here constitute a suggestive illustration of how man's personality is active in determining the quality of his interaction with nature.

REFERENCES AND NOTES

1. A. Court, *Tornado Incidence Maps*, ESSA technical memorandum ERLTM-NSSL 49 (U.S. Department of Commerce, 1970). Available from Clearinghouse for Federal Scientific and Technical Information, Port Royal Road, Springfield, Va. 22151.
2. Two types of tornado alert have been formulated by the National Weather Service. A tornado *watch* is a probability statement concerning the occurrence of a tornado (or tornadoes) within a given area (usually between 10,000 and 30,000 square miles) and is issued at least 6 hours before the possible event. A tornado *warning* is a message denoting that a tornado is imminent and that persons should be prepared to take cover immediately.
3. U. Linehan, *Tornado Deaths in the United States* (Washington, D.C.: Government Printing Office, 1957), p. 16. See also Reed (*4*), who notes: "In Arkansas one person in 44 residing in the destroyed area was killed, versus one in 407 in Iowa." Region I includes Alabama, Mississippi, Tennessee, Kentucky, Arkansas, most of Georgia, Oklahoma, and eastern Texas, and the southern part of Missouri.
4. J. Reed, *Proceedings of the Seventh Conference on Severe Local Storms* (Boston: American Meteorological Society, 1971), p. 192.
5. A. Sadowski, *Potential Casualties from Tornadoes* (Washington, D.C.: National Weather Service, 1965). Potential casualties were calculated by multiplying the area of the average tornado by the number of tornadoes in a 2° square, and then dividing this sum by the area of the 2° square. The quotient was multiplied by the quotient of the population of a 2° square divided by the area of a 2° square.
6. "A tornado-death may be regarded as a 24-hour period, between an instant after midnight on one day and midnight the same day, during which one or more deaths occurred and/or during which one or more persons received tornado-induced injuries that subsequently proved fatal" (3, p. 3).
7. This decade was selected because, beginning in 1953, tornado data became more reliable as a result of the implementation in 1952 of a more elaborate detection network by the National Weather Service.
8. R. Skaggs, *Mon. Weather Review* 97 (1969): 103; J. Lee, *Mon. Weather Review* 86 (1958): 219.
9. U.S. Department of Commerce, *Storm Data, 1–10* (Washington, D.C.: Government Printing Office, 1959–1968).
10. G. Harman and J. Hook, *Economic Geographer* 32 (1956): 95.
11. S. Flora, *Tornadoes in the United States* (Norman: University of Oklahoma Press, 1954), p. 71.
12. S. Bigler, *Research No. 41: The Tornadoes at Dallas, Texas, April 2, 1957* (Washington, D.C.: Government Printing Office, 1960), pp. 159–68.
13. T. Fujita, *Weatherwise* 23 (1970): 4.
14. F. Bates, *Bulletin of the American Meteorological Society* 43 (1962): 288.
15. J. Brouillette, *A Tornado Warning System: Its Functioning on Palm Sunday in Indiana* (Disaster Research Center, Columbus: Ohio State University, 1966), p. 9.
16. D. Adams, *The Minneapolis Tornadoes, May 6, 1965, Notes on the Warning Process, Research Report No. 16* (Disaster Research Center, Columbus: Ohio State University, 1965), p. 17.

17. B. Hudson, *Journal of Social Issues* 10 (1954) : 53.

18. W. Throop and A. MacDonald, Jr., *Psychol. Rep.* 28 (1971) : 175. This bibliography on internal-external locus of control cites over 300 references to work done through 1969.

19. T. D. Graves, *Time Perspective and the Deferred Gratification Patterns in a Tri-ethnic Community,* Research Report No. 5, Tri-ethnic Research Project (Institute of Behavioral Science, Boulder: University of Colorado, 1961).

20. J. Rotter, *Psychol. Monogr. Gen. Appl.* 80 (1966) : 1; H. M. Lefcourt, *Psychol. Bull.* 65 (1956) : 206; V. C. Joe, *Psychol. Rep.* 28 (1971) : 619.

21. The data analyzed here are drawn from our larger study, which involves a total sample of 420 interviews from four different areas of the country— Kansas-Oklahoma, Alabama, Illinois, and Massachusetts-Connecticut. For the particular problem addressed in this article, a sample of 57 respondents was chosen from Illinois and Alabama, controlling for education, income, sex, age, and occupation.

22. Using the chi-square one-tailed test, the differences shown in Tables 2 and 3 are significant at the $P < .05$ level.

23. Only examples of the data themselves can adequately convey the two very different meanings of "luck" used here by the two groups of respondents. Illinoisans define luck as a *random* phenomenon: for example, "The survivors of a tornado are lucky to be alive . . . it is a hit-or-miss thing"; or, "The survivors of a tornado are lucky, it could so easily have been them." Alabamians, on the other hand, define luck as *nonrandom* good fortune: for example, "The survivors of a tornado are lucky, it wasn't their time"; or, "The survivors of a tornado are very lucky, but tragedies cannot be questioned; it's all God's Will."

24. T. Fujita of the University of Chicago has developed a scale of tornado intensity that correlates wind speed with extent of property damage shown in aerial photographs. Since January 1971, state weather officials have been evaluating tornadoes according to Fujita's criterion photographs. At this time, only the data for January through April were available. As the geography of tornado occurrence is seasonal, moving northward during the late spring and early summer, it is too early to compare the North and South on this measure of storm violence.

CHAPTER

Coping with Environmental Threat:

Great Plains
Farmers and the
Sudden Storm

JOHN H. SIMS
THOMAS FREDERICK SAARINEN

Reprinted from the *Annals* of the
Association of American Geographers
59, no. 4 (1969): 677–86, by permission
of the Association of American Geographers and the authors.

The effects of weather and climate on man can be studied in a variety of ways. One approach is to observe human behavior under different environmental conditions, as discussed in the final chapter on suicides and weather. Another approach is illustrated in the following chapter by Sims and Saarinen where a measurement technique used primarily by psychologists in the assessment of emotional disturbance is applied to a non-clinical population to explore its response to an environmental hazard.

The technique used here is a variant of the Thematic Apperception Test. Simply put, the subject is shown a somewhat ambiguous picture and asked to tell a story about it. Variations in the stories are interpreted as reflecting variations in the psychodynamics and cognitive styles of the storytellers. The object of such an indirect method is to by-pass the subject's defenses; thus, in telling an "innocent" story, he is unaware that he's revealing aspects of his psychology. The application of such a method for investigating the relationship between man and his environment is quite recent and holds considerable promise. In this study the technique is used to explore how Great Plains wheat farmers react to the threat of a crop-destroying storm.

The stories of the farmers are not greatly surprising. Their first responses are generally rational, task-oriented ones; they work to save the harvest. But, interestingly, such efforts are supplemented by appeals to a transcendental authority, an arational coping behavior, although such prayers may indeed serve to temporarily lessen anxiety. Unlike the Southerners' responses to the threat of tornado, the Great Plains wheat farmers, when faced with an environmental threat, respond first with action, with *rational,* if you will, behavior; only when that fails do they move to "explain" their fate by resorting to a belief in a higher authority.

ABSTRACT. A trend toward increasing use in geographical research of methods and concepts developed and tested in other social sciences seems likely to provide new insights into the effects of weather and climate on human behavior. Psychological reactions of a sample of Great Plains wheat farmers to the threat of a sudden storm are examined by means of a variant of the Thematic Apperception Test. The pictured situation is assessed as an unpredictable environmental press potentially in opposition to the inner need to achieve. The primary reaction to the threat is the mobilization of one's own resources towards rational, task-oriented action. However, uncertainty remains and this is reflected in a subsidiary theme in which attempts to alleviate anxiety are made by the essentially religious appeal to transcendental powers to lessen or stay the environmental threat. It is suggested that the TAT could prove useful for measuring many aspects of the man-environment relationships including that of regional personality.

The effect of environment on human behavior is a topic which has stimulated man's curiosity through the centuries (1). One important aspect of the man-environment relationship involves an assessment of the effects of weather and climate upon human behavior. During the heyday of the environmental determinists many provocative ideas were advanced in attempts to answer this question. But, perhaps as a result of incautious generalizations often based on inconclusive data, the topic and its investigators fell into disrepute. Lee over a decade ago urged that these earlier works be reexamined in light of newly acquired knowledge (2). There appears to be a growing interest to do as he suggested, in geography and in many other disciplines (3).

The greatest obstacle hampering investigations of the relationship between weather and human behavior is the difficulty of measurement. How can long range or short term effects of weather and climate on man be measured? What we really want to know are the psychological effects but, because they are easier to measure, we often study the physiological effects. Or the results of behavior indicated by the land use pattern are measured. Both approaches are useful but each leaves much unexplained.

What is really needed are new methods, concepts, and measuring techniques (4). This need has been recognized in much of the recent work often referred to as perception in geography. Concepts and methods developed and tested in other social science disciplines have been utilized in this branch of geographic research. They represent the first strong infusion of psychological ideas into geography. In reviewing some pioneer studies of this type, Burton, Kates, and White list use of the following behavioral science techniques: structured and unstructured interviews, thematic apperception tests, content analysis of news media, models of decision-making, benefit-cost analysis, new and extended uses of probability theory, as well as new uses of such traditional geographical methods as land-use mapping and air-photo techniques (5).

The introduction of new methods has been accompanied by increasing interaction between geographers and other social scientists who have become interested in environmental problems on a broad inter-disciplinary basis (6). For example, Craik a psychologist, speaks of the timid emergence of psychologists from their laboratory retreats in search of phenomena of real human significance to study (7). Craik outlines a number of techniques psychologists might use in studying environmental behavior (8). Geographers might well profit by examination and testing of some of these methods.

The paper which follows illustrates the use of such a psychological technique which makes it possible to trace the sequence of events involved in a decision-making situation posed by a particular weather event. The study is concerned with the general issue of how men mobilize their inner resources in contending with environmental threat. Specifically it explores, in depth, the reactions of Great Plains wheat farmers to an impending storm.

THE THEMATIC APPERCEPTION TEST

The technique used is a variant of the Thematic Apperception Test, or TAT (9). For those readers unfamiliar with the form of the TAT and its psychological rationale, these are briefly discussed. The standard test consists of a series of ambiguous pictures about which the Subject is asked to tell stories. Since the stimuli of the pictures are ambiguous, the thoughts, feelings, attitudes, and actions with which the story teller endows the persons portrayed in the pictures, are indicative of the personality of the story teller himself. What happens, in effect, when asked to interpret an ambiguous stimulus, is that one projects onto the stimulus one's view of himself and his relation to the world.

Experience has shown that particular pictures tend to produce stories which are revealing of particular dimensions of personality, for example, achievement motivation, or relations with authority

Figure 1. *Card C*

figures. This fact allows the researcher to select pictures from the standard TAT set, or to design new pictures, which will elicit personality data specifically relevant to his interests. The picture used for this study (labelled Card C and reproduced in Figure 1) is a photograph of a farmer in the process of harvesting wheat with a storm approaching. Its purpose, to force stories concerned with how Great Plains farmers cope with such a potential danger to their crops.

This picture was presented as part of an interview and test battery to a random sample of ninety-six male Great Plains farmers drawn from Nebraska, Kansas, Oklahoma, and Colorado during the summer of 1964 (see Figure 2) (*10*). The present paper is based on the analysis of sixty cases randomly selected from that sample.

GROUP INTERPRETATION TECHNIQUE
The Schaw-Henry method was used for analyzing the TAT stories (*11*). This technique abstracts from the story a thema which has three parts: "Basic Stem," a statement of the story's starting situation; "Coping Mechanisms," the hero's actions in response to that situation; "Resolution," what happens as a result of what the hero has done. In addition, a judgment of whether the hero's needs have been met is made. This judgment is termed accordingly, a "Good Outcome," a "Bad Outcome," or, if the story is left unresolved, a "No Outcome." Once abstracted, the themas are stated in Murray's need-press terminology (*12*). In this way, the idiosyncratic expression of the stories is translated into a consistent vocabulary which permits their summation for the characterization of groups. Examples of how story material is abstracted into themas are given in the context of the following analysis.

ENVIRONMENTAL THREAT IN CONFLICT WITH NEED ACHIEVEMENT
All of the Great Plains wheat farmers of this sample, without exception, depict the situation presented in Card C as one in which an environmental threat may deprive the farmer of his wheat crop. In need-press terms, this basic stem is coded: press Environmental Threat in conflict with need Achievement (pEThreat c nAch.). Some examples are:

> Well, there he is. This is a western Kansas farmer. He's worked all year and now he's got the crop within his reach and the rainclouds or hail storm is approaching.

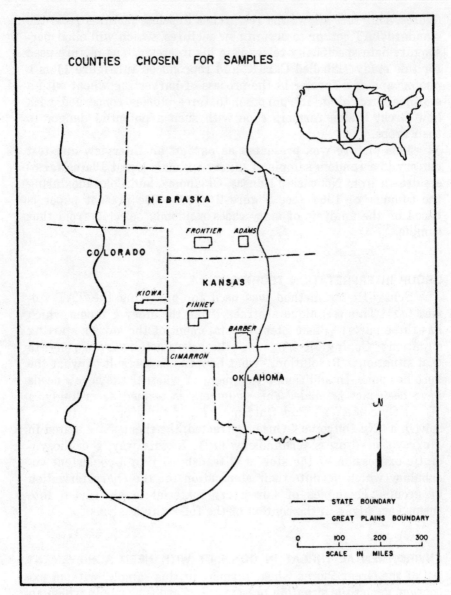

Figure 2

Harvesting grain and it looked like a bad storm coming up and
it could destroy all.

Well, that looks like the fellow's hopes of a full year's work
could be gone in fifteen minutes with that hail.

The atypicality of Card C (in comparison to standard projective
test pictures) in conjunction with the fact that every member of

the sample defined the situation it presents in the same way, raises an issue which requires a brief methodological discussion. Card C does not constitute a truly ambiguous stimulus for this sample. Given that they are Great Plains farmers, the situation shown in the photograph is not amenable to a wide variety of interpretations by them. Indeed, the very fact that 100 percent of the sample presented the exact same basic stem argues that such responses are more likely the product of the "demanding" stimulus properties of the card rather than a function of the farmers' psycho-dynamics. Such a possibility makes interpretation impossible for we do not know whether the basic stem is a projection or simply the forced identification of a well-known situation. In other words, are the story-tellers revealing that their own achievement needs are in conflict with envirnomental forces (as opposed for instance, to their being in harmony with nature), or are they simply telling us that they recognize a storm cloud when they see one and that they are well aware of what this can mean to a farmer in the midst of a harvest? Because we do not know the answer to this question, our interest in the stories to Card C lies not in how the sample describes the initial situation, but in what they see the farmer doing about the impending storm, and what results as a consequence of what he does. For these questions clearly do offer the possibility of a variety of response.

COPING WITH ENVIRONMENTAL THREAT

Almost all of the sample (ninety-three percent) reacted to the environmental threat by taking immediate action. The farmers see the necessity for working as fast as possible to save the crop or salvage at least a portion of it. This is coded simply: need Work Fast (nWkF). The following excerpts illustrate both elements of this coping mechanism, the action itself and the strong sense of urgency which accompanies it:

> . . . he's determined to get every kernel he can before the storm sets in.

> . . . he's pushing his machine to capacity to try to get every bushel before the storm hits.

> . . . he's harvesting like mad to get his wheat cut before the hail storm comes.

For forty percent of the farmers, this is the only method of handling the situation presented. Another fifty-three percent also use need Work Fast, but in conjunction with other coping mechanisms. These additional modes of handling the conflict between achievement needs and environmental threat are of two major types. Those of the first type share, in common with need Work Fast, the qualities of being rational and task-oriented. The first specific mechanism so categorized is coded: need Risk (nRk) and means essentially the immediate action of working fast taken to an extreme: that is, the determination to continue harvesting the crop until it becomes too dangerous or impossible to carry on. The following examples illustrate this additional fervor:

> He probably cut that just as long as he can before it hits. . .
> But he ain't going to leave 'til he's pounded out of there.

> He's just going like the dickens hoping to get done . . . He'll probably stay 'til he gets caught in the rain and blowing 'cause they usually do.

This method of handling the situation was presented by five men, just over eight percent of the sample.

Another variety of coping mechanism classified here is that coded: need Question Judgment (nQuesJudg.). An example follows:

> Well, they're cutting wheat, wheat's pretty fair. He didn't have a whole lot of wheat that year and he tried to cut it himself. Right now he's wondering whether he should have hired help or not. It just depends on what the cloud does. In the next hour that cloud will tell the tale whether his judgment was wrong in cutting it himself or whether he should have hired help.

Although this coping mechanism fails to meet strictly the qualification of being realistic, for such doubts contribute nothing to meeting the crisis, it is nevertheless seen as belonging here for two reasons. First, because of its involvement with the task at hand, for, though idle, such speculations are relevant to the achievement need. Second, such reflections do show respect for the reality principle, albeit expressed in the past. There were two examples of this coping mechanism, or just over three percent of the sample.

The final coping mode of this type was coded: need Problem Solve (nProbSol.). In this case the farmer was engaged in figuring out how best to go about the harvesting task. In sum then, 13.3 percent of the sample presented such additional rational, task-oriented coping mechanisms.

The second major type of coping mechanism found in the

farmers' stories to Card C are classified under the rubric arational-philosophical. Although in all but one of these stories, the awareness of the necessity to work fast is present, they manifest, in addition, either a hopeful or a fatalistic theme. In the first of these categories, expressed by just under a quarter of the sample, are three varieties of idle hopes or vain wishes—those who wish they had more combines or power, those who wish they could somehow delay the storm, and those who hope the storm will pass them by. Some examples are shown below.

> He wishes that combine could go ten times faster . . . He wishes he had started sooner. He wishes that it would go away.

> . . . he sure wishes it would hold off awhile. "If only I could get a few more rounds," he says.

> Please hold off one more day 'til I get through with it.

> They're probably hoping it goes around and they don't get any.

The second category of arational-philosophical coping mechanisms has a fatalistic tone. Rather than being directed toward wishing or hoping, energy is again "wastefully" spent, only here in terms of expressing a readiness to accept whatever fate hands out. For example:

> He has that crop within his grasp but it could be gone in thirty minutes. He'll be happy for what he's got, sad about what he lost. But he'll take the bitter with the sweet and be thankful for what he's got.

> Can't always get it off before the good Lord takes it back again.

> . . . looks like a big storm acomin'. Could be like some of the others and blow over, or demolish him. Oh, I've come out on top once or twice.

About an eighth of the farmers employed such fatalistic themes. Thus, in sum, 36.6 percent of the sample presented coping mechanisms classified under the grouping of arational-philosophical.

A review of our analysis of coping mechanisms shows the following: ninety-three percent of the sample present need Work Fast as the only or primary method of handling the environmental threat to their achievement needs; 13.3 percent employ additional coping mechanisms which, similar to need Work Fast, are rational

	Type of coping mechanism	N	%
	RATIONAL, TASK-ORIENTED		
____	need Work Fast	24	40.0
____	need Work Fast; need Risk	5	8.3
____	need Work Fast; need Question Judgment	2	3.3
	need Problem Solve	1	1.7
		32	53.3
	ARATIONAL, PHILOSOPHICAL		
____	need Work Fast: *need Wish*	6	10.0
____	need Work Fast: *need Fatalism*	6	10.0
____	need Work Fast: *need Hope*	8	13.3
	need Fatalism	2	3.3
		22	36.6
	MISCELLANEOUS		
____	need Work Fast: *press Physical Danger*	4	6.7
____	need Work Fast: *need Humor*	1	1.7
	No Coping Mechanism	1	1.7
		6	10.1
	Total	60	100.0

need Work Fast (93.3%)

Table 1. *Coping Mechanisms to Card C*
Source: Analysis of authors.

and task-oriented; and 36.6 percent present additional coping mechanisms which are of an arational-philosophical nature (*13*). Table 1 presents a convenient overview of these various coping mechanisms.

HOW UNCERTAINTY IS HANDLED
What do these coping mechanisms tell us about Great Plains farmers? It is clear, in terms both of frequency and primacy, that this sample's overwhelmingly distinctive coping style in dealing with environmental threats of this nature is a truly efficacious one, in that what they choose to do holds the realistic possibility of producing the intended effect, namely, saving the crop.

However, one other theme appears with sufficient frequency to merit our attention—that which we have labelled arational-philosophical. In direct contrast to the farmers' primary coping style, what these coping mechanisms have in common is the absence of efficacy; none of them holds any realistic promise of producing the desired effect. But, if they do not serve the farmers' need to achieve, they do serve another need. In our judgment, they may be seen as ways of handling anxiety aroused by possible achievement failure owing to uncontrollable external forces. We see wishing and hoping as essentially religious appeals to transcendental powers to modify the threatening situation; to change the direction of the storm, to hold it back to obtain more time, or to have more machine power. Fatalism is also essentially religious; it is at one and the same time, a way, established before the fact, of handling the anticipated trauma which would accompany crop failure (It is God's will), and an act of propitiation which hopefully will prevent the wrath of God or Nature. (Willingness to accept God's will regardless of what It may bring is an act of placatory humility.) Both of these kinds of coping mechanisms are ways of confronting and trying to handle forces outside of the control of man. Both acknowledge man's impotence in the face of a powerful and capricious Nature. Implicit in them is the belief that rational action is insufficient in such circumstances.

However, it is important to reemphasize two points: one, this appeal to higher powers is presented by only a third (36.6 percent) of the sample; second, with only one exception, such coping mechanisms are second choices, they follow the rational, task-oriented modes of coping, such as need Work Fast. (It is as though some of the farmers felt it necessary to cover their bets.) Thus, although important, the arational-philosophical type of coping theme is a subordinate one for this sample.

Type of coping mechanism	Good outcome		Bad outcome		No outcome		Total	
	N	%	N	%	N	%	N	%
Exclusively RATIONAL, TASK-ORIENTED	1	3.1	13	40.6	18	56.3	32	100
Contain element of ARATIONAL, PHILOSOPHICAL	3	13.6	2	9.1	17	77.3	22	100
MISCELLANEOUS	1	16.7	0	0	5	83.3	6	100
Total	5	8.3	15	25	40	66.7	60	100

Table 2. *Outcomes to Card C*

Source: Analysis of authors.

Given the situation depicted on Card C and the primary use of efficacious modes of coping with it, how is the situation resolved? Do the farmers conclude their stories with achievement, by managing to get the harvest in before the storm breaks? Does the storm pass over, or does it wreak its destruction? The story outcomes are presented in Table 2.

OUTCOME UNPREDICTABLE

The most impressive findings shown in Table 2 appear in the No Outcome column. We see first, that regardless of what type of coping mechanism is used, the majority of farmers in each instance leave their stories unresolved. In all, two-thirds of the entire sample are uncertain about what the effects of the labor and/or of their hoping and wishing will be. Some examples of this type of resolution are:

> Sometimes it comes down, sometimes it backs off. You never know.

Could be like some of the others and blow over, or demolish him.

I wouldn't know what the outcome would be. If it hails he's done. If the wind blows very hard he's done too. If it don't hail and don't rain he can go ahead and work tomorrow. I'd wait until the storm passed and then give you an outcome.

This inconclusiveness implies a conviction already identified in connection with emotional-philosophical coping mechanisms, namely, a limited faith in the power or rational action to bring about achievement in the face of a capricious Nature. We emphasize that it is a faith which is limited, but not absent. There are two reasons for this caution: first, Card C presents an extreme situation, that of a possibly violent storm. Perhaps, then, what we are getting here is a correspondingly extreme response. Thus, it could be argued that given more normal weather conditions, belief in the efficacy of rational action to bring about achievement might not appear so limited. Secondly, it is clear that these farmers have not abandoned faith in rational action even in the face of this extreme situation because one, they engage in it, and two, they end their stories in inconclusiveness—and if lack of resolution means that rational action may not work, it also means that it may. The essential point then, made by the high percentage of No Outcome is that for these farmers, achievement is removed from the universe of predictable things. For it is seen as a product of the interaction of two variables: one is man, and his actions can be anticipated; the other is Nature, and its actions can not. And because it is impossible to assess the extent to which Nature will be capricious, the efficacy of rational action in accomplishing achievement is problematic.

The second finding of importance in Table 2 is the ratio between Good Outcomes (8.2 percent) and Bad Outcomes (twenty-five percent). Some examples of these types of resolution follow:

The storm went around and he made it alright.

The cloud came over and he got a three inch rain, no hail, a lot of wind. Couldn't harvest for three days. But finished his harvest and everyone was happy.

I'd say the cloud missed him and he made a crop.

The clouds moved in and the wind began to blow and the hail followed along. Within a few minutes the ground was white with hail and the crop was a complete loss.

Hail finished his wheat up. I had one like that, hail six inches deep.

If that is this country, I'd say the outcome would be that the wheat was hailed out.

For this third of the sample which does conclude its stories, the ratio is 3 to 1 in favor of negative resolutions. In these pessimistic outcomes we can again identify the two participants involved in the achievement endeavor—man and Nature. For these men however, it is no longer a matter of limited faith in man's rational attempts to control Nature; for them, when man and Nature are combatants rather then partners, man loses, the resolution of the conflict is no longer an open question. These men see Nature not only as capricious but as negatively so. For them the sudden storm means sudden destruction, whereas for those who leave the outcome open, there remains the chance that just as the storm blew up it may blow over.

Combining the No Outcomes (66.7 percent) with the Bad Outcomes (25 percent), we account for 91.7 percent of the sample. We conclude then, that the dynamic theme manifested by Great Plains farmers in their resolutions to Card C is one of, at best, limited belief in man's ability to achieve in the face of an unpredictable Nature correlated with a belief that Nature's capriciousness is not necessarily destructive, and at worst, is one of resignation to the fact that man cannot achieve in the face of an unpredictable Nature because its capriciousness is destructive.

One final series of findings shown in Table 2 remains to be discussed: the greater percentages of Good Outcomes and No Outcomes and the correlative lesser percentage of Bad Outcomes which follow the use of a combination of rational, task-oriented with arational-philosophical coping mechanisms alone. It is important to emphasize that these shifts towards Optimistic Outcomes are not the result of greater faith in, or greater use of, rational efforts. Virtually all of the farmers take those actions. The use of rational, task-oriented coping mechanisms then, is a constant, and the effect on outcomes must be attributed to the use of arational-philosophical coping modes. Why would such devices exert such an influence? We can suggest two possibilities: one, they may, as we have already suggested, act to reduce anxiety, thereby lessening the perception of the seriousness of the environmental threat and consequently increasing the ease with which a Good Outcome may be entertained. Or, a second possibility, they may express genuine conviction that a benevolent transcendental power is on their side, and that with His or Its help, the chances of achievement are improved.

THE SUDDEN STORM AS AN ENVIRONMENTAL THREAT

We have now examined each component of the stories told to Card C—basic stem, coping mechanism, and resolution-outcome. When the modal responses of these components are sequentially ordered, they reveal the following dynamic thema: an unpredictable environmental press is seen to be potentially in opposition to the inner need to achieve; the primary reaction to the threat is the mobilization of one's own resources towards rational, task-oriented action; however, because the environmental threat is by nature capricious, it is impossible to know whether one's efforts will be efficacious.

A subsidiary, but significant contrapuntal theme, is the essentially religious appeal to transcendental powers to lessen or stay the environmental press. Such an appeal acts to alleviate the anxiety aroused by the environmental threat and increases the probability of successful achievement, attained not through one's own efforts, but "by the grace of" higher powers.

The sudden storm portrayed in Card C exemplifies but one type of environmental threat: unpredictable, immediate, it precludes preparation, and methods of confronting it are restricted to reactive rather than initiatory behaviors. The psychodynamics revealed in the stories to Card C must be viewed within that context. How Great Plains farmers would handle environmental threats of a different nature, for example, an extended drought, is of course another question. The authors are currently involved in exploring, via the TAT, a variety of environmental hazards in an attempt to further delineate man's psychodynamic repertoire of methods by which he copes with the forces of Nature.

THE TAT AS A GEOGRAPHIC RESEARCH TECHNIQUE

The TAT is a very flexible technique which can be used to examine a wide variety of environmental dimensions and man's attitudes toward them. It can provide deeper insights than the conventional geographic techniques into the reactions of individuals confronted by any number of different environmental situations. For example, by careful selection or design of cards, it could be useful for systematic investigation of various environmental hazards and man's coping with them (14). One could vary the amount of time a man would have in order to prepare for a stress, or one could vary the amount of information given in characterizing a hazard and see how responses would differ. One could also choose two or more cultures with the same environmental hazard and see whether methods of handling differed.

On a broader more general sense, the TAT could perhaps be used to measure the degree to which regional differences in personality exist, if at all. A favorite device of regional novelists is to express the unique flavor of a place by means of personality traits of local characters. It has been suggested that personality is a significant element of regional analysis and that it may well be one of the most powerful forces for regional change (15). But quite apart from any directly practical applications the TAT could well enrich geographic literature by providing a means to explore what Wright referred to as the most fascinating "terrae incognitae" of all, those that lie in the minds and hearts of man (16).

NOTES

1. For a review of some of the key questions involved in the man-land relationship in the history of Western thought see C. J. Glacken, *Traces on the Rhodian Shore* (Berkeley and Los Angeles: University of California Press, 1967); and F. Thomas, *The Environmental Basis of Society* (New York and London: The Century Co., 1925; Reprint by Johnson Reprint Corporation, 1965).

2. D. H. K. Lee, "Physiological Climatology," Chapter 22 in P. E. James and C. F. Jones, eds., *American Geography; Inventory and Prospect* (Syracuse: Syracuse University Press, 1954), p. 473.

3. For a review of articles devoted to this subject in the major American geographical journals in the period 1916–1966, see W. R. D. Sewell, R. W. Kates, and L. E. Phillips, "Human Response to Weather and Climate; Geographical Contributions," *Geographical Review* 58 (1968): 262–80. Most directly related to the plea of Lee, in other disciplines, is the research summarized in the massive textbook of C. W. Tromp, *Medical Biometeorology; Weather, Climate and the Living Organism* (Amsterdam: Elsevier Publishing Company, 1963). An indication of the current interest in behavioral aspects of man-environment relationships is the listing of thirty disciplines and 270 individuals in *1967 Directory of Behavior and Environmental Design* (Providence, Rhode Island: Research and Design Institute, 1967); and of 160 social scientists from over fifty universities and institutions in J. Ochs, H. J. Barnett, and G. Ault, *Environmental Social Scientists* (St. Louis: Institute for Urban and Regional Studies, 1968); in addition, one could cite the following journals, nearly all originating in the past few years, which are devoted almost exclusively to the same topic: *Man and His Environment, Milieu, Landscape, Architectural Psychology, Newsletter of Architectural Psychology, Design Methods Group Newsletter*, and *Journal of Environmental Research and Development*.

4. This point is also stressed in A. Pred, *Behavior and Location; Foundations for a Geographic and Dynamic Location Theory*, Part 1 (Lund Studies in Geography, Series B, No. 27, Lund: C. W. K. Gleerup, 1967), p. 11.

5. I. Burton, R. W. Kates, and G. F. White, *The Human Ecology of Extreme Geophysical Events*, Natural Hazard Research Working Paper No. 1, Department of Geography (Toronto: University of Toronto Press, 1968), pp. 6–8. On interviews, see W. Roder, "Attitudes and Knowledge on the Topeka Plain," pp. 62–83, and I. Burton, "Invasion and Escape on the Little Calumet," pp. 84–92 in G. F. White, ed., *Papers on Flood Problems*, Department of Geography Research Paper No. 70 (Chicago: University of Chicago Press, 1961). On the apperception test, see T. F. Saarinen, *Perception of the Drought Hazard on Great Plains*, Department of Geography Research Paper No. 106 (Chicago: University of Chicago Press 1966). On analysis of news media, see J. F. Rooney, *The Urban Snow Hazard, an Analysis of the Disruptive Impact of Snowfall at Ten Cities in Central and Western United States*, Unpublished Ph.D. dissertation, Clark University, 1966. For studies on decision-making models, see G. F. White, "The Choice of Use in Resource Management," *Natural Resources Journal* 1 (1961): 23–40; R. W. Kates, *Hazard and Choice Perception in Flood Plain Management*, Department of Geography Research Paper No. 78 (Chicago: University of Chicago Press, 1962). On benefit-cost analysis, see G. F. White, *Choice of Adjustment to Floods*, Department of Geog-

raphy Research Paper No. 93 (Chicago: University of Chicago Press, 1964). On new methods, see G. F. White et al, *Changes in the Urban Occupance of Flood Plains in the United States*, Department of Geography Research Paper No. 57 (Chicago: University of Chicago Press, 1958); I. Burton, *Types of Agricultural Occupance of Flood Plains in the United States*, Department of Geography Research Paper No. 75 (Chicago: University of Chicago Press, 1962); I. Burton, R. W. Kates, R. Mather, and R. E. Snead, *The Shores of Megalopolis: Coastal Occupance and Human Adjustment to Flood Hazard* (Elmer, N.J.: C. W. Thornthwaite Associates Laboratory of Climatology Publications in Climatology, Vol. 18, 1965).

6. This has been evident at national meetings of the Association of American Geographers since April 20, 1965, when at Columbus, Ohio, a pair of psychologists appeared on the program at a special symposium on environmental perception and behavior arranged by R. W. Kates. Edited versions of the papers presented are to be found in D. Lowenthal, ed., *Environmental Perception and Behavior*, Department of Geography Research Paper No. 109 (Chicago: University of Chicago Press, 1967). Other major examples of interaction between psychologists and geographers is the series of articles in R. W. Kates and J. F. Wohwill, eds., "Man's Response to the Physical Environment," *The Journal of Social Issues* 22 (1966); the work underway by Lowenthal and his associates as reported by D. Lowenthal, "Environmental Perception Project," *Man and His Environment*, Vol. 1 (1968), pp. 3–6; the collaboration between social psychologists and geographers at the University of Chicago currently in preparation under the title *Attitudes Toward Water: An Interdisciplinary Exploration* (forthcoming); or the symposium on "Behavior Models in Geography," at the Association of American Geographers meeting in Washington, D.C., on August 21, 1968. A review of many recent studies on environmental attitudes showing the interdisciplinary nature of this type of work is to be seen in G. F. White, "Formation and Role of Public Attitudes," in H. Jarret, ed., *Environmental Quality in a Growing Economy* (Baltimore: Johns Hopkins Press, 1966), pp. 105–27.

7. K. H. Craik, "The Comprehension of the Everyday Physical Environment," *Journal of the American Institute of Planners* 34 (1968): 30.

8. Craik, "The Comprehension of the Everyday Physical Environment," p. 31.

9. H. A. Murray, *Thematic Apperception Test: Pictures and Manual* (Cambridge, Mass.: Harvard University Press, 1943).

10. Although the data analyzed here have not been previously treated, they were collected as part of a larger study; see Saarinen, note 5.

11. L. C. Schaw and W. F. Henry, "A Method for the Comparison of Groups: A Study in Thematic Apperception," *Genetic Psychology Monographs* 54 (1956): 207–53.

12. H. A. Murray, *Explorations in Personality* (New York: Oxford University Press, 1938) and B. Aron, *A Manual for Analysis of the Thematic Apperception Test* (Berkeley, Calif.: Berg, 1949).

13. Other coping mechanisms presented by six members of the sample (9.6 percent) could not be classified as either rational, task-oriented, or arational-philosophical. They are described here to show what are, for this group, possible but atypical coping modes. Four of these six farmers emphasized the physical danger posed by the storm. For example; ". . . I'd be getting for home instead of staying on the machinery. That's one thing I've got respect for is lightning." Another farmer displayed a grim sense of humor: "Well, he's harvesting like mad trying to get his wheat cut before the hail storm comes. (Laugh) One consolation is that it's going to bring rain." Finally, one farmer, after describing the conflict

situation presented by the card, failed to offer any means of coping with it. These various coping mechanisms form a group labelled "Miscellaneous."

14. For a discussion of the range of environmental hazards see I. Burton and R. W. Kates, "The Perception of Natural Hazards in Resource Management," *Natural Resources Journal* 3 (1964): 412–41; see also Burton, Kates, and White, note 5.

15. R. D. Campbell, "Personality as an Element of Regional Geography," *Annals* of the Association of American Geographers 58 (1968): 748–59. For an indication of the role of personality in economic growth, see the following paper and books by D. C. McClelland: "The Achievement Motive in Economic Growth," paper delivered at North American Conference on the Social Implications of Industrialization and Technological Change, Chicago, 1960; *The Achievement Motive* (New York: Appleton-Century-Crofts, 1953); *The Achieving Society* (Princeton, N.J.: Van Nostrand, 1961).

16. J. K. Wright, "Terrae Incognitae, The Place of Imagination in Geography," Chapter 5 in J. K. Wright, *Human Nature in Geography* (Cambridge, Mass.: Harvard University Press, 1966), p. 88.

CHAPTER

A Comparative Study of the Role of Values in Social Action in Two Southwestern Communities

EVON Z. VOGT
THOMAS F. O'DEA

Reprinted from the *American Sociological Review* 18, no. 6 (1953): 645–54, by permission of the American Sociological Association and the authors.

The authors are indebted to the Rockefeller Foundation (Social Science Division) for the financial support of the research reported in this paper as part of the Comparative Study of Values in Five Cultures Project of the Laboratory of Social Relations at Harvard University. They also wish to express their appreciation to Ethel M. Albert, Wilfrid C. Bailey, Clyde Kluckhohn, Anne Parsons, and John M. Roberts for criticisms and suggestions in the preparation of the paper.

The consequences of different cultural values interacting with virtually identical physical environments are illustrated in this study of two communities only 40 miles apart in western New Mexico. The Mormon community, Rimrock, and Homestead, a community settled by migrants from Texas and Oklahoma do, indeed, share many values characteristic of the American culture—achievement, success, progress, and man seen as dominant over nature. However, they differ dramatically in one area: the Homesteaders confront life as individualists—every man for himself; the Mormons join hands and work together. Vogt and O'Dea argue that it is this difference that accounts for the Mormons' more successful manipulation of the land as well as a more socially responsible community.

But serious questions can be raised about this "explanation" of the different accomplishments of the two communities. Would the isolated farm families of Homestead have responded differently to community problems if, like the townspeople of Rimrock, they had enjoyed the assurance of future income provided by irrigation farming? Perhaps it was the Homestead ranchers' realistic fears of drought that kept them from donating to community causes. And though cooperative and close in their relations, could the Mormons of Rimrock have survived their early years without the help of the mother church? Such questions must be carefully explored before final conclusions can be drawn about the factors which account for the differences between the two communities.

It is one of the central hypotheses of the Values Study Project that value-orientations play an important part in the shaping of social institutions and in influencing the forms of observed social action. By value-orientations are understood those views of the world, often implicitly held, which define the meaning of human life or the "life situation of man" and thereby provide the context in which day-to-day problems are solved (1). The present article is an outgrowth of one phase of the field research carried out in western New Mexico. It presents the record of two communities composed of people with a similar cultural background and living in the same general ecological setting.

The responses of these two communities to similar problems were found to be quite different. Since the physical setting of the two villages is remarkably similar, the explanation for the differences was sought in the manner in which each group viewed the situation and the kind of social relationships and legitimate expectations which each felt appropriate in meeting situational challenges. In this sphere of value-orientations a marked difference was found. Moreover, the differences in response to situation in the two cases were found to be related to the differences between the value-orientations central to these communities.

We do not deny the importance of situational factors. Nor do we intend to disparage the importance of historical convergence of value-orientations with concrete situations in explaining the centrality of some values as against others and in leading to the deep internalization of the values we discuss. But the importance of value-orientations as an element in understanding the situation of action is inescapably clear. All the elements of what Parsons has called the action frame of reference—the actors, the means and conditions which comprise the situation, and the value-orientations of the actors enter into the act (2). The primacy of any one in any individual case does not permit generalization. Yet the present study testifies to the great importance of the third element—the value-orientations—in shaping the final action which ensues.

FOCUS OF THE INQUIRY
The inquiry is focused upon a comparison of the Mormon community of *Rimrock* (3) with the Texan community of *Homestead,* both having populations of approximately 250 and both located (forty miles apart) on the southern portion of the Colorado Plateau in western New Mexico. The natural environmental setting is virtually the same for the two villages: the prevailing elevations stand at 7,000 feet; the landscapes are characterized by mesa and canyon

country; the flora and fauna are typical of the Upper Sonoran Life Zone with stands of pinyon, juniper, sagebrush, and blue gramma grass and some intrusions of Ponderosa pine, Douglas fir, Englemann spruce and Gambel oak from a higher life zone; the region has a steppe climate with an average annual precipitation of 14 inches (which varies greatly from year to year) and with killing frosts occurring late in the spring and early in the autumn (4). The single important environmental difference between the two communities is that Rimrock is located near the base of a mountain range which has elevations rising to 9,000 feet, and a storage reservoir (fed by melting snow packs from these higher elevations) has made irrigation agriculture possible in Rimrock, while in Homestead there is only dry-land farming. Today both villages have subsistence patterns based upon combinations of farming (mainly irrigated crops of alfalfa and wheat in Rimrock, and dry-land crops of pinto beans in Homestead) and livestock raising (mainly Hereford beef cattle in both villages).

Rimrock was settled by Mormon missionaries in the 1870s as part of a larger project to plant settlements in the area of northern Arizona. Rimrock itself, unlike the Arizona sites, was established as a missionary outpost and the intention of the settlers was the conversion of the Indians, a task concevied in terms of the *Book of Mormon*, which defines the American Indian as "a remnant of Israel."

The early settlers were "called" by the Church, that is, they were selected and set out by the Church authorities. The early years were exceedingly difficult and only the discipline of the Church and the loyalty of the settlers to its gospel kept them at the task. Drought, crop diseases, and the breaking of the earth and rock dam which they had constructed for the storage of irrigation water added to their difficulties, as did the fact that they had merely squatted on the land and were forced to purchase it at an exorbitant price to avoid eviction. The purchase money was given by the Church authorities in Salt Lake City, who also supplied 5,000 pounds of seed wheat in another period of dearth. The original settlers were largely from northern Utah although there were also some converts from the southern states who had been involved in unsuccessful Arizona settlements a few years earlier.

As the emphasis shifted from missionary activities to farming, Rimrock developed into a not unusual Mormon village, despite its peripheral position to the rest of Mormondom. Irrigation farming was supplemented by cattle raising on the open range. In the early 1930s the Mormons began to buy range land, and Rimrock's economy shifted to a focus upon cattle raising. Today villagers own a total of 149 sections of range land and about four sections of irrigated or irrigable land devoted to gardens and some irrigated pastures in the immediate vicinity of the village. The family farm is still the basic economic unit, although partnerships formed upon a kinship basis and devoted to cattle raising have been important in raising the economic level of the village as a whole. In recent years some of the villagers—also on the basis of a kinship partnership—purchased the local trading post which is engaged in trading with the Indians as well as local village business. In addition to 12 family partnerships which own 111 sections of land, there is a village cooperative which owns 38 sections. Privately-owned commercial facilities in the village include two stores, a boarding house, two garages, a saddle and leather shop, and a small restaurant. With this economic variety there is considerable difference in the distribution of wealth.

The Church is the central core of the village and its complex hierarchical structure, including the auxiliary organizations which activate women, youth, and young children, involves a large portion of the villagers in active participation. The church structure is backed up and impenetrated by the kinship structure. Moreover, church organization and kinship not only unify Rimrock into a social unit, they also integrate it into the larger structure of the Mormon Church and relate it by affinity and consanguinity to the rest of Mormondom.

Rimrock has been less affected by secularization than most Mormon villages in Utah and is less assimilated into generalized American patterns. (5). Its relative isolation has both kept such pressures from impinging upon it with full force and enhanced its formal and informal ties with the Church, preserving many of the characteristics of a Mormon village of a generation ago.

Homestead was settled by migrants from the South Plains area of western Texas and Oklahoma in the early 1930s. The migration represented a small aspect of that vast movement of people westward to California which was popularized in Steinbeck's *Grapes of Wrath* and which was the subject of investigation by many governmental agencies in the 1930s and 1940s (6). Instead of going on to California, these homesteaders settled in a number of semi-arid farming areas in northern and western New Mexico and proceeded to develop an economy centered around the production of pinto beans. The migration coincided with the period of national depression and was due in part to severe economic conditions on the South Plains which forced families to leave their Texas and Oklahoma communities, in part to the attraction of land available for homesteading which held out the promise of family-owned farms for families who had previously owned little or no land or who had lost their land during the depression. The land base controlled by the homesteaders comprises approximately 100 sections. Each farm unit is operated by a nuclear family; there are no partnerships. Farms now average two sections in size and are scattered as far as twenty miles from the crossroads center of the community which contains the two stores, the school, the post office, two garages, a filling station, a small restaurant, a bean warehouse, a small bar, and two church buildings. Through the years, farming technology has shifted almost completely from horse-drawn implements to mechanized equipment.

With the hazardous farming conditions (periodic droughts and early killing frosts) out-migration from Homestead has been relatively high. A few of these families have gone on to California, but more of them have moved to irrigated farms in the middle Rio Grande Valley and entered an agricultural situation which in its physical environmental aspects is similar to the situation in the Mormon community of Rimrock.

THE MORMON CASE

In broad perspective these two villages present local variations of generalized American culture. They share the common American value-orientations which emphasize the importance of achievement and success, progress and optimism, and rational mastery over nature. In the Mormon case, these were taken over from the nineteenth century American milieu in western New York where the Church was founded, and reinterpreted in terms of an elaborate theological conception of the universe as a dynamic process in which God and men are active collaborators in an eternal progression to greater power through increasing mastery (7). The present life was and is conceived as a single episode in an infinity of work and mastery. The result was the heightening for the Mormons of convictions shared with most other Americans. Moreover, this conception was closely related to the belief in the reopening of divine revelation through the agency first of Joseph Smith, the original Mormon prophet, and later through the institutionalized channels of the Mormon Church. The Mormons conceived of themselves as a covenant people especially chosen for a divine task. This task was the building of the kingdom of God on earth and in this project—attempted four times unsuccessfully before the eventual migration to the west—much of the religious and secular socialism of the early nineteenth century found a profound reflection. The Mormon prophet proposed the "Law of Consecration" in an attempt to reconcile private initiative with cooperative endeavor. Contention led to its abandonment in 1838 after some five years of unsuccessful experiment. Yet this withdrawal did not limit, but indeed rather enhanced, its future influence in Mormon settlement. The "Law of Consecration" was no longer interpreted as a blueprint prescribing social institutions of a definite sort, but its values lent a strong cooperative bias to much of later Mormon activity (8). In the context of the notion of peculiarity and reinforced by outgroup antagonism and persecution, these values became deeply embedded in Mormon orientations. The preference for agriculture combined with an emphasis upon community and lay participation in church activities resulted in the formation of compact villages rather than isolated family farmsteads as the typical Mormon settlement pattern (9).

While Rimrock and Homestead share most of the central value-orientations of general American culture, they differ significantly in the values governing social relationships. Rimrock, with a stress upon community cooperation, an ethnocentrism resulting from the notion of their own peculiarity, and a village pattern of settlement, is more like the other Mormon villages of the West than it is like Homestead.

The stress upon *community cooperation* in Rimrock contrasts markedly with the stress upon *individual independence* found in Homestead. This contrast is one of emphasis, for individual initiative is important in Rimrock, especially in family farming and cattle raising, whereas cooperative activity does occur in Homestead. In Rimrock, however, the expectations are such that one must show his fellows or at least convince himself that he has good cause for *not* committing his time and resources to community efforts while in Homestead cooperative action takes place *only* after certainty has been reached that the claims of other individuals upon one's time and resources are legitimate.

Rimrock was a cooperative venture from the start, and very early the irrigation company, a mutual non-profit corporation chartered under state law, emerged from the early water association informally developed around—and in a sense within—the Church. In all situations which transcend the capacities of individual families or family combinations, Rimrock Mormons have recourse to cooperative techniques. Let us examine four examples.

The "Tight" Land Situation
Rimrock Mormons, feeling themselves "gathered," dislike having to migrate to non-Mormon areas. However, after World War II the 32 returned veterans faced a choice between poverty and under-

employment or leaving the community. This situation became the concern of the Church and was discussed in its upper lay priesthood bodies in the village. It was decided to buy land to enable the veterans to remain. The possibilities of land purchase in the area were almost nonexistent and it appeared that nothing could be done, when unexpectedly the opportunity to buy some 38 sections presented itself. At the time, the village did not have the needed 10,000 dollars for the down payment, so the sum was borrowed from the Cooperative Security Corporation, a Church Welfare Plan agency, and the land was purchased. The patterns revealed here—community concern over a community problem, and appeal to and reception of aid from the general authorities of the Church—are typically Mormon. However, Mormon cooperation did not end here. Instead of breaking up the purchased land into plots to be individually owned and farmed, the parcel was kept as a unit, and a cooperative Rimrock Land and Cattle Company was formed. The company copied and adapted the form of the mutual irrigation company. Shares were sold in the village, each member being limited to two. A quota of cattle per share per year to be run on the land and a quota of bulls relative to cows were established. The cattle are privately owned, but the land is owned and managed cooperatively. The calves are the property of the owners of the cows. The project, which has not been limited to veterans, supplements other earnings sufficiently to keep most of the veterans in the village.

The Graveling of the Village Streets

The streets of Rimrock were in bad repair in the fall of 1950. That summer a construction company had brought much large equipment into the area to build and gravel a section of a state highway which runs through the village. Before this company left, taking its equipment with it, villagers, again acting through the Church organization, decided that the village should avail itself of the opportunity and have the town's streets graveled. This was discussed in the Sunday priesthood meeting and announced at the Sunday sacrament meeting. A meeting was called for Monday evening, and each household was asked to send a representative. The meeting was well attended, and although not every family had a member present, practically all were represented at least by proxy. There was considerable discussion, and it was finally decided to pay 800 dollars for the job which meant a 20 dollar donation from each family. The local trader paid a larger amount, and, within a few days after the meeting, the total amount was collected. Only one villager raised objections to the proceedings. Although he was a man of importance locally, he was soon silenced by a much poorer man who invoked Mormon values of progress and cooperation and pledged to give 25 dollars which was 5 dollars above the norm.

The Construction of a High School Gymnasium

In 1951 a plan for the construction of a high school gymnasium was presented to the Rimrock villagers. Funds for materials and for certain skilled labor would be provided from state school appropriations, providing that the local residents would contribute the labor for construction. The plan was discussed in a Sunday priesthood meeting in the church, and later meetings were held both in the church and in the schoolhouse. Under the leadership of the principal of the school (who is also a member of the higher priesthood), arrangements were made whereby each able-bodied man in the community would either contribute at least 50 hours of labor or 50 dollars (the latter to be used to hire outside laborers) toward the construction. The original blueprint was extended to include a row of classrooms for the high school around the large central gymnasium.

Work on the new building began in late 1951, continued through 1952, and is now (in 1953) nearing completion. The enterprise was not carried through without difficulties. A few families were sympathetic at first but failed to contribute full amounts of either labor or cash, and some were unsympathetic toward the operation from the start. The high school principal had to keep reminding the villagers about their pledges to support the enterprise. But in the end the project was successful, and it represented an important cooperative effort on the part of the majority.

The Community Dances

The Mormons have always considered dancing to be an important form of recreation—in fact a particularly Mormon form of recreation. Almost every Friday evening a dance is held in the village church house. These dances are family affairs and are opened and closed with prayer. They are part of the general Church recreation program and are paid for by what is called locally "the budget." The budget refers to the plan under which villagers pay 15 dollars per family per year to cover a large number of entertainments, all sponsored by the Church auxiliary organization for youth, the Young Men's Mutual Improvement Association, and the Young Women's Mutual Improvement Association. The budget payment admits all members of the family to such entertainments.

Observation of these dances over a six months period did not reveal any tension or fighting. Smoking and drinking are forbidden to loyal Mormons, and those who smoked did so outside and away from the building. At dances held in the local school there has been evidence of drinking, and at times fighting has resulted from the presence of non-villagers. But on the whole the Rimrock dances are peaceful family affairs.

Rimrock reveals itself responding to group problems *as a group*. The economic ethic set forth by Joseph Smith in the Law of Consecration is seen in the dual commitment to private individual initiative (family farms and family partnerships in business and agriculture) and to cooperative endeavor in larger communal problems (irrigation company, land and cattle company, graveling the streets, and construction of school gymnasium). For the Mormons, cooperation has become second nature. It has become part of the institutionalized structure of expectations, reinforced by religious conviction and social control.

THE HOMESTEADER CASE

The value-stress upon individual independence of action has deep roots in the history of the homesteader group (*10*). The homesteaders were part of the westward migration from the hill country of the Southern Appalachians to the Panhandle country of Texas and Oklahoma and from there to the Southwest and California. Throughout their historical experience there has been an emphasis upon a rough and ready self-reliance and individualism, the Jacksonianism of the frontier West. The move to western New Mexico from the South Plains was made predominantly by isolated nuclear families, and Homestead became a community of scattered, individually-owned farmsteads—a geographical situation and a settlement pattern which reinforced the stress upon individualism.

Let us now examine the influence of this individualistic value-orientation upon a series of situations comparable to those that were described for Rimrock.

The "Tight" Land Situation

In 1934 the Federal Security Administration, working in conjunction with the Land Use Division of the Department of Agriculture, proposed a "unit re-organization plan." This plan would have enabled the homesteaders to acquire additional tracts of land and permit them to run more livestock and hence depend less upon the more hazardous economic pursuit of dry-land pinto bean farming. It called for the use of government funds to purchase large ranches near the Homestead area which would be managed cooperatively by a board of directors selected by the community. The scheme collapsed while it was still in the planning stages, because it was clear that each family expected to acquire its own private holdings on the range and that a cooperative would not work in Homestead.

The Graveling of the Village Streets

During the winter of 1949–50 the construction company which was building the highway through Rimrock was also building a small section of highway north of Homestead. The construction company offered to gravel the streets of Homestead center if the residents who lived in the village would cooperatively contribute enough funds for the purpose. This community plan was rejected by the homesteaders, and an alternative plan was followed. Each of the operators of several of the service institutions—including the two stores, the bar, and the post office—independently hired the construction company truck drivers to haul a few loads of gravel to be placed in front of his own place of business, which still left the rest of the village streets a sea of mud in rainy weather.

The Construction of a High School Gymnasium

In 1950 the same plan for the construction of a new gymnasium was presented to the homesteaders as was presented to the Mormon village of Rimrock. As noted above, this plan was accepted by the community of Rimrock, and the new building is now nearing completion. But the plan was rejected by the residents of Homestead at a meeting in the summer of 1950, and there were long speeches to the effect that "I've got to look after my own farm and my own family first; I can't be up here in town building a gymnasium." Later in the summer additional funds were provided for labor; and with these funds adobe bricks were made, the foundation was dug, and construction was started—the homesteaders being willing to work on the gymnasium on a purely business basis at a dollar an hour. But as soon as the funds were exhausted, construction stopped. Today a partially completed gymnasium, and stacks of some 10,000 adobe bricks disintegrating slowly with the rains, stand as monuments to the individualism of the homesteaders.

The Community Dances

As in Rimrock, the village dances in Homestead are important focal points for community activity. These affairs take place several times a year in the schoolhouse and are always well-attended. But while the dances in Rimrock are well-coordinated activities which carry through the evening, the dances in Homestead often end when tensions between rival families result in fist-fights. And there is always the expectation in Homestead that a dance (or other cooperative activity such as a picnic or rodeo) may end at any moment and the level of activity reduced to the component nuclear families which form the only solid core of social organization within the community.

The individualistic value-orientation of the homesteaders also has important functional relationships to the religious organization of the community. With the exception of two men who are professed atheists, all of the homesteaders define themselves as Christians. But denominationalism is rife, there being ten different denominations represented in the village: Baptist, Presbyterian, Methodist, Nazarene, Campbellite, Holiness, 7th Day Adventist, Mormon, Catholic, and Present Day Disciples.

In the most general terms, this religious differentiation in Homestead can be interpreted as a function of the individualistic and factionalizing tendencies in the social system. In a culture with a value-stress upon independent individual action combined with a "freedom of religion" ideology, adhering to one's own denomination becomes an important means of expressing individualism and of focusing factional disputes around a doctrine and a concrete institutional framework. In turn, the doctrinal differences promote additional factionalizing tendencies, with the result that competing churches become the battleground for a cumulative and circularly reinforcing struggle between rival small factions within the community (11).

To sum up, we may say that the strong commitment to an individualistic value-orientation has resulted in a social system in which inter-personal relations are strongly colored by a kind of factionalism and in which persons and groups become related to one another in a competitive, feuding relationship. The homesteaders do not live on their widely separated farms and ignore one another, as it might be possible to do. On the other hand, they do not cooperate in community affairs as closely as does a hive of bees. They interact, but a constant feuding tone permeates the economic, social and religious structure of the community.

RELATIONSHIP BETWEEN THE TWO COMMUNITIES

Although there is some trading in livestock, feed, and other crops, the most important contacts between the two communities are not economic but are social and recreational. The village baseball teams have scheduled games with one another for the past two decades, and there is almost always joint participation in the community dances and in the summer rodeos in the two communities. Despite Mormon objections to close associations with "gentiles," there is also considerable inter-dating between the two communities among the teen-age groups, and three intermarriages have taken place.

In general, the homesteaders envy and admire the Mormons' economic organization, their irrigated land, and more promising prospects for good crops each year. On the other hand, they regard the Mormons as cliquish and unfriendly and fail completely to understand why anyone "wants to live all bunched up the way the Mormons do." They feel that the Mormons are inbred and think they should be glad to get "new blood" from intermarriages with homesteaders. They add, "That Mormon religion is something we can't understand at all." Finally, the homesteaders say that Mormons "used to have more than one wife, and some probably still do; they dance in the church, they're against liquor, coffee, and tobacco, and they always talk about Joseph Smith and the *Book of Mormon.*"

The Mormons consider their own way of life distinctly superior to that of the homesteaders in every way. Some will admit that the homesteaders have the virtue of being more friendly and of "mixing more with others," and their efforts in the face of farming hazards are admired, but Homestead is generally regarded as a rough and in some ways immoral community, especially because of the drinking, smoking, and fighting (particularly at dances) that takes place. They also feel that Homestead is disorganized and that the churches are not doing what they should for the community. For the past few years they have been making regular missionary trips to Homestead, but to date they have made no conversions.

COMPARISONS AND CONCLUSIONS

In the case of Rimrock and Homestead, we are dealing with two communities which are comparable in population, in ecological setting, and which are variants of the same general culture. The two outstanding differences are: (a) irrigation versus dry-land farming and associated differences in settlement pattern, compact village versus isolated farmstead type; (12) (b) a value stress upon cooperative community action versus a stress upon individual action. The important question here involves the relationship (if any) between these two sets of variables. Is the cooperation in Rimrock directly a function of an irrigation agriculture situation with a compact village settlement pattern, the rugged individualism in Homestead, a function of a dry-land farming situation with a scattered settlement pattern? Or did these value-orientations arise out of earlier historical experience in each case, influence the types of communities which were established in western New Mexico, and later persist in the face of changed economic situations? We shall attempt to demonstrate that the second proposition is more in accord with the historical facts as we now know them.

Nelson has recently shown that the general pattern of the Mormon village is neither a direct function (in its beginnings) of the requirements of irrigation agriculture, nor of the need for protection against Indians on the frontier. Rather, the basic pattern was a social invention of the Mormons, motivated by a sense of urgent need to prepare a dwelling place for the "Savior" at "His Second Coming." The "Plat of the City of Zion" was invented by Joseph Smith, Sidney Rigdon, and Frederick G. Williams in 1833 and has formed the basis for the laying out of most Mormon villages, even those established in the Middle West before the Mormons migrated to Utah (13).

It is very clear that both the compact village pattern and the cooperative social arrangements centered around the church existed before the Mormons engaged in irrigation agriculture and had a strong influence upon the development of community structure not only in Utah but in the Mormon settlements like Rimrock on the periphery of the Mormon culture area. There is no objective reason in the Rimrock ecological and cultural setting (the local Navahos and Zunis did not pose a threat to pioneer settlements in the 1880s) why the Mormons could not have set up a community which conformed more to the isolated farmstead type with a greater stress upon individualistic social relations. Once the Mormon community was established, it is clear that the cooperation required by irrigation agriculture of the Mormon type and the general organization of the church strongly reinforced the value stress upon communal social action.

It is of further significance that as the population expanded and the Rimrock Mormons shifted from irrigation agricultural pursuits to dry-land ranching in the region outside of the Rimrock valley, the earlier cooperative patterns modeled on the mutual irrigation company were applied to the solution of economic problems that are identical to those faced by the Homesteaders. Moreover, in midwestern and eastern cities to which Mormons have recently moved, church wards have purchased and cooperatively worked church welfare plan farms.

In Homestead, on the other hand, our evidence indicates that the first settlers were drawn from a westward-moving population which stressed a frontier-type of self-reliance and individualism. They were searching for a place where each man could own his own farm and be his own "boss." Each family settled on its isolated homestead claim, and there emerged from the beginning an isolated

farmstead type of settlement pattern in which the nuclear family
was the solidary unit. The service center which was built up later
simply occupied lots that were sold to storekeepers, filling station
operators, the bartender, and others, by the four families who
owned the four sections which joined at a crossroads. Only two of
these four family homes were located near the service center at the
crossroads. The other two families continued to maintain their
homes in other quarters of their sections and lived almost a mile
from "town." In 1952 one of the former families built a new home
located over a mile from the center of town, and commented that
they had always looked forward to "getting out of town."

There is no objective reason in the Homestead ecological setting why there could not be more clustering of houses into a compact village and more community cooperation than actually exists.
One would not expect those farmers whose farms are located 15 or
20 miles from the service center to live in "town" and travel out to
work each day. But there is no reason why those families living
within 2 or 3 miles of the village center could not live in town and
work their fields from there. In typical Mormon villages a large
percentage of the farms are located more than three miles from
the farm homes. For example, in Rimrock over 31 percent, in
Escalante over 38 percent, and in Ephriam over 30 percent of the
farms are located from three to eight or more miles from the center
of the villages (14).

It is clear that the homesteaders were operating with a set of
individualistic property arrangements (drawn, of course, from our
generalized American culture) and that their strong stress upon
individualism led to a quite different utilization of these property
patterns (than was the case with the Mormons) and to the establishment of a highly scattered type of community. Once Homestead
was established, the individualism permitted by the scattered dry-
land farming pattern, and encouraged by the emphasis upon the
small nuclear family unit and upon multi-denominationalism in
church affiliation reacted on and strongly reinforced the value
stress upon individual independence. It is evident that the homesteaders continue to prefer this way of life, as shown by their remarks concerning the "bunched up" character of a Mormon village
and the fact that a "number of families have recently moved "out
of town" when they built new houses.

Of further interest is the fact that when homesteader families
move to irrigated farms in the middle Rio Grande Valley, the stress
upon individual action tends to persist strongly. They do not readily
develop cooperative patterns to deal with this new setting which is
similar to the situation in the irrigated valley of the Mormons at

Rimrock. Indeed, one of the principal innovations they have been promoting in one region along the Rio Grande where they are replacing Spanish-Americans on the irrigated farming land is a system of meters on irrigation ditches. These meters will measure the water flowing into each individual farmer's ditches, and effectively eliminate the need for more highly organized cooperative arrangements for distributing the available supply of water.

In conclusion, we should like to reiterate that we are strongly cognizant of situational factors. If the Rimrock Mormons had not been able to settle in a valley which was watered by melting snow packs from a nearby mountain and which provided the possibilities for the construction of storage reservoir, they certainly could not have developed an irrigation agricultural system at all. In the case of Rimrock, however, the actual site of settlement was selected from among several possible sites in a larger situation. The selection was largely influenced by Mormon preconceptions of the type of village they wished to establish. In fact, Mormons chose the irrigable valleys throughout the inter-montane west. On the other hand, the physical environmental features for the development of irrigation were simply not present in the Homestead setting, and the people had no alternative to dry-land farming. There is no evidence to suggest that had they found an irrigable valley, they would have developed it along Mormon lines. In fact, the homesteaders' activities in the Rio Grande Valley suggest just the opposite. It is clear that the situational facts did not *determine* in any simple sense the contrasting community structures which emerged. Rather, the situations set certain limits, but within these limits contrasting value-orientations influenced the development of two quite different community types. It would appear that solutions to problems of community settlement pattern and the type of concrete social action which ensues are set within a value framework which importantly influences the selections made with the range of possibilities existing within an objective situation.

NOTES

1. C. Kluckhohn, "Values and Value-Orientations in the Theory of Action: An Exploration in Definition and Classification," T. Parsons and E. A. Shils, eds., *Toward a General Theory of Action* (Cambridge: Harvard University Press, 1951), p. 140.

2. T. Parsons, *The Structure of Social Action* (Glencoe, Ill.: Free Press, 1949), pp. 43–86; T. Parsons, *Essays in Sociological Theory* (Glencoe, Ill.: Free Press, 1949), pp. 32–40; T. Parsons, *The Social System* (Glencoe, Ill.: Free Press, 1951), pp. 3–24.

3. "Rimrock" and "Homestead" are pseudonyms used to protect the anonymity of our informants.

4. For additional ecological details on the region see E. Z. Vogt, *Navaho Veterans: A Study of Changing Values* (Peabody Museum of Harvard University, Papers, Vol. 41, No. 1, 1951), pp. 11–12; and J. Landgraf, *Land-Use in the Rimrock Area of New Mexico: An Anthropological Approach to Areal Study* (Peabody Museum of Harvard University, Papers, forthcoming, 1953).

5. L. Nelson, *The Mormon Village* (Salt Lake City: University of Utah Press, 1952), pp. 275–85.

6. See especially the reports of the Tolan Committee, U.S. Congress, "House Committee to Investigate the Interstate Migration of Destitute Citizens," 76th Congress, 3rd Session, Vol. 6, Part 6, 1940.

7. The data from Rimrock was based upon seven months field experience in the community during 1950–51. Additional data on this community will be provided in O'Dea's forthcoming monograph on *Mormon Values: The Significance of a Religious Outlook for Social Action*.

8. The "Law of Consecration" became the basis of the Mormon pattern of cooperative activity also known as "The United Order of Enoch." Cf. J. A. Geddes, *The United Order Among the Mormons* (Salt Lake City: Desert News Press, 1924); E. J. Allen, *The Second United Order Among the Mormons* (New York: Columbia University Press, 1936).

9. L. Nelson, *The Mormon Village*, pp. 25–54.

10. The data from Homestead are based upon a year's field work in the community during 1949–50. Additional data on this community will be provided in Vogt's forthcoming monograph on *The Homesteaders: A Study of Values in a Frontier Community*. See also Vogt, "Water Witching: An Interpretation of a Ritual Pattern in a Rural American Community," *Scientific Monthly* 75 (September, 1952).

11. This relationship between churches and factionalizing tendencies has also been observed by Bailey in his unpublished study of a community in west Texas, in the heart of the ancestral home region of the present residents of Homestead. Cf. W. C. Bailey, "A Study of Texas Panhandle Community; A Preliminary Report on Cotton Center, Texas," Values Study Files, Harvard University.

12. Cf. L. Nelson, *The Mormon Village*, p. 4.

13. L. Nelson, *The Mormon Village*, pp. 28–38.

14. See L. Nelson, *The Mormon Village*, pp. 99 and 144 for data on Escalante and Ephriam.

CHAPTER

Uncertainty in Nature, Cognitive Dissonance, and the Perceptual Distortion of Environmental Information:

Weather Forecasts and New England Beach Trip Decisions

ROBERT L. A. ADAMS

Reprinted from *Economic Geography*
49, no. 4 (October, 1973): 287–97,
by permission of the publisher and the author.

The research upon which this article is based was supported by grants from the National Science Foundation (GS3184), Collaborative Research on Natural Hazards.

The reader's initial reaction to the following chapter may be one of impatience, or at least puzzlement: what is the relevance of studying the factors affecting a person's decision to go to the beach considering the seriousness of environmental problems facing society? But the study, while light in subject matter, makes a heavy point—how man organizes information about the physical world to fit his personal desires and commitments.

Adams shows that persons with strong desires or commitments to go to the beach tend to interpret weather forecasts as favorable. If the forecasts suggest a high probability of rain, the potential beach users may unconsciously interpret them to mean merely a "chance of showers." Conversely, those whose commitments are weak interpret the chance of rain as even more likely to occur than intended in the forecast message.

These observations tend to illustrate the theory of cognitive dissonance which asserts that man struggles to attain consistency among his cognitions (attitudes, beliefs, values). When these are not in agreement, a discomforting dissonance is created, and one seeks to reduce it. This can be done in essentially three ways: (1) by changing one's own cognition or belief in order to attain harmony with the presently dissonant fact; (2) by changing the *external,* dissonant producing factor; (3) by reducing the problem to trivia, defining it as unworthy of one's attention.

There is considerable research concerning when and how much people will distort information in order to achieve cognitive harmony. To date, the results are mixed and more research is needed. Nevertheless, this study clearly shows that even in deciding about something as inconsequential as a trip to the beach, something is going on other than the rational judgment of information and the cool calculation of risk.

A word of caution: to test Adams' conclusions, it would be necessary to observe how a person feels when he is *actually* planning to go to the beach and listening to a weather forecast—not what he thinks he would do given a hypothetical situation. Such an effort would be no small research task. And we must point out that this present study takes a major step away from the traditional laboratory approach of psychologists toward a more realistic situation.

During the summer months, the coastal beaches of New England are the foci of millions of day-use recreational occasions; undertakings which, for most people, involve a non-trivial allocation of leisure time and a significant amount of effort. Beach trip decisions must, however, be made in the context of variable weather, a renowned New England phenomenon which elicited the following comment from Samuel Clemens (1876):

> There is a sumptuous variety about the New England weather that compels the stranger's admiration—and regret. The weather is always doing something there; always attending strictly to business; always getting up new designs and trying them on the people to see how they will go. But it gets through more business in spring than in any other season. In the spring I have counted one hundred and thirty-six different kinds of weather inside of four-and-twenty hours.

Although the variability of summer weather would have taxed less severely the enumerative powers of Clemens, it does present a decision making situation involving environmental uncertainty to the prospective beach user, particularly when the proposed trip involves substantial amounts of travel and on-site time.

The author recently completed a study which focused upon these decisions, i.e., the interplay between weather, weather information, and one-day, recreational, beach trip decisions in New England (1971). The data upon which this study was based were obtained largely through the mechanism of a detailed interview schedule which was designed to yield insights into the ways people use, perceive, and evaluate weather information in making their weather/beach-trip decisions. This schedule was administered during the month of August, 1970 at two of the most popular beaches serving the Boston metropolitan region, northeastern Massachusetts, and southeastern New Hampshire (1). Interviewees were selected on a random basis with a resulting total sample size of 458 parties who were engaged in a major, day-use, recreational occasion (2).

This article is devoted to a small portion of these data, i.e., to that portion which was collected to test the application of the theory of cognitive dissonance to beach-trip decision making behavior vis-à-vis weather information. This important body of social-psychological theory is based upon the notion that man does not wish to appear irrational to himself or to others. Briefly, in a simplified behavioral sense, the theory states that men seek consistency between their cognitions of how they act and their cognitions of how they should act based upon the information they have acquired. However, such accordant relationships are often difficult to achieve. For instance, having committed himself to a particular course of action, a person may be faced with information that is discordant with that commitment. In such instances, dissonance (psychological stress or discomfort) is produced due to the lack of congruity between his cognition of his commitment (*3*) and his cognition of the discordant information. However, the presence of dissonance nurtures pressures to reduce or eliminate that dissonance; much as, for example, hunger gives rise to forces to reduce or eliminate hunger. In the above case, the individual could reduce the dissonance by changing his commitment (chosen course of action) or altering his perception of the meaning, importance, or validity of the discrepant information. Any of these adjustments would promote a greater cognitive consistency. The mode of dissonance reduction chosen would be determined according to which of the elements (commitment or information) would be least resistant to change in that particular case (Abelson, 1968; Brehm and Cohen, 1962; Festinger, 1957 and 1964).

At the outset of the study, it was felt that this theory embodied the promise of possible relevance to weather/beach-trip decision making behavior. In this connection, it would be expected that people who have plans to go to the beach on a given day would make trip decisions consistent with their evaluation of prospective weather conditions. Provided that the weather information they received indicates that these conditions will clearly be good, this information is then consistent with their plan to go to the beach and no dissonance will occur. If, however, the information received predicts the occurrence of unfavorable conditions, a dissonance producing juxtaposition is presented. To reduce this dissonance the decision maker can resort to a number of strategies; for instance, he might cancel the trip (change his commitment) so as to achieve congruity with the unfavorable weather information, or he may maintain his original commitment to go to the beach and alter his perception of the importance, validity, and meaning of the discrepant weather information. Translated into a specific research objective, the author was particularly interested in whether or not these decision makers, in the face of dissonance producing weather information with its inherent uncertainty, engage in the perceptual distortion of such information in order to justify their particular trip decisions.

To provide the data necessary for accomplishment of this research objective, the subjects' responses to a uniform, hypothetical situation were monitored. During the course of the interview every fourth respondent (*4*) was asked a question which required him to interpret the meaning of a suboptimal weather forecast statement (5), and to indicate how that forecast would have influenced his beach-trip decision that day, had it been necessary to base the decision upon that weather information alone. The question was stated as follows:

> Now I would like you to pretend that it had been necessary for you to decide *last night* whether or not you would make *this trip* to the beach today. In that case you'd have only had a weather forecast to help you decide what today would be like. Right? What if the 11 o'clock forecast last night had predicted a 60 percent chance of rain for today, knowing how much you wanted to go to the beach, would you still have planned to come?
> Yes...... No......
>
> Given this forecast *last night,* what would you have felt were the chances that it would actually be rainy today?
> ...... almost certain
> ...... very likely
> ...... likely
> ...... a chance
> ...... a small chance
> ...... not likely

In constructing this question, the intent was to present the subjects with dissonance producing weather information, then to record their theoretical behavioral responses to, and interpretations of, that information.

It was hypothesized that the theoretical behavioral response to this question would be governed by how strongly the respondent was committed, in a tentative sense, to completing his intended beach trip. Through the use of a surrogate measure, a means was thus devised by which the sample population could be stratified according to the relative strength of their tentative commitments to completing their planned trips. During the course of the interview each subject was asked to respond to the following hypothetical situation:

> Let's pretend that when you were about ready to leave for the beach today both the weather and the weather forecast had been *very uncertain*, and you felt the chances were about 50–50 that it would turn out either *really good or really bad,* but couldn't decide which. Would you still have come to the beach or would you have stayed home?
> Come .... Stay ....
> Why? (Probe for reasons behind answer.)

The intent here was to present everyone with an ambiguous weather situation where the perceived chances of obtaining acceptable or unacceptable weather were equal, such that the trip decision would have to be based heavily upon the evaluation of extra-weather variables. It was expected that those individuals with a "strong tentative commitment" to the trip would "still come" while those with a relatively "weak tentative commitment" would have "stayed home." As a check upon this expectation and in order to gain further insights into the factors underlying these decisions, each respondent was probed for the rationale behind his decision.

Of the 454 subjects who answered this question, 76 percent said they would still have made their intended trips to the beach while 24 percent indicated that they would have cancelled their trips. As shown by Table 1, the respective positive or negative decisions that were made appear to have been the consequences of the decision makers' evaluations of certain sets of extra-weather forces that bounded their particular, prospective trips. Despite the ambiguous weather situation, those subjects who indicated that they would still have made their trips cited, as reasons for their decisions, various personal and situational constraints which made alteration of their intended course of action difficult. Those who would have opted not to make their trips not only were relatively free from the above constraints but were generally influenced by their obverse which made cancellation comparatively easy. Consequently, for the purpose of further analysis, the former group ("still come") was regarded as having relatively strong tentative commitments to their trips on the day in question, and the latter group ("stay home") having relatively weak tentative commitments to theirs.

Having devised a way to thus stratify the respondents, it remained to test the notion that there would be an association between the strength of the tentative commitment to one's trip and his response to the aforementioned weather forecast question. Table 2 was generated, resulting in a statistically significant confirmation of the existence of the hypothesized relationship. As expected, when faced with the unfavorable forecast information, those subjects with the weaker tentative commitments showed a greater propensity to cancel their proposed trips.

It is, thus, suggested that the respondents with the stronger tentative commitments were greater risk takers in their choices of behavioral commitment. However, Table 3 raises doubts as to the validity of this risk taking explanation. If the trip decision, in the face of a 60 percent chance of rain, was mainly a function of the willingness to gamble, it would be expected that those making

Theoretical Behavioral Response	Reasons for Response	Number	Percent
	Plans and Preparations Completed		28
	children anticipating trip	41	
	trip planned and prepared	33	
	special occasion (guests, friends, etc.)	12	
	took day off specifically for beach	6	
Would	**Strong Motivation**		21
	worth the gamble	38	
Still	like beach so much	30	
	Cost of Failure Low		19
Have	if encounter bad weather do something else in the area	37	
	just a short drive	24	
Come	**Limited Opportunity**		16
	last or few opportunities left	23	
To	regular day off	14	
	on vacation, main chance to go	11	
Beach	weather has been so bad	5	
	Lack of Attractive Alternatives		14
(N = 277)ᵃ	nothing else to do	25	
	get away from home or city	20	
	Other		1
	any weather acceptable	8	
	favorable outcomes in past	1	
	Total	323	99
	Available Alternatives		36
Would	do something at home	29	
	go to closer beach	3	
Have	**Other Opportunities To Go**		28
	will be able to go tomorrow or some other day	25	
Cancelled	**Weak Motivation**		20
	not worth the gamble	18	
That Trip	**Cost of Failure Too High**		17
	drive too long	12	
(N = 86)ᵃ	health reasons (cold, etc.)	3	
	Total	90	101

Table 1. *Reasons for Theoretical Behavioral Response to Hypothetical, Ambiguous Weather Situation*

ᵃ The question which probed for the reasons behind the subject's response was added to the schedule after the first six days of interviewing. This accounts for the deviation between these figures and the total sample size as previously stated.

Forecast	Strength of Tentative Commitment	Behavioral Commitment		Total Percent	N
		Go to Beach	Cancel Trip		
60 percent chance of rain	Strong	60	40	100	65
	Weak	19	81	100	21

Table 2. *Choice of Behavioral Commitment Stratified by Strength of Tentative Commitment to the Beach Trip*

Chi square = 10.65 (significant at the .01 level).

positive decisions and those making negative decisions would have perceived similar probabilities of the day being rainy, but with the former group being willing to accept the level of risk involved. However, as illustrated in Table 3, the perceived likelihood of the day being rainy varied significantly according to the choice of behavioral commitment, with the tendency, in each case, being consistent with that choice of commitment. Sufficient evidence is thus

Forecast	Behavioral Commitment	Perceived Likelihood of Day Being Rainy[a]				Total Percent	N
		"Almost certain" or "very likely"	"Likely"	"A chance"	"Small chance" or "not likely"		
60 percent chance of rain	Go to Beach	16	30	40	14	100	43
	Cancel Trip	46	40	12	2	100	43

Table 3. *Perceived Likelihood of the Day Being Rainy Stratified by Choice of Behavioral Commitment*

Chi square = 21.84 (significant at the .001 level).
[a] Here, and for the remaining Tables in this section, the data on the perceived likelihood of the day being rainy were compressed due to the low frequency of response on the extreme categories —"almost certain" and "not likely."

presented to conclude that the choice of behavioral commitment was not purely the function of differences in risk taking propensity. The origin of these differing perceptions, however, remains unclear.

As exhibited in Table 3, the relationships between the perceived likelihood of rain and the choice of behavioral commitment are, in general, consonant. These data do not, however, clearly indicate whether the consonant relationships arose because these decision makers distorted their perceptions of the likelihood of rain to conform with their respective behavioral commitments or whether these subjects actually, and initially, interpreted the forecast information as indicated, irrespective of any commitment, and subsequently based their trip decisions upon these interpretations. Or, to rephrase the question, are the different distributions of the perceived likelihood of rain shown in Table 3 the causes or the consequences of the different choices of behavioral commitment? In an attempt to resolve this question, a supplementary scheme was devised for analyzing the data on the perceived likelihood of rain. Earlier the sample population was stratified on the basis of the relative strengths of the tentative commitments to completing the intended beach trips on the day of the interview. On the basis of this stratification Table 4 was generated.

Forecast	Strength of Tentative Commitment	Perceived Likelihood of Day Being Rainy				Total Percent	N
		"Almost certain" or "very likely"	"Likely"	"A chance"	"Small chance" or "not likely"		
60 percent chance of rain	Strong	25	35	32	8	100	65
	Weak	52	33	5	10	100	21

Table 4. *Perceived Likelihood of the Day Being Rainy Stratified by the Strength of the Tentative Commitment to the Trip*

Chi square = 8.70 (significant at .05 level).

Again a significant difference in the perceived likelihood of the day being rainy is noted, with the more strongly committed population tending to perceive a lower likelihood of the day being rainy than the population with the weaker tentative commitment. An explanation of this difference, however, may be found in the disparate character of the two populations. For various reasons the former population found it difficult to cancel their intended trips on the day in question, while the latter population regarded the prospective trip cancellation as being relatively easy. As a consequence of this difference, these two populations exhibited opposing tendencies in their choices of behavioral commitment vis-à-vis the forecast of a 60 percent chance of rain (see Table 2). It would, therefore, seem apparent that the differences in the perceived likelihood of rain shown in Table 4 resulted from perceptual distortion of the meaning of the forecast information. In other words, it seems evident that these differences resulted from one, or both, of the following:

1. When faced with the forecast of a 60 percent chance of rain, the majority of those people with strong tentative commitments to their trips chose to go to the beach anyway; and, therefore, in order to justify these decisions, a significant portion of these people diminished the perceived likelihood of rain.

2. When faced with similar forecast information, the majority of those people with weak tentative commitments to their trips chose to cancel their planned occasions; and, therefore, in order to justify these decisions, a significant portion of these people magnified the perceived likelihood of rain.

It is concluded that the difference between the distributions of the perceived likelihood of rain revealed in Table 3 may more appropriately be viewed as the consequence, rather than the cause, of the opposing choices of behavioral commitment. However, it still remains unclear as to whether this difference in the perceived likelihood of rain arose because both populations ("go to beach" and "cancel trip") perceptually distorted the forecast information so as to conform with their respective behavioral commitments or because only one of those populations engaged in such distortion.

In order to resolve this problem an additional body of data was drawn into the analysis. The following control question was presented to the interviewees on an alternating basis with the previously described forecast test question:

This question has *nothing to do* with planning a beach trip. I am merely interested in what weather forecasts mean to you. O.K.? Now generally speaking, when you hear a weather forecast which predicts a 60 percent chance of rain for the next day, do you plan on it being *rainy?*

Yes...... No......

When a forecast predicts a 60 percent chance of rain for the next day, what do you feel the chances are that it will actually be rainy?

...... almost certain
...... very likely
...... likely
...... a chance
...... a small chance
...... not likely

In including this question in the interview schedule, the intent was to present a control group with the same forecast information as the former test group; however, the control group would be asked to evaluate the forecast in merely a general sense, without reference to any beach trip commitment. A "no commitment" control population would be generated whose evaluation of the likelihood of a rainy day could be compared with that of the committed "go to beach" and "cancel trip" test populations. As the control group was asked to evaluate the forecast without reference to a beach trip decision, it was hypothesized that these people would be under no pressure to perceptually distort the meaning of the forecast (6). As can be seen in Table 5, the evaluation of the control population was relatively neutral, i.e., less optimistic than the "go to beach" group and less pessimistic than the "cancel trip" group. These data thus support the conclusion that a significant percentage of both test populations did indeed perceptually distort the meaning of the forecast so as to justify their respective choices of behavioral commitment (7).

Finally, as a check upon the conclusions drawn from Table 4, Table 6 was generated. The former table depicts the evaluations of a forecast with reference to a particular beach trip; the latter

Perceived Likelihood of Day Being Rainy

Forecast	Population	"Almost certain" or "very likely"	"Likely"	"A chance"	"Small chance" or "not likely"	Total Percent	N
60 percent chance of rain	"Go to beach"	16	30	40	14	100	43
	Control (no commitment)	31	32	27	10	100	121
	"Cancel trip"	46	40	12	2	100	43

Table 5. *Perceived Likelihood of the Day Being Rainy: Control Versus Test Populations*

Chi square = 16.88 (significant at .01 level).

depicts the evaluation of the same forecast but with no reference to a beach trip, i.e., the perceptions of the control population. The organization of Table 6 thus poses an irrelevant relationship, as the control population was asked to interpret the meaning of the forecast without reference to any commitment; therefore, variations in the strength of their tentative commitments to their planned recreational occasions should have no bearing upon their interpretations of an unrelated forecast statement. Consequently, the data in Table 6 add support to the conclusions drawn from Table 4, for while a significant relationship is revealed in the latter case, no relationship is revealed in Table 6. The conclusion that beach users do engage in the perceptual distortion of forecast information, as a mode of dissonance reduction in making their weather/beach-trip decisions, is thus corroborated.

These findings present ample evidence to support the notion that the theory of cognitive dissonance has application to weather forecast, beach trip, decision making behavior. The related decision making process is diagrammed in Figure 1 where it has been compartmentalized and ordered for the purpose of summary discussion; however, in reality, it is more likely that the components are considered in combination with constant feedback. In this context it was revealed that the subjects, when faced with a forecast

Forecast (no reference to beach trip)	Strength of Tentative Commitment	Perceived Likelihood of Day Being Rainy					
		"Almost certain" or "very likely"	"Likely"	"A chance"	"Small chance" or "not likely"	Total Percent	N
60 percent chance of rain	Strong	31	31	28	10	100	93
	Weak	32	36	25	7	100	28

Table 6.   *Perceived Likelihood of the Day Being Rainy: Control Population Stratified by Relative Strength of Tentative Commitment*

Chi square = 0.25 (not significant at .05 level).

Tentative Commitment to the Beach Trip	Cognition Discordant with Tentative Commitment	Choice of Behavioral Commitment	Cognition Discordant with Behavioral Commitment	Mode of Dissonance Reduction
		Go to beach	Forecast of possible rain	Diminish perceived chances of rain
Variations in intensity	Forecast of possible rain			
		Cancel trip	Loss of recreational experience—weather outcome still in doubt	Magnify perceived chances of rain

Figure 1.   *Schema of Dissonance Reducing Behavior in the Weather Forecast, Beach Trip, Decision Making Process*

of suboptimal weather, tended to make trip decisions (behavioral commitments) which were consistent with the strength of their tentative commitments, i.e., people with relatively strong tentative commitments found it more difficult to cancel their trips, and, therefore, were more likely to behaviorally commit themselves to completing those trips. However, regardless of the choice of behavioral commitment, a dissonance producing situation appeared to remain. If the decision was made to go to the beach, dissonance persisted due to the individual's awareness of the unfavorable forecast. On the other hand, if the decision was made to cancel the trip, the individual was aware of losing a desired recreational experience when the weather outcome was still in doubt, i.e., dissonant cognitions. In both cases it was demonstrated that a significant percentage of the subjects attempted to justify their trip decisions by perceptually distorting the meaning of the forecast information. Through such perceptual distortion, these individuals achieved a greater consistency between their behavioral and informational cognitions thereby reducing or eliminating the dissonant aspects of their decisions (8). By virtue of these findings, it may be concluded that much of the weather information, beach trip, decision making behavior discussed herein does not conform with the notions conventionally embodied in risk taking theory. Risk taking involves a conscious gamble in the face of uncertainty where there is the perceived threat of loss or failure (Kogan and Wallach, 1967). However, to the extent that beach users perceptually distort the meaning of weather information so as to justify their particular trip decisions, they behave more as risk manipulators than as risk takers.

While the author's study was confined to the weather/beach-trip situation, the notion is offered that similar dissonance reducing behavior may underlie, in varying modes and degrees, much of the spectrum of man/nature decision making behavior. In terms of the cost consequences of failure, the time horizons of the decisions, and the amount of uncertainty involved, weather/beach-trip decisions are at the relatively common, repetitive, trivial end of this spectrum. At the opposite end are the long term, life-implicating decisions that man makes with respect to extreme natural events, i.e., floods, earthquakes, tornadoes, etc. These latter types of decisions have been the foci of an extensive, interdisciplinary research effort which has been organized under the title of Collaborative Research on Natural Hazards (9). One of the major objectives of this effort has been to provide an explanation of man's persistent settlement of areas which are subject to recurrent natural hazards. A possible explanation of this phenomenon lies in the assertion that such behavior is the outcome of man's innate, or situational, proclivity to gamble, and, thus, is a form of calculated irrationality and falls under the rubric of risk taking behavior. However, natural hazards research has met with little success in attempting to relate the precepts of risk taking theory to man/natural hazard behavior (Kates, 1971). It is the author's notion that this lack of success may be attributed, at least in part, to the possible propensity of these decision makers to behave more as dissonance reducing rationalizers than as risk takers.

In support of this notion the work of Burton and Kates dealing with man's response to the uncertainty of extreme natural hazards is cited (Burton, 1972; Burton and Kates, 1963; Burton, Kates, Mather, Snead, 1965; Kates, 1962). In interviewing floodplain dwellers and occupants of coastal zones subject to storms, they encountered common individual efforts on the part of these resource users to dispel hazard uncertainty. In this context the most common mechanism employed was to find a determinate, repetitive, or cyclic order in the occurrence of these hazards, e.g., "we get storms once in ninety years, we're not due for another." Although no such order exists, placing one's belief in such renders the future a mere extension of the past and, thus, eliminates uncertainty (10). A second tactic of the respondents was to deny or denigrate the existence or reoccurrence of the hazard, e.g., "that was a freak, won't happen again." In this case the future is not only certain but also hazard free. A final view held is that the future is completely indeterminate and in the hands of a higher power, e.g., "it's in the hands of God." In this last instance, rather than being plagued with uncertainty, the individual assumes a "come what will" attitude in the face of a completely inscrutable higher power (11). Burton and Kates attribute these responses to uncertainty to neither ignorance nor irrationality but to the inability of the layman, unlike members of the scientific-technical community, to either assimilate probabilistic information in hazard related decisions or to cope with the inherent uncertainty therein. The authors, therefore, regard these responses as resulting largely from a desire on the part of the layman to render the indeterminate determinate; consequently, these resource users tend to assume attitudinal stances toward the uncertainty of natural hazards which make the future occurrence of these phenomena knowable (Burton and Kates, 1963, p. 437).

While the author concurs with the observations of Burton and Kates regarding the inability of the layman to assimilate and cope with probabilistic information, it is felt that the above responses to the uncertainty of natural hazards merit additional comment in two senses. First, these inhabitants of hazardous regions would appear to be characterized by neither a high risk taking propensity nor risk taking behavior in general. For rather than consciously gambling in the face of uncertainty, these decision makers employed various mechanisms to dispel that uncertainty, and, thereby, greatly reduced or eliminated the risky aspects of their hazard related decisions. To this end, then, they behaved similar to the beach users in the author's study, i.e., more as risk manipulators than as risk takers. Secondly, to the extent that these individuals, in dispelling uncertainty, enhanced the security of their expectations of the future, their perceptual manipulations of risk may appropriately be viewed as attempts to justify their particular commitments to hazard prone locations. These subjects appeared to behave not as risk takers but as rationalizers engaging in the perceptual distortion of environmental information for the purpose of reducing cognitive dissonance.

Why then do people continue to live in tectonically active areas where the threat of an earthquake is high? Why do people rebuild their previously devastated homes on the same floodplain that is recurrently plagued by rampaging waters? Dissonance theory offers a plausible explanation for such apparently logic-defying instances of human behavior. The need to change one's behavioral commitment in such situations has been eliminated by employing alternative mechanisms to reduce any dissonance that one's hazard related posture may have created. Having thus dispelled dissonance, one's behavior takes on an air of apparent rationality; and perceived rationality, in such instances, renders the *status quo* secure. While evidence has been presented in this article to support this notion, further research is needed to verify the general application of dissonance theory to man's decision making behavior vis-à-vis extreme natural hazards. In this connection, much could be learned from studies designed to test hypothetical relationships between variations in the perceived threat of specific natural hazards and variations in commitment to the related hazardous situations.

NOTES

1. These were Crane Beach, Ipswich, Massachusetts and Hampton Beach State Park, Hampton Beach, New Hampshire. An important factor in the selection of these beaches was the fact they serve primarily the *major*, day-use, recreational occasion, i.e., a beach trip which in terms of preparation, travel, and on-site time involved the greater portion of a day. Such an expenditure of time, money, and effort by these recreationists lends a non-trivial nature to their weather/beach-trip decisions.

2. In actuality a dual sampling scheme was employed. During periods when the beaches were uncrowded, all parties on the beach were enumerated and respondents then were selected on a strictly random basis. However, when enumeration became impossible because of crowding, a random, areal sampling mechanism was employed such that respondents were selected on the basis of randomly designated locations on the beach.

3. The presence of a commitment is central to the theory of cognitive dissonance; for without a commitment of some sort (an overt act, a decision, a plan, etc.) informational cognitions can neither be consonant nor dissonant, i.e., they would be irrelevant.

4. This question was asked on an alternating basis with three other questions. One of these alternate questions was identical in wording to the question referred to here, except for the insertion of "a 40 percent chance of rain." The analysis of these data supported in every way the conclusions drawn from the analysis of the data presented in this report; however, the data gathered from this alternate question are not included here for the sake of brevity.

5. Although personal observations are the most important sources of weather information upon which these decisions are based, substantial use is made of forecast information, i.e., 71 percent of the sample indicated that they always or usually made a special point of consulting a weather forecast before undertaking a beach trip. Despite the high level of use made of actual forecast information, however, the hypothetical format of this question was chosen so as to promote within-sample comparability through informational control.

6. Although it was intended that the control question should be devoid of commitment, an error was made in the format which in effect introduced this element into the question. The respondent should not have been asked if he felt the next day would be rainy before he was asked to qualitatively interpret the quantitative probabilistic statement. For in responding to the first question, the subject committed himself to a particular polar evaluation of the forecast information which may have influenced his subsequent answer to the second part of the question, the qualitative interpretation of the likelihood of a rainy day. Consequently, it is the author's opinion that the distribution of responses for the "no commitment" population (see Table 5) shows higher frequencies of response toward the extremes than would have been the case had the first question not been asked. Had the above error not been made, it is believed that the differences between the control and test populations would have been even greater than those revealed in Table 5.

7. It is important to note that such perceptual distortion was not engaged in by all members of these populations. Indeed, a perusal of the distributions depicted in Table 5 indicates that approximately only 20 percent of those decision makers exhibited such dissonance reducing behavior. While

this percentage is significant in both a statistical and practical sense, the reader is cautioned against imparting an excessive level of generalization to these findings.

8. Although a relationship has been demonstrated between the perceptual distortion of forecast information and the choice of behavioral commitment, it is not clear that all such perceptual distortion arose entirely as a post-behavioral commitment phenomenon. In this connection, the author believes that it is possible, even likely, that in reality some perceptual distortion may take place prior to the choice of a behavioral commitment (trip decision) as an outgrowth of a strong tentative commitment. In other words, a very strong desire to go to the beach may promote a more optimistic interpretation of the forecast information leading to a positive trip decision which then may be further justified by additional perceptual distortion. However, any attempt to separate perceptual distortion into post-tentative commitment and post-behavioral commitment stages would be difficult, if not impossible. Furthermore, such a separation would likely do injustice to reality for it is probable that the assessment of one's tentative commitment, the evaluation of weather information, and the choice of behavioral commitment are considered in a simultaneous and reiterative fashion. The important point is that during this process the meaning of the weather information is distorted; whether this distortion arises from the commitment to a plan (tentative commitment) or the commitment to a decision (behavioral commitment) is of secondary import. Intuitively, however, one would expect the latter type of commitment to be the greater motivating force due to its more compelling nature.

9. Collaborative Research on Natural Hazards is a National Science Foundation funded research program under the direction of Ian Burton (University of Toronto), Robert Kates (Clark University), and Gilbert White (University of Colorado). See I. Burton, R. Kates, and G. White, *The Human Ecology of Extreme Geophysical Events*, Natural Hazard Research Paper No. 1 (Toronto: University of Toronto Press, 1968); R. Kates, *Hazard and Choice Perception in Flood Plain Management*, Department of Geography Research Paper No. 78 (Chicago: University of Chicago, 1962).

10. That the layman often sees such order in nature is, in a way, not surprising in view of the fact that the scientific community has expended a vast number of man-hours seeking to unveil just such order. Secondly, the layman tends to view the occurrence of events in human scales of time, e.g., "once in a lifetime." In the context of such generalized time scales, a rough ordering of events may indeed exist or be recalled by the individual.

11. It should be noted that such responses were elicited from a significantly large, but minority, portion of the samples.

LITERATURE CITED

R. Abelson, et al, *Theories of Cognitive Consistency: A Sourcebook* (Chicago: Rand McNalley and Co., 1968).

R. L. A. Adams, Weather, Weather Information, and Outdoor Recreation Decisions: A Case Study of the New England Beach Trip, Unpublished Ph.D. dissertation, Clark University, 1971.

J. Brehm and A. Cohen, *Explorations in Cognitive Dissonance* (New York: John Wiley and Sons, Inc., 1962).

I. Burton, *Types of Agricultural Occupance of Floodplains in the United States*, Department of Geography Research Paper No. 75 (Chicago: University of Chicago Press, 1962).

I. Burton and R. Kates, "The Perception of Natural Hazards in Resource Management," *Natural Resources Journal* 3 (October, 1963): 412–41.

I. Burton, R. Kates, J. Mather, and R. Snead, *The Shores of Megalopolis: Coastal Occupance and Human Adjustment to Flood Hazard* (Elmer, N.J.: C. W. Thornthwaite Associates Publications in Climatology 18, 3, 1965).

I. Burton, R. Kates, and G. White, *The Human Ecology of Extreme Geophysical Events*, Natural Hazard Research Paper No. 1 (Toronto: University of Toronto Press, 1968).

S. Clemens (Mark Twain), "The Weather," a speech, New York, 1867.

L. Festinger, *A Theory of Cognitive Dissonance* (Evanston, Ill.: Row, Peterson, 1957).

———, *Conflict, Decision, and Dissonance* (Stanford: Stanford University Press, 1964).

R. Kates, *Hazard and Choice Perception in Flood Plain Management*, Department of Geography Research Paper No. 78 (Chicago: University of Chicago Press, 1962).

———, "Natural Hazard in Human Ecological Perspective: Hypotheses and Models," *Economic Geography* 47 (1971): 438–51.

R. Kogan and M. Wallach, "Risk Taking as a Function of the Situation, the Person, and the Group," *New Dimensions in Psychology III* (New York: Holt, Rinehart and Winston, 1967).

CHAPTER

10

Environmental Perceptions and Attitudes of Engineers and Public Health Officials

W. R. DERRICK SEWELL

Reprinted from *Environment and Behavior* 3, no. 1 (March, 1971): 23–59, by permission of the publisher, Sage Publications, Inc., and the author.

W. R. Derrick Sewell's major research interests are in resources management, particularly on behavioral aspects. He is the author of numerous monographs and articles on resources problems, and is coeditor of a forthcoming volume on *Perceptions and Attitudes in Resources Management*.

The reason for this study was supported by grants from Resources for the Future, Inc., Washington, D.C., and from the National Advisory Committee on Water Resources Research, Department of Energy, Mines and Resources, Ottawa, Ontario. The author wishes to thank those who assisted in the study, notably Miss J. Elizabeth McMeiken and Mr. John Rostron of the University of Victoria, who undertook library research, carried out interviews, and contributed many useful ideas. The author also wishes to acknowledge the helpful comments and criticisms of Dr. Harold D. Foster of the University of Victoria on earlier drafts of the paper.

For many college students, it is an introductory course in anthropology that first forces them to think about the fact that their own ways of life are not the only ways of life; that their own values and attitudes and ways of relating to others are neither especially true nor inevitable, but constitute merely one version, one possibility among many lifestyles, all of which are equally authentic. Although this lesson may set us back on our heels somewhat (after all, what *we* do is what seems "natural"), it is easily learned because the contrasts between modern Western man and members of the so-called primitive societies are so stark and dramatic. And we are properly impressed with the power of the social forces which transform the universal child into the member of a particular society.

When such a relativistic perspective is used to view different groups *within the same society*—for instance, blacks and whites, the rich and the poor, Jews, Protestants, and Catholics—the differences in life patterns, although greatly diminished, still remain powerful. Although all are Americans-of-today, we readily accept the proposition that the different circumstances of their upbringings have produced general differences in values and attitudes, in knowledge and skills, in world perspectives, and in styles of life.

But rarely do we go further and apply the same logic, but with a narrower focus—for instance, to a group of men, all from the same society and all of the same race, socioeconomic status and religion, but who belong to different *professions*. Yet just as societies mold men in their own images, so does the training and practice of a profession.

We tend to take a naively circumscribed view of professional training, defining it as the communication of knowledge and skill. Indeed, that's an important part of it, but it is not all. In dissecting a corpse, the medical student is not only learning about anatomy, he is also beginning to adopt the aloofness, the distancing from patients, and the cool familiarity with death which characterize the professional physician. Professionalization, a form of adult socialization, is a comprehensive process, involving areas of attitude and value and belief which go far beyond the prescribed circumference of the profession's defining work.

What Sewell superbly demonstrates in this study is a general fact often overlooked—when society turns to an expert for advice, it always gets more than it bargains for. In addition to his professional *expertise,* it gets his professional *biases;* along with his skills come his prejudices, of which he, himself, is, by the way, quite unaware.

Specifically, this paper looks at members of two professions which are critically involved in the management of environmental quality—engineers and public health officials. Sewell shows that membership in either of these professions means far more than a guarantee of possession of certain skills. It also means that only certain environmental problems are seen, that only certain solutions are considered and proposed, and that only certain attitudes are taken toward the government and toward the public. In other words, the professionalization processes that have produced the expert's skills have, at the same time, limited his vision.

Of course, the careful reader will perceive that Sewell himself demonstrates a point he makes, for his conclusions regarding the contributions of professionals and the general public to the solution of environmental problems go well beyond his evidence and reflect not his expertise as an economist and geographer but his beliefs about the desirability of change and the efficacy of participatory democracy.

One of the most significant characteristics of modern society is its overwhelming dependence upon experts. This dependence appears to stem from three main forces: the growing complexity of problems faced by society, the fear of the individual that his own judgment may result in disastrous consequences, and the salesmanship of the experts. Advances in science and technology have produced problems which are beyond the capability of the individual to handle on his own, because he feels he has either insufficient knowledge or insufficient power. At one time, an individual could repair his own automobile, design and build his own house, or solve a family problem without advice from outside. Those days have now gone. Bombarded with increasingly complex gadgetry, by new discoveries about man and his physical world, and by new ideas about how to do things, the individual has turned to the expert to help him decide what course of action to follow. The experts have helped promote this process both by offering advice and by helping create problems to solve.

There is considerable competition among experts for recognition, for some are accorded higher status than others (Sommer, 1963). Those who have attained the highest status are those who have specialized on problems relating to one or more of the following four areas:

a. the development and use of technology
b. human health
c. human rights and obligations
d. finance

It is in these areas that the average individual believes he has the least capability of understanding the problem or selecting a solution, that the personal costs of being wrong are especially high, and that the opportunity for the exercise of mysticism by experts is particularly great. As a consequence, it is the professionals that have the highest social status among experts, and among them, scientists, technologists, engineers, doctors, psychologists, lawyers, and economists appear to have attained the highest standing. This is reflected both in the salaries they earn and in the power they exercise, either as individuals or as groups. Increasingly they have assumed not only the responsibility for solving problems and recommending means for attaining goals, but also for defining the goals themselves.

The role of the professional has become institutionalized both in industry and in government. It is reflected in internal organization on the one hand, and in the process of decision-making on the other. Businesses and government agencies are now organized principally upon the basis of specialization, with divisions or departments established to handle particular processes or problems. The larger firms, for example, have a legal division, a financial division, a design division, a research division, and a marketing division. The same is true of government agencies (Corson and Paul, 1966). In the latter case, a whole department may be devoted to one particular kind of problem such as the management of fisheries or the construction of highways. Typically such divisions or departments are staffed by one kind of professional. Thus Departments of Water Resources are usually staffed by engineers, while Departments of Fisheries or Wildlife are manned mainly by biologists.

The exercise of professional expertise is also an integral part of the policy-making process. Professionals are called in at the various stages of problem definition, the analysis of alternative solutions, selection of solutions, and sometimes implementation as well. Typically, however, only a few types of professionals are involved. This is especially the case in the management of natural resources and in matters relating to the quality of the environment.

The specialization which has accompanied professionalization of management and policy-making has resulted inevitably in a compartmentalized or fragmented approach. This approach, however, is now being seriously challenged, both on conceptual and practical grounds. Those who challenge it suggest that its underlying assumptions are invalid. Reality, they point out, is not composed of a number of discrete facets which can be dealt with independently of each other. On the contrary, it is composed of a number of interlocking systems which together make up the physical and human environments. The causes of any problem, therefore, can only be identified by examining each of these systems and the interrelationships between them, and likewise the effectiveness of a solution can only be assessed by tracing the consequences in each system. Holism, therefore, is now advocated as the relevant approach to environmental quality problems (Nicholson, 1970; Shepard and McKinley, 1969; Watt, 1968).

Support for holism is based in part on the recognition of the interdependence of things, but also upon the fact that the fragmented approach has often failed to deal effectively with the problems at hand. Despite major inputs of expertise, for example, the condition of the environment has become progressively worse (de Bell, 1970; Cooley and Wandesforde-Smith, 1970). Today many of the nation's major bodies of water are so polluted that they constitute a severe hazard to human health, as well as to that of fish and wildlife. Costs of restoring them are staggering. The condition of the atmosphere in most major cities is also appalling and in some has reached crisis proportions. The solutions recommended by experts seem to have been ineffectual. Air pollution, for example, continues to increase despite the imposition of regulations and the installation of new devices on cars. The posting of signs that swimming is hazardous fails to keep bathers out of the water (Hewings, 1968). The construction of roads to wilderness areas tends to result not in the provision of wilderness experience, but in the opportunity to move the city temporarily out into the country. The Long Beach National Park on Vancouver Island, B.C., is an excellent example. Aiming to provide a national wilderness preserve, the Canadian federal government set aside a large uninhabited area on the west coast of Vancouver Island. Vigorous advertising of this "recreational paradise" and the provision of high quality access roads, however, have resulted in a massive influx of recreationists, most of whom are equipped with every modern convenience, including bathtubs and TV. The area has suddenly taken on the appearance of a temporary town. Its inhabitants have brought with them all the things they wished to leave behind—overcrowding, noise, and pollution! In this case, park planning has clearly failed to attain its intended objectives.

How has it come about that the experts have failed to diagnose problems correctly and offer effective solutions? Is it because they have a very constricted view of the problems with which they deal? Is it because they feel constrained to consider solutions other than those rooted in the conventional wisdom of their discipline? Is it because environmental experts appear to be more conversant with science and technology than with human behavior? The answers to these questions are not immediately clear for, as Craik (1970a) has pointed out, the perceptions and attitudes of environmental experts have never been studied in any systematic fashion. It seems, however, that with such answers we would be in a much better position to assess the role of various professionals in environmental decision-making, and, hopefully, to devise means whereby their contributions could be made more effective.

Two studies undertaken during the past three years at the University of Victoria have helped shed some light on how experts perceive the problems with which they deal, and the solutions which they recommend. These studies have also helped identify some of the factors which influence such perceptions. The research was intended to be exploratory, aiming principally to develop a methodology and to identify factors that might be examined in greater depth in subsequent investigations. Nevertheless, the findings do have some implications both for research and for public policy in the environmental quality field.

ENGINEERS AND PUBLIC HEALTH OFFICIALS

The studies were focused upon two groups of professionals who play critical roles in environmental quality management: engineers and public health officials. Both have a long tradition of involvement in this area. Problems resulting from alterations in the physical environment are typically referred to engineers, since they are believed to have the necessary training and experience to deal with them. This is especially the case with problems which affect man's economic well-being. Thus engineers are usually called in to deal with alterations in the environment stemming from natural hazards such as floods, hurricanes, or earthquakes to problems resulting from traffic congestion, industrial conglomeration, or mining operations. In such instances, economic costs can be clearly identified, and since the problems seem physical in origin, the expertise of the engineer is regarded as particularly appropriate (Gerstl and Hutton, 1966; Vallentine, 1967).

Public health officials have also been dealing with environmental quality problems for a long time (Brockington, 1961). The kinds of problems on which they work, however, differ from those involving engineers. Public health officials are mainly concerned with those aspects of environmental alteration that result in adverse effects on human health, such as the effects of disposal of industrial and municipal wastes into bodies of water.

The two groups of professionals play similar roles in the policy-making process. They act as technical advisers and administrators, and sometimes as decision makers as well. In these capacities, they are instrumental in defining the problems to be solved, determining the solutions to be considered, and, frequently, in selecting the strategy actually adopted. Inevitably, in doing so they give expression to their views as to what society wants and as to how it will react to what is provided.

The engineers' study was intended as a pilot investigation, designed to test methods of identifying attitudes and perceptions of a professional group. The emphasis was upon technique evaluation rather than on information collection. Its results provided guidance for the second study, which probed perceptions and attitudes of public health officials. In this case, a considerable amount of data was gathered, enabling much more sophisticated analysis. Sufficient information was obtained in the engineers' study, however, to enable some comparisons to be made with results of the public health officials' study.

ORGANIZATION OF THE STUDIES

The study of engineers was undertaken in the summer of 1967. It was based upon a sample of 30 engineers, specializing in water resources problems, and drawn from government agencies, firms of private consultants, and from universities, all in Vancouver and Victoria, B.C. Care was taken to include engineers involved at various levels of responsibility and having differing degrees of experience. The sample was believed to be reasonably representative of the universe from which it was drawn. There are approximately 359 engineers specializing in water problems in the two cities. The sample thus represented about 10 percent of the universe. It was randomly selected from lists of engineers supplied by the Association of Professional Engineers of British Columbia, which noted levels of responsibility and degrees of experience. Those selected were contacted first by telephone and then by letter. None refused to participate.

The public health officials' study was undertaken in the summer of 1969, based upon interviews with 40 officials who were located in the 20 health units which together cover the province of British Columbia. The sample was highly representative of the universe from which it was drawn, since it covered almost 95 percent of all those who could have been selected. A Medical Health Officer and a Public Health Inspector were selected from each health unit and then contacted by letter and by telephone. Only one unit refused to cooperate in the study. Its omission, however, did not bias the results unduly. The remainder of the sample covered officials from a wide spectrum of experience and interests and from a wide range of environmental conditions.

The Medical Health Officer (MHO) and the Public Health Inspector (PHI) work together as a team, but they perform quite separate functions. The MHO is ultimately responsible to the provincial Department of Health and to local Boards of Health. He is mainly an administrator, charged with the responsibility of interpreting government policy, and ensuring it is carried out. The Inspector is the field representative of the Department of Health and is generally regarded as "its eyes and ears" in the region in which he operates. He carries out various tests to determine water quality and acts as a sounding board to receive complaints and suggestions for policy change.

The various public health officials maintain contacts with each other through communication between health units and with their head office in Victoria. They also maintain contacts with personnel in other agencies, with representatives of industry, and with the general public (see Figure 1).

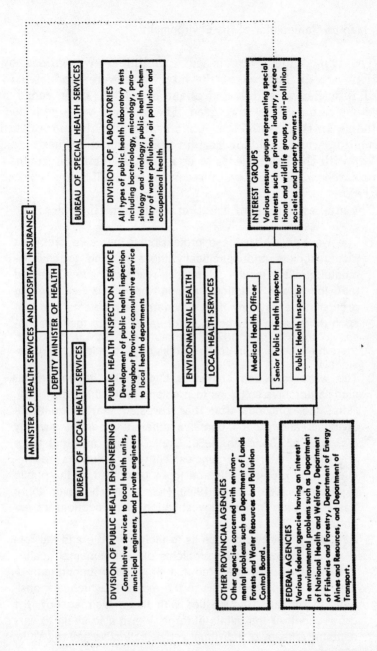

Figure 1. *Provincial Health Branch Organization: Environmental Health*

Source: Province of British Columbia, Health Branch, Department of Health Services and Hospital Insurance *Seventy-second Annual Report of the Public Health Services of British Columbia, For Year Ended December 31, 1968* (Victoria, B.C.: Queen's Printer, 1969), p. 5 with modifications.

188 Man as Manipulator of His Environment

The two studies were based upon interviews, guided by a questionnaire. In both cases, the interviews were conducted by a skilled interviewer and lasted about one hour. Open-ended and forced-choice questions were used. The answers were recorded in shorthand. In the case of the public health officials, more detailed information was sought on certain matters, and a questionnaire was left with the respondents to be mailed at their convenience to the researchers. Replies were received from all those who participated.

The studies sought information on three main topics:

1. The ways in which these professionals perceive problems facing society and specifically those relating to environmental quality. Results of previous research have suggested that there are variations among individuals and among groups in the ways in which they perceive problems, and that such differences may account for variations in their responses to them (Craik, 1970b; White, 1966). So far, however, there have been no in-depth studies of perceptions of professionals.

2. The ways in which engineers and public health professionals perceive solutions to problems with which they deal. Here, too, previous work has revealed that different individuals and groups perceive different kinds of strategy (Kates, 1962; Saarinen, 1966; Craik, 1970a), and that there are often major divergencies between solutions recommended by professionals and those perceived by the public (Appleyard, 1969; Lucas, 1966). Here again, however, there has been little in-depth investigation of perceptions of experts.

3. Attitudes of the two groups as to their own role and the role of others in dealing with problems of environmental quality. Other studies have indicated that views differ among individuals and among groups as to the extent to which responsibility for initiating action lies with them, their agency, the government, or the public at large. Views also seem to vary as to the efficacy of individual versus collective action (White, 1966).

It is important not only to identify perceptions and attitudes, but also to account for variations in them. To this end, information was sought on possible influences identified in other studies, such as socioeconomic characteristics, training, experience, present responsibilities, and views about man's relationship to nature (Kluckhohn and Strodtbeck, 1961; White, 1966). The latter dimension has been found to be a significant factor in explaining variations in perceptions and attitudes relating to human adjustment to the environment in a variety of contexts (Lowenthal, 1967).

ANALYSIS OF THE RESULTS

The information gathered in the study was coded and subsequently punched onto computer cards. The data relating to engineers was subjected to simple techniques of correlation analysis and tests of significance. That relating to the public health officials was analyzed in greater detail, using three main phases of analysis, namely the development of correlation matrices, factor analysis, and stepwise multiple regression. A correlation matrix was developed to identify relationships between the different variables derived from the information gathered in the study. Significant intercorrelations were found among 66 of the 313 variables, and these were used in further analysis.

Factor analysis was used to examine data relating to

a. perceptions of problems
b. perceptions of solutions
c. attitudes as to the roles of the public, public health officials, and the government, on the one hand, and factors hypothesized as possible influences and such perceptions and attitudes, on the other.

Stepwise multiple regression analysis was then used to determine the extent to which the influences identified in the latter case (designated independent variables) explained variations in the factors identified in the former case (designated dependent variables).

Perceptions of Problems

An attempt was made to determine the views of the two groups of professionals as to what the major problems facing British Columbia are, and how environmental quality problems ranked among these issues. As indicated in Table 1, most of the public health officials identified environmental quality problems as the major issue facing the province, followed by various other social problems such as poverty, unemployment, and education. Air pollution and water pollution were seen as the major causes of environmental deterioration, followed by land pollution in various forms. Little

	Frequency of Mention	
	Public Health Officials	Engineers
Number One Problem Facing the Province		
Environmental quality	32	5
Social problems (poverty, unemployment, education)	20	20
Urban growth and transportation	9	15
Lack of health facilities	8	—
Politics	6	—
Drugs, alcoholism, crime	4	10
Quality of the Environment is Deteriorating in B.C.		
Air	35	10
Water	34	20
Land	26	—
Other	3	—
Measures of Water Quality		
Colli count	39	N1
BOD	36	N1
COD	18	N1
Visual characteristics	12	N1
Turbidity	12	N1
Taste	—	N1
Smell	—	N1
Major Concern About Water Quality		
Hazard to health	31	5
Impairment to aesthetic values	9	5
Increased costs of production	—	15
N1 = No information solicited.		

Table 1.   *Perceptions of Problems*

mention was made, however, of such things as noise, billboards, or powerlines.

These results contrast somewhat with the findings of the engineers' study. In this case, problems of unemployment, labor unrest, and juvenile delinquency were seen as the major issues facing British Columbia. Environmental deterioration ranked far down the list. Of the various forms of pollution, water pollution was regarded as the most important. These findings, however, should be interpreted with caution. The engineers' study was undertaken in 1967, some two years before there was widespread public concern about environmental quality in British Columbia. If the study were undertaken today, the results might be quite different. It is interesting to note, nevertheless, that the close relationship between problems on which the respondent worked and the perceived importance of the problem observed in the case of the public health officials was not found in the case of the engineers.

Other indications of the ways in which professionals perceive problems are found in the terms in which they describe them and the means they use to identify them. Both groups of professionals in this study described environmental quality problems in technical terms, principally in terms of 'standards' used by the public health profession. Thus coliform counts and BOD levels were used to describe the degree of water pollution. Little mention was made, however, of parameters which are typically used by members of the general public to describe such pollution, such as color, smell, or taste.

It was also clear that both groups of professionals generally relied on measurements of physical attributes to assess the "seriousness" of a problem. The degree of public awareness or the extent of complaints was not normally regarded as an index of "seriousness." The public health officials noted that they did not usually go out to assess public awareness by surveys. The only measure they had was the number of complaints received by them or the number of letters to newspapers.

A final indication of the ways in which the two groups of professionals perceived water quality was in the extent to which they saw it as a health problem rather than as an impairment to aesthetic beauty or a cost of production. Interestingly, most of the public health officials saw it mainly as a health problem. Half the engineers viewed it as a factor increasing costs of production, and the remainder perceived it either as a hazard to health or as an impairment of aesthetic values.

Perceptions of Solutions
The solutions proposed by the two groups were clearly influenced by the conventional wisdom and practices of their respective professions. The public health officials felt that the way to handle environmental quality problems was to discuss the matter first with the offender and suggest he find means of reducing the pollution, and if he did not do so, to subject him to court proceedings (see Table 2). This has long been the approach used by Departments of Public Health, but it has often been unsuccessful. The more powerful the offender, the more likely it is he will be able to ignore the regulations. Those interviewed were well aware of the fact that this had been the case in British Columbia, but most of them were uncritical of the policies and procedures used to combat pollution in the province (see Table 2). Most of the officials were

	Frequency of Mention	
	Public Health Officials	Engineers
Strategy Generally Recommended		
Warning followed by litigation	40	2
Construction of facilities	—	28
Provision of subsidies	—	—
Imposition of charges	—	—
Public pressure	—	—
Present Legislation		
Adequate	3	15
Weaknesses of Present Approach		
Lack of staff and facilities	10	—
Lack of time, money and research	16	—
Inadequate enforcement	20	20
Suggested Improvements		
Enforcement and control	18	N1
Better testing facilities	11	N1
Improved criteria	9	N1
N1 = No information solicited.		

Table 2.   *Perceptions of Solutions*

dissatisfied with present pollution legislation, but, in the main, their criticisms related to the lack of rigor of its application rather than to its relevance as a solution to the pollution problem.

There are various alternatives to legislation and regulation as strategies to deal with pollution, such as the imposition of charges for the use of water bodies, the provision of subsidies for effluent treatment, the development of nonpolluting processes or products, or the imposition of public pressure on polluters (Bower and Sewell, 1970). None of these, however, was mentioned (see Table 2). Suggestions were offered for a more forceful attack on pollution problems, but these all reflected the generally conservative bias of the officials. Tougher standards, more finances for laboratory facilities, and higher fines for offenders were among the suggestions most frequently offered (see Table 2). No radical departures from existing policies or procedures were suggested.

The engineers, too, perceived solutions in very conventional terms, reflecting standard practices of the profession, on the one hand, and an adherence to established government policy, on the other. Thus, the solution to declining water quality was generally perceived as the provision of additional water to increase the assimilative capacity of the water body, or installation of effluent processing facilities. Other alternatives, such as those noted above, were mentioned by a few of the engineers but were dismissed as being "unrealistic" or "unacceptable by the public." The engineers, too, seemed reasonably satisfied with present legislation and with the present approach to pollution problems in the province. Their main criticism was the lack of enforcement of regulations.

Attitudes as to Roles and Responsibilities

Attitudes as to one's own role in dealing with problems, and the roles of others, appear to have an important bearing on one's perception of problems and on action proposed or taken (White, 1966; Lowenthal, 1966). The results of the engineers' study seemed to suggest that this was an especially important dimension (see Table 3), and so it was decided to probe it in greater depth in the public health officials' study.

One indication of role assessment is the way in which an individual perceives his own job or agency in relation to other individuals or groups having responsibilities or interests in the same field. The public health officials were asked to list the various groups having an interest in environmental quality. As indicated in Table 3, health officials were mentioned by far the most frequently, followed by recreation and service clubs, various antipollution groups, property owners' associations, and other government agencies. The groups noted in this list are those with whom the public health officials normally have to deal, and the frequency of mention may be a partial indication of their perceived importance.

Another indication is the extent to which the professional feels he is better equipped than others to handle the job assigned to him. As might be expected, both the public health officials and the engineers were convinced that their training and experience enabled them to deal with water quality problems better than others. Both suggested that the record clearly showed this to be the case. The officials pointed out that there had been no major outbreak of any communicable disease arising from poor water quality in the province since the first Public Health Act was passed in British Columbia in 1893. The engineers claimed that it was only where technology had been applied in British Columbia that major improvements had been achieved in water quality. The fact that it was now possible to swim at beaches in Vancouver was viewed as an excellent illustration of the efficacy of sewage treatment facilities.

The two groups of professionals saw themselves in a variety of roles in dealing with environmental quality problems. About 25

	Frequency of Mention	
	Public Health Officials	**Engineers**
Groups Concerned with Environmental Quality		
Health officials	28	–
Recreation and service clubs	19	–
Educators	14	–
Anti-pollution committees	13	–
Civic officials and chambers of commerce	12	–
Lakeshore property owners and rate payers associations	10	–
Provincial and federal agencies	4	–
Specific Roles		
Adviser	10	27
Decision maker	4	–
Adviser and decision maker	26	3
Consultations		
Internal		
Within own office or other regional offices	39	30
With head office	32	30
External		
Other provincial or federal agencies	16	10
Municipal councils	29	5
Private agencies	11	5
Other (pressure groups, etc.)	9	3
Perceived Opposition		
"Abnormal" minority groups	13	N1
Politicians	26	N1
Industrialists and developers	6	N1
Individual members of the public	10	N1
Attitude of PHO as to Areas of Responsibility		
Department of Health		
(1) all aspects of quality	20	N1
(2) sewage disposal and treatment	15	N1
(3) garbage disposal and treatment	11	N1
(4) recreation	3	N1
(5) ind. and comm. effluents	2	N1
(6) drinking water	4	N1
Pollution Control Board		
(1) all aspects of quality	3	N1
(2) sewage disposal and treatment	0	N1
(3) garbage disposal and treatment	1	N1
(4) recreation	2	N1
(5) ind. and comm. effluents	15	N1
(6) drinking water	0	N1
N1 = No information solicited.		

Table 3.   *Perceptions of Roles*

percent of the public health officials regarded their role as being that of a technical adviser (see Table 3). Almost one-third of them, however, considered that they were decision makers as well as advisers. The need to make quick decisions in the field (within the broad limits imposed by law and policy) no doubt accounts for this view. In contrast, the engineers saw themselves principally as technical advisers, even though government engineers as well as consulting engineers were involved in the study. Only those concerned with issuing water licenses thought they had any kind of a decision-making role. The decision makers, suggested the engineers, are the politicians. As one of them put it: "They make the policy and to a considerable extent they interpret it too. Our role is generally defined by Terms of Reference which set out in detail what the task is, and what actions we are expected to perform in undertaking it."

A further indication of the way in which professionals perceive their role is the extent to which they feel that other groups have something useful to contribute to the solution of problems on which they work. To this end, both groups were asked which other agencies or professions they consulted and how often, and in what ways they tried to assess public opinion. Contacts within an agency or a firm appeared to be very frequent (see Table 3). Consultation among peers was, in fact, an integral part of practice in both professions. Beyond the agency or firm, however, contacts became much less frequent and were generally very formal.

Public health officials seem reluctant to contact officials in other agencies or to establish formal links with groups in the general public. At least two partial explanations might be offered for this reluctance. One is that continuous contacts with other agencies might lead to a sharing of responsibility. This, as the views expressed on the perceived roles of the Department of Health and the Pollution Control Branch seem to suggest, is clearly not what the public health officials want. They wish to retain complete jurisdiction over control of pollution, at least as far as health considerations are concerned, and are willing to concede only that part involving major industries, which the officials feel require much greater power to control than the Department of Health can exercise (see Table 3).

Engineers are similarly jealous of the role they perceive for themselves. They, too, have very few continuous external contacts. The rationale given is that they are sufficiently aware of the overall picture to be able to cast the problem into a broad framework, and they only need to call in outside opinions when they require specialized advice on a certain aspect. They feel that they are much more likely to be effective in the decision-making process than many other types of professional because they are "precise and accurate, and have a reputation for offering workable solutions." They contrast the "practical view" taken by the engineer with the "idealism" that characterizes proposals of many other professions, notably planners. "Our projects usually get built," said one of the engineers, "whereas theirs usually end up on the shelf."

The engineers were even less anxious to establish direct and continuous links with the public than were the public health officials. Most of them thought that "the public is not well informed and therefore cannot make rational judgments" or that "consulting the public makes planning much more difficult, and generally it delays or even precludes any action being taken." Most of those interviewed thought that the conventional methods of consulting public opinion were satisfactory as guides, namely, the public hearing, the referendum, and the ballot box. "Here the public is presented with a clear choice of alternatives," said one of them. "Like any shopper you can decide whether to take it or leave it."

The problem of consulting public opinion poses a somewhat different problem for the public health official than it does for the engineer. The effectiveness of the former in performing his tasks depends very much upon the extent to which his recommendations and regulations are understood and accepted by the public, and the extent to which he is able to overcome opposition (real or imaginary) from various groups. One way of dealing with this problem is to carry out programs of public education through talks and lectures, and through encouraging the organization of anti-pollution groups. Many public officials engage in such activities. However, most of them seem to feel that they are facing a dilemma in this regard: if they educate the public, they may acquire increased support for their programs, but, at the same time, they may be offered more advice than they desire as to what those programs should be!

In summary, it seems that the perceptions and attitudes of the two groups of professionals studied have all the characteristics of a closed system. Their views seem to be highly conditioned by training, adherence to standards and practices of the respective professions, and allegiance to the agency's or firm's goals or mission. Both groups believe they are highly qualified to do their respective jobs and that they act in the public interest. Contact with representatives of other agencies or the general public, however, is considered either unnecessary or potentially harmful. There appears to be general satisfaction with past policies and practices, and few, if any, major alterations are suggested.

FACTORS CONDITIONING PERCEPTIONS AND ATTITUDES

The analyses of perceptions of problems, solutions, and attitudes as to roles and responsibilities tend to confirm impressions gathered from other indicators of these views—such as statements of leading engineers or public health officials in professional journals or in public hearings—and the courses of action they have recommended in the past to deal with certain problems. To an important extent, these perceptions and attitudes differ from those which appear to be held by other professionals and by members of the general public, as statements in the technical and popular press and at public hearings clearly testify. What then, are the factors that account for such divergencies in viewpoint? Are they rooted in the individual's training and experience, where he has lived, his interactions with others, or his views about the relationship of man to nature? Data were gathered on various factors which it was believed might have an influence upon perceptions and attitudes. These were examined by factor analysis to determine which were the most significant. Stepwise multiple regression was then used to discover the extent to which any of these factors could explain variations in the perceptions and attitudes.

As noted earlier, the factor analysis isolated some 21 variables reflecting perceptions and attitudes of public health officials. These are noted in Table 4 and fall into five main groups, namely those relating to:

1. perceptions of problems
2. perceptions of solutions
3. role of the public
4. role of public health officials
5. role of other government agencies

These were treated as dependent variables.

The analysis also revealed five main independent variables relating to possible influences upon perceptions and attitudes, namely:

1. years in the profession
2. rank and mobility
3. distinction between Medical Health Officers
   (MHO) and Public Health Inspectors (PHI)
4. nature over man
5. man over nature

The analysis revealed some important relationships between the two sets of factors.

Years in the Profession
The hypothesis that the amount of time one spends in an occupation conditions one's perceptions and attitudes about the problems with which it is concerned was clearly borne out by the analysis. As Table 5 indicates, the concern of the public health official about environmental quality problems tends to decline the longer he has

Dependent Variables

Perception of Problems

1. Multiple quality criteria. (The range of criteria used in determining the extent of pollution.)
2. Pesticides, noise and purification. (Concern about problems of increasing use of pesticides, levels of noise, and the use of chlorination or fluoridation.)
3. Environmental quality and sewage disposal. (Sewage disposal seen as a major factor in environmental deterioration.)
4. Broad perspective. (Major issues and environmental quality problems perceived in a broad context.)

Perception of Solutions

5. Improved facilities. (The need for better laboratory facilities.)
6. Improved administration and standards. (The need for better administration and more rigorous application of standards.)
7. More meaningful water quality parameters. (The need to improve present bacteriological and chemical criteria.)
8. Adequate legislation. (Lack of dissatisfaction with present legislation.)

Role of Public

9. Dissatisfaction with role of public. (Public viewed as either apathetic or obstructive.)
10. Satisfaction with role of public. (Public viewed as well informed, active and nonobstructive.)
11. Opposition from vested interests. (Opposition received from pressure groups, especially property owners and rate payers.)
12. Organize groups. (Encouragement of local groups to obtain information and where appropriate, call for action.)

Role of Public Health

13. Water quality as a health problem. (Water quality viewed mainly as a human health problem and principally a responsibility of Department of Health.)
14. Intra-agency consultation. (Propensity to consult with colleagues within the agency.)
15. Extra-agency consultation. (Propensity to consult with people in other agencies or the general public.)
16. Adviser and decision maker. (Role viewed as a combination of adviser and decision maker.)
17. MHO as a health administrator. (MHO viewed as an administrator rather than as a physician or civic official.)

Role of Government

18. Water quality as department of health problem. (Water quality viewed as a problem that should be handled mainly by department of health.)
19. Focus on physical criteria. (Physical criteria viewed as relevant parameters in assessing water quality.)
20. Provincial versus municipal consultations. (Propensity to consult provincial rather than municipal officials on water quality matters.)
21. Consultations with other provincial and federal agencies.

Independent Variables

Background and Professional Characteristics

1. Medical Health Officer/Public Health Inspector. (Distinction between the two posts.)
2. Rank and mobility. (Seniority and the extent to which the individual has transferred between posts.)
3. Years in public health.

Views Toward the Environment

4. Nature over man.
5. Man over nature.

Table 4.   *Summary Listing of Dependent and Independent Variables*

Dependent Variable Entering the Equation	Sign	R	R^2	Increase in R^2	T-value To Enter Equation	T-value In Final Equation	Level of Significance
Environmental quality and sewage disposal	-	.423	.179	.179	2.874	3.511	.005
Dissatisfaction with role of public	-	.585	.342	.163	3.041	2.176	.025
Extra-agency consultation	-	.633	.401	.059	1.868	2.714	.005
Improved administration and standards	-	.674	.454	.054	1.840	2.735	.005
Organize groups	-	.706	.498	.044	1.737	1.660	.10
Adviser and decision maker	+	.727	.529	.030	1.475	1.672	.05
Intra-agency consultation	-	.748	.560	.031	1.474	1.781	.05
Consultation with other provincial and federal agencies	+	.766	.587	.027	1.453	2.250	.025
Pesticides, noise, and purification	-	.786	.618	.031	1.546	1.437	.10
M.H.O. roles as a health administrator	-	.802	.643	.025	1.426	1.426	.10

Table 5. *Influence of Years in the Profession: Results of Multiple Regression Analysis*

been in the profession, as do his desire to involve the public more directly in decision-making, his propensity to consult with others outside his agency, his concern about the effectiveness of present administrative arrangements, and his skepticism about the validity of water quality standards. It seems also that the longer an official has been in an agency, the less anxious he is to promote change in either its structure, its policies, or the matters with which it concerns itself. In the present study, it was mainly the younger, less-experienced officials who tended to be most aware of deteriorating environmental conditions and most skeptical about the ability of present administrative arrangements and policies to improve these conditions. It was they, too, who were the most anxious to provide the public with a more direct link into the planning and policy-making processes.

One possible interpretation of the findings is that the longer a public health official has been in the profession, the more likely he is to become adjusted to his physical and institutional environments. He is less prone to want to move elsewhere or to propose modifications to agency structure, standards of environmental quality, or public policies. So long as deterioration of environmental quality does not appear to be resulting in hazards to human health, the public health official does not feel any particular motivation to promote action or policy change. Modification of policies or expansion of responsibilities would obviously further complicate his task, a task which he believes is complicated enough already!

Years spent in public health appeared to be a good predictor of variations in perceptions and attitudes. As shown in Table 5, it accounted for more than 64 percent of the variance in ten significant dependent variables.

Rank and Mobility
Several sociologists (Eiduson, 1962; Gerstl and Hutton, 1966; Gross, 1958) and others (Caldwell, 1967; Marshall, 1966) have suggested that an individual's view about the problems with which he deals and about his role in dealing with them are conditioned by his position in the employment hierarchy, and by his identification with the organization for which he works. It appears that those who occupy positions in the lower echelons generally feel divorced from responsibility for making decisions. They often develop an attitude of being a cog in a very large machine. As they ascend the ladder of responsibility, however, their feeling of commitment and of identification with the organization's goals seems to grow (Zytowski, 1968).

The extent to which an individual has moved from one post to another also appears to have an influence upon his perceptions and attitudes. In some occupations, notably the academic profession and industrial management, transfers from one location to another are a generally accepted means of moving up the hierarchy (Gerstl and Hutton, 1966; Caplow and McGee, 1958). In many government agencies, experience in the field is often a prerequisite for obtaining a post at the head office (Corson and Paul, 1966; Caplow and McGee, 1958). Having ascended to the top rung of the ladder, however, the individual then tends to become more sedentary. Generally there is nowhere else to go, except to another organization, and there is also the knowledge that others are anxious to reach the top positions. The individual, therefore, can be expected to defend both his own position and the aims and policies of the organization for which he works.

Seniority and mobility were found in the analysis to be closely related, and were combined into a single factor for the regression studies. This factor seems to have an important influence on perceptions of public health officials, accounting for more than fifty percent of the variance in six variables (see Table 6). The more senior the official, the more likely it is that he has transferred at least five times, that he has a fairly narrow view of problems facing society, and that he identifies solutions in terms of the conventional practice of his agency. It seems also that seniority affects perceptions of the role of the public. The more senior officials are much more skeptical about involving the public in planning and policymaking than are the junior officials. Finally, it appears that seniority brings with it an increasing degree of dedication and commitment to the agency. The more senior officials spend a good deal of time outside their office hours informing themselves about environmental problems (such as through reading journals or attending meetings) and trying to inform the public.

These findings provide some interesting comparisons and contrasts with the results of the engineers' study. As in the case of public health officials, seniority is attained partly through experience acquired through working in a variety of places on a variety of problems. No characteristic patterns could be detected in transfers. It seems, however, that engineers may transfer at least three times before they settle into a post for more than five years. Like the senior public health officials, the senior engineers indicate both a close allegiance to the agency for which they worked and support for past recommendations made by it. In contrast to the public health officials, however, they tend to perceive a wider range of

Dependent Variable Entering the Equation	Sign	R	R^2	Increase in R^2	T-value		Level of Significance
					To Enter Equation	In Final Equation	
Broad perspective	-	.514	.264	.264	3.695	5.041	.005
Environmental quality and sewage disposal	+	.580	.336	.072	2.008	2.089	.025
Organize groups	+	.631	.398	.062	1.913	2.520	.02
Adviser and decision maker	-	.667	.445	.047	1.713	1.609	.10
Adequate legislation	+	.695	.483	.038	1.607	1.731	.05
Dissatisfaction with role of public	-	.717	.514	.031	1.452	1.510	.10
Pesticides, noise, and purification	+	.728	.530	.016	1.037	1.037	a

Table 6. *Influence of Rank and Mobility: Results of Multiple Regression Analysis*

a. Statistically insignificant.

problems facing society, and their off-duty activities were much less related to their work. In particular, they were seldom involved in public lecturing or in organizing groups.

Distinction between the Medical Health Officer (MHO) and the Public Health Inspector (PHI)

As noted earlier, responsibilities relating to public health in British Columbia are shared between Medical Health Officers and Public Health Inspectors. The essential difference between them is that the former are principally administrators, while the latter are the field representatives. This distinction appears to have an important bearing on their perceptions, attitudes, and behavioral responses. MHO's participate much more actively in intra-agency consultation than do PHI's, and especially with their head office. PHI's, in contrast, are much more frequently in contact with representatives of private industry and the general public. While MHO's are generally fairly skeptical about involving the public in policy-making, the PHI's tend to support such involvement.

The two groups also differed in their views as to their roles as advisers and decision makers. The former saw themselves as both advisers and decision makers, whereas the latter tended to consider themselves as advisers only. This, of course, reflects the kinds of functions which they perform in the agency, particularly in connection with environmental policy.

Differences in perceptions resulting from differences in functions performed by subgroups of a profession were also observed in the case of the engineers. The government engineers saw themselves as public servants, using their talents and training to promote the general welfare. All were strongly attached to the agency for which they worked and referred constantly to its goals, activities, and achievements. They spent much less time describing projects on which they had worked themselves. They contrasted their role with that of the consulting engineer. The latter, they thought, was brought in only to answer specific questions on a specialized topic and was not answerable to the public. "Consulting engineers," said one of the government engineers, "do not have to be as aware of government policy or of potential public reaction as we do. They are able to operate in a detached manner, whereas we have to be ready to field comments and criticisms long after the report is completed or the project is built."

The consulting engineers tended to concur with the government engineers' image of them. They, too, saw themselves as specialists on specific topics, participating as advisers in the planning and policy-making process when called upon to do so. They con-

Dependent Variable Entering the Equation	Sign	R	R^2	Increase in R^2	T-value To Enter Equation	T-value In Final Equation	Level of Significance
Intra-agency consultation	+	.724	.524	.524	6.476	6.580	.005
Adviser and decision maker	+	.755	.570	.046	1.964	3.115	.005
Opposition with vested interests	+	.772	.596	.026	1.517	0.713	a
Dissatisfaction with role of public	+	.786	.618	.022	1.455	1.868	.05
Extra-agency consultation	-	.796	.634	.016	1.158	1.216	.10
Improved facilities	+	.802	.643	.010	1.003	2.319	.025
Environmental quality and sewage disposal	+	.811	.658	.015	1.132	1.064	a
Provincial versus municipal consultations	-	.818	.669	.011	1.021	1.290	.10
Focus on physical criteria	+	.828	.686	.017	1.264	1.469	.10

Table 7. *Influence of Distinction between MHO and PHI: Results of Multiple Regression Analysis*

a. Statistically insignificant.

trasted their role with that of the government engineer. The latter, they thought, carried out important functions as watchdogs, planners, and administrators, but their job was neither as challenging nor as precarious as that of the consulting engineer. As one of them suggested, "The consulting engineer can afford much less to be wrong than the government engineer."

Man's Relationship to Nature

As noted earlier, several studies have shown that views about man's relationship to nature have an important bearing upon perceptions of and attitudes toward the environment. The views of the public health officials on this relationship were sought in several ways. First, the respondents were asked whether they thought technology had the answer to most problems faced by man. Next, they were asked for their views on three technological innovations now on the horizon and likely to alter the environment in important ways: namely the large-scale diversion of water from Alaska to Mexico (the NAWAPA scheme; Sewell, 1967); the purposeful modification of the weather (Fleagle, 1968); and the Supersonic Transport plane (SST; Shurcliff, 1969). Finally, they were asked who should be put in charge of decisions about the control of nature. Their views in these connections were then correlated with their perceptions of problems, solutions, and responsibilities.

Opinion was sharply divided on the extent to which man is in control of nature and vice versa. Just over one-half of the public health officials felt that technology could not solve many of the major problems now faced by man (see Table 8). The rationale given for this view was that there are some problems that are not amenable to the technological fix—like the Watts riot, poverty, or drug addiction—and that, in many cases, technological solutions create more problems than they solve. In contrast, those who felt

	Frequency of Mention	
	Public Health Officials	Engineers
Does Technology Have the Answer to all Problems?		
Yes	16	24
No	24	6
What Are its Deficiencies?		
Cannot deal with problems of human relations	15	6
Is limited by time or money	15	4
Creates problems	7	5

Table 8. *The Efficacy of Technology*

that technology does have the answer pointed to the fantastic material progress made in the past three decades as a result of technological advances. To the technological optimists, the only limitations were money and the need to develop institutional means of ensuring the adoption of innovations.

Opinions were also divided on the desirability of the three technological innovations, with roughly half in favor of them and half against. Those who favored them spoke of improvements in income, additions to food supply, and more rapid communications. Those who were against them pointed out uncertainties as to impacts on the environment, and the lack of a clearly demonstrated need for the innovation.

Man now has the technological capacity to make vast alterations in the environment and perhaps even destroy it. To provide another indication as to attitudes toward the man-nature relationship, the respondents were asked to suggest a group of persons to whom they would entrust the control of technology and decisions as to its use. Opinion was divided on this matter, too (see Table 9). Varying proportions of scientists and laymen were proposed. The only point of agreement was that no one would trust a group of politicians, a group of laymen, or a group of scientists to make such decisions!

| | n of Respondents | |
	Public Health Officials	Engineers
Scientists	7	7
Politicians	8	1
Scientists and politicians	10	2
Scientists and the general public	15	20

Table 9. *Allocation of Responsibility for Control of Technology*

The views of the public health officials on the role of technology were paralleled to a surprising degree by the views of the engineers. Knowing that the fundamental goal of the engineering profession is the control of nature, one would naturally assume that engineers would feel highly confident that technology has the answer to most problems, and that major technological innovations would be looked on with favor (Hertz, 1970). Analysis of the answers to the questions on technology reveals that while most engineers are confident about the ability of technology to solve human problems, they have reservations about the desirability of certain kinds of innovations. If anything, their reservations were even stronger than those of the public health officials (see Table 10). There was general support for the SST, based on the view that reductions in travel time were still a desirable social goal. Some mentioned problems of noise, but these were believed to be surmountable. Attempts to alter the weather drew much less support, and most of the engineers thought such attempts should be strictly controlled, pending much better understanding of the processes involved. There was almost unanimous opposition to the proposed NAWAPA scheme, based partly on technical and economic considerations, but mainly on the fact that it involved export of Canadian water. Mention of the scheme seemed to trigger considerable emotion in many of the

	n of Respondents	
	Public Health Officials	Engineers
Weather Modification		
Aware of the innovation	39	30
Is it feasible?	32	26
How far should we go?		
Do not attempt it	19	–
Small-scale	10	26
Large-scale	11	4
SST		
Advantageous innovation	9	18
Disadvantageous innovation	31	12
Advantages		
Increased speed of communication	9	16
Increased trade	4	7
Increased understanding	2	2
Challenge to the imagination	2	16
Disadvantages		
Noise	20	10
Space requirements	10	8
Jet contrails	2	2
Ecological disturbances	2	–
NAWAPA Scheme		
Advantageous innovation	18	8
Disadvantageous innovation	22	22
Advantages		
Solution to growing water needs	16	8
Source of revenue	8	6
Challenge to technology	6	8
Disadvantages		
Involves water export	22	22
Cheaper alternatives available	18	14
No demonstrated need	8	12
Potential ecological disaster	3	4

Table 10. *Views on Three Technological Innovations*

Dependent Variable Entering the Equation	Sign	R	R^2	Increase in R^2	T-value To Enter Equation	T-value In Final Equation	Level of Significance
Dissatisfaction with role of public	-	.315	.099	.099	2.045	1.424	.10
Water quality as a health problem	+	.412	.170	.071	1.771	1.852	.05
Adequate legislation	-	.492	.242	.072	1.858	1.179	a
Pesticides, noise, and purification	-	.522	.273	.030	1.209	1.412	.10
Extra-agency consultation	+	.547	.299	.027	1.142	1.050	a
Improved administration and standards	-	.565	.319	.020	0.964	1.053	a
Intra-agency consultation	+	.580	.336	.017	0.933	.898	a
Opposition from vested interests	-	.591	.349	.013	.785	.785	a

Table 11. *Influence of Views on Nature's Control Over Man: Results of Multiple Regression Analysis*

a. Statistically insignificant.

respondents, revealing a variety of attitudes about resource owner-ship, economic dependence, and so on.

Views about man's relationship to nature appear to have an important influence on perceptions and attitudes. In the public health officials' study, those who regarded water quality mainly as a health problem, those who were skeptical about public involve-ment in environmental health decisions, and those who were par-ticularly concerned about pesticides, noise pollution, and water purification tended to hold the view that nature is in control of man (see Table 11).

The view that man is in control of nature, however, appeared to be an even better predictor of perceptions and attitudes. It ac-counted for 47 percent of the explained variance in nine significant variables (see Table 12). Those who held this view also tended to feel that consultation beyond the public health unit is generally not essential, that public involvement often leads to unsatisfactory re-sults, that present water quality criteria are valid, and that pesti-cides, noise, and water purification problems are not a matter for great concern. One possible interpretation of these results might be that the public health official not only sees man in control of nature, but also sees his own official role as occupying an especially vital position in helping man to deal with problems involving the physical environment. Believing that his background and experi-ence furnish him with the necessary expertise, and that others are either less capable or disinterested in dealing with the problems with which he concerns himself, he feels a strong personal commit-ment to his job. At the same time, he is cognizant that other pro-fessionals, other agencies, and the general public are developing a concern about the environment. This poses a dilemma. On the one hand, it could mean that there will be vastly increased public recog-nition and support for his work. On the other, it could result in criticism, opposition, and perhaps an erosion of his position.

IMPLICATIONS OF THE RESULTS
FOR ENVIRONMENTAL QUALITY MANAGEMENT

The solution to the emerging environmental crisis will require at least three major changes in the present approach to environmental quality management. First, it will necessitate the adoption of a ho-listic rather than a fragmented view of the problem. Instead of water pollution being considered in isolation from air pollution or land pollution, and instead of the physical dimensions being con-sidered apart from the human dimensions, a conscious attempt will need to be made to consider them together. Likewise, the overall

Dependent Variable Entering the Equation	Sign	R	R^2	Increase in R^2	T-value		Level of Significance
					To Enter Equation	In Final Equation	
Extra-agency consultation	-	.352	.124	.124	2.316	3.386	.005
Focus on physical criteria	-	.462	.213	.090	2.050	1.627	.10
Environmental quality and sewage disposal	+	.536	.287	.074	1.930	2.196	.025
Opposition with vested interests	-	.586	.343	.056	1.727	2.139	.025
Adviser and decision maker	-	.624	.389	.046	1.600	1.672	.05
Satisfaction with role of public	-	.642	.412	.023	1.153	1.416	.10
Pesticides, noise, and purification	-	.658	.433	.021	1.089	1.457	.10
Broad perspective	+	.674	.454	.021	1.088	1.157	a
Water quality as a health problem	+	.683	.467	.012	0.843	1.647	.10

Table 12.   Influence of Views on Man's Control Over Nature: Results of Mutiple Regression Analysis

a Statistically insignificant.

effects of the adoption of any solution on the environment and on man will need to be taken into account in policy decisions.

Second, it will be necessary to involve the public much more directly in the planning process. It is already clear that the public feels alienated in this process, and that conventional means of consulting public opinion do not accurately reveal their preferences. Presenting the public with a few discrete alternatives has the advantage of simplifying the choice process, but unless the alternatives reflect the values held by the public rather than those of the planners, they may all be rejected.

Third, and as a corollary of the first two requirements, there will need to be changes in administrative structures, laws, and policies to ensure that a broader view is taken, enabling the various aspects of environmental quality problems to be considered in an integrated fashion, and ensuring that the public enjoys a satisfactory sense of participation.

The results of the two studies reported on here seem to suggest that such changes will not be easily accomplished. In fact, the likelihood is that they will be vigorously opposed. Holism, for example, is an antithesis to the approach upon which different professions depend for their recognition and is likely to be rejected by them. It is possible that some attempt will be made to broaden the viewpoint of certain professions by establishing training programs which expose members to ideas and methods of other disciplines, and by setting up formal and informal links among professions. This process is, in fact, already under way, generally under the banner of environmental science or environmental studies. Almost always, however, one discipline or profession dominates the scene, and only in rare instances does it appear that several professions can work together in a truly integrated fashion on a problem of mutual concern.

It also seems that professionals, particularly in the physical sciences and the natural sciences, are skeptical about involving the public in policy-making. For the most part, they appear to take the view either that the public is not well informed or that so many different opinions will appear that policy-making will become impossible. The alternative is to present the public with solutions conceived by the planners. The only choice then is to accept or reject them. If they are rejected, the problem remains unsolved. As the rows of unimplemented plans on planners' shelves testify, this is frequently the case.

Finally, it is clear that experts are not in favor of institutional change, especially if it means that their own role will be altered. Accordingly, they resist suggestions that new agencies should be established, new laws should be passed, new solutions should be tried, or that other professions should become involved. Such resistance appears to increase with seniority. There is, in fact, an inverse relationship between the perception of the need for change and power to accomplish it.

It is obvious that society will always need experts and expertise. The question now is the kinds of experts and expertise needed to solve environmental problems. Unless our present experts broaden their views and integrate their activities, they may well contribute more to the promotion of the environmental crisis than to its solution.

REFERENCES

D. Appleyard, "City Designers and the Pluralistic City," in L. Rodwin et al, eds., *Regional Planning for Development* (Cambridge, Mass.: M.I.T. Press, 1969).

C. F. Brockington, "Organization and Administration of Health Services," in W. Hobson, ed., *The Theory and Practice of Public Health* (London: Oxford University Press, 1961), pp. 305–20.

B. T. Bower and W. R. D. Sewell, *Selecting Strategies for Management of Air Quality* (Ottawa: Queen's Printer, 1970).

L. Caldwell, *Politics, Professionalism, and Environment* (Bloomington, Ind.: University of Indiana Institute of Public Administration, 1967).

T. Caplow and R. J. McGee, *The Academic Marketplace* (New York: Basic Books, 1958).

R. L. Cooley and G. Wandesforde-Smith, *Congress and the Environment* (Seattle: University of Washington Press, 1970).

J. Corson and R. S. Paul, *Men Near the Top* (Baltimore: Johns Hopkins Press, 1966).

K. H. Craik, "The Environmental Dispositions of Environmental Decision-Makers," *Annals of the American Academy of Political and Social Science* (May, 1970a): 87–94.

———, "Environmental Psychology," in T. M. Newcomb, ed., *New Directions in Psychology* (New York: Holt, Rinehart and Winston, 1970b), pp. 1–122.

G. De Bell, ed., *The Environmental Handbook* (New York: Ballantine, 1970).

B. T. Eiduson, *Scientists: Their Psychological World* (New York: Basic Books, 1962).

R. G. Fleagle, *Weather Modification: Science and Public Policy* (Seattle: University of Washington Press, 1968).

J. E. Gerstl and S. B. Hutton, *Engineers: The Anatomy of a Profession* (London: Tavistock, 1966).

E. Gross, *Work and Society* (New York: Thomas Y. Crowell, 1958).

D. B. Hertz, "The Technological Imperative—Social Implications of Professional Technology," *Annals of the American Academy of Political and Social Science* (May, 1970): 95–106.

J. Hewings, *Water Quality and the Hazard to Health*, Natural Hazard Research Working Paper No. 3, Department of Geography (Toronto: University of Toronto Press, 1968).

R. W. Kates, *Hazard and Choice Perception in Flood Plain Management*, Department of Geography Research Paper No. 78 (Chicago: University of Chicago Press, 1962).

F. R. Kluckhohn and F. L. Strodtbeck, *Variations in Value Orientations* (Evanston, Ill.: Row, Peterson, 1961).

D. Lowenthal, *Environmental Perception and Behavior*, Department of Geography Research Paper No. 109 (Chicago: University of Chicago Press, 1967).

———, "Assumptions behind Public Attitudes," in H. Jarrett, ed., *Environmental Quality in a Growing Economy* (Baltimore: Johns Hopkins Press, 1966).

R. C. Lucas, "The Contribution of Environmental Research to Wilderness Policy Decisions," *Journal of Social Issues* 22 (October, 1966): 116–26.

H. Marshall, "Politics and Efficiency on Water Development," in A. V. Kneese and S. C. Smith, eds., *Water Research* (Baltimore: Johns Hopkins Press, 1966), pp. 291–310.

M. Nicholson, *The Environmental Revolution* (London: Hodder and Stoughton, 1970).

T. F. Saarinen, *Perceptions of the Drought Hazard in the Great Plains*, Department of Geography Research Paper No. 105, (Chicago: University of Chicago Press, 1966).

W. R. D. Sewell, "NAWAPA: Pipedream of Practical Possibility?" *Bulletin of Atomic Scientists* (September, 1967): 8–13.

P. Shepard and D. McKinley, eds., *The Subversive Science: Essays Towards an Ecology of Man* (New York: Houghton-Mifflin, 1969).

W. A. Shurcliff, *SST and the Sonic Boom Handbook* (New York: Ballantine, 1969).

R. Sommer, *Expertland* (Garden City, N.Y.: Doubleday, 1963).

H. R. Valentine, *Water in the Service of Man* (Harmondsworth, Middlesex: Penguin, 1967).

K. E. Watt, *Ecology and Resource Management* (New York: McGraw-Hill, 1968).

G. F. White, "Formation and Role of Public Attitudes," in H. Jarrett, ed., *Environmental Quality in a Growing Economy* (Baltimore: Johns Hopkins Press, 1966), pp. 105–27.

D. G. Zytowski, *Vocational Behavior* (New York: Holt, Rinehart and Winston, 1968).

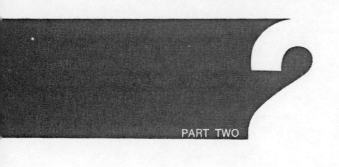

PART TWO

MAN AS
MANIPULATED BY
HIS ENVIRONMENT

CHAPTER

The Experience
of Living in Cities

STANLEY MILGRAM

Reprinted from *Science* 167 (13 March 1970): 1461–68, by permission of the American Association for the Advancement of Science and the author. Copyright 1970 by the American Association for the Advancement of Science.

This article is based on an address given 2 September 1969 at the 77th annual meeting of the American Psychological Association in Washington, D.C.

A fifty-one minute cinematic treatment of this article is available to educational and civic groups. It is entitled *The City and the Self* and is distributed by Time-Life Films, 43 West 16th Street, New York, NY ·10011.

Milgram begins his analysis of city life by noting three commonplace facts of urban experience—the large numbers of people present, the high density (that is, many people in little space), and the great variety of the population. But, he argues, if the actual experience of living in cities is to be understood, these social facts must be given psychological meaning. That is, we must consider what are the *internal* consequences for the individual who is surrounded by 220,000 people within a ten-minute walk from his office.

Milgram introduces the concept of *overload* as a useful idea for understanding the psychological experience of urban living: "This term, drawn from systems analysis, refers to a system's inability to process inputs from the environment because there are too many inputs for the system to cope with, or because successive inputs come so fast that input *A* cannot be processed when input *B* is presented." When overload occurs, adaptations must be made if the system is to remain viable. He argues that city life constitutes a steady stream of such overload experiences which demand those social behaviors which characterize the city dweller.

For example, since it is impossible to have moral and social involvement with thousands of people, such interactions must be restricted. One way is to maintain relationships at a superficial level (the nodding acquaintance with the neighbor of ten years); another is to disregard people entirely (to walk past the drunk fallen on the sidewalk, or more tragically, to ignore an attack victim's cries for help). Milgram examines such seemingly callous behaviors and others—willingness to trust and assist strangers, to be courteous, to maintain anonymity—using the concept of overload as an analytical tool, and always reviewing the relevant researches, so that his points are based on evidence as well as on argument.

Toward the end of the paper, Milgram continues his examination of urban life by penetrating the unexplored territory of city "atmosphere," that is, the special qualities that distinguish one city from another and make living in New York different from Los Angeles or Chicago. Again, he is painstaking in his use of data, careful in his speculations, and imaginative in his suggestions for further research on the character of cities and the lives of their inhabitants.

"When I first came to New York it seemed like a nightmare. As soon as I got off the train at Grand Central I was caught up in pushing, shoving crowds on 42nd Street. Sometimes people bumped into me without apology; what really frightened me was to see two people literally engaged in combat for possession of a cab. Why were they so rushed? Even drunks on the street were bypassed without a glance. People didn't seem to care about each other at all."

This statement represents a common reaction to a great city, but it does not tell the whole story. Obviously cities have great appeal because of their variety, eventfulness, possibility of choice, and the stimulation of an intense atmosphere that many individuals find a desirable background to their lives. Where face-to-face contacts are important, the city offers unparalleled possibilities. It has been calculated by the Regional Plan Association (1) that in Nassau County, a suburb of New York City, an individual can meet 11,000 others within a 10-minute radius of his office by foot or car. In Newark, a moderate-sized city, he can meet more than 20,000 persons within this radius. But in midtown Manhattan he can meet fully 220,000. So there is an order-of-magnitude increment in the communication possibilities offered by a great city. That is one of the bases of its appeal and, indeed, of its functional necessity. The city provides options that no other social arrangement permits. But there is a negative side also, as we shall see.

Granted that cities are indispensable in complex society, we may still ask what contribution psychology can make to understanding the experience of living in them. What theories are relevant? How can we extend our knowledge of the psychological aspects of life in cities through empirical inquiry? If empirical inquiry is possible, along what lines should it proceed? In short, where do we start in constructing urban theory and in laying out lines of research?

Observation is the indispensable starting point. Any observer in the streets of midtown Manhattan will see (i) large numbers of people, (ii) a high population density, and (iii) heterogeneity of population. These three factors need to be at the root of any sociopsychological theory of city life, for they condition all aspects of our experience in the metropolis. Louis Wirth (2), if not the first to point to these factors, is nonetheless the sociologist who relied most heavily on them in his analysis of the city. Yet, for a psychologist, there is something unsatisfactory about Wirth's theoretical variables. Numbers, density, and heterogenity are demographic facts but they are not yet psychological facts. They are external to the individual. Psychology needs an idea that links the individual's *experience* to the demographic circumstances of urban life.

One link is provided by the concept of overload. This term, drawn from systems analysis, refers to a system's inability to process inputs from the environment because there are too many inputs for the system to cope with, or because successive inputs come so fast that input A cannot be processed when input B is presented. When overload is present, adaptations occur. The system must set priorities and make choices. A may be processed first while B is kept in abeyance, or one input may be sacrificed altogether. City life, as we experience it, constitutes a continuous set of encounters with overload, and of resultant adaptations. Overload characteristically deforms daily life on several levels, impinging on role performance, the evolution of social norms, cognitive functioning, and the use of facilities.

The concept has been implicit in several theories of urban experience. In 1903 George Simmel (*3*) pointed out that, since urban dwellers come into contact with vast numbers of people each day, they conserve psychic energy by becoming acquainted with a far smaller proportion of people than their rural counterparts do, and by maintaining more superficial relationships even with these acquaintances. Wirth (*2*) points specifically to "the superficiality, the anonymity, and the transitory character of urban social relations."

One adaptive response to overload, therefore, is the allocation of less time to each input. A second adaptive mechanism is disregard of low-priority inputs. Principles of selectivity are formulated such that investment of time and energy are reserved for carefully defined inputs (the urbanite disregards the drunk sick on the street as he purposefully navigates through the crowd). Third, boundaries are redrawn in certain social transactions so that the overloaded system can shift the burden to the other party in the exchange; thus, harried New York bus drivers once made change for customers, but now this responsibility has been shifted to the client, who must have the exact fare ready. Fourth, reception is blocked off prior to entrance into a system; city dwellers increasingly use unlisted telephone numbers to prevent individuals from calling them, and a small but growing number resort to keeping the telephone off the hook to prevent incoming calls. More subtly, a city dweller blocks inputs by assuming an unfriendly countenance, which discourages others from initiating contact. Additionally, social screening devices are interposed between the individual and environmental inputs (in a town of 5000 anyone can drop in to chat with the mayor, but in the metropolis organizational screening devices deflect inputs to other destinations). Fifth, the intensity of inputs is diminished by filtering devices, so that only weak and relatively superficial forms of involvement with others are allowed. Sixth, specialized institutions are created to absorb inputs that would otherwise swamp the individual (welfare departments handle the financial needs of a million individuals in New York City, who would otherwise create an army of mendicants continuously importuning the pedestrian). The interposition of institutions between the individual and the social world, a characteristic of all modern society, and most notably of the large metropolis, has its negative side. It deprives the individual of a sense of direct contact and spontaneous integration in the life around him. It simultaneously protects and estranges the individual from his social environment.

Many of these adaptive mechanisms apply not only to individuals but to institutional systems as well, as Meier (4) has so brilliantly shown in connection with the library and the stock exchange.

In sum, the observed behavior of the urbanite in a wide range of situations appears to be determined largely by a variety of adaptations to overload. I now deal with several specific consequences of responses to overload, which make for differences in the tone of city and town.

SOCIAL RESPONSIBILITY

The principal point of interest for a social psychology of the city is that moral and social involvement with individuals is necessarily restricted. This is a direct and necessary function of excess of input over capacity to process. Such restriction of involvement runs a broad spectrum from refusal to become involved in the needs of another person, even when the person desperately needs assistance, through refusal to do favors, to the simple withdrawal of courtesies (such as offering a lady a seat, or saying "sorry" when a pedestrian collision occurs). In any transaction more and more details need to be dropped as the total number of units to be processed increases and assaults an instrument of limited processing capacity.

The ultimate adaptation to an overloaded social environment is to totally disregard the needs, interests, and demands of those whom one does not define as relevant to the satisfaction of personal needs, and to develop highly efficient perceptual means of determining whether an individual falls into the category of friend or stranger. The disparity in the treatment of friends and strangers ought to be greater in cities than in towns; the time allotment and willingness to become involved with those who have no personal claim on one's time is likely to be less in cities than in towns.

Bystander Intervention in Crises

The most striking deficiencies in social responsibility in cities occur in crisis situations, such as the Genovese murder in Queens. In 1964, Catherine Genovese, coming home from a night job in the early hours of an April morning, was stabbed repeatedly, over an extended period of time. Thirty-eight residents of a respectable New York City neighborhood admit to having witnessed at least a part of the attack, but none went to her aid or called the police until after she was dead. Milgram and Hollander, writing in *The Nation* (5), analyzed the event in these terms:

> Urban friendships and associations are not primarily formed on the basis of physical proximity. A person with numerous close friends in different parts of the city may not know the occupant of an adjacent apartment. This does not mean that a city dweller has fewer friends than does a villager, or knows fewer persons who will come to his aid; however, it does mean that his allies are not constantly at hand. Miss Genovese required immediate aid from those physically present. There is no evidence that the city had deprived Miss Genovese of human associations, but the friends who might have rushed to her side were miles from the scene of her tragedy.
>
> Further, it is known that her cries for help were not directed to a specific person; they were general. But only individuals can act, and as the cries were not specifically directed, no particular person felt a special responsibility. The crime and the failure of community response seem absurd to us. At the time, it may well have seemed equally absurd to the Kew Gardens residents that not one of the neighbors would have called the police. A collective paralysis may have developed from the belief of each of the witnesses that someone else must surely have taken that obvious step.

Latané and Darley (6) have reported laboratory approaches to the study of bystander intervention and have established experimentally the following principle: the larger the number of bystanders, the less the likelihood that any one of them will intervene in an emergency. Gaertner and Bickman (7) of The City University of New York have extended the bystander studies to an examination of help across ethnic lines. Blacks and whites, with clearly identifiable accents, called strangers (through what the caller represented as an error in telephone dialing), gave them a plausible story of being stranded on an outlying highway without more dimes, and asked the stranger to call a garage. The experimenters found that the white callers had a significantly better chance of obtaining assistance than the black callers. This suggests that ethnic allegiance may well be another means of coping with overload: the city dweller can reduce excessive demands and screen out urban heterogeneity by responding along ethnic lines; overload is made more manageable by limiting the "span of sympathy."

In any quantitative characterization of the social texture of city life, a necessary first step is the application of such experimental methods as these to field situations in large cities and small towns. Theorists argue that the indifference shown in the Genovese case would not be found in a small town, but in the absence of solid experimental evidence the qeustion remains an open one.

More than just callousness prevents bystanders from participating in altercations between people. A rule of urban life is respect for other people's emotional and social privacy, perhaps because physical privacy is so hard to achieve. And in situations for which the standards are heterogeneous, it is much harder to know whether taking an active role is unwarranted meddling or an appropriate response to a critical situation. If a husband and wife are quarreling in public, at what point should a bystander step in? On the one hand, the heterogeneity of the city produces substantially greater tolerance about behavior, dress, and codes of ethics than is generally found in the small town, but this diversity also encourages people to withhold aid for fear of antagonizing the participants or crossing an inappropriate and difficult-to-define line.

Moreover, the frequency of demands present in the city gives rise to norms of noninvolvement. There are practical limitations to the Samaritan impulse in a major city. If a citizen attended to every needy person, if he were sensitive to and acted on every altruistic impulse that was evoked in the city, he could scarcely keep his own affairs in order.

Willingness to Trust and Assist Strangers
We now move away from crisis situations to less urgent examples of social responsibility. For it is not only in situations of dramatic need but in the ordinary, everyday willingness to lend a hand that the city dweller is said to be deficient relative to his small-town cousin. The comparative method must be used in any empirical examination of this question. A commonplace social situation is staged in an urban setting and in a small town—a situation to which a subject can respond by either extending help or withholding it. The responses in town and city are compared.

One factor in the purported unwillingness of urbanites to be helpful to strangers may well be their heightened sense of physical (and emotional) vulnerability—a feeling that is supported by urban crime statistics. A key test for distinguishing between city and town behavior, therefore, is determining how city dwellers compare with town dwellers in offering aid that increases their personal vulnerability and requires some trust of strangers. Altman, Levine, Nadien, and Villena (8) of The City University of New York devised a study to compare the behaviors of city and town dwellers in this respect. The criterion used in this study was the willingness of householders to allow strangers to enter their home to use the telephone. The student investigators individually rang doorbells, explained that they had misplaced the address of a friend nearby, and asked to use the phone. The investigators (two males and two females) made 100 requests for entry into homes in the city and 60 requests in the small towns. The results for middle-income housing developments in Manhattan were compared with data for several small towns (Stony Point, Spring Valley, Ramapo, Nyack, New City, and West Clarkstown) in Rockland County, outside of New York City. As Table 1 shows, in all cases there was a sharp increase in the proportion of entries achieved by an experimenter when he moved from the city to a small town. In the most extreme

Experimenter	Entries achieved (%)	
	City*	Small town†
Male		
No. 1	16	40
No. 2	12	60
Female		
No. 3	40	87
No. 4	40	100

Table 1. *Percentage of Entries Achieved by Investigators for City and Town Dwellings* (See text)

* Number of requests for entry, 100. † Number of requests for entry, 60.

case the experimenter was five times as likely to gain admission to homes in a small town as to homes in Manhattan. Although the female experimenters had notably greater success both in cities and in towns than the male experimenters had, each of the four students did at least twice as well in towns as in cities. This suggests that the city-town distinction overrides even the predictably greater fear of male strangers than of female ones.

The lower level of helpfulness by city dwellers seems due in part to recognition of the dangers of living in Manhattan, rather than to mere indifference or coldness. It is significant that 75 percent of all the city respondents received and answered messages by shouting through closed doors and by peering out through peepholes; in the towns, by contrast, about 75 percent of the respondents opened the door.

Supporting the experimenters' quantitative results was their general observation that the town dwellers were noticeably more friendly and less suspicious than the city dwellers. In seeking to explain the reasons for the greater sense of psychological vulnerability city dwellers feel, above and beyond the differences in crime statistics, Villena (8) points out that, if a crime is committed in a village, a resident of a neighboring village may not perceive the crime as personally relevant, though the geographic distance may be small, whereas a criminal act committed anywhere in the city, though miles from the city-dweller's home is still verbally located within the city; thus, Villena says, "the inhabitant of the city possesses a larger vulnerable space."

Civilities

Even at the most superficial level of involvement—the exercise of everyday civilities—urbanites are reputedly deficient. People bump into each other and often do not apologize. They knock over another person's packages and, as often as not, proceed on their way with a grumpy exclamation instead of an offer of assistance. Such behavior, which many visitors to great cities find distasteful, is less common, we are told, in smaller communities, where traditional courtesies are more likely to be observed.

In some instances it is not simply that, in the city, traditional courtesies are violated; rather, the cities develop new norms of noninvolvement. These are so well defined and so deeply a part of city life that *they* constitute the norms people are reluctant to violate. Men are actually embarrassed to give up a seat on the subway to an old woman; they mumble "I was getting off anyway," instead of making the gesture in a straightforward and gracious way. These norms develop because everyone realizes that, in situations of high population density, people cannot implicate themselves in each others' affairs, for to do so would create conditions of continual distraction which would frustrate purposeful action.

In discussing the effects of overload I do not imply that at every instant the city dweller is bombarded with an unmanageable number of inputs, and that his responses are determined by the excess of input at any given instant. Rather, adaptation occurs in the form of gradual evolution of norms of behavior. Norms are evolved in response to frequent discrete experiences of overload; they persist and become generalized modes of responding.

Overload on Cognitive Capacities: Anonymity

That we respond differently toward those whom we know and those who are strangers to us is a truism. An eager patron aggressively cuts in front of someone in a long movie line to save time only to confront a friend; he then behaves sheepishly. A man is involved in an automobile accident caused by another driver, emerges from his car shouting in rage, then moderates his behavior on discovering a friend driving the other car. The city dweller, when walking through the midtown streets, is in a state of continual anonymity vis-à-vis the other pedestrians.

Anonymity is part of a continuous spectrum ranging from total anonymity to full acquaintance, and it may well be that measurement of the precise degrees of anonymity in cities and towns would help to explain important distinctions between the quality of life in each. Conditions of full acquaintance, for example, offer security and familiarity, but they may also be stifling, because the individual is caught in a web of established relationships. Conditions of complete anonymity, by contrast, provide freedom from routinized social ties, but they may also create feelings of alienation and detachment.

Empirically one could investigate the proportion of activities in which the city dweller or the town dweller is known by others at given times in his daily life, and the proportion of activities in the course of which he interacts with individuals who know him. At his job, for instance, the city dweller may be known to as many people as his rural counterpart. However, when he is not fulfilling his occupational role—say, when merely traveling about the city—the urbanite is doubtless more anonymous than his rural counterpart.

Limited empirical work on anonymity has begun. Zimbardo (9) has tested whether the social anonymity and impersonality of the big city encourage greater vandalism than do small towns. Zimbardo arranged for one automobile to be left for 64 hours near the Bronx campus of New York University and for a counterpart to be left for the same number of hours near Stanford University in Palo Alto. The license plates on the two cars were removed and the hoods were opened, to provide "releaser cues" for potential vandals. The New York car was stripped of all removable parts within the first 24 hours, and by the end of 3 days was only a hunk of metal rubble. Unexpectedly, however, most of the destruction occurred during daylight hours, usually under the scrutiny of observers, and the leaders in the vandalism were well-dressed, white adults. The Palo Alto car was left untouched.

Zimbardo attributes the difference in the treatment accorded the two cars to the "acquired feelings of social anonymity provided by life in a city like New York," and he supports his conclusions with several other anecdotes illustrating casual, wanton vandalism in the city. In any comparative study of the effects of anonymity in city and town, however, there must be satisfactory control for other confounding factors: the large number of drug addicts in a city like New York; the higher proportion of slum-dwellers in the city; and so on.

Another direction for empirical study is investigation of the beneficial effects of anonymity. The impersonality of city life breeds its own tolerance for the private lives of the inhabitants. Individuality and even eccentricity, we may assume, can flourish more readily in the metropolis than in the small town. Stigmatized persons may find it easier to lead comfortable lives in the city, free of the constant scrutiny of neighbors. To what degree can this assumed difference between city and town be shown empirically? Judith Waters (10), at The City University of New York, hypothesized that avowed homosexuals would be more likely to be accepted as tenants in a large city than in small towns, and she dispatched letters from homosexuals and from normal individuals to real estate agents in cities and towns across the country. The results of her study were inconclusive. But the general idea of examining the protective benefits of city life to the stigmatized ought to be pursued.

Role Behavior in Cities and Towns

Another product of urban overload is the adjustment in roles made by urbanites in daily interactions. As Wirth has said (2): "Urbanites meet one another in highly segmental roles. . . . They are less dependent upon particular persons, and their dependence upon others is confined to a highly fractionalized aspect of the other's round of activity." This tendency is particularly noticeable in transactions between customers and individuals offering professional or sales services. The owner of a country store has time to become well acquainted with his dozen-or-so daily customers, but the girl at the checkout counter of a busy A & P, serving hundreds of customers a day, barely has time to toss the green stamps into one customer's shopping bag before the next customer confronts her with his pile of groceries.

Meier, in his stimulating analysis of the city (4), discusses several adaptations a system may make when confronted by inputs that exceed its capacity to process them. Meier argues that, according to the principle of competition for scarce resources, the scope and time of the transaction shrink as customer volume and daily turnover rise. This, in fact, is what is meant by the "brusque" quality of city life. New standards have developed in cities concerning what levels of services are appropriate in business transactions (see Figure 1).

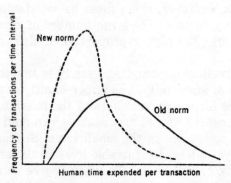

Figure 1. Changes in the demand for time for a given task when the overall transaction frequency increases in a social system.

Reprinted from *A Communications Theory of Urban Growth* by R. L. Meier, by permission of The M.I.T. Press, Cambridge, Massachusetts. Copyright 1962 by The M.I.T. Press.

McKenna and Morgenthau (*11*), in a seminar at The City University of New York, devised a study (i) to compare the willingness of city dwellers and small-town dwellers to do favors for strangers that entailed expenditure of a small amount of time and slight inconvenience but no personal vulnerability, and (ii) to determine whether the more compartmentalized, transitory relationships of the city would make urban salesgirls less likely than small-town salesgirls to carry out, for strangers, tasks not related to their customary roles.

To test for differences between city dwellers and small-town dwellers, a simple experiment was devised in which persons from both settings were asked (by telephone) to perform increasingly onerous favors for anonymous strangers.

Within the cities (Chicago, New York, and Philadelphia), half the calls were to housewives and the other half to salesgirls in women's apparel shops; the division was the same for the 37 small towns of the study, which were in the same states as the cities. Each experimenter represented herself as a long-distance caller who had, through error, been connected with the respondent by the operator. The experimenter began by asking for simple information about the weather for purposes of travel. Next the experimenter excused herself on some pretext (asking the respondent to "please hold on"), put the phone down for almost a full minute, and then picked it up again and asked the respondent to provide the phone number of a hotel or motel in her vicinity at which the experimenter might stay during a forthcoming visit. Scores were assigned the subjects on the basis of how helpful they had been. McKenna summarizes her results in this manner:

> People in the city, whether they are engaged in a specific job or not, are less helpful and informative than people in small towns; . . . People at home, regardless of where they live, are less helpful and informative than people working in shops.

However, the absolute level of cooperativeness for urban subjects was found to be quite high, and does not accord with the stereotype of the urbanite as aloof, self-centered, and unwilling to help strangers. The quantitative differences obtained by McKenna and Morgenthau are less great than one might have expected. This again points up the need for extensive empirical research in rural-urban differences, research that goes far beyond that provided in the few illustrative pilot studies presented here. At this point we have very limited objective evidence on differences in the quality of social encounters in city and small town.

But the research needs to be guided by unifying theoretical concepts. As I have tried to demonstrate, the concept of overload helps to explain a wide variety of contrasts between city behavior and town behavior: (i) the differences in role enactment (the tendency of urban dwellers to deal with one another in highly segmented, functional terms, and of urban sales personnel to devote limited time and attention to their customers); (ii) the evolution of urban norms quite different from traditional town values (such as the acceptance of noninvolvement, impersonality, and aloofness in urban life); (iii) the adaptation of the urban dweller's cognitive processes (his inability to identify most of the people he sees daily, his screening of sensory stimuli, his development of blasé attitudes toward deviant or bizarre behavior, and his selectivity in responding to human demands); and (iv) the competition for scarce facilities in the city (the subway rush; the fight for taxis; traffic jams; standing in line to await services). I suggest that contrasts between city and rural behavior probably reflect the responses of similar people to very different situations, rather than intrinsic differences in the personalities of rural and city dwellers. The city is a situation to which individuals respond adaptively.

FURTHER ASPECTS OF URBAN EXPERIENCE

Some features of urban experience do not fit neatly into the system of analysis presented thus far. They are no less important for that reason. The issues raised next are difficult to treat in quantitative fashion. Yet I prefer discussing them in a loose way to excluding them because appropriate language and data have not yet been developed. My aim is to suggest how phenomena such as "urban atmosphere" can be pinned down through techniques of measurement.

The "Atmosphere" of Great Cities

The contrast in the behavior of city and town dwellers has been a natural starting point for urban social scientists. But even among great cities there are marked differences in "atmosphere." The tone, pacing, and texture of social encounters are different in London and New York, and many persons willingly make financial sacrifices for the privilege of living within a specific urban atmosphere which they find pleasing or stimulating. A second perspective in the study of cities, therefore, is to define exactly what is meant by the atmosphere of a city and to pinpoint the factors that give rise to it. It may seem that urban atmosphere is too evanescent a quality to be reduced to a set of measurable variables, but I do not believe the matter can be judged before substantial effort has been made in this direction. It is obvious that any such approach must be comparative. It makes no sense at all to say that New York is "vibrant" and "frenetic" unless one has some specific city in mind as a basis of comparison.

In an undergraduate tutorial that I conducted at Harvard University some years ago, New York, London, and Paris were selected as reference points for attempts to measure urban atmosphere. We began with a simple question: Does any consensus exist about the qualities that typify given cities? To answer this question one could undertake a content analysis of travelbook, literary, and journalistic accounts of cities. A second approach, which we adopted, is to ask people to characterize (with descriptive terms and accounts of typical experiences) cities they have lived in or visited. In advertisements placed in the *New York Times* and the *Harvard Crimson* we asked people to give us accounts of specific incidents in London, Paris, or New York that best illuminated the character of that particular city. Questionnaires were then developed, and administered to persons who were familiar with at least two of the three cities.

Some distinctive patterns emerged (*12*). The distinguishing themes concerning New York, for example, dealt with its diversity, its great size, its pace and level of activity, its cultural and entertainment opportunities, and the heterogeneity and segmentation ("ghettoization") of its population. New York elicited more descriptions in terms of physical qualities, pace, and emotional impact than Paris or London did, a fact which suggests that these are particularly important aspects of New York's ambiance.

A contrasting profile emerges for London; in this case respondents placed far greater emphasis on their interactions with the inhabitants than on physical surroundings. There was near unanimity on certain themes: those dealing with the tolerance and courtesy of London's inhabitants. One respondent said:

> When I was 12, my grandfather took me to the British Museum . . . one day by tube and recited the *Aeneid* in Latin for my benefit. . . . He is rather deaf, speaks very loudly and it embarrassed the hell out of me, until I realized that nobody was paying any attention. Londoners are extremely worldly and tolerant.

In contrast, respondents who described New Yorkers as aloof, cold, and rude referred to such incidents as the following:

> I saw a boy of 19 passing out anti-war leaflets to passersby. When he stopped at a corner, a man dressed in a business suit walked by him at a brisk pace, hit the boy's arm, and scattered the leaflets all over the street. The man kept walking at the same pace down the block.

We need to obtain many more such descriptions of incidents, using careful methods of sampling. By the application of factor-analytic techniques, relevant dimensions for each city can be discerned.

The responses for Paris were about equally divided between responses concerning its inhabitants and those regarding its physical and sensory attributes. Cafés and parks were often mentioned as contributing to the sense that Paris is a city of amenities, but many respondents complained that Parisians were inhospitable, nasty, and cold.

We cannot be certain, of course, to what degree these statements reflect actual characteristics of the cities in question and to what degree they simply tap the respondents' knowledge of widely held preconceptions. Indeed, one may point to three factors, apart from the actual atmospheres of the cities, that determine the subjects' responses.

1. A person's impression of a given city depends on his implicit standard of comparison. A New Yorker who visits Paris may well describe that city as "leisurely," whereas a compatriot from Richmond, Virginia, may consider Paris too "hectic." Obtaining reciprocal judgment, in which New Yorkers judge Londoners, and Londoners judge New Yorkers, seems a useful way to take into account not only the city being judged but also the home city that serves as the visitor's base line.

2. Perceptions of a city are also affected by whether the ob-

server is a tourist, a newcomer, or a longer-term resident. First, a tourist will be exposed to features of the city different from those familiar to a long-time resident. Second, a prerequisite for adapting to continuing life in a given city seems to be the filtering out of many observations about the city that the newcomer or tourist finds particularly arresting; this selective process seems to be part of the long-term resident's mechanism for coping with overload. In the interest of psychic economy, the resident simply learns to tune out many aspects of daily life. One method for studying the specific impact of adaptation on perception of the city is to ask several pairs of newcomers and old-timers (one newcomer and one old-timer to a pair) to walk down certain city blocks and then report separately what each has observed.

Additionally, many persons have noted that when travelers return to New York from an extended sojourn abroad they often feel themselves confronted with "brutal ugliness" (*13*) and a distinctive, frenetic atmosphere whose contributing details are, for a few hours or days, remarkably sharp and clear. This period of fresh perception should receive special attention in the study of city atmosphere. For, in a few days, details which are initially arresting become less easy to specify. They are assimilated into an increasingly familiar background atmosphere which, though important in setting the tone of things, is difficult to analyze. There is no better point at which to begin the study of city atmosphere than at the moment when a traveler returns from abroad.

3. The popular myths and expectations each visitor brings to the city will also affect the way in which he perceives it (see *14*). Sometimes a person's preconceptions about a city are relatively accurate distillations of its character, but preconceptions may also reinforce myths by filtering the visitor's perceptions to conform with his expectations. Preconceptions affect not only a person's perceptions of a city but what he reports about it.

The influence of a person's urban base line on his perceptions of a given city, the differences between the observations of the long-time inhibitant and those of the newcomer, and the filtering effect of personal expectations and stereotypes raise serious questions about the validity of travelers' reports. Moreover, no social psychologist wants to rely exclusively on verbal accounts if he is attempting to obtain an accurate and objective description of the cities' social texture, pace, and general atmosphere. What he needs to do is to devise means of embedding objective experimental measures in the daily flux of city life, measures that can accurately index the qualities of a given urban atmosphere.

EXPERIMENTAL COMPARISONS OF BEHAVIOR

Roy Feldman (15) incorporated these principles in a comparative study of behavior toward compatriots and foreigners in Paris, Athens, and Boston. Feldman wanted to see (i) whether absolute levels and patterns of helpfulness varied significantly from city to city, and (ii) whether inhabitants in each city tended to treat compatriots differently from foreigners. He examined five concrete behavioral episodes, each carried out by a team of native experimenters and a team of American experimenters in the three cities. The episodes involved (i) asking natives of the city for street directions; (ii) asking natives to mail a letter for the experimenter; (iii) asking natives if they had just dropped a dollar bill (or the Greek or French equivalent) when the money actually belonged to the experimenter himself; (iv) deliberately overpaying for goods in a store to see if the cashier would correct the mistake and return the excess money; and (v) determining whether taxicab drivers overcharged strangers and whether they took the most direct route available.

Feldman's results suggest some interesting contrasts in the profiles of the three cities. In Paris, for instance, certain stereotypes were borne out. Parisian cab drivers overcharged foreigners significantly more often than they overcharged compatriots. But other aspects of the Parisians' behavior were not in accord with American preconceptions: in mailing a letter for a stranger, Parisians treated foreigners significantly better than Athenians or Bostonians did, and, when asked to mail letters that were already stamped, Parisians actually treated foreigners better than they treated compatriots. Similarly, Parisians were significantly more honest than Athenians or Bostonians in resisting the temptation to claim money that was not theirs, and Parisians were the only citizens who were more honest with foreigners than with compatriots in this experiment.

Feldman's studies not only begin to quantify some of the variables that give a city its distinctive texture but they also provide a methodological model for other comparative research. His most important contribution is his successful application of objective, experimental measures to everyday situations, a mode of study which provides conclusions about urban life that are more pertinent than those achieved through laboratory experiments.

TEMPO AND PACE

Another important component of a city's atmosphere is its tempo or pace, an attribute frequently remarked on but less often studied.

Does a city have a frenetic, hectic quality, or is it easygoing and leisurely? In any empirical treatment of this question, it is best to start in a very simple way. Walking speeds of pedestrians in different cities and in cities and towns should be measured and compared. William Berkowitz (16) of Lafayette College has undertaken an extensive series of studies of walking speeds in Philadelphia, New York, and Boston, as well as in small and moderate-sized towns. Berkowitz writes that "there does appear to be a significant linear relation between walking speed and size of municipality, but the absolute size of the difference varies by less than ten percent."

Perhaps the feeling of rapid tempo is due not so much to absolute pedestrian speeds as to the constant need to dodge others in a large city to avoid collisions with other pedestrians. (One basis for computing the adjustments needed to avoid collisions is to hypothesize a set of mechanical manikins sent walking along a city street and to calculate the number of collisions when no adjustments are made. Clearly, the higher the density of manikins the greater the number of collisions per unit of time, or, conversely, the greater the frequency of adjustments needed in higher population densities to avoid collisions.)

Patterns of automobile traffic contribute to a city's tempo. Driving an automobile provides a direct means of translating feelings about tempo into measurable acceleration, and a city's pace should be particularly evident in vehicular velocities, patterns of acceleration, and latency of response to traffic signals. The inexorable tempo of New York is expressed, further, in the manner in which pedestrians stand at busy intersections, impatiently awaiting a change in traffic light, making tentative excursions into the intersection, and frequently surging into the street even before the green light appears.

VISUAL COMPONENTS

Hall has remarked (17) that the physical layout of the city also affects its atmosphere. A gridiron pattern of streets gives the visitor a feeling of rationality, orderliness, and predictability but is sometimes monotonous. Winding lanes or streets branching off at strange angles, with many forks (as in Paris or Greenwich Village), create feelings of surprise and esthetic pleasure, while forcing greater decision-making in plotting one's course. Some would argue that the visual component is all-important—that the "look" of Paris or New York can almost be equated with its atmosphere. To investigate this hypothesis, we might conduct studies in which only blind, or at least blindfolded, respondents were used.

We would no doubt discover that each city has a distinctive texture even when the visual component is eliminated.

SOURCES OF AMBIANCE

Thus far we have tried to pinpoint and measure some of the factors that contribute to the distinctive atmosphere of a great city. But we may also ask, Why do differences in urban atmosphere exist? How did they come about, and are they in any way related to the factors of density, large numbers, and heterogeneity discussed above?

First, there is the obvious factor that, even among great cities, populations and densities differ. The metropolitan areas of New York, London, and Paris, for example, contain 15 million, 12 million, and 8 million persons, respectively. London has average densities of 43 persons per acre, while Paris is more congested, with average densities of 114 persons per acre (18). Whatever characteristics are specifically attributable to density are more likely to be pronounced in Paris than in London.

A second factor affecting the atmosphere of cities is the source from which the populations are drawn (19). It is a characteristic of great cities that they do not reproduce their own populations, but that their numbers are constantly maintained and augmented by the influx of residents from other parts of the country. This can have a determining effect on the city's atmosphere. For example, Oslo is a city in which almost all of the residents are only one or two generations removed from a purely rural existence, and this contributes to its almost agricultural norms.

A third source of atmosphere is the general national culture. Paris combines adaptations to the demography of cities *and* certain values specific to French culture. New York is an admixture of American values and values that arise as a result of extraordinarily high density and large population.

Finally, one could speculate that the atmosphere of a great city is traceable to the specific historical conditions under which adaptations to urban overload occurred. For example, a city which acquired its mass and density during a period of commercial expansion will respond to new demographic conditions by adaptations designed to serve purely commercial needs. Thus, Chicago, which grew and became a great city under a purely commercial stimulus, adapted in a manner that emphasizes business needs. European capitals, on the other hand, incorporate many of the adaptations which were appropriate to the period of their increasing numbers and density. Because aristocratic values were prevalent at the time of the growth of these cities, the mechanisms developed for coping with overload were based on considerations other than pure efficiency. Thus, the manners, norms, and facilities of Paris and Vienna continue to reflect esthetic values and the idealization of leisure.

COGNITIVE MAPS OF CITIES

When we speak of "behavior comparisons" among cities, we must specify which parts of the city are most relevant for sampling purposes. In a sampling of "New Yorkers," should we include residents of Bay Ridge or Flatbush as well as inhabitants of Manhattan? And, if so, how should we weight our sample distribution? One approach to defining relevant boundaries in sampling is to determine which areas form the psychological or cognitive core of the city. We weight our samples most heavily in the areas considered by most people to represent the "essence" of the city.

The psychologist is less interested in the geographic layout of a city or in its political boundaries than in the cognitive representation of the city. Hans Blumenfeld (20) points out that the perceptual structure of a modern city can be expressed by the "silhouette" of the group of skyscrapers at its center and that of smaller groups of office buildings at its "subcenters" but that urban areas can no longer, because of their vast extent, be experienced as fully articulated sets of streets, squares, and space.

In *The Image of the City* (21), Kevin Lynch created a cognitive map of Boston by interviewing Bostonians. Perhaps his most significant finding was that, while certain landmarks, such as Paul Revere's house and the Boston Common, as well as the paths linking them, are known to almost all Bostonians, vast areas of the city are simply unknown to its inhabitants.

Using Lynch's technique, Donald Hooper (22) created a psychological map of New York from the answers to the study questionnaire on Paris, London, and New York. Hooper's results were similar to those of Lynch: New York appears to have a dense core of well-known landmarks in midtown Manhattan, surrounded by the vast unknown reaches of Queens, Brooklyn, and the Bronx. Times Square, Rockefeller Center, and the Fifth Avenue department stores alone comprise half the place specifically cited by respondents as the haunts in which they spent most of their time. However, outside the midtown area, only scattered landmarks were recognized. Another interesting pattern is evident: even the best-known symbols of New York are relatively self-contained, and the pathways joining them appear to be insignificant on the map.

The psychological map can be used for more than just sampling techniques. Lynch (*21*) argues, for instance, that a good city is highly "imageable," having many known symbols joined by widely known pathways, whereas dull cities are gray and nondescript. We might test the relative "imagibility" of several cities by determining the proportion of residents who recognize sampled geographic points and their accompanying pathways.

If we wanted to be even more precise we could construct a cognitive map that would not only show the symbols of the city but would measure the precise degree of cognitive significance of any given point in the city relative to any other. By applying a pattern of points to a map of New York City, for example, and taking photographs from each point, we could determine what proportion of a sample of the city's inhabitants could identify the locale specified by each point (see Figure 2). We might even take the subjects

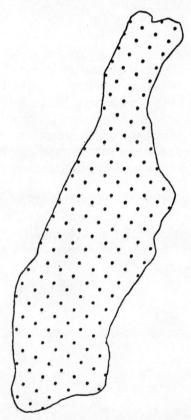

Figure 2. To create a psychological map of Manhattan, geographic points are sampled, and, from photographs, the subjects attempt to identify the location of each point. To each point a numerical index is assigned indicating the proportion of persons able to identify its location.

blindfolded to a point represented on the map, then remove the blindfold and ask them to identify their location from the view around them.

One might also use psychological maps to gain insight into the differing perceptions of a given city that are held by members of its cultural subgroups, and into the manner in which their perceptions may change. In the earlier stages of life, whites and Negroes alike probably have only a limited view of the city, centering on the immediate neighborhood in which they are raised. In adolescence, however, the field of knowledge of the white teen-ager probably undergoes rapid enlargement; he learns of opportunities in midtown and outlying sections and comes to see himself as functioning in a larger urban field. But the process of ghettoization, to which the black teen-ager is subjected, may well hamper the expansion of his sense of the city. These are speculative notions, but they are readily subject to precise test.

CONCLUSION

I have tried to indicate some organizing theory that starts with the basic facts of city life: large numbers, density, and heterogeneity. These are external to the individual. He experiences these factors as overloads at the level of roles, norms, cognitive functions, and facilities. These overloads lead to adaptive mechanisms which create the distinctive tone and behaviors of city life. These notions, of course, need to be examined by objective comparative studies of cities and towns.

A second perspective concerns the differing atmospheres of great cities, such as Paris, London, and New York. Each has a distinctive flavor, offering a differentiable quality of experience. More precise knowledge of urban atmosphere seems attainable through application of the tools of experimental inquiry.

REFERENCES AND NOTES

1. *New York Times* (25 June 1969).
2. L. Wirth, *American Journal of Sociology 44* (1938): 1. Wirth's ideas have come under heavy criticism by contemporary city planners, who point out that the city is broken down into neighborhoods, which fulfill many of the functions of small towns. See, for example, H. J. Gans, *People and Plans: Essays on Urban Problems and Solutions* (New York: Basic Books, 1968); J. Jacobs, *The Death and Life of Great American Cities* (New York: Random House, 1961); G. D. Suttles, *The Social Order of the Slum* (Chicago: University of Chicago Press, 1968).
3. G. Simmel, *The Sociology of Georg Simmel*, K. H. Wolff, ed., (New York: Macmillan, 1950). [English translation of G. Simmel, *Die Grosstadte und das Geistesleben Die Grossstadt* (Dresden: Jansch, 1903)].
4. R. L. Meier, *A Communications Theory of Urban Growth* (Cambridge, Mass.: M.I.T. Press, 1962).
5. S. Milgram and P. Hollander, *Nation* 25 (1964): 602.
6. B. Latané and J. Darley, *American Scientist* 57 (1969): 244.
7. S. Gaertner and L. Bickman, unpublished research, Graduate Center, The City University of New York.
8. D. Altman, M. Levine, M. Nadien, J. Villena, unpublished research, Graduate Center, The City University of New York.
9. P. G. Zimbardo, paper presented at the Nebraska Symposium on Motivation, 1969.
10. J. Waters, unpublished research, Graduate Center, The City University of New York.
11. W. McKenna and S. Morgenthau, unpublished research, Graduate Center, The City University of New York.
12. N. Abuza (Harvard University), "The Paris-London-New York Questionnaires," unpublished.
13. P. Abelson, *Science* 165 (1969): 853.
14. A. L. Strauss, ed. *The American City: A Sourcebook of Urban Imagery* (Chicago: Aldine, 1968).
15. R. E. Feldman, *Journal of Personality and Social Psychology* 10 (1968): 202.
16. W. Berkowitz, personal communication.
17. E. T. Hall, *The Hidden Dimension* (New York: Doubleday, 1966).
18. P. Hall, *The World Cities* (New York: McGraw-Hill, 1966).
19. R. E. Park, E. W. Burgess, R. D. McKenzie, *The City* (Chicago: University of Chicago Press, 1967), pp. 1–45.
20. H. Blumenfeld, in *The Quality of Urban Life* (Beverly Hills, Calif.: Sage, 1969).
21. K. Lynch, *The Image of the City* (Cambridge, Mass.: M.I.T. and Harvard University Press, 1960).
22. D. Hooper (Harvard University) unpublished.
23. Barbara Bengen worked closely with me in preparing the present version of this article. I thank Dr. Gary Winkel, editor of *Environment and Behavior*, for useful suggestions and advice.

CHAPTER

A Social-Psychological Model of Human Crowding Phenomena

DANIEL STOKOLS

Reprinted from the *Journal of the American Institute of Planners* 38, no. 2 (March, 1972): 72–83, by permission of the publisher and the author.

Three photographs in the original paper have been deleted for this publication.

The preparation of this paper was supported by United States Public Health Service Grant 5-T01 MH 07325. The author wishes to express his appreciation to John Schopler, Marilyn Rall, Bepi Pinner, and C. David Jenkins for their comments and suggestions concerning the issues discussed in this paper. Thanks are also due to Nehemia Friedland and Jeannette Stokols for their critical readings of the manuscript; and to Sidney Cohn and Vaida D. Thompson for their comments on an earlier version of the paper.

Most previous studies of the effects of crowding have emphasized factors external to man, such as population density and physical closeness. In the following chapter, however, Stokols goes a step further by pointing out that, although the amount and arrangement of space are important aspects of crowding, other *non-physical* factors are equally important, if not more so. For example, the degree to which a person experiences himself competing with others affects his feeling of being crowded. This feeling, then, is not solely the result of a physical environmental condition; it is a psychological experience largely dependent upon the presence of stress on the individual.

Stokols argues that the average citizen and the professional expert tend to view the phenomenon of crowding from very different perspectives. Urban planners and designers consider it from the *macro* or sociological point of view, ". . . where the main concern is with the effects of large scale urban population density upon societal and cultural integration." But it is at the *micro* level that crowding is experienced by the individual and this necessarily involves questions of personality and of specific situations.

242 Man as Manipulated by His Environment

Previous research on crowding has generally lacked a theoretical perspective. Moreover, there has been a tendency to view crowding in terms of spatial considerations alone and a failure to distinguish between the physical condition (density) and the psychological experience (crowding). In the present discussion, a heuristic model of human crowding phenomena is proposed which permits an integration of various theoretical perspectives and the derivation of experimental hypotheses. Although the limitation of space remains as the essential ingredient of crowding, the proposed model introduces personal and social variables which have a direct bearing on a person's perception of spatial restriction as well as on his attempts to cope with this constraint. The relation between the dimensions of the model is examined in terms of social-psychological theory. Finally, a program for future research is discussed.

Within the past decade, growing concern for the quality of the physical and social environment has prompted scientists from various academic disciplines to concentrate their research efforts upon contemporary ecological problems. A fundamental assumption underlying ecologically oriented research has been that an understanding of the relationship between organisms and their environment, gained through scientific inquiry, will ultimately provide guidelines for social planning and urban design.

Among the ecological phenomena which have attracted the attention of behavioral scientists are those related to spatial limitation and crowding. Problems of spatial restriction represent formidable topics for scientific inquiry due to their high degree of complexity. Like most concomitants of overpopulation and urbanization, such as pollution and scarcity of resources, crowding phenomena are highly interrelated with other societal problems—for example, poverty and racial discrimination. Hence, at the urban level it is difficult to separate the behavioral effects of spatial limitation from those of other variables.

Another source of complexity which hinders a comprehensive understanding of crowding is the variety of levels at which it is manifested throughout society. We can speak of a crowded home, neighborhood, or city. The types of variables which interact with spatial restriction undoubtedly vary from one level to the next. Consequently, the effects of crowding on human behavior are probably different at each level.

Finally, the ambiguity of vocabulary used to describe crowding phenomena has also made it difficult to subject problems of spatial limitation to empirical study. For instance, many writers often use the terms "density" and "crowding" interchangeably rather than distinguishing between the physical condition, density, and the psychological experience, crowding. Such confusion not only impairs the precise specification of independent and dependent variables, but also obstructs the development of a broad theoretical perspective from which to approach crowding phenomena.

In order for crowding to be rendered amenable to scientific inquiry, some of the above-mentioned complexities and ambiguities must be recognized, and an attempt must be made to resolve them. In this article I develop an analysis of human crowding phenomena and propose a conceptual model of crowding situations and their effects on human behavior. First, however, a brief review of previous approaches to the study of crowding is presented. A consideration of the contributions, as well as the inadequacies, of these approaches provides the foundation on which the proposed framework is developed.

Previous Research on Crowding

There have been four basic lines of behavioral research which relate to the issue of crowding: animal studies, correlational surveys utilizing census tract data, experiments on the human use of space, and experimental studies directly concerned with the effects of crowding on human behavior.

The well-known animal studies of Calhoun (1962, 1966) and his associates (Marsden, 1970) exemplify the first approach. By limiting the amount of space available to a community of Norwegian rats, Calhoun observed a phenomenon known as the "behavioral sink," that is, the simultaneous gathering of several animals at specific points in the community (for example, feeding areas) over long periods of time. Calhoun linked the crowded conditions of the behavioral sink to pathological behaviors exhibited by certain animals in the community: the neglect of maternal duties, hyper- and homosexuality, and the withdrawal of individual animals from social interaction.

An experiment by Christian, Flyger, and Davis (1960) provides further evidence regarding the detrimental effects of crowding upon animal populations. In this study, a herd of deer was confined to a small island and allowed to reproduce. As the number of deer increased, a pronounced decrease in reproductivity was observed.

The correlational studies of Schmitt (1957, 1966), Chombart

de Lauwe (1959), Winsborough (1965), and Mitchell (1971), which have relied upon census tract data, are examples of the second type of crowding research. The typical approach of such surveys is to correlate various measures of population density (for example, number of persons per net acre or per dwelling unit) with several indices of social and medical pathology (for example, rates of crime, tuberculosis, and suicide). Usually, the effects of variables, such as income level and education, are controlled through the technique of partial correlation.

The findings of these surveys suggest that population density is generally associated with social disorganization. Winsborough, however, has demonstrated that the positive correlation between density and pathology disappears when certain measures of social status are utilized as control variables. And Schmitt (1963) has observed that in Hong Kong, density per acre is not invariably associated with behavioral anomalies; other factors such as cultural traditions and the nature of residential land use seem to mediate the relationship between population density and human behavior.

The ecological research of Barker (1965, 1968) on behavior settings, and the work of Hall (1959, 1966) and Sommer (1967, 1969) on proxemics (the use of space in everyday behavior) represent the third type of investigation of crowding. Although these studies do not focus directly upon the behavioral effects of crowding, their inquiry into the perception and use of space is certainly germane to a consideration of problems arising from spatial restriction.

Barker, in his naturalistic studies on "undermanned" versus "overmanned" behavior settings, found that students of small schools generally achieved satisfaction by being competent, accepting challenges, and engaging in group activities, while students of large schools derived satisfaction more frequently out of vicarious, rather than direct, participation in group functions. The main implication of Hall's work on proxemics is that people differ in their habits, attitudes, and values concerning the use of space and interpersonal distance, and that differences along these dimensions are largely culture-bound. Finally, the message of Sommer's research regarding "personal space" is that the perception of spatial relations among objects is significantly influenced by the type of activity which generally occurs in a given area.

Experimental investigations directly concerned with the effects of spatial limitation on human behavior reflect the most recent approach to the study of crowding phenomena. Such studies have generally been of two types, those which define crowding in terms of group size and those which manipulate it in terms of room size.

The research of Ittelson, Proshansky, and Rivlin (1970), Hutt and Vaizey (1966), and Griffit and Veitch (1971) represent the first type of investigation, while those of Freedman (1970) and Freedman, Klevansky, and Ehrlich (1971) represent the second. Results from the first set of studies indicate that members of larger groups are more aggressive and asocial than those of smaller ones, regardless of whether the setting is a psychiatric ward, a playground, or a psychological experiment. The second set of experiments, however, demonstrates that when group size is kept constant but room size is varied, the task performance of subjects in the small room is no less efficient than that of subjects in the large room. Freedman did observe, though, in the small room condition, that interpersonal relations within female groups were more intimate and friendly than the affective behaviors manifested in male groups.

From the four categories of research outlined above, a preliminary picture of crowding phenomena begins to emerge. The animal studies portray crowding as a stress situation which develops over time. The physical condition of spatial limitation, which places constraints upon certain social activities (for example, allocation of food and sexual behavior), represents the necessary condition for crowding phenomena. As population density increases, spatial constraints become more acute until, finally, they eventuate in social disorganization and physiological pathology. Situations of crowding, then, are characterized both by the element of spatial restriction and by the manifestation of its deleterious effects on organisms over time.

The research on human populations, however, indicates that spatial restriction is not inevitably associated with social maladies. The survey studies, for instance, suggest that in Asian societies cultural traditions serve to offset the detrimental effects of high population density. Experiments concerning the human use of space provide further evidence that cultural norms mediate the perception and adjustment of interpersonal space. Such research also suggests that the type of activity performed in a given area largely determines whether the amount of available space is perceived as adequate or too limited. Finally, the laboratory investigations of human crowding demonstrate that when group size is held constant and the physical consequences of spatial restriction (for example, high temperature, stuffiness, limited movement) are controlled, high density exerts virtually no ill effects on human task performance. The research on human subjects, then, considered in light of the animal studies, indicates that spatial restriction serves as a necessary antecedent of, but not always a sufficient condition for, the arousal of crowding stress.

Although previous empirical approaches provide some insights into the nature of human crowding phenomena, interpretation of the findings from each line of inquiry is rendered difficult by methodological or conceptual inadequacies. For example, the applicability of data from animal research to the analysis of human crowding is limited by problems of ecological validity (Brunswik, 1956) which arise whenever one generalizes from communities of rats to societies of men. The findings of survey studies are plagued by the causal ambiguities of correlational research. The results from experiments on personal space, while interesting, do not relate specifically to the experience of human crowding. And the more direct experimental investigations of human crowding have not been guided by any coherent theoretical perspective.

The lack of a conceptual framework concerning crowding has led to a failure in laboratory studies to distinguish between the different types of variables which mediate the experience of crowding stress, such as spatial, temporal, social, and personal factors. Hence, most investigators have defined crowding in terms of spatial considerations alone. Moreover, there has been little consensus among experimenters regarding the specification of independent and dependent variables. Thus, in some studies the manipulation of density has been accomplished through variations in group size, while in others it has been effected through the use of small and large rooms.

Direct experimental investigation appears to be the most advanced and promising approach to the analysis of human crowding. In order to resolve some of the ambiguities which have previously hindered research, a conceptual framework for the experimental study of human crowding is introduced in the ensuing discussion.

A Conceptual Framework for the Analysis of Human Crowding

An elementary definition of crowding. Before the concept of human crowding can be framed as a psychological research topic, some attempt must be made to define, or describe, this concept. As a preliminary definition, we will assume that a state of crowding exists, and is perceived as such by an individual, when the individual's demand for space exceeds the available supply of such space. A similar conceptualization of crowding has been proposed by Kwan (1967) and by Proshansky, Ittelson, and Rivlin (1970).

While the above definition is rudimentary, it enables us to draw a crucial distinction between the concepts of *density* and *crowding*. Density denotes a physical condition involving the limitation of space. Crowding, on the other hand, refers to a situation in which the restrictive aspects of limited space are perceived by the individuals exposed to them. The recognition of spatial inadequacy arouses the experience of psychological and physiological stress. Thus, density is a univariate condition of limited space, without motivational overtones, whereas crowding is a multivariate phenomenon, resulting from the interaction of spatial, social, and personal factors, and characterized by the adverse manifestations of stress.

Some additional distinctions. In order to delineate, more specifically, the scope of the proposed model, four additional distinctions regarding the conceptualization of crowding are required. First, it is important to differentiate between crowding as a *stressor situation* and the experience of crowding as a *syndrome of stress*. The first concept refers to sources of crowding stress, that is, those variables whose interaction evokes the experience of being crowded. The second concept connotes the experience of crowding itself and its various levels of impact within the individual or group, that is, the manifestations of physiological and psychological stress, or social disorganization. Each of the above meanings is represented as a separate dimension of the proposed model.

Secondly, we can distinguish between *nonsocial* and *social* crowding. In the first case, a person's supply of useable space is restricted at what he perceives to be an inadequate level by purely physical factors. For example, an astronaut may feel crowded because of the cramped quarters of his space capsule, or a person sitting at a table may feel crowded if his desk is overly cluttered with books, papers, and a typewriter. Among the major types of variables affecting an individual's experience of nonsocial crowding are: spatial factors including the amount and arrangement of space, stressor variables such as noise or glare which heighten the salience of physical constraints, and personal characteristics including idiosyncratic skills and traits.

In situations of social crowding, the individual's awareness of spatial restriction is related directly to the presence of other persons, as well as to his relationship to them. The number of people in a given area largely determines the proportion of space available to each person. While situations of nonsocial crowding involve spatial restriction caused by physical variables alone, conditions of social crowding introduce social constraints on available space and imply competition with other persons for scarce resources (for example, space and materiel).

An individual may feel crowded in the midst of strangers, but quite comfortable and secure in the presence of an equal number of friends. The factors which determine one's experience of social crowding include the variables already mentioned in relation to nonsocial crowding, as well as social factors such as group structure and activity variables. The ensuing discussion focuses upon social crowding situations because they involve a greater number of component variables than do nonsocial situations and thereby afford a more complete application of the proposed model of crowding.

A third major distinction can be drawn between situations of *crowding* and those of *undercrowding*. The first situation involves an acute restriction of space, while the latter is characterized by an excessive abundance of space (that is, a situation in which an individual's supply of space greatly exceeds his demand for space; *uncrowded* situations, on the other hand, are those in which there is a balance between an individual's supply of and demand for space). Each type of situation elicits characteristic forms of stress. While crowded persons may feel constrained and infringed upon, undercrowded individuals tend to experience a need for enclosure and affiliation with others. The present discussion is concerned mainly with crowding situations, although the proposed model of crowding can be extended to a consideration of undercrowded conditions.

The fourth and final distinction concerns the levels at which human response to crowding can be considered. Two basic levels of crowding phenomena are distinguishable: the sociological, or *macrocosmic*, level; and the psychological, or *microcosmic*, level. The first represents the level at which most urban designers and environmental behavioral scientists approach crowding. Its main concern is with the effects of large scale urban population density upon societal and cultural integration. The psychological, or microcosmic, level is primarily concerned with the impact of perceived spatial restriction on the individual's behavior. The experience of crowding is viewed as a syndrome of psychological stress, the intensity of which is determined by several independent factors. This article deals primarily with the microcosmic level.

An Equilibrium Model of Human Response to Crowding
Because the individual and the environment are the basic units involved in crowding phenomena, the variables which mediate an individual's perception of and response to crowding can be subsumed under two major categories: qualities of the physical and social environment, and personal attributes of the individual. Qualities of the physical environment include the amount and arrangement of available space, as well as stressors which affect the salience and immediacy of spatial variables (for example, noise, glare, and length of exposure time). Features of the social environment include variables which are introduced by the presence of other per-

sons (for example, status allocation, the division of labor, and group size). Finally, personal attributes of the individual include momentary states of arousal (for example, hunger and sexual arousal), idiosyncratic skills and weaknesses related to effective operation in the environment (for example, intelligence, strength, and agility), and personality characteristics (for example, internal-external locus of control and comparison level).

The present model applies to situations involving spatial restriction in which personality and social factors interact with physical variables to induce psychological or physiological stress in the individual. The experience of such stress provokes behavioral, perceptual, or cognitive responses designed to alleviate physical discomfort or psychological strain. Hence, the model represents a multivariate schema of response to crowding in that it incorporates several distinct sets of input and output variables. Moreover, the relationship between input and output factors is one of equilibrium in the sense that extremes in one type of variable are compensated for through adjustments in other types of variables so as to maintain a state of equilibrium between the individual and the environment.

As illustrated in Figure 1, the model consists of four basic dimensions: environmental variables, E; personal attributes, P; intensity and type of stress, S; and adaptive and maladaptive responses to stress, R. There are five major phases of crowding phenomena which are inherent in the model. Their numerical ordering denotes a chronological sequence of events: (1) the interaction between E and P variables which determines their respective salience and immediacy to the individual; (2) the perception of that subset of interactions between E and P variables which induces crowding stress in the individual (that is, psychological and physiological strain); (3) the provocation of tension-reducing responses in the person (these may include cognitive, perceptual, or behavioral adjustments); (4a) the enactment of specific responses aimed at modifying either environmental qualities or (4b) personal attributes (for example, moving to a less crowded area, or adjusting one's perception of the situation so as to render it more tolerable); and (5a) the adaptive or maladaptive consequences of environmental, as well as (5b) personal adjustments.

In the present framework, a response is adaptive to the extent that it relieves either environmental or personal sources of strain and breaks the cycle of crowding stress (in Figure 1, this is represented by the broken arrows). A response is maladaptive to the degree that it intensifies strain due to environmental and personal factors and thereby perpetuates the cycle of crowding stress (in

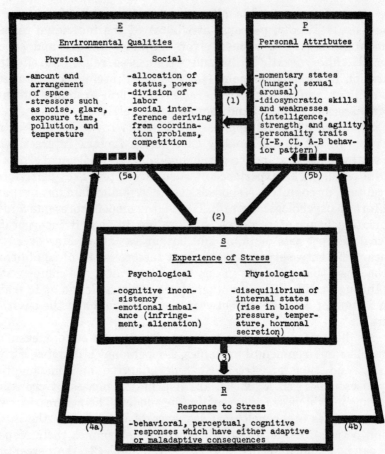

Figure 1.   *An Equilibrium Model of Human Response to Crowding*

this case, the arrows of [5a] and [5b] in Figure 1 would be solid).

According to the present analysis, all crowding situations involve stress, and occurrence of this stress cannot be predicted on the basis of spatial considerations alone. Rather, the experience of crowding must be understood as a phenomenon which develops over time, and whose development pattern and intensity are determined through a combination of environmental and personal factors. If several people occupy a small room in which there is a relatively small amount of space per person, yet these people feel completely comfortable and unrestricted, then a situation of crowding does not exist. On the other hand, if fewer persons in a larger room feel restricted and infringed upon by each other, then a state of crowding does exist.

Regardless of the specific environmental and personal factors involved, all situations of crowding seem to involve similar manifestations of stress. The basic forms of crowding stress have already been mentioned, namely, psychological and physiological strain. Psychological stress can be characterized as two types: cognitive inconsistency stemming from the realization that one's demand for space exceeds the available supply of such space, and emotional imbalance resulting from feelings of infringement, alienation, and lack of privacy. Physiological stress involves a disequilibrium in one's internal response systems (for example, increased blood pressure, temperature, or adrenalin secretion) and can be triggered by purely spatial variables, as evidenced in the discomfort of feeling cramped. It may also arise through the interaction of spatial variables with social and personality factors. A person with high affiliative needs, for example, who finds himself in a small room with several unfriendly strangers, may experience physiological symptoms of anxiety stemming from feelings of alienation and detachment. Thus, physiological stress is often aroused by psychological strain.

In the present model, the experience of crowding stress provokes tension-reducing responses which occur in order to reduce physical or psychological discomfort. The particular form of one's response to crowding will be a function of the relative intensity of environmental and personal factors and of the degree to which they can be modified. When spatial variables can be readily altered, a person who feels crowded will most likely adopt a behavioral mode of response. For example, an individual can increase his amount of personal space by leaving the crowded situation. In cases where overt behavioral adjustments of spatial variables are limited, perceptual and cognitive modes of reducing crowding stress will be more likely to occur. In such situations, a person may modify his standards of spatial adequacy so as to alleviate the sensation of crowding.

Adaptive responses to crowding are those which reduce the stressful effects of perceived spatial restriction. The reduction of stress is accomplished through the effective adjustment of either physical, social, or personal factors. Maladaptive responses, on the other hand, are those which fail to alleviate the experience of crowding stress. For example, a person's decision to remain at a crowded party with several strangers would be adaptive if it eventually led to pleasant interaction and friendship with other persons. The decision to remain, however, would be maladaptive if the person was unable to strike up a conversation with someone at the party and left feeling alienated and depressed.

Derivation of Hypotheses From Social-Psychological Theory
The major features of the proposed model of human crowding have
been delineated above; hypotheses regarding the interaction of its
various components remain to be specified. In the ensuing discussion, the relationships between the four dimensions of the model
are considered in terms of social-psychological theory. A set of experimental hypotheses is derived by examining examples of situations in which environmental and personal factors engender the
experience of crowding.

ENVIRONMENTAL AND PERSONAL
SOURCES OF CROWDING STRESS

Some of the environmental and personal factors which yield conditions of crowding are categorized in Figure 1. Because these variables are quite numerous, only a representative sample will be discussed. It should be emphasized that the variables included in each
box of Figure 1 are not intended to comprise an exhaustive inventory of the parameters of crowding. Rather, they reflect the variety
of factors, within each of the four dimensions of the model, which
may contribute to an individual's experience of crowding. Determination of the relative salience and importance of each factor,
across various situations of crowding, is a task for future research.

Physical variables. The amount and arrangement of space are
probably the most salient physical dimensions of a crowded situation. The amount of space available to a person represents a crucial
determinant of his behavioral freedom. As space becomes scarce,
the number of behavioral alternatives available to an individual decreases. Although the amount of space sets limits on one's range of
behavioral freedom, the intensity of spatial restriction can be altered, somewhat, through various arrangements of the available
space. For example, a small room may be made to appear larger by
surrounding it with mirrored walls or by judiciously arranging
furniture. As Michelson (1970) points out, the arrangement of
dwelling space in Japan may be one factor which mitigates the
adverse effects of high population density there.

In light of the research on crowding, mentioned earlier,
spatial limitation appears to be a variable whose latent unpleasant
properties are activated only through its interaction with other
aspects of the specific situation. The immediacy and salience of reduced space are intensified, for instance, through the operation of
physical stress factors such as temperature and noise. Griffit and
Veitch (1971) observed that interpersonal affective responses were
significantly more negative under conditions of high temperature

and high density than under those of comfortable temperature and low density. Also, it is plausible that noise, through its unwelcomed infringement on the individual's personal space, also serves to increase the salience of spatial restriction and thereby intensify the experience of crowding.

Social factors. The presence of other persons introduces several factors which may heighten the individual's sense of spatial restriction. The type of activity engaged in with others will directly affect the salience of limited space. The impact of activity variables on the experience of crowding is evident at a football game, where thousands of people are packed into a giant stadium. While the game is being played, everyone is completely engrossed in the action, and the limitation of space goes unnoticed or is forgotten. As soon as the game ends, however, the restrictions of spatial limitation are immediately felt. Each person becomes concerned with exiting the stadium as quickly as possible. It is at this point that the individual must coordinate his actions with those of other persons. The necessity of behavioral coordination as a means of limiting social interference and insuring the efficient use of space (for example, avoidance of traffic jams) represents one social factor which may intensify the experience of crowding.

The extent to which an individual perceives himself to be competing with others for scarce resources represents another social variable which heightens the salience of limited space. In the previous example, access to the stadium exits represents a commonly desired resource. The individual's realization that the other fans are competing with him for a direct path to the exits is likely to exacerbate his sensation of spatial restriction. In other situations, competition may concern nonspatial commodities such as power and prestige. In such instances, competitive feelings arouse a tendency to view the presence of others as a threat to the individual's general welfare and an infringement on his privacy. In the context of spatial limitation, these perceptions are likely to promote the experience of crowding and a heightened concern for personal space.

For a group which is characterized by a high degree of organization and clearly defined goals, the susceptibility or immunity of its members to crowding stress can be considered in terms of the two basic aspects of group structure suggested by Homans (1950), the internal and external systems. The first facet of social structure encompasses those factors which promote cohesion and minimize conflict among group members (for example, a well-defined leadership hierarchy, status consensus, and widely held norms). The second system of social structure concerns variables which enable the group to adapt to the demands of its external environment (for example, the division of labor, which facilitates task efficiency).

The internal and external systems operate to maintain social equilibrium. To the extent that these systems are weak, group structure breaks down and its members experience stress. Since limited space can be characterized as an external contingency which threatens the group's equilibrium, the capacity of the internal and external systems to deal effectively with spatial constraints determines whether or not members of the group will experience crowding stress. For example, if the group members are unable to coordinate their activities efficiently, the restrictions of limited space are likely to become salient. Or, if the "correspondence of outcomes" (Thibaut and Kelley, 1959), that is, the commonality of interest, among group members is low, interpersonal relations within the group will tend to be quite competitive. As noted earlier, intragroup competition interferes with the ability of each member to cope with spatial constraints and thereby promotes the experience of crowding.

Personal factors. This set of variables includes momentary states of arousal, idiosyncratic skills, weaknesses, and personality traits which affect an individual's ability to cope with the limitation of space. It is quite plausible that certain personal attributes serve to protect an individual from the ill effects of crowding, while others tend to predispose him to the dissatisfactions and health hazards of crowding situations.

The temporary states of hunger and sexual arousal, for example, may heighten a person's experience of crowding by making salient his competition with others for scarce resources, or by increasing his need for privacy. Under conditions of spatial limitation, then, prolonged hunger and sexual deprivation would intensity an individual's frustration, dissatisfaction, and sense of crowding.

Idiosyncratic skills and weaknesses will also have some bearing upon a person's ability to cope with spatial constraints. An intelligent person, for example, will be more able to find creative solutions to problems of crowding than will an unintelligent one. Similarly, a strong person will be able to exert control over limited resources more readily than will a weak person. And, under conditions of limited space, an agile individual will find it easier to coordinate his actions with those of other people than will a clumsy one. The personal traits of intelligence, strength, and agility, thus, would contribute to the minimization of crowding stress.

The dimension of "internal-external locus of control" (Rotter, 1966) represents a personality characteristic that may be quite relevant to the intensity of the individual's crowding experience. This dimension concerns the degree to which a person perceives the quality of his experiences as being under either personal or environmental control. In situations of crowding, it is plausible that "internal" individuals will be able to perform more efficiently than "external" individuals within the constraints of spatial restriction. This would be especially true if behavioral modes of alleviating crowding stress were available. But if conditions of crowding are prolonged and unrelievable, "internals" may experience more frustration with being confined and unable to exert their usual control over the situation. "Externals," however, perceiving themselves to be generally under environmental control anyway, might experience relatively less dissatisfaction with spatial restriction. In situations such as these, "externals" may be more readily adaptable to crowding stress than "internals."

The concept of "comparison level," as formulated by Thibaut and Kelley (1959), is also relevant to a consideration of personal factors which affect the individual's perception of crowding. Comparison level (CL) is a criterion of outcome acceptability with which an individual evaluates the attractiveness of a situation in terms of what he expects or feels he deserves. Individuals who are generally used to having large amounts of space at their disposal (for example, individuals raised in a rural setting) would be likely to develop a higher CL regarding the amount of space considered to be adequate in any situation than would individuals who have had more experience with spatial limitations (for example, residents of a large city). Hence, the former would be more apt to experience frustration over spatial constraints than the latter. This conceptualization may explain Cassel's (1970) observation that newcomers to a situation of crowding tend to be more vulnerable to its adverse effects than persons who have had previous experience with crowded situations.

Another individual characteristic which may mediate the experience of crowding is the coronary-prone behavior pattern described by Jenkins (1971). This behavioral syndrome is characterized by extremes of competitiveness, impatience, and overinvolvement with work. Individuals who manifest this pattern are referred to as "Type A's," whereas individuals who tend to be patient, easygoing, and relaxed are labelled "Type B's."

In situations of crowding, Type A's should be highly susceptible to the dissatisfactions and bodily imbalances caused by spatial restriction, while Type B's should be relatively resistant to these strains. The characteristics of impatience, competitiveness, and restlessness, embodied in the coronary-prone behavior pattern, would be likely to arouse an accentuated sense of frustration and anxiety under conditions of prolonged and unalterable crowding.

THE EXPERIENCE OF, AND RESPONSE TO, CROWDING STRESS

Psychological stress. Two manifestations of psychological stress in situations of crowding have been distinguished above, cognitive inconsistency and emotional imbalance. In many instances, the former type of stress precipitates the latter.

Cognitive inconsistency, in the context of crowding phenomena, has been characterized as the recognized disparity between an individual's supply of and demand for space. A person's realization that he is unable to supplement his supply of space evokes an awareness that his range of behavioral freedom is restricted. According to Brehm (1966), such an awareness should provoke "psychological reactance," that is, a motivational state involving feelings of preemption and infringement, and resulting in behavior directed toward the reestablishment of threatened or eliminated freedom. A similar conclusion is reached by Proshansky, Ittelson, and Rivlin (1970), who consider crowding to be a situation involving the restriction of an individual's behavioral choice. They point out that a person's reactance against crowding will be especially intense if his restriction of freedom is due to the presence of other persons who infringe upon his privacy.

In situations of crowding, then, psychological reactance can be viewed as the motivational or emotional consequence of cognitive inconsistency stemming from the recognized discrepancy between one's supply of and demand for space. According to the present model, an individual will alleviate his reactance to crowding through an appropriate adjustment of either environmental variables, personal factors, or both. Furthermore, his adoption of a behavioral, perceptual, or cognitive mode of response will depend upon the relative intensity and flexibility of these factors.

Brehm's reactance theory, Festinger's (1957) dissonance theory, and the cognitive consistency theory of Rosenberg and Abelson (1960) provide a basis for considering some of the manifestations and determinants of the three modes of response to psychological stress under conditions of crowding. According to Brehm, the greater the magnitude of an individual's reactance, the more he will attempt to reestablish his lost or threatened freedom. The magnitude of reactance will depend upon the importance of that freedom to the individual, as well as upon the degree of freedom of behavior eliminated or threatened. Brehm discusses two basic means of reestablishing freedom. The first involves a direct reestablishment of freedom through the enactment of the forbidden or threatened behavior. When there are restraints against this type of response, the second mode of reestablishing freedom, which involves the symbolic attainment of freedom "by implication," will occur. In this case, the person will engage in behavior similar to that which has been prevented.

An example of direct reestablishment of freedom would be an individual's exit from an overly crowded room. If, however, the person was confined to the crowded area, then he might attempt to reestablish his freedom symbolically, by withdrawing from social interaction. This type of behavior would symbolize, or approximate, the unavailable behavioral option of leaving the room. Through this mode of response, the person would reestablish his autonomy by implication.

The methods of alleviating reactance, discussed by Brehm, represent behavioral modes of inconsistency-resolution. Yet, in certain situations of crowding, the costs of attempting to reestablish one's behavioral freedom, either directly or indirectly, far outweigh the potential advantages of such action. Conditions of crowding may arise from which it is physically impossible to withdraw and within which withdrawal from social interaction would be maladaptive. The members of a jury, for example, may find themselves operating under such conditions, especially if their chamber is cramped and their deliberation prolonged. In such situations, where reactance against spatial restriction cannot be alleviated behaviorally, a perceptual or cognitive mode of stress-resolution must be employed.

The members of the jury might alleviate their reactance by becoming thoroughly engrossed in deliberation so as to minimize the salience of their spatial restriction. By concentrating on the gravity of their decision rather than on the discomforts of their chamber, they are able to alleviate the strain of feeling crowded. This type of reactance-resolution represents a perceptual mode of response to crowding. By focusing upon the task dimensions of the situation, the spatial constraints which cannot be eliminated directly or indirectly become less noticeable and hence less stressful.

The adjustment of cognitive elements so as to render them less discrepant represents an alternative mode of reactance-resolution and is especially adaptive in situations where reestablishment of freedom is either impossible or too costly. The jurors, in our example, realizing that they must remain together until a final verdict is reached, make an implicit decision to give up the freedom of voluntarily leaving the jury chamber. Such a decision should elicit reactance against behavioral restriction to the extent that room space is inadequate and the deliberation prolonged. In terms of Festinger's (1957) dissonance theory, reactance against spatial and temporal stress factors can be characterized as a cognitive element, dissonant with the decision to remain in the situation. Cognitive dissonance, deriving from the discrepancy between the discomforts of crowding and the decision to endure them, can be alleviated, essentially, by increasing the desirability of the chosen alternative (remaining in the jury chamber) and decreasing the desirability of the rejected alternative (leaving the chamber). For example, the jurors may attempt to convince themselves that the case on which they are deliberating is extremely interesting and unique. Participating in jury deliberation would therefore seem enjoyable. Or they may persuade themselves that withdrawal from the jury would represent a dishonorly abdication of civil duty.

According to the cognitive consistency theory of Rosenberg and Abelson (1960), the jurors' attitude toward remaining in the chamber should become more favorable to the extent that their action can be instrumentally linked to positively evaluated objects or values. For example, the decision to remain on the jury may be judged as a good, wise, useful, or moral action if it is associated with the "pursuit of justice" or the attainment of valuable experience. In terms of reactance-resolution, the more favorable the jurors feel about their decision to remain in the chamber, the more tolerable will be their spatial restriction and the less reactance they will feel toward it.

Physiological stress. It has so far been assumed that the individual will be able, ultimately, to alleviate his psychological reactance against crowding through the utilization of behavioral, perceptual, or cognitive modes of inconsistency resolution. Yet under certain conditions, the person will be unable to cope successfully with psychological stress resulting from involuntary or prolonged exposure to crowding. The maladaptive consequences of inappropriate (or inadequate) response to crowding will be manifested as feelings of frustration, alienation, and impatience, but they become particularly noticeable and potentially dangerous as manifestations of physiological disorders.

Physiological stress arising from reactance against the experience of crowding can be quite detrimental to an individual's health and general well-being. Researchers in the medical and public health professions have continually emphasized the general relationship between stress and physiological maladies (Cannon, 1932; Levine and Scotch, 1970; Selye, 1956). Rene Dubos (1968) reports that "physiological tests have revealed that crowding commonly results in an increased secretion of various hormones which affect the whole human physiology. An adequate hormonal activity is essential for well-being, but any excess has a variety of harmful effects" (p. 153).

Cassel (1970) has also discussed the relationship between hormonal disequilibrium and the incidence of disease. He contends that crowding increases the risk of disease by heightening social and emotional strain, rather than by increasing the opportunity for spread of infection. Cassel proposes that the role of social factors is to increase the susceptibility of the organism to disease through "the activation of inappropriate neuroendocrine arousal mechanisms" (p. 18).

In certain instances, physiological imbalance may have adaptive value for the individual, especially if it continues to provoke responses which finally eventuate in an alleviation of crowding stress. A detailed analysis of human adaptation to physiological stress is provided by Dubos (1965) and Selye (1956). For the purposes of the present discussion, though, it is sufficient to point out that prolonged exposure to the psychological and physiological stresses of crowding can have detrimental consequences for the individual's health.

A SET OF EXPERIMENTAL HYPOTHESES CONCERNING CROWDING

The preceding analysis of human crowding phenomena suggests several hypotheses which can be tested experimentally.

1. The limitation of space will engender an experience of crowding to the extent that it introduces noxious physical effects (for example, rise in temperature, stuffiness) or places constraints on personal or social activities (e.g., the restriction of free movement).

2. Under conditions of spatial limitation:

(a) a noisy situation will be perceived as more crowded than a quiet one;

(b) a cluttered area will appear more crowded than one in which physical objects are neatly arranged;

(c) situations involving social interference (for example, competition) will be perceived as more crowded than those in which such interference is absent;

(d) individuals who perceive their reinforcements, in general, to be internally controlled will feel more crowded as time of exposure to the situation increases, and

(e) persons who are, by nature, aggressive or impatient

will experience a stronger sensation of being crowded than individuals who are characteristically easygoing and relaxed.

In order to test the above hypotheses, independent variables representing physical, social, and personal sources of crowding stress can be factorially combined to assess their additive and interactive impact upon the individual. This approach permits an orthogonal manipulation of factors such as the amount and arrangement of space, noise level, or social interference. The quantity of available space per person, for example, can be varied through the use of large and small rooms, as suggested by Freedman (1970). Personality measures may also be included in the design as group composition variables or covariates.

The experimental analysis of human crowding also requires careful specification of dependent measures designed to assess the experience of crowding. Four types of assessments may be employed: subjective reports of discomfort (for example, in terms of feeling "cramped") or of dislike for other people in the group; observational indices of stress in terms of reduced eye contact with others, hostile remarks, or facial expressions; performance criteria relating to task efficiency; and physiological indicators of strain such as increased blood pressure or galvanic skin response.

Although the proposed model is primarily concerned with the psychological aspects of crowding phenomena, the experimental approach outlined here is potentially relevant to macrocosmic levels of crowding. Since urban crowding can be conceptualized as an aggregation of microcosmic crowding phenomena, the understanding of crowding at the psychological level could have broad implications for dealing with sociological manifestations of crowding.

REFERENCES

R. G. Barker, "Explorations in Ecological Psychology," *American Psychologist* 20, no. 1 (1965): 1–14.

———, *Ecological Psychology* (Stanford: Stanford University Press, 1968).

J. Brehm, *A Theory of Psychological Reactance* (New York: Academic Press, 1966).

E. Brunswik, *Perception and the Representative Design of Psychological Experiments* (Berkeley: University of California Press, 1956).

J. B. Calhoun, "Population Density and Social Pathology," *Scientific American* 206 (February, 1962): 139–48.

———, "The Role of Space in Animal Sociology," *The Journal of Social Issues* 22, no. 4 (1966): 46–59.

W. B. Cannon, *The Wisdom of the Body* (New York: W. W. Norton, 1932).

J. Cassel, "Health Consequences of Population Density and Crowding," unpublished manuscript, School of Public Health, University of North Carolina, Chapel Hill, 1970.

P. Chombart de Lauwe, *Famille et Habitation* (Paris: Editions du Centre National de la Recherche Scientifique, 1959.)

J. Christian, V. Flyger, and D. Davis, "Factors in the Mass Mortality of a Herd of Sika Deer *Cervus nippon*," *Chesapeake Science* 1 (1960): 79–95.

R. Dubos, *Man Adapting* (New Haven: Yale University Press, 1965).

———, *So Human an Animal* (New York: Scribners, 1968).

L. Festinger, *A Theory of Cognitive Dissonance* (Evanston, Ill.: Row, Peterson, and Co., 1957).

J. Freedman, "The Effects of Crowding on Human Behavior," unpublished manuscript, Department of Psychology, Columbia University, 1970.

J. Freedman, S. Klevansky, and P. Ehrlich, "The Effect of Crowding on Human Task Performance," *Journal of Applied Social Psychology* 1 (1971): 7–25.

W. Griffit and R. Veitch, "Hot and Crowded: Influences of Population Density and Temperature on Interpersonal Affective Behavior," *Journal of Personality and Social Psychology* 17, no. 1 (1971): 92–98.

E. Hall, *The Silent Language* (Greenwich, Conn.: Premier Books, 1959).

———, *The Hidden Dimension* (Garden City, N.Y.: Doubleday, 1966).

G. Homans, *The Human Group* (New York: Harcourt, Brace, and World, 1950).

C. Hutt and M. Vaizey, "Differential Effects of Group Density on Social Behavior," *Nature* 209 (March 26, 1966): 1371–2.

W. Ittelson, H. Proshansky, and L. Rivlin, "The Environmental Psychology of the Psychiatric Ward," in Proshansky, Ittelson, and Rivlin, eds., *Environmental Psychology* (New York: Holt, Rinehart and Winston, 1970).

C. D. Jenkins, "Psychologic and Social Precursors of Coronary Disease," *New England Journal of Medicine* 284 (February 4, 1971): 244–55; (February 11, 1971): 307–17.

W. T. Kwan, "Overcrowding as a Form of Environmental Stress—a Preliminary Inquiry," departmental paper, Department of City and Regional Planning, University of North Carolina, Chapel Hill, 1967.

S. Levine and N. Scotch, *Social Stress* (Chicago: Aldine Publishing Co., 1970).

H. Marsden, "Crowding and Animal Behavior," paper presented at American Psychological Association 1970 annual convention.

W. H. Michelson, *Man and His Urban Environment: A Sociological Approach* (Reading, Mass.: Addison-Wesley, 1970).

R. Mitchell, "Some Social Implications of High Density Housing," *American Sociological Review* 36 (February, 1971): 18–29.

H. Proshansky, W. Ittelson, and L. Rivlin, "Freedom of Choice and Behavior in a Physical Setting," in Proshansky, Ittelson, and Rivlin, eds., *Environmental Psychology* (New York: Holt, Rinehart and Winston, 1970), pp. 173–82.

M. Rosenberg and R. Abelson, "An Analysis of Cognitive Balancing," in C. Hovland and M. Rosenberg, eds., *Attitude Organization and Change* (New Haven: Yale University Press, 1960), pp. 112–63.

J. B. Rotter, "Generalized Expectancies of Internal versus External Control of Reinforcement," *Psychological Monographs* 80 (1, Whole No. 609, 1966).

R. S. Schmitt, "Density, Delinquency and Crime in Honolulu," *Sociology and Social Research* 41 (March-April, 1957): 274–76.

R. C. Schmitt, "Implications of Density in Hong Kong," *Journal of the American Institute of Planners* 29, no. 3 (1963): 210–17.

———, "Density, Health, and Social Disorganization," *Journal of the American Institute of Planners* 32, no. 1 (1966): 38–40.

H. Selye, *The Stress of Life* (New York: McGraw-Hill, 1956).

R. Sommer, *Personal Space—the Behavioral Basis of Design* (Englewood Cliffs, N.J.: Prentice Hall, 1969).

J. Thibaut and H. H. Kelley, *The Social Psychology of Groups* (New York: Wiley, 1959).

H. Winsborough, "The Social Consequences of High Population Density," *Law and Contemporary Problems* 30, no. 1 (1965): 120–26.

CHAPTER

Some Sources of Residential Satisfaction in an Urban Slum

MARC FRIED
PEGGY GLEICHER

Reprinted from the *Journal of the American Institute of Planners* 27, no. 4 (November, 1961): 305–15, by permission of the publisher and the authors.

Marc Fried received his doctorate from the Department of Social Relations at Harvard. Professionally a clinical psychologist, he has devoted himself largely to interdisciplinary research.

Peggy Gleicher received her Bachelor's Degree from Brooklyn College. She has done graduate work at Columbia and has had long-standing contact, in several capacities, with social research organizations.

This report is part of a study entitled "Relocation and Mental Health: Adaptation Under Stress," conducted by the Center for Community Studies in the Department of Psychiatry of the Massachusetts General Hospital and the Harvard Medical School. The research is supported by the National Institute of Mental Health, Grant No. 3M 9137-C3. We are grateful to Erich Lindemann, the Principal Investigator, and to Leonard Duhl of the Professional Services Branch, NIMH, for their continued help and encouragement. Edward Ryan has contributed in many ways to the final formulations of this paper, and Chester Hartman and Joan Levin have given criticism and advice.

In the following chapter Fried and Gleicher raise essentially the same question in Boston as did Hollingshead and Rogler in Puerto Rico: why, in the name of all that's holy (and middle class) do people object to being better off? In answering that question, Hollingshead and Rogler emphasized the cultural codes of conduct and value that were violated by the regulations governing occupancy of new and improved housing. In contrast, Fried and Gleicher stress what the slum resident is forced to give up when urban renewal demands his relocation.

With but a moment's consideration, the reader will identify some of the important losses suffered by the relocated slum dweller. Perhaps most immediately obvious is the simple comfort of familiarity, of knowing one's way around, versus the uneasiness associated with the new and alien. But more important, surely, is the network of local social relationships that is weakened or destroyed by dispersion. Fried and Gleicher indeed acknowledge and describe these effects of relocation and they go on to surprise us.

They argue that the lower-class slum resident conceptualizes living space in a very different way from the middle-class resident. For the latter, home tends to be defined by the four walls of the dwelling unit, extending perhaps to the surrounding lawn. Beyond this, space becomes public, that is, belongs to everyone, hence, no one. In striking contrast, the lower-class resident does not make these sharp distinctions between public and private space; for him, home is a locale, an area. The neighborhood is an extension of the dwelling place and evokes the same sense of belonging. Hence, when you relocate him, you dislocate him; he cannot transfer his home, he cannot take it with him.

In a speculative but persuasive conclusion, the authors suggest the following causal sequence and raise a serious and frightening question:

> If the local spatial area and an orientation toward localism provide the core of social organization and integration for a large proportion of the working class, and if, as current behavioral theories would suggest, social organization and integration are primary factors in providing a base for effective social functioning, what are the consequences of dislocating people from their local areas?

Urban renewal planning has assumed that social benefits would accrue to the former residents of slums. But the meanings that the slum areas have for their residents and the consequent effects that relocation would have for them have not been adequately understood. Prior to being located from Boston's West End redevelopment area, most residents experienced profound satisfaction from living in the area. Their satisfaction derived, in large part, from the close associations maintained among the local people and from their strong sense of identity to the local places. In turn, people and places provided a framework for personal and social integration.

The gradual deterioration of older urban dwellings and the belief that such areas provide a locus for considerable social pathology have stimulated concern with altering the physical habitat of the slum. Yet the technical difficulties, the practical inadequacies, and the moral problems of such planned revisions of the human environment are also forcing themselves upon our attention most strikingly (1). While a full evaluation of the advantages and disadvantages of urban renewal must await studies which derive from various disciplines, there is little likelihood that the vast sums currently available will be withheld until there is a more systematic basis for rational decisions. Thus it is of the utmost importance that we discuss all aspects of the issue as thoroughly as possible and make available even the more fragmentary findings which begin to clarify the many unsolved problems.

Since the most common foci of urban renewal are areas which have been designated as slums, it is particularly important to obtain a clearer picture of so-called slum areas and their populations. Slum areas undoubtedly show much variation, both variation from one slum to another and heterogeneity within urban slum areas. However, certain consistencies from one slum area to another have begun to show up in the growing body of literature. It is quite notable that the available systematic studies of slum areas indicate a very broad working-class composition in slums, ranging from highly skilled workers to the nonworking and sporadically working members of the "working" class. Moreover, even in our worst residential slums it is likely that only a minority of the inhabitants (although sometimes a fairly large and visible minority) are afflicted with one or another form of social pathology. Certainly the idea that social pathology in any form is decreased by slum clearance finds little support in the available data. The belief that poverty, delinquency, prostitution, and alcoholism magically inhere in the buildings of slums and will die with the demolition of the slum has a curious persistence but can hardly provide adequate justification for the vast enterprise of renewal planning.

In a larger social sense, beyond the political and economic issues involved, planning for urban renewal has important human objectives. Through such planning we wish to make available to a larger proportion of the population some of the advantages of modern urban facilities, ranging from better plumbing and decreased fire hazards to improved utilization of local space and better neighborhood resources. These values are all on the side of the greater good for the greatest number. Yet it is all too apparent that we know little enough about the meaning and consequences of differences in physical environment either generally or for specific groups. Urban renewal may lead, directly and indirectly, to improved housing for slum residents. But we cannot evaluate the larger effects of relocation or its appropriateness without a more basic understanding than we now have of the meaning of the slum's physical and social environment. This report is an initial essay toward understanding the issue. We shall consider some of the factors that give meaning to the residential environment of the slum dweller. Although the meaning of the environment to the resident of a slum touches only one part of the larger problem, it is critical that we understand this if we are to achieve a more effectively planned and designed urban environment (2).

II

THE SIGNIFICANCE OF THE SLUM ENVIRONMENT
People do not like to be dispossessed from their dwellings, and every renewal project that involves relocation can anticipate considerable resistance, despite the best efforts to insure community support (3). It is never quite clear whether most people object mainly to being forced to do something they have not voluntarily elected to do: or whether they simply object to relocation, voluntary or involuntary. There is, of course, considerable evidence for the commitment of slum residents to their habitat. Why this should be so is less clear and quite incomprehensible in the face of all middle-class residential values. In order to evaluate the issue more closely we shall consider the problem of the meaning and functional significance of residence in a slum area. Although we are primarily concerned with a few broadly applicable generalizations, a complete

analysis will take better account of the diversities in the composition of slum populations.

The fact that more than half the respondents in our sample (4) have a long-standing experience of familiarity with the area in which they lived before relocation suggests a very basic residential stability. Fifty-five percent of the sample first moved to or were born in the West End approximately 20 years ago or more. Almost one-fourth of the entire sample was born in the West End. Not only is there marked residential stability within the larger area of the West End, but the total rate of movement from one dwelling unit to another has been exceedingly low. Table 1 gives the distribution of movement from one dwelling unit to another within the ten years prior to the interview. It is readily evident that the largest proportion of the sample has made very few moves indeed. In fact, a disproportionate share of the frequent moves is made by a small group of relatively high-status people, largely professional and semipro-

Moves	Number	Per cent
Totals	473	100
None	162	34
One	146	31
Two	73	15
Three or more	86	19
No answer	6	1

Table 1.   *Number of Moves in Previous Ten Years*

fessional people who were living in the West End only temporarily. Regardless of which criterion we use, these data indicate that we cannot readily accept those impressions of a slum which suggest a highly transient population. An extremely large proportion shows unusual residential stability, and this is quite evenly distributed among the several levels of working-class occupational groups.

The Slum Environment as Home

What are the sources of this residential stability? Undoubtedly they are many and variable, and we could not hope to extricate the precise contribution of each factor. Rents were certainly low. If we add individually expended heating costs to the rental figures reported we find that 25 percent were paying $34 a month or less, and 85 percent paying $54 a month or less. But though this undoubtedly played a role as a background factor, it can hardly account for the larger findings. Low rental costs are rarely mentioned in discussing aspects of the West End or of the apartment that were sources of satisfaction. And references to the low West End rents are infrequent in discussing the sources of difficulty which people expected in the course of moving. In giving reasons for having moved to the last apartment they occupied before relocation, only 12 percent gave any type of economic reason (including decreased transportation costs as well as low rents). Thus, regardless of the practical importance that low rents must have had for a relatively low income population, they were not among the most salient aspects of the perceived issues in living in the West End.

On the other hand, there is considerable evidence to indicate that living in the West End had particular meaning for a vast majority of West End residents. Table 2 shows the distribution in response to the question, "How do you feel about living in the West End?", clearly indicating how the West End was a focus for very positive sentiments.

Feelings	Number	Per cent	
Totals	473	*100*	
Like very well	174	*37* ⎫	*75*
Like	183	*38* ⎭	
Mixed like-dislike	47	*10* ⎫	*14*
Indifferent	18	*4* ⎭	
Dislike	25	*5* ⎫	*10*
Dislike very much	23	*5* ⎭	
No answer	3	*1*	

Table 2.   *Feelings about the West End*

That the majority of West Enders do not remain in or come back to the West End simply because it is practical (inexpensive, close to facilities) is further documented by the responses of the question, "Which neighborhood, this one or any other place, do you think of as your real home, that is where you feel you really belong?" It is quite striking that fully 71 percent of the people named the West End as their real home, only slightly less than the proportion who specify liking the West End or liking it very much. Although there is a strong relationship between liking the West End and viewing it as home, 14 percent of those who view the West End as home have moderately or markedly negative feelings about the area. On the other hand, 50 percent of those who do not regard the

West End as home have moderately or markedly positive feelings about the area. Thus, liking the West End is not contingent on experiencing the area as that place in which one most belongs. However, the responses to this item give us an even more basic and global sense of the meaning the West End had for a very large proportion of its inhabitants.

These responses merely summarize a group of sentiments that pervade the interviews, and they form the essential context for understanding more discrete meanings and functions of the area. There are clearly differences in the details, but the common core lies in a widespread feeling of belonging someplace, of being "at home" in a region that extends out from but well beyond the dwelling unit. Nor is this only because of familiarity, since a very large proportion of the more recent residents (64 percent of those who moved into the West End during 1950 or after) also showed clearly positive feelings about the area. And 39 percent of those who moved in during 1950 or after regard the West End as their real home (5).

Types of Residential "Belonging"

Finer distinctions in the quality and substance of positive feelings about the West End reveal a number of variations. In categorizing the qualitative aspects of responses to two questions which were analyzed together ("How do you feel about living in the West End?" and "What will you miss most about the West End?"), we distinguished three broad differences of emphasis among the positive replies. The three large categories are: (1) *integral belonging:* sense of *exclusive* commitment, taking West End for granted as home, thorough familiarity and security; (2) *global commitment:* sense of profound gratification (rather than familiarity), pleasure in West End and enjoyment; and (3) *discrete satisfaction:* specific satisfying or pleasurable opportunities or atmosphere involving no special commitment to *this* place.

Only a small proportion (13 percent) express their positive feelings in terms of logically irreplaceable ties to people and places. They do so in often stark and fundamental ways: this is my home; it's all I know; everyone I know is here; I won't leave. A larger group (38 percent) are less embedded and take the West End less for granted but, nonetheless, express an all-encompassing involvement with the area which few areas are likely to provide them again. Their replies point up a less global but poignant sense of loss: it's one big happy family; I'll be sad; we were happy here; it's so friendly; it's handy to everything and everyone is congenial and friendly. The largest group (40 percent) are yet further removed from a total commitment but, in spite of the focused and discrete nature of their satisfaction with the interpersonal atmosphere or the convenience of the area, remain largely positive in feeling.

Differences in Foci of Positive Feelings

Thus, there is considerable variability in the depth and type of feeling implied by liking the West End; and the West End as home had different connotations for different people. For a large group, the West End as home seems to have implied a comfortable and satisfying base for moving out into the world and back. Among this group, in fact, the largest proportion were more concerned with accessibility to other places than with the locality itself. But for more than half the people, their West End homes formed a far more central feature of their total life space.

There is a difference within this larger group between a small number for whom the West End seems to have been the place *to* which they belonged and a larger number for whom it seems rather to have been the place *in* which they belonged. But for the larger group as a whole the West End occupied a unique status, beyond any of the specific attributes one could list and point to concretely. This sense of uniqueness, of home, was not simply a function of social relationships, for the place in itself was the object of strong positive feelings. Most people (42 percent) specify both people and places or offer a global, encompassing reason for their positive feelings. But almost an equally small proportion (13 percent and 10 percent, respectively) select out people or places as the primary objects of positive experience.

With respect to the discrete foci for positive feelings, similar conclusions can be drawn from another question: "Which places do you mostly expect to miss when you leave the West End?" In spite of the place-orientation of the question, 16 percent specify some aspect of interpersonal loss as the most prominent issue. But 40 percent expect to miss one of the places which is completely identified with the area or, minimally, carries a specific local identity. The sense of the West End as a local region, as an area with a spatial identity going beyond (although it may include) the social relationships involved, is a common perception. In response to the question: "Do you think of your home in the West End as part of a local neighborhood?" (6) 81 percent replied affirmatively. It is this sense of localism as a basic feature of lower-class life and the functional significance of local interpersonal relationships and of local places which have been stressed by a number of studies of the working class (7) and are documented by many aspects of our data.

In summary, then, we observe that a number of factors contribute to the special importance that the West End seemed to bear for the large majority of its inhabitants.

1. Residence in the West End was highly stable, with relatively little movement from one dwelling unit to another and with minimal transience into and out of the area. Although residential stability is a fact of importance in itself, it does not wholly account for commitment to the area.

2. For the great majority of the people, the local area was a focus for strongly positive sentiments and was perceived, probably in its multiple meanings, as home. The critical significance of belonging in or to an area has been one of the most consistent findings in working-class communities both in the United States and in England.

3. The importance of localism in the West End, as well as in other working-class areas, can hardly be emphasized enough. This sense of a local spatial identity includes both local social relationships and local places. Although oriented around a common conception of the area as "home," there are a number of specific factors dominating the concrete meaning of the area for different people.

We now turn to a closer consideration of two of these sets of factors: first, the interpersonal networks within which people functioned and, in the subsequent section, the general spatial organization of behavior.

III

SOCIAL RELATIONSHIPS IN PHYSICAL SPACE

Social relationships and interpersonal ties are not as frequently isolated for special attention in discussing the meaning of the West End as we might have expected. Despite this relative lack of exclusive salience, there is abundant evidence that patterns of social interaction were of great importance in the West End. Certainly for a great number of people, local space, whatever its independent significance, served as a locus for social relationships in much the same way as in other working-class slum areas (8). In this respect, the urban slum community also has much in common with the communities so frequently observed in folk cultures. Quite consistently, we find a strong association between positive feelings about the West End and either extensive social relationships or positive feelings about other people in the West End (9). The availability of such interpersonal ties seems to have considerable influence on feelings about the area, but the absence of these ties does not preclude a strongly positive feeling about the West End. That is, despite the prominence of this pattern, there seem to be alternative sources of satisfaction with the area for a minority of the people.

The Place of Kinship Ties

Following some of the earlier studies of membership in formal organizations, which indicated that such organizational ties were infrequent in the working class, increasing attention has been given to the importance of kinship ties in lower-class groups (10). Despite the paucity of comparative studies, most of the investigations of working-class life have stressed the great importance of the extended-kinship group. But the extended-kinship group, consisting of relationships beyond the immediate family, does not seem to be a primary source of the closest interpersonal ties. Rather, the core of the most active kinship ties seems to be composed of nuclear relatives (parents, siblings, and children) of both spouses (11). Our data show that the more extensive these available kinship ties are within the local area, the greater the proportion who show strong positive feeling toward the West End. These data are given in Table 3 and show a quite overwhelming and consistent trend in

Extensiveness of kin in West End	Number of respondents	Feelings about West End (per cent)			
		Totals	Strongly positive	Positive	Mixed negative
None	193	100	29	46	25
Few	150	100	37	38	25
Some	67	100	45	31	24
Many	52	100	58	27	15

Table 3.   *Extensiveness of Kin in West End by Feelings about West End*

this direction. Other relationships point to the same observation: the more frequent the contact with siblings or the more frequent the contact with parents or the greater the desire to move near relatives, the greater the proportion who like the West End very well.

The Importance of the Neighbor Relationship

Important as concrete kinship ties were, however, it is easy to overestimate their significance and the relevance of kinship contacts for positive feelings about the residential area. Studies of the lower class have often neglected the importance of other interpersonal patterns in their concentration on kinship. Not only are other social relationships of considerable significance, but they also seem

Preference for relatives or friends	Number of respondents	Feelings about West End (per cent)			
		Totals	Strongly positive	Positive	Mixed negative
Relatives preferred	232	100	39	39	22
Mixed preferences	81	100	35	32	33
Friends preferred	148	100	36	42	22

Table 4.   *Preference for Relatives or Friends by Feelings about West End*

to influence feelings about the area. The similar effects of both sets of relationships is evident in Table 4, which presents the association between feelings about the West End and the personal importance of relatives versus friends (*12*). A greater proportion (50 percent) have a strong preference for relatives, but a large group (31 percent) indicates a strong preferential orientation to friends. More relevant to our immediate purpose, there is little difference among the three preference groups in the proportions who have strong positive feelings about the West End.

In view of the consistency in the relations between a wide variety of interpersonal variables and feelings about the West End, it seems likely that there are alternative paths to close interpersonal ties of which kinship is only one specific form (*13*). In fact, the single most powerful relation between feelings about the West End and an interpersonal variable is provided by feelings about West End neighbors (see Table 5). Although the neighbor relationship may subsume kinship ties (i.e., when the neighbors are kin), the association between feelings about neighbors and feelings about the West End is stronger than the association between feelings about the West End and any of the kinship variables. Beyond this fact, the frequent references to neighbors and the stress on *local* friendships lead us to suggest that the neighbor relationship was one of

Closeness to neighbors	Number of respondents	Feelings about West End (per cent)			
		Totals	Strongly positive	Positive	Mixed negative
Very positive	78	100	63	28	9
Positive	265	100	37	42	21
Negative	117	100	20	39	41

Table 5.   *Closeness to Neighbors by Feelings about West End*

the most important ties in the West End. And, whether based on prior kinship affiliation or not, it formed one of the critical links between the individual (or family) and the larger area and community.

Localism in Close Interpersonal Ties
Since the quality of feeling about the West End is associated with so wide a diversity of interpersonal relationships, it is not surprising that the majority of people maintained their closest ties with West Enders. The distribution of relationships which were based in the West End or outside the West End are given in Table 6. The striking proportion whose closest ties are all or mostly from

Five closest persons	Number	Per cent
Totals	473	*100*
All West End	201	*42*⎱ *60*
Mostly West End	85	*18*⎰
Equally West End and outside	13	*3*
Mostly outside West End	70	*15*⎱ *25*
All outside West End	46	*10*⎰
Unspecified	58	*12*

Table 6.   *West End Dwelling of Five Closest Persons*

the West End is clearly evident. As we would expect on the basis of the previous results, the more exclusively a person's closest relationships are based in the West End, the greater the likelihood that he will have strong positive feelings about the West End.

A few significant factors stand out clearly from this analysis.

1. Although the kinship relationship was of considerable importance in the West End, as in other working-class communities, there were a number of alternative sources of locally based interpersonal ties. Among these, we suggest that the neighbor relationship is of particular importance, both in its own right and in its effect on more general feelings about the area.

2. There is considerable generality to the observation that the greater one's interpersonal commitments in the area, in the form of close contact or strongly positive feelings, the greater the likelihood of highly positive feelings about the area as a whole. This observation holds for all the forms of interpersonal relationship studied.

What is perhaps most striking about the social patterns of the West End is the extent to which all the various forms of interpersonal ties were localized within the residential area. Local physical space seems to have provided a framework within which some of the most important social relationships were embedded. As in many a folk community (14) there was considerable overlap in the kinds of ties which obtained: kin were often neighbors; there were many interrelated friendship networks; mutual help in household activities was both possible and frequent; many of these relationships had a long and continuous history; and the various ties often became further intertwined through many activities within a common community.

The street itself, favorite recreation areas, local bars, and the settlement houses in the area all served as points of contact for overlapping social networks. Thus the most unique features of this working-class area (although common to many other working-class areas) were: (a) the interweaving and overlap of many different types of interpersonal contacts and role relationships, and (b) the organization and concrete manifestation of these relationships within a common, relatively bounded spatial region. It is these characteristics which seem to have given a special character and meaning both to the quality of interpersonal relationships and to the area within which these relationships were experienced.

We have repeatedly stressed the observation that, granting the importance of local social relationships, the meaning of "localism" in the West End included places as well as people. It is difficult to document the independent significance of either of these factors, but the importance of the physical space of the West End and the special use of the area are evident in many ways. Previously we indicated the importance of physical areas and places as sources of satisfaction in the West End. We now wish to consider more systematically the way in which the physical space of the area is subjectively organized by a large proportion of the population. In understanding the importance of such subjective spatial organization in addition to the significance of local social relationships, we can more adequately appreciate the enormous and multiply derived meaning that a residential area may have for people.

IV

SUBJECTIVE SPATIAL ORGANIZATION

There is only a fragmentary literature on the psychological, social, or cultural implications of spatial behavior and spatial imagery.

The orientation of the behavioral sciences to the history, structure, and dynamics of social relationships has tended to obscure the potential significance of the nonhuman environment generally and, more specifically, that aspect of the nonhuman environment which we may designate as significant space. Although there have been a number of important contributions to this problem, we are far from any systematic understanding of the phenomena (15). We do not propose to discuss the problems or concepts, but only to start with a few very primitive considerations and to observe the working-class relationship to space in several respects. We are primarily concerned with the way in which space is organized or structured in defining the usable environment and in providing restrictions to or freedom for mobility in space (16). In this way we may hope to see more broadly the constellation of forces which serve to invest the residential environment of the working class with such intense personal meaning.

Spatial Usage Patterns in the Middle Class

There are undoubtedly many differences among people in the way space is organized, according to personality type, physiological disposition, environmental actualities, social roles, and cultural experience. We wish to focus only on some of those differences which, at the extremes, distinguish the working class quite sharply from higher-status groups. Although we do not have comparative data, we suggest that in the urban middle class (most notably among relatively high-status professional and business groups) space is characteristically used in a highly *selective* way. The boundary between the dwelling unit and the immediate environs is quite sharp and minimally permeable. It is, of course, possible to go into and out of the dwelling unit through channels which are specifically designated for this purpose. But walls are clear-cut barriers between the inside of the dwelling unit and the outer world. And even windows are seldom used for any interchange between the inner world of the dwelling unit and the outside environment (except for sunlight and air). Most of us take this so much for granted that we never question it, let alone take account of it for analytic purposes. It is the value of the "privacy of the home." The dwelling unit may extend into a zone of lawn or garden which we tend and for which we pay taxes. But, apart from this, the space outside the dwelling unit is barely "ours."

As soon as we are in the apartment hallway or on the street, we are on a wholly *public* way, a path to or from someplace rather than on a bounded space defined by a subjective sense of belonging (17). Beyond this is a highly individualized world, with many common properties but great variability in usage and subjective meaning. Distances are very readily transgressed; friends are dispersed in many directions; preferred places are frequently quite idiosyncratic. Thus there are few physical areas which have regular (certainly not daily) widespread common usage and meaning. And contiguity between the dwelling unit and other significant spaces is relatively unimportant. It is primarily the channels and pathways between individualized significant spaces which are important, familiar, and common to many people. This orientation to the use of space is the very antithesis of that localism so widely found in the working class.

The Territorial Sense in the Working Class

Localism captures only a gross orientation toward the social use of an area of physical space and does not sufficiently emphasize its detailed organization. Certainly, most middle-class observers are overwhelmed at the degree to which the residents of any working-class district and, most particularly, the residents of slums are "at home" in the street. But it is not only the frequency of using the street and treating the street outside the house as a place, and not simply as a path, which points up the high degree of permeability of the boundary between the dwelling unit and the immediate environing area. It is also the use of all channels between dwelling unit and environment as a bridge between inside and outside: open windows, closed windows, hallways, even walls and floors serve this purpose. Frequently, even the sense of adjacent human beings carried by noises and smells provides a sense of comfort. As Edward Ryan points out: (18)

> Social life has an almost uninterrupted flow between apartment and street: children are sent into the street to play, women lean out the windows to watch and take part in street activity, women go "out on the street" to talk with friends, men and boys meet on the corners at night, and families sit on the steps and talk with their neighbors at night when the weather is warm.

It is not surprising, therefore, that there is considerable agreement between the way people feel about their apartments and the way they feel about the West End in general (see Table 7). Without attempting to assign priority to feelings about the apartment or to feelings about the West End, it seems likely that physical barriers which are experienced as easily permeable allow for a ready generalization of positive or negative feelings in either direction.

Feelings about apartment	Number of respondents	Feelings about West End (per cent)			
		Totals	Like very well	Like	Mixed-dislike
Like	367	100	43	40	17
Mixed-indifferent	41	100	20	42	39
Dislike	60	100	12	30	58

Table 7.   *Feelings about the Apartment by Feelings about West End*

We would like to call this way of structuring the physical space around the actual residential unit a *territorial* space, in contrast to the selective space of the middle class. It is territorial in the sense that physical space is largely defined in terms of relatively bounded regions to which one has freedom or restriction of access, and it does not emphasize the path function of physical space in allowing or encouraging movements to or from other places (*19*). There is also evidence, some of which has been presented in an earlier section, that it is territorial in a more profound sense: that individuals feel different spatial regions belong to or do not belong to them and, correspondingly, feel that they belong to (or in) specific spatial regions or do not belong (*20*).

Spatial Boundaries in the Local Area

In all the previous discussion, the West End has been treated as a whole. People in the area did, in fact, frequently speak of the area as a whole, as if it were an entity. However, it is clear that the area was differently bounded for different people. Considering only the gross distinction between circumscribing the neighborhood as a very small, localized space in contrast to an expansive conception of the neighborhood to include most of the area, we find that the sample is about equally split (see Table 8). It is apparent, there-

Neighborhood	Number	Per cent
Totals	473	100
Much of West End: all of area, West End specified, most of area, large area specified	191	40
Part of West End: one or two streets or less, a small area, a store	207	44
People, not area: the people around	17	4
Not codeable	58	12

Table 8.   *Area of West End "Neighborhood"*

fore, that the territorial zone may include a very small or a very large part of the entire West End, and for quite a large proportion it is the former. For these people, at least, the boundary between dwelling unit and street may be highly permeable; but this freedom of subjective access does not seem to extend very far beyond the area immediately adjacent to the dwelling unit. It is also surprising how little this subjective sense of neighborhood size is affected by the extensiveness of West End kin or of West End friends. This fact tends to support the view that there is some degree of independence between social relationships and spatial orientations in the area (21).

Thus, we may say that for almost half the people, there is a

Area	Number	Per cent	
Totals	473	100	
Just own block	27	6 ⎫	
A few blocks	65	14 ⎬ 20	
Large part	66	14 ⎫	
Most of it	237	50 ⎬ 64	
Uncodeable	78	16	

Table 9.   Area of West End Known Well

subjective barrier surrounding the immediately local area. For this large group, the barrier seems to define the zone of greatest personal significance or comfort from the larger area of the West End. However, it is clearly not an impermeable barrier. Not only does a large proportion of the sample fail to designate this boundary, but even for those who do perceive this distinction, there is frequently a sense of familiarity with the area beyond (22). Thus, when we use a less severe criterion of boundedness than the local "neighborhood" and ask people how much of the West End they know well, we find that a very large proportion indeed indicate their familiarity with a large part or most of the area (see Table 9) (23). Although almost half the people consider "home ground" to include only a relatively small local region, the vast majority is easily familiar with a greater part of the West End. The local boundaries within the West End were, thus, boundaries of a semipermeable nature although differently experienced by different people.

The Inner-Outer Boundary
These distinctions in the permeability of the boundaries between dwelling units and street and across various spaces within the

larger local region are brought even more sharply into focus when we consider the boundary surrounding the West End as a whole. The large majority may have been easily familiar with most or all of the West End. But it is impressive how frequently such familiarity seems to stop at the boundaries of the West End. In comparison with the previous data, Table 10 demonstrates the very sharp delineation of the inner space of the West End from the outer space surrounding the West End. The former is generally well explored and essentially familiar, even though it may not be considered the area of commitment. The latter is either relatively unknown by many people or, if known, it is categorized in a completely different way. A relatively large proportion are familiar with the immediately adjacent areas which are directly or almost directly contiguous with the West End (and are often viewed as extensions of the West End), but only slightly more than a quarter (26 percent) report familiarity with any other parts of the Boston area. Thus there seems to be a widely experienced subjective

Area	Number	Per cent
Totals	473	*101*
West End only: no other area, none	141	*30*
Adjacent area: North End, esplanade	216	*46*
Contiguous areas: East Boston, Cambridge	98	*21*
Nearby areas: Revere, Malden, Brookline	12	*3*
Metropolitan Boston, beyond "nearby" areas	1	*0*
Outside Boston area	3	*1*
No answer	2	*0*

Table 10.   *Familiar Areas of Boston*

boundary surrounding the larger local area and some of its immediate extensions which is virtually impermeable. It is difficult to believe that people literally do not move out of this zone for various activities. Yet, if they do, it apparently does not serve to diminish the psychological (and undoubtedly social) importance of the boundary (*24*).

These data provide considerable evidence to support, if they do not thoroughly validate, the view that the working class commonly organizes physical space in terms of a series of boundaries. Although we do not mean to imply any sense of a series of concentric boundaries or to suggest that distance alone is the critical dimension, there seems to be a general tendency for the permeability of these boundaries to decrease with increasing distance from the dwelling unit. Significant space is thus subjectively defined as a series of contiguous regions with the dwelling unit and its immediately surrounding local area as the central region. We have referred to this way of organizing physical space as *territorial* to distinguish it from the more highly *selective* and individualized use of space which seems to characterize the middle class. And we suggest that it is the territorial conception and manner of using physical space which provides one of the bases for the kind of localism which is so widely found in working-class areas.

In conjunction with the emphasis upon local social relationships, this conception and use of local physical space gives particular force to the feeling of commitment to, and the sense of belonging in, the residential area. It is clearly not just the dwelling unit that is significant but a larger local region that partakes of these powerful feelings of involvement and identity. It is not surprising, therefore, that "home" is not merely an apartment or a house but a local area in which some of the most meaningful aspects of life are experienced.

V

CONCLUSIONS

The aims of urban renewal and the sources of pressure for renewal are manifold: among the objectives we may include more rational and efficient use of land, the elimination of dilapidated buildings, increase in the municipal tax base, and the improvement of living conditions for slum dwellers. Although the social benefit to the slum dweller has received maximum public attention, it is always unclear how the life situation (or even the housing situation) of the working-class resident of a slum is supposed to be improved by slum clearance or even slum improvement. Public housing has not proved to be an adequate answer to this problem for many reasons. Yet public housing is the only feature of renewal programs that has even attempted to deal seriously with this issue.

In recent years, a number of reports have suggested that concern about slum conditions has been used to maneuver public opinion in order to justify use of eminent domain powers and demolition, largely, for the benefit of middle- and upper-status groups. Although we cannot evaluate this political and economic issue, we do hope to understand the ways in which dislocation from a slum and relocation to new residential areas has, in fact, benefited or damaged the working-class residents involved. It is all too apparent, however, that the currently available data are inadequate for clarifying some of the most critical issues concerning the effects of residential relocation upon the subject populations.

We know very little about slums and the personal and social consequences of living in a slum. We know even less about the effects of forced dislocation from residential areas on people in general and on working-class people specifically. But rational urban planning which, under these circumstances, becomes urban *social* planning, requires considerable knowledge and understanding of people and places affected by the plans. It is incumbent upon us to know both what is wrong with the slum and with slum life and what is right about slums and living in slums (25). It is essentially this question, formulated as the meaning and consequences of living in a slum, that has motivated our inquiry into the sources of residential satisfaction in an urban slum. In turn, this study provides one of the bases for understanding the ways in which dislocation and relocation affect the patterns of personal and social adaptation of former residents of a slum.

In studying the reasons for satisfaction that the majority of slum residents experience, two major components have emerged. On the one hand, the residential area is the region in which a vast and interlocking set of social networks is localized. And, on the other, the physical area has considerable meaning as an extension of home, in which various parts are delineated and structured on the basis of a sense of belonging. These two components provide the context in which the residential area may so easily be invested with considerable, multiply determined meaning. Certainly, there are variations both in the importance of various factors for different people and in the total sense which people have of the local area. But the greatest proportion of this working-class group (like other working-class slum residents who have been described) shows a fairly common experience and usage of the residential area. This common experience and usage is dominated by a conception of the local area beyond the dwelling unit as an integral part of home. This view of an area as home and the significance of local people and local places are so profoundly at variance with typical middle-class orientations that it is difficult to appreciate the intensity of meaning, the basic sense of identity involved in living in the particular area. Yet it seems to form the core of the extensive social integration that characterizes this (and other) working-class slum populations.

These observations lead us to question the extent to which, through urban renewal, we relieve a situation of stress or create further damage. If the local spatial area and an orientation toward localism provide the core of social organization and integration for a large proportion of the working class, and if, as current behavioral theories would suggest, social organization and integration are primary factors in providing a base for effective social functioning, what are the consequences of dislocating people from their local areas? Or, assuming that the potentialities of people for adaptation to crisis are great, what deeper damage occurs in the process? And, if there are deleterious effects, are these widespread or do they selectively affect certain predictable parts of the population? We emphasize the negative possibilities because these are closest to the expectations of the population involved and because, so frequently in the past, vague positive effects on slum populations have been arbitrarily assumed. But it is clear that, in lieu of or along with negative consequences, there may be considerable social benefit.

The potential social benefits also require careful, systematic evaluation, since they may manifest themselves in various and sometimes subtle ways. Through a variety of direct and intervening factors, the forced residential shift may lead to changes in orientations toward work, leading to increased satisfaction in the occupational sphere; or, changes may occur in the marital and total familial relationship to compensate for decreased kinship and friendship contacts and, in turn, lead to an alternative (and culturally more syntonic) form of interpersonal satisfaction; or, there may be either widespread or selective decreases in problems such as delinquency, mental illness, and physical malfunctioning.

A realistic understanding of the effects, beneficial and/or deleterious, of dislocation and relocation from an urban slum clearly requires further study and analysis. Our consideration of some of the factors involved in working-class residential satisfaction in the slum provides one basis for evaluating the significance of the changes that take place with a transition to a new geographic and social environment. Only the careful comparison of pre-relocation and post-relocation data can begin to answer these more fundamental questions and, in this way, provide a sound basis for planning urban social change.

NOTES

1. H. Gans, "The Human Implications of Current Redevelopment and Relocation Planning," *Journal of the American Institute of Planners* 25, no. 1 (February, 1959) : 15–25.

2. This is one of a series of reports on the meaning and significance of various aspects of working-class life. This group of studies will provide a basis for a subsequent analysis of the impact of relocation through a comparison of the pre-relocation and the post-relocation situation. The population of the original area was predominantly white, of mixed ethnic composition (mainly Italian, Polish, and Jewish). The many ethnic differences do not vitiate the larger generalizations of this study.

3. This does not seem limited to contemporary relocation situations. Firey reports a similar phenomenon in Boston during the nineteenth century. W. Firey, *Land Use in Central Boston* (Cambridge: Harvard University Press, 1947).

4. These data are based on a probability sample of residents from the West End of Boston interviewed during 1958–1959. The sampling criteria included only households in which there was a female household member between the ages of 20 and 65. The present analysis is based on the pre-relocation data from the female respondents. Less systematic pre-relocation data on the husbands are also available, as well as systematic post-relocation data for both wives and husbands and women without husbands.

5. It is possible, of course, that we have obtained an exaggerated report of positive feelings about the area because of the threat of relocation. Not only does the consistency of the replies and their internal relationships lead us to believe that this has not caused a major shift in response, but, bearing in mind the relative lack of verbal facility of many of the respondents and their frequent tendencies to give brief replies, we suspect that the interview data often lead to underestimating the strength of sentiment.

6. This question is from the interview designed by Leo Stole and his associates for the Yorkville study in New York.

7. The importance of localism in working-class areas has been most cogently described by R. Hoggart, *The Uses of Literacy* (London: Chatto and Windus, 1857), and by M. Young and P. Wilmott, *Family and Kinship in East London* (Glencoe: The Free Press, 1957). In our own data, the perception of the area as a local neighborhood is largely independent of the individual's own commitment to the area.

8. Many of the studies of working-class areas make this point quite clear. Cf. Hoggart, op. cit.; Young and Wilmott, op. cit.; H. Gans, *The Urban Villagers* (Glencoe: The Free Press, forthcoming) ; J. M. Mogey, *Family and Neighbourhood* (London: Oxford University Press, 1956) ; M. Kerr, *People of Ship Street* (London: Routledge and Kegan Paul, 1958).

9. The associations between feelings about the West End and interpersonal variables include interpersonal relationships outside the West End as well. Thus there is the possibility that an interrelated personality variable may be involved. We shall pursue this in subsequent studies.

10. The importance of kinship ties for working-class people was particularly brought to the fore by F. Dotson, "Patterns of Voluntary Association Among Urban Working Class Families," *American Sociological Review* 25 (1951) : 687–693.

11. This point is made by Young and Wilmott, op. cit. In this regard as in

many others, the similarity of the East End of London and the West End of Boston is quite remarkable.

12. The "Preference for Relatives or Friends" item is based on four separate questions presenting a specific situation and asking if the respondent would prefer to be associated with a relative or friend in each situation.

13. We do not mean to imply that this exhausts the special importance of kinship in the larger social structure. There is also evidence to suggest that some of the basic patterns of the kinship relationship have influenced the form of interpersonal ties more generally in the urban working class. This issue is discussed in M. Fried and E. Lindemann, "Sociocultural Factors in Mental Health and Illness," *American Journal of Orthopsychiatry* 31 (1961): 87–101, and will be considered further in subsequent reports.

14. W. Goodenough gives an excellent description of a similar pattern on Truk. Cf. W. Goodenough, *Property, Kin, and Community on Truk* (New Haven: Yale University Publications in Anthropology, No. 46, 1951).

15. There are a number of rich and provocative discussions of selected aspects of space-oriented behavior. Cf. P. Schilder, *The Image and Appearance of the Human Body* (London: Kegan Paul, Trench, Trubner, and Co., 1935): and *Mind: Perception and Thought in Their Constructive Aspects* (New York: Columbia University Press, 1942); E. Homburger Erikson, "Configurations in Play—Clinical Notes," *Psychoanalytic Quarterly* 6 (1937): 139–214; H. A. Witkin, *Personality Through Perception* (New York: Harper, 1954); Edward T. Hall, "The Language of Space," *Landscape* (Fall, 1960). The studies of the animal ecologists and the experimental studies of spatial orientation have considerable bearing on these issues. A recent contribution to the literature of urban planning, K. Lynch's *The Image of the City* (Cambridge: The Technology Press, 1960) bears directly on the larger problems of spatial orientation and spatial behavior in the urban environment, and its analytic framework has proved useful in the present formulations.

16. We shall not touch on a related problem of considerable interest, the basic modes of conceiving or experiencing space in general. We assume a close relation between general conceptions of space and ways of using spatial aspects of specific parts of the environment, but an analysis of this problem is beyond the scope of the present discussion.

17. The comment of one reader to an early draft of this paper is worth quoting, since it leads into a fascinating series of related problems. With respect to this passage, Chester Hartman notes, "We tend to think of this other space as anonymous and public (in the sense of belonging to everyone, i.e., no one) when it does not specifically belong to us. The lower-class person is not nearly so alienated from what he does not own." To what extent is there a relationship between a traditional expectation (even if occasionally belied by reality) that only *other* people own real property, that one is essentially part of a "property-less class" and a willingness to treat any property as common? And does this provide a framework for the close relationship between knowing and belonging in the working class in contrast to the middle-class relationship between owning and belonging? Does the middle-class acceptance of legal property rights provide a context in which one can *only* belong if one owns. From a larger psychological view, these questions are relevant not merely to physical space and physical objects but to social relationships as well.

18. This comment is a fragment from a report on ethnographic observations made in the area.

19. These formulations, as previously indicated, refer to modal patterns and do not apply to the total population. Twenty-six percent do select out the "accessibility" of the area, namely, a path function. The class difference,

however, is quite striking since 67 percent of the highest-status group give this response, but only 19 percent of the lowest-status group and between 28 percent and 31 percent of the middle- (but still low-status) groups select out various types of "accessibility."

20. Without attempting, in this report, a "depth" psychological analysis of typical patterns of working-class behaviors, we should note the focal importance of being accepted or rejected, of belonging or being an "outsider." Preliminary evidence from the post-relocation interviews reveals this in the frequent references to being unable to obtain an apartment because "they didn't want us" or that the landlord "treated us like dirt." It also emerges in the frequently very acute sensitivity to gross social-class differences, and a sharp sense of not belonging or not fitting in with people of higher status. Clarification of this and related problems seems essential for understanding the psychological and social consequences of social-class distinctions and has considerable implication for urban residential planning generally and urban renewal specifically.

21. The social-class patterning is also of interest. Using the occupation of the head of household as the class criterion, there is almost no difference among the three working-class status levels in the area included as a neighborhood (the percentages who say "much or all of the area" for these three groups are, respectively, 51 percent, 46 percent, and 48 percent). But only 38 percent of the high-status group include much or all of the West End in their subjective neighborhood.

22. Of those who include only part of the West End in their designation of their neighborhood, 68 percent indicate they know a large part or most of the West End well. Naturally, an even higher percentage (87 percent) of those who include much or all of the West End in their neighborhood are similarly familiar with a large part or all of the area.

23. We used the term "neighborhood" for want of a better term to designate the immediate local area of greatest significance. On the basis of his ethnographic work, however, E. Ryan points out that this term is rarely used spontaneously by West Enders.

24. Unfortunately, we do not have data on the actual frequency of use of the various areas outside the West End. Thus we cannot deal with the problem of the sense of familiarity in relation to actual usage patterns. However, in subsequent reports, we hope to pursue problems related to the bases for defining or experiencing physical-spatial boundaries and the various dimensions which affect the sense of commitment to and belonging in physical areas.

25. There is, of course, the evident danger of considering a social pattern on the basis of "right" and "wrong" which, inevitably, merely reproduce our own transitory values. A careful and thorough analysis, however, provides its own correctives to our all-too-human biases.

CHAPTER

The Social Effects
of the Physical Environment

IRVING ROSOW

Reprinted from the *Journal of the
American Institute of Planners* 27, no.
2 (May, 1961): 127–33, by permission
of the publisher and the author.

    Irving Rosow is a sociologist, with
his Ph.D. from Harvard. He has taught
at Wayne State University, Harvard,
Purdue, and Western Reserve, where
he studied the effects of different
social environments on the lives of old
people. His research includes studies
conducted in Germany and England
as well as in the United States.

    This article originally appeared
under the title "Specialists' Perspectives and Spurious Validation in
Housing," in *Marriage and Family*
19, no. 3 (August, 1957). [Copyright by
the National Council on Family
Relations.]

The chapters by Hollingshead and Rogler and by Fried and Gleicher identified some of the unanticipated and unwanted consequences of slum clearance and public housing. But what of the desirable and *planned for* effects of new housing? To what extent is it possible to control social interaction through the manipulation of the physical environment: can we decrease crime and juvenile delinquency, diminish anxiety and depression, increase racial integration, and create a sense of community, by controlling the way we build? These are the questions raised by Rosow.

His answer is a sobering one: with the exception of reducing social pathologies, such as crime, disease, and mortality, there is little hard evidence to support the contention that social change can be accomplished through planned communities. Racial and social class divisions remain, and what community integration does occur fails to endure. The moral seems to be that when man moves into a new house he, sometimes for better but more often for worse, takes himself along.

Rosow also takes a penetrating look at the concept of housing "livability"—that organization of space which best accommodates the needs of the occupants. He finds there is often a considerable disparity between designer and occupant as to what constitutes a "desirable" use of space: for example, the architect plans a study area in a bedroom where the "younger generation can do its lessons in privacy," but typically, such "privacy" is experienced as isolation and the teenager is happier (and more productive) with his "homework scattered over the living room floor." Thus, as in the chapters by Hollingshead and Rogler and by Fried and Gleicher, this paper highlights the differences in values and lifestyles that so often, once again, separate environmental planners from environmental users.

The assumption of housers that planned manipulation of the physical environment can change social patterns in determinate ways seems to be only selectively true. It applies mainly to the extreme housing situations—removing people from substandard housing, providing for highly individual needs, and catering to an intellectual-aesthetic minority for whom housing values are extremely salient. It applies less to average housing situations, where the consequences of livability and community integration may be as effectively realized simply by new housing, as such, without the benefit of planned neighborhoods. People in general may be far less sensitive to the discrepancy between the real and the ideal in housing than are the professionals.

Much of the force behind the movement for housing reform is epitomized by one of its most articulate exponents: "The tenants' entire social life may hang on the smallest whim of the greenest draftsman or rent collector" (*3*). Although it is an extreme statement—and one which, if taken too literally, imposes a severe responsibility—it sums up a basic operational assumption of idealistic housing practitioners. As a movement and ideology, housing and planning rest on the premise that by the manipulation of the physical environment, we can control social patterns. If housing exerts an independent influence on how people live, then the creation of certain housing conditions can change social relationships. We can affect the choice of friends, family adjustments, and generally how people spend their time. All this is subject, of course, to given cost limitations. But apparently, within these restrictions, different housing decisions may have different social consequences. The problem of the housers is to learn more about how and in what way factors of design do indeed affect patterns of social life.

In this paper, we should like to assess this premise against the findings of a growing body of housing research. This is by no means a systematic, exhaustive coverage of the literature or of housers' working "hypotheses." It is more of an interim clarification, now that "some of the early research returns are in," of those assumptions which tend to be more effective than others in realizing social policies which are at once the housers' goals and guides.

The assumptions may be classified into several general categories to which they refer: (1) social pathology and social efficiency; (2) "livability" of the dwelling unit; (3) neighborhood structure and integration; and (4) aesthetics. Our concern here is mainly, though not exclusively, with low- and middle-income public housing or similar planned neighborhoods.

SOCIAL PATHOLOGY

The housers have effectively won their point that slum clearance pays dividends in terms of social welfare and hard cash. The correlation between poor housing and the incidence of crime, disease, juvenile delinquency, morality, et cetera, have been established beyond doubt. Planners no longer have to deal seriously with the objection that correlations do not prove causal relationships. Enough work has already shown re-housing to be sufficient condition to produce a sharp, significant decline in these morbidities (5, 6, 40). Slum clearance and the elimination of obviously substandard housing have reduced some virulent social problems and contributed to health and welfare among underprivileged groups.

Furthermore, Rumney, among others, has demonstrated impressively that the dividends of re-housing are not only to be reaped in social values like health, but also in dollars and cents (38, 39). Slums have been highly profitable rental and speculative properties to their owners, but largely at public expense. Municipalities have subsidized slums indirectly. For thirteen major cities, the public expenditures on blighted areas have exceeded revenues from them by ratios of 2.2 to 9.9. (39). In other words, the direct costs of public services (relief, police and fire, welfare, et cetera) were between two and ten times as high as the taxes which these areas contributed to the public coffers. These ratios are reversed for high-rental residential districts which tend to yield considerably more revenue than expense, thereby providing the funds for slum services. Despite certain difficulties with such indices (14), the over-all outline is clear. Depressed housing areas represent social and financial liabilities which are greatly eased by clearance and re-housing.

LIVABILITY

The factor of livability is the most instrumental aspect of design and is most commonly related to the individual dwelling unit (33, 34, 35). It refers to the utilitarian organization of space and facilities which best accommodates the needs of the occupants and minimizes frictions and frustrations from factors of layout and design (17). According to one sociologist of housing:

> Modern architecture does its best to accommodate in the most utilitarian manner the informal aspects of private family living. . . . Room arrangements [are favored] that serve the everyday life of the family and reduce household chores to a minimum. . . . Relaxation and informality in the relations between different family members are promoted (32).

Livability thus becomes an expression of the "functional" goals of modern architecture and design, and its norms are efficiency. It implies a careful adaptation of design to use, and frequently specific features or space are designed for specific purposes.

But there is evidence of "nonconforming" usage. Many features are neglected, used for purposes other than those intended, the activity takes place elsewhere, or does not take place at all in the confines of the plan. This applies both to the dwelling unit and to the neighborhood.

In the private dwellings, for example, study space is commonly provided in the "children's bedroom where, at desks or built-in desk shelves, the younger generation can do its lessons in privacy." This nominally removes them from the distractions of family intercourse without imposing undue restraint on the rest of the family. Yet the picture of the teenager with homework scattered over the living room floor and the radio or TV set blaring in his ear has become almost a stereotype, although to the writer's knowledge it has not been examined in research.

Other features have had a varying fate in nonconforming usage. The short-lived experiment with the tiny "Pullman" kitchen is a case in point. Another, in private houses, is the basement recreation room which matures into a conventional storage space. Or in residential suburbs, the façade of house after house may have enormous "picture windows" which are covered by venetian blinds or drapes (often made-to-measure) to give some privacy to the occupants.

Similar nonconforming usage is found in community facilities, with the community center a conspicuously neglected amenity (16). In one interracial development, for example, a professionally-staffed community center was created to promote interracial activities and contact. But only 15 percent of the women reported meeting women of the other race in the center compared with almost 60 percent who named the community laundry (25).

These few illustrations are typical. They can be multiplied, although these suffice to make the point here. Nonconforming usage is important because it almost invariably represents fixed installations which become an economic liability. The space and cost might have been otherwise invested. The occupants are thereby penalized in some sense for incorrect predictions about use or the plasticity of habits.

In mass housing, livability of the domicile necessarily takes on a more restricted meaning than the ideals represented by modern architecture. Cost limitations and family patterns which vary in time, in stage of the family cycle, and from one group to another forbid detailed attention to individual preferences and force standardization of design. In effect, this reduces livability largely to considerations of housekeeping and mechanics—choices of kitchen layout; easy-to-clean wall, floor, and window surfaces; convenient storage, et cetera. Not only are these decisions sharply restricted by cost factors (viz. consolidating fixtures about plumbing cores), but they frequently involve choices between space and appliances. In this respect, public housing may represent rather few differences from *any* new housing. This is especially true to the extent that, aside from *gross blunders* of design, housekeeping ease may be increased more by appliances than by design decisions. The availability, for example, of a clothes dryer may save more time and exasperation than a brilliant subtle detail of planning.

Beyond housekeeping mechanics, livability problems can essentially be reduced to factors of space which afford the room for group activities *and* for privacy. In the arrangement of space the designer can make ingenious decisions which minimize frictions. Thus this is most true in relatively expensive residential housing. In middle- and low-income dwellings, the cost limitations severely restrict the amount of space available. And only so many alternatives exist as realistic choices. The different livability consequences between them may be even more limited.

The effect of the space variable on livability is not simply in crowding (whether persons per room or use-crowding) or space for social activities. Usually there is enough room for those activities in which the family engages together, although larger social affairs such as parties, et cetera, may suffer in small dwellings. The basic problem boils down to privacy. To some extent it is possible to isolate part of the dwelling by clever design: careful solutions of circulation, sound insulation from closet placement, et cetera. But real privacy requires room for comfortable retirement; and unless this space is "manufactured," the lack of privacy may become a source of friction and frustration. The difficulty of creating space without sacrificing other indispensables is a problem of which designers are only too well aware.

The problem of livability may be viewed in a somewhat different perspective. We may properly ask under what conditions livability factors are positive causes of frustration, friction, and tension, and the extent to which they are significant in the social adjustment of the family. In Westgate, a prefabricated housing project for married students, there were extremely serious livability difficulties (*20*). Notwithstanding Festinger reported:

> This general satisfaction [with living in the community] existed in spite of, and seemed to compensate for, many physical inadequacies of the houses. At the time of our study there were many physical nuisances in the houses. Some were incompletely equipped, the grounds were muddy and had not yet been landscaped, they were difficult to heat in the winter, and the like. One example of the reaction to such physical inadequacies will suffice, however, to illustrate the point. At the time of the investigation many of the houses had trouble with the roofs. The houses were prefabricated, and many of the roofs had not been assembled properly . . . in the interviews about one-third of the residents reported that the roofs leaked. Any rain accompanied by a moderately strong wind would apparently raise the roof slightly, and water would pour down the walls. One family reported in a particular strong rain the roof had started to blow off; the husband had to go outside and hold the roof down until the wind subsided.
>
> It is remarkable, however, that even such *serious physical inconveniences did not create a strong impression on the residents*. Typically the reaction was, "Oh yes, there are many things wrong with these houses, but we love it here and wouldn't want to move."
>
> The adequate and satisfying social life was sufficient to override many inconveniences. The result was a rather happy social and psychological existence (*19*). [Italics inserted.]

This is not to recommend such Spartan trials as built-in housing features. But housing attitudes are far too complex to ascribe them specifically to livability frustrations which may be much less relevant than housers suppose. The adjustment of family members to one another is a function of social and personal factors to which the dwelling may contribute relatively little. In another study, for example, of thirty-three families who built homes, five had absolutely no dissatisfaction with their previous dwelling and the complaints of the others centered about highly discrete details which were annoying (*36*).

The almost standard response of housers to such evidence is, "Aha, but these people don't know what it can be like to live in a well-designed dwelling." This is largely true. But on the other hand, there is little evidence that satisfaction with new housing is directly related to livability resulting *from design per se* except when there is a significant improvement in housing, especially where people came from substandard housing, or occupants are particularly conscious of housing in highly literate, sophisticated terms.

This brings us to a second point regarding space and privacy. There is evidence of important class differences in the meaning and valuation of privacy. In a study of fifty families in New York state, Cutler found that exactly one half of the people in lower class families complained about the lack of privacy in comparison with only 10 percent of the middle class and none of the upper class (9). Furthermore, in defining the elements of privacy, lower class respondents mentioned having a room of one's own twice as frequently as upper class people (70 percent versus 34 percent). Conversely, 44 percent of the upper class compared with 8 percent of the lower class mentioned such factors as outdoor privacy, rooms that could be closed off, extra baths, extra guest rooms, and the maid living away from the family. In other words, higher social groups take for granted amenities which the lower classes would like. The lower class groups basically want more space than they have available. Although satisfaction with housing is clearly related to size of dwelling (8, 9, 13)—which is in turn related to many other features as well—crowding, privacy, and space limitations may not be so important to working-class groups as to other segments of the population. Dean found in a Steubenville sample that although 21 percent of the semiskilled and unskilled workers were doubled-up with relatives, only 6 percent specifically complained about this in terms of overcrowding, whereas in the white collar group 6 percent were living with relatives, but 29 percent complained of overcrowding (13). This is consistent with other findings in which space was subordinate to other features in housing complaints of working-class groups.

Thus, conceptions of privacy and adequate space have different class meanings; and there is little evidence that these assume drastic importance in family adjustment *provided* that some adequate space standards are met and that the class culture does not demand private space for highly individual personal activities. Chapin, for example, observes:

Thus privacy becomes a value. One may question the validity of imputing to others the desires, needs, and wants that are characteristic in this respect of nervously high-strung sophisticated, and responsive intellectual persons. Perhaps the common run of home occupants is not as sensitive to deprivation of privacy as some, but it is safer to assume that some individuals born to the common run of humanity will be sensitive. . . . Privacy is needed for thinking, reflection, reading and study, and for aesthetic enjoyment and contemplation. In-

trusions on the fulfillment of personal desires need to be shut
off. . . . (7)

This is a statement of highly personal goals pursued in the home.
As Chapin indicates, it tends to be highly class-selective in its relevance—or indeed, to characterize particular social types within
classes, particularly middle and upper class intellectuals and aes-
thetes. Their needs can ultimately only be satisfied with space,
which again involves cost more than design factors.

In general there tends to be an incompatability between highly
individuated housing goals and standardization imposed by mass
housing. Virtually the only manipulable variable in large scale
projects is the diversification of dwelling-unit sizes within the
overall budget. This is perhaps the most opportune way to juggle
space to satisfy the needs of specialized groups—whether by providing larger units for larger families and those with high privacy
activities or by smaller units for smaller families (young and old
couples, et cetera).

The provision of space poses additional problems, since large
increments of floor space may have to be provided to realize small
increments of actual free space. In studies of the Pierce Foundation, for example, middle class families tended to fill free space with
furnishings so that from one family to another, similar amounts of
open space were found despite different sizes of comparable rooms.
Some of these furnishings were for storage and others for decora-
tion. It is important to note, however, when the designer assumes
that he is squeezing out several more cubic feet of open space in
reality he may be creating a "vacuum" which the occupant will
"abhor" and fill at the earliest possible opportunity.

Further, although surveys and the like may reveal considerable
agreement about the *categories* of housing complaints or desired
housing features, the research on livability has not "weighted"
these factors, especially by class and social typology variables, to
reveal how important housing values actually are to different
groups. Who is willing to sacrifice how much of what (including
money) to get the kind of housing he wants? For example, a New
York realtor not long ago expressed amazement at his middle class
tenants who preferred to give up a bedroom and sleep on a studio
couch in the living room in order to own a car. Or as one houser
put it:

> We are inclined to look down our noses at the family who
> lives in a shack so they can own an automobile, or the six per-
> sons who live in one room and yet pool their resources to buy
> a television set; but are we sure we are right? (*18*)

Nowhere does the problem of relative class values become so acute
as the question of livability. The planners, designers, architects, and
housers must operate with assumptions about how people do live,
how they want to live, how they would live if given a chance (*37*).
Most of them conventionally assume that the people for whom they
are designing must be "educated" to appreciate and exploit the
housing advantages being placed at their disposal. When the tenants fail to respond, this is often written off as "no fair test" because the housing itself was too restricted and not enough design
influence was brought to bear. On the contrary, there is ample reason to believe that design factors generally represent only conditions of the physical environment which do not significantly alter
human outlooks apart from the significant social experience which
housing may not provide. And it remains to be seen how the average new project or even the better ones which have been built with
strong cost restrictions can affect the relations of family members
to one another—for those people who did not come from substandard housing. Or more precisely, it is an open question whether
livability factors can be significantly separated from the sheer
fact of re-housing lower class groups or custom-building for upper
class families. The intermediate range may be slightly but not substantially affected by livability provisions.

In summary, the factors of livability which can be influenced
by design tend to apply selectively to class groups and to those with
highly specialized housing needs. It is mainly the lower class group,
moving into new housing from conspicuously poor dwellings, who
benefit most from factors of livability. The more specialized needs
of people with strong privacy desires can scarcely be met in new
dwellings except at high cost.

COMMUNITY INTEGRATION

Intimately bound up with the planning movement is a reaction to
the fragmentation and segmentalization of urban life. There is an
effort to recapture an "organic" environment in which people will
be integrated into communities on a residential basis. This is epitomized in the controversy over the neighborhood plan in its various
names and guises (*1, 10, 11, 15, 24, 31, 42*).

A series of studies has amply demonstrated the effect of residential placement on group formation and the selection of friends
(*4, 16, 20, 21, 23, 28, 29, 30*, et al). The evidence is well-known and
so clear that it warrants little elaboration. In planned communities
friendship groups are determined by two variables: proximity of
neighbors and orientation of dwellings. People select their friends

primarily from those who live nearby and those whom their home faces.

The full significance of these patterns, however, is less clear. Housers interpret this to mean that people are indeed being integrated into community or neighborhood structures. But these patterns are adumbrated by several factors: deviant cases in which planned communities did *not* result in this spontaneous cohesiveness *(12, 19)*; that they characterized the earliest period in the life of the community, but then became instable and gave way to the extension of friendships farther afield, outside the neighborhood *(16, 22)*; that the neighborhood community developed a system of social stratification which was not solidary in its effects *(12, 16, 21, 23, 26, 29)*; that community integration was most directly related to homogeneous social composition and inversely related to length of residence *(22)*. In other words, when people of a similar type (viz. students, war plant workers, et cetera) are brought together into a new community for a relatively impermanent period, considerable social solidarity springs up. But the longer people stay and the more diversified the group, the more is solidarity affected by status differentiation and the establishment of friendships elsewhere.

The deeper issues presented here center about the significance of homogeneous social composition. Some critics of the neighborhood concept have contended that homogeneous communities tend to formalize social segregation and defeat the very democratic objectives which neighborhood planners seek *(24)*. According to others, the contrary desire to establish socially heterogeneous communities will not necessarily achieve democratic aims. Some argue that there is no reason to assume that people will spontaneously or willingly enter heterogeneous planned neighborhoods any more than similar unplanned neighborhoods *(22)*. If they do, there is no assurance that they will interact harmoniously, but may, on the contrary, perpetuate existing differences *(12, 26, 43)*.

Some changes are perceptible. For example, in interracial housing, attitudes toward Negroes became more favorable on closer contact *(25)*. In two projects with internal segregation of Negroes, between two-thirds and three-fourths of the white occupants favored segregation while in two others with no internal segregation, about 40 percent of the whites favored segregation. These attitudes were accompanied by extremely sharp differences in association between the races. In the segregated projects, less than 5 percent of the white women knew any Negro woman by first name or engaged in such cooperative activity as baby-sitting, shopping together, helping in illness, et cetera. In contrast to this, the proportion of white women in the non-segregated projects varied from one-fourth to three-fourths who had such associations with Negroes. The occupancy patterns evidently served to reinforce negative attitudes in the segregated projects.

Jahoda and West indicate the strong influence exerted by previous interracial experience on attitudes (25). Of those whites who had previously lived in racially mixed neighborhoods, 19 percent expected trouble and 17 percent found relations better than they had expected; but of those who had no prior biracial experience, 56 percent expected trouble and 43 percent were pleasantly surprised by the absence of conflict. But under the best conditions, among the whites who had both previous residential experience and worked with Negroes, only 45 percent favored interracial housing. Although whites' desire to move from an interracial project was directly related with their expectations of a Negro invasion, among those who expected no change in the proportion of Negro residents, 50 percent nonetheless planned to move—not necessarily, of course, as a reflection of their racial attitudes. In this project, the management's policy of a "quota" system maintained a stable proportion of the races through time. But in the same town, a comparable project without a "quota" showed the proportion of Negroes gradually reaching between 80–90 percent.

Unquestionably, the influence of greater contact on racial images had an impact on stereotypes, but the overall picture is one of accommodation rather than community integration. Changes in attitude ultimately depended on more than sheer contact. Jahoda and West indicate, "But in part, also, the more favorable expectations [of whites] are the result of that kind of sustained interracial contact which displaces racial stereotypes" (25). [Italics inserted.)

The factor of residential mobility has bearing both on the necessary condition of sustained contact in changing racial stereotypes and on the friendship patterns of homogeneous communities. Apparently about three-fourths of the American people changed their residence during the 1940–50 decade (2). Furthermore, among the working classes most eligible for planned projects, there is the highest residential mobility and the lowest integration into the local neighborhood. Higher class groups who are less mobile and have longer residential tenure have more friends within their immediate neighborhoods. Nonetheless, in terms of sources of friendships, the lower class groups draw upon immediate neighbors more than twice as frequently as middle and upper class groups (33 percent versus 14 percent) (41). The reasons for the mobility may vary—economic opportunity, desire to own a home, middle class aspirations, changing stages in the family cycle, et cetera (14, 36). The motives are less important than the implications for the integration of the community. High mobility is not a condition favoring *sustained* contacts necessary to change racial attitudes. Nor is either high mobility or long tenure in planned neighborhoods conducive to the sustained solidarity and friendship patterns observed in the newly formed communities.

One may properly inquire what the alternative friendship patterns may have been in homogeneous *unplanned* neighborhoods. Apparently they were of a similar character to those of the planned neighborhood. Lower class groups draw heavily upon the local area for their friendships, but because they move frequently, their friends are spread about; upper class people have more diverse sources of friendships, but with more stable residence they gradually extend their local contacts and become integrated into the community (*41*). Planned communities of a given density and layout provide X–number of conveniently located neighbors with whom friendships are established. It remains to be shown that unplanned neighborhoods of equal density and equally homogeneous composition do not provide the identical patterns of friendship formation and group structure.

We may here be the innocent victims of a research bias. Housing research has concentrated heavily on the planned community and findings have been interpreted as changed social patterns, although no base point for change was established. In fact, we may have inadvertently discovered basic patterns which have been operating in urban environments but which were not intensively investigated prior to the modern housing developments.

Under these circumstances, one is forced to ask anew, "What are the social patterns which housing and design have changed?" If anything, one is impressed perhaps less by the changes than by the continuities and the persistence of previous social patterns— with the exception of the easing of social pathology by the movement from substandard housing areas. There is little conclusive evidence of more than ephemeral changes in social patterns through the medium of planned communities. Particularly, the integration of the community does not seem to be significantly greater than is found in homogeneous, unplanned neighborhoods. Stratification and racial divisions remain effective forces.

Thus, to all intents and purposes, it remains to be established how planning does significantly more than shift or re-group active —not latent—social relations into new settings.

AESTHETICS

The final factor which concerns us is the commitment of planners and housers to an aesthetic way of life. In this, their assumptions of psychological effects of aesthetic atmosphere may be on firmer ground. Light, air, greenery, variety of color, materials, forms—within the dwelling unit and the neighborhood—may create interest which affects people's moods. In extreme cases this is clear. One need only allude to women's customary responses to blue fluorescent light.

There is reason to suspect class differentials on the importance of the variable of aesthetics. But planners have here a more intangible factor which, despite its subjectivity, may have subtle effects on mood and thereby potentially affect tolerance thresholds and the texture of social interaction. Very little research has been done on the psychological impact of different aesthetic environments (beyond some preliminary research into effects of colors), so there is little ground on which to evaluate the importance of design from this standpoint. Certainly we know its importance in merchandising—although housers may not be identified with the aesthetics in some proven packaging. In housing, however, we would expect the aesthetic element to involve much more of a Gestalt perception process rather than segmental responses. Aesthetic judgments will have to await further research.

REFERENCES

1. American Public Health Association, Committee on the Hygiene of Housing, *Planning the Neighborhood* (Chicago: Public Administration Service, 1948).
2. C. Bauer, "Social Questions in Housing and Community Planning," *Journal of Social Issues* 7, nos. 1 and 2 (1951): 1–34. Special Housing Issue.
3. C. Bauer, "Good Neighborhoods," *Annals* 242 (1945): 104–15.
4. T. Caplow and R. Forman, "Neighborhood Interaction in an Homogeneous Community," *American Sociological Review* 15 (June, 1950): 357–66.
5. F. S. Chapin, "The Effects of Slum Clearance and Rehousing on Family and Community Relationships in Minneapolis," *American Journal of Sociology* 43 (1938): 744–63.
6. F. S. Chapin, "An Experiment on the Social Effects of Good Housing," *American Sociological Review* 5 (December, 1940): 868–79.
7. F. S. Chapin, "Some Factors Related to Mental Hygiene," *Journal of Social Issues* 7, nos. 1 and 2 (1951). Special Housing Issue.
8. H. Cottam, *Housing and Attitudes Toward Housing in Rural Pennsylvania* (State College, Pa.: Pennsylvania State College School of Agriculture, 1942).
9. V. Cutler, *Personal and Family Values in the Choice of a Home* (Ithaca, N.Y.: Cornell University Agricultural Experimental Station, 1947).
10. J. Dahir, *Communities for Better Living* (New York: Harper and Bros., 1950).
11. J. Dahir, *The Neighborhood Unit Plan* (New York: Russell Sage Foundation, 1947).
12. R. Danhof, "The Accommodation and Integration of Conflicting Cultures in a Newly Established Community," *American Journal of Sociology* 48 (1943): 14–43.
13. J. Dean, "The Ghosts of Home Ownership," *Journal of Social Issues* 7, nos. 1 and 2 (1951). Special Housing Issue.
14. J. Dean, "The Myths of Housing Reform," *American Journal of Sociology* 54 (1949): 271–88.
15. R. Dewey, "The Neighborhood, Urban Ecology and City Planners," *American Sociological Review* 15 (August, 1950): 502–07.
16. R. Durant, *Watling* (London: P. S. King and Son, 1939).
17. Federal Public Housing Authority, *The Livability Problem of 1000 Families* (Washington: National Housing Agency, 1945).
18. C. Ferrier, "Frontiers of Housing Research," *Land Economics* 25 (1949), supplement.
19. L. Festinger, "Architecture and Group Membership," *Journal of Social Issues* 7, nos. 1 and 2 (1951). Special Housing Issue.
20. L. Festinger, S. Schachter, and K. Back, *Social Pressures in Informal Groups* (New York: Harper and Bros., 1950).
21. W. Form, "Status Stratification in a Planned Community," *American Sociological Review* 10 (October, 1945): 605–13.
22. W. Form, "Stratification in Low and Middle Income Housing Areas," *Journal of Social Issues* 7, nos. 1 and 2 (1951): 109–31. Special Housing Issue.
23. H. Infield, "A Veterans' Cooperative Land Settlement and its Sociometric Structure," *Sociometry* 6 (1947): 50–70.

24. R. Isaacs, "The Neighborhood Theory," *Journal of the American Institute of Planners* 14 (1948): 15–23.
25. M. Jahoda and P. S. West, "Race Relations in Public Housing," *Journal of Social Issues* 7, nos. 1 and 2 (1951). Special Housing Issue.
26. R. Jevrons and J. Madge, *Housing Estates* (Bristol, Eng.: University of Bristol, 1946).
27. C. Killbourn and M. Lantis, "Elements of Tenant Instability in a War Housing Project," *American Sociological Review* 11 (February, 1946): 57–64.
28. L. Kuper, *Living in Towns* (London: Cresset Press, 1953).
29. R. Merton, "Patterns of Interpersonal Influence and Communication Behavior in a Local Community," in P. Lazarsfeld and F. Stanton, eds., *Communications Research, 1948–49* (New York: Harper and Bros., 1949).
30. R. Merton, "The Social Psychology of Housing," in W. Dennis, ed., *Current Trends in Social Psychology* (Pittsburgh: University of Pittsburgh Press, 1948), pp. 163–217.
31. C. Perry, *Housing for the Machine Age* (New York: Russell Sage Foundation, 1939).
32. S. Riemer, "Architecture for Family Living," *Journal of Social Issues* 7, nos. 1 and 2 (1951). Special Housing Issue.
33. S. Riemer, "Designing the Family Home," in H. Becker and R. Hill, eds., *Family, Marriage and Parenthood* (Boston: D. C. Heath, 1948).
34. S. Riemer, "Maladjustment to the Family Home," *American Sociological Review* (October, 1945): 442–48.
35. S. Riemer, "Sociological Perspective in Home Planning," *American Sociological Review* 12 (April, 1947): 155–59.
36. I. Rosow, "Home Ownership Motives," *American Sociological Review* 13 (1948): 751–55.
37. I. Rosow, "Housing Research and Administrative Decisions," *Journal of Housing* 8 (1951): 285–87.
38. J. Rumney and S. Shuman, *The Cost of Slums in Newark* (Newark, 1946).
39. J. Rumney, "The Social Costs of Slums," *Journal of Social Issues* 7, nos. 1 and 2 (1951). Special Housing Issue.
40. J. Rumney and S. Shuman, *The Social Effects of Public Housing* (Newark: Newark Housing Authority, 1944).
41. J. Smith, W. Form, and G. Stone, "Local Intimacy in a Middle-Sized City," *American Journal of Sociology* 60 (November, 1954): 276–85.
42. F. Sweetser, Jr., "A New Emphasis for Neighborhood Research," *American Sociological Review* 7 (August, 1942): 525–33.
43. H. Wright, *Rehousing Urban America* (New York: Columbia University Press, 1935).

CHAPTER

Physical Distance and Persuasion

STUART ALBERT
JAMES M. DABBS, JR.

Reprinted from the *Journal of Personality and Social Psychology* 15, no. 3 (1970): 265–70, by permission of the American Psychological Association and the authors. Copyright 1970 by the American Psychological Association.

This research was supported by United States Public Health Service Grant CH-00044. The authors would like to thank Veronica Bassil, Judith Bailey, and Jim Hradski for their help in collecting data.

One aspect of our environment that has received attention has been the influence of spatial arrangement on human behavior. Past research suggests that the persuasiveness of a speaker may be influenced by the physical distance between himself and the listener. In the following chapter, Albert and Dabbs seek to measure the influence distance exerts upon the acceptance or rejection of a message.

Their findings: With an increase in distance, attitude change was less; although, under conditions of close distance, but with a hostile speaker, attitude change did not occur. Further, the findings suggest that a person's attention to the content of the message was greatest at a relatively middle distance (4 to 5 feet), while for closer or farther distances the person focused more upon the speaker's physical appearance. The listener also tended to ascribe greater expertness to the speaker at the middle distance.

Seldom does spatial arrangement seem to have a very direct effect upon communication; it is, rather, a *contributing* factor. That is, its power depends upon other conditions, such as whether the speaker is hostile or friendly. Nevertheless, physical distance may have undesirable effects on our interaction with our fellowman of which we are unaware. It may, for example, explain why someone does not seem to be listening to what you are saying, regardless of how important you think the message is. And the simple fact of where you sit in the classroom may effect your attention to the lecture. Indeed, does the commonplace phenomenon of so many students choosing to sit at the back of the room suggest something about their expected acceptance of the lecture?

The following chapter clearly demonstrates the difficulty one encounters in trying to measure the effects upon man of even as straightforward and easily measured an environmental dimension as physical distance.

A friendly or hostile speaker delivered two persuasive messages to a subject seated at 1–2, 4–5, and 14–15 feet away from him. Attitude change decreased linearly with distance, becoming negative for the hostile speaker at the close distance. Selective attention to the message was greatest at the middle distance, while at either the close or far distances, attention was apparently shifted to the physical appearance of the speaker. For one of the messages the inferred expertise of the communicator was judged greatest at the middle distance. The results are discussed in terms of Hall's concept of optimal spatial zones and in terms of acceptance and resistance forces, particularly reactance, underlying persuasion.

There has been continued interest in the psychological properties and significance of human spatial behavior (Hall, 1966; Mehrabian, 1969; Sommer, 1967). The goal of the present research was to understand the effects of different distances between speaker and listener on the process of communication and persuasion. The specific hypotheses to be tested were stimulated on the basis of three potential functional relationships between distance and the acceptance of influence.

1. The imposition of extremely close physical distances between individuals constitutes an invasion of "personal space" (Sommer, 1969), the adverse consequences of which, documented by Garfinkel (1964) and Felipe and Sommer (1966), include feelings of embarrassment, bewilderment, and actual flight. Increasing proximity may therefore increase forces of resistance; or expressed in Brehm's (1966) terms, proximity may cause the arousal of reactance and thereby result in the rejection of influence.

2. Especially when interindividual distances exceed the boundaries of personal space, the opposite relationship has been found; namely, that spatial closeness is associated with the attribution and arousal of positive attitudes and may thus facilitate the acceptance of influence (Leipold, 1963; Little, 1965; Mehrabian, 1968a, 1968b; Rosenfeld, 1965).

3. Probably reflecting the joint operation of both the positive and negative relationships mentioned above, Hall has proposed a series of culturally defined spatial zones and an analysis that implies that the acceptance of influence is curvilinearly related to distance (Hall, 1966). Certain spatial zones are appropriate for certain kinds of communication, and placement of a communicator outside of the appropriate spatial

zone will lower his effectiveness through such processes as distraction from the content of the message itself, the arousal of defensive reactions, the attribution of manipulative intent to the speaker, or the listener's inference that the speaker is treating him in a negative manner ranging from discontent to disdainful avoidance.

To explore a hypothesized curvilinear relationship between distance and persuasion, three distances were selected: a middle distance which would seem most appropriate, a far distance which would appear inappropriately large, and a close distance sufficiently small to entail the invasion of personal space.

Tolerance for spatial invasion, however, could likely be raised or lowered (and consequently persuasion increased or decreased) by endowing the speaker with positive or negative characteristics. Whatever the characteristics of the speaker, they should become more important as proximity is increased, both because they are more visible and because the evaluation of a speaker's intent becomes all the more crucial as the boundaries of personal space are approached and crossed. This expected polarization of speaker characteristics is in accord with the everyday observation that neutral interaction is virtually nonexistent at close distances. In order to study the possible interactive effects of these magnification and polarization processes on persuasion, a manipulation of speaker manner (friendly versus hostile) was added to that of distance.

In summary, to investigate the hypotheses (a) that persuasion should be maximum when the physical distance separating a speaker and a listener is intermediate, and (b) that a positive speaker is more persuasive than a negative speaker, and that this difference is accentuated at close distances, a friendly or hostile speaker delivered face-to-face persuasive communications to a subject seated at either 1–2, 4–5, or 14–15 feet from the speaker.

Measures of attitude change, recall for the content of the communication, and selective attention to different elements in the persuasion situation were obtained. Shifts in the subject's dispersal of attention were expected to clarify the concept of spatial boundary. Dependent variables also included the perception of communicator expertise, trustworthiness, status, liking, and social distance. Finally, a social schemata task was included before and after to assess further forces of acceptance and resistance to persuasive influence.

METHOD

Subjects and speaker. Subjects were 90 unpaid male University of Michigan students from an introductory psychology subject pool.

There were 15 subjects per condition, except for occasional missing data. The speaker was a 22-year-old male senior at the University of Michigan who had had some acting experience.

Design. Each subject was exposed to two messages always in the same order. These messages were delivered by a consistently friendly or hostile communicator seated either at 1–2, 4–5, or 14–15 feet away. Two messages were included to give some generality over attitude topics. The first message was highly factual and was always presented first so that differential recall for its contents might be obtained prior to any adaptation to the different speaker-listener distances. The resulting design had two between-subjects factors: speaker manner (friendly/hostile) and distance (close, medium, far). Message was not included as a within-subject factor since the sequence of messages was purposely not counterbalanced, and therefore, any effect of message would be difficult to interpret.

Messages. All subjects heard two 5-minute messages, the first on population control and the second on self-disclosure. The speaker introduced the messages as prepared discussions in the field of public health. The population message was intended to serve as a basis for measuring recall, and it presented a relatively constant flow of technical information and suggestions on how to deal with the problem of overpopulation. It was also aimed at convincing subjects that overpopulation was a serious problem and that creative proposals were being developed to cope with it. The self-disclosure message was less factual and argued in favor of the need for increased openness and honesty in interpersonal relationships. The speaker delivered the messages from a manuscript with which he was very familiar. He was coached until he could deliver the messages smoothly while carrying out the manipulations described below.

Speaker's distance. The subject entered a 15 × 24-foot conference room and was seated near the corner along the shorter side of a 6 × 13-foot rectangular table. There were no other chairs at the table. A wall behind the subject and a movie screen to one side blocked him from radically changing the position of his chair. The speaker entered, took a chair from near the wall, and slid it to one of three points along the larger side of the table. He sat down and began to talk with his face 1–2, 4–5, or 14–15 feet away from the subject's face. Pretests suggested that distances were uncomfortably close, about average, or uncomfortably far for this kind of communication. The close distance corresponds to Hall's upper boundary for intimate space, the medium to social-consultive space, and the far distance to the beginning of public space.

Speaker's manner. The speaker's manner, consistently either friendly or hostile toward a given subject, was manipulated by letting the subject see a staged interaction between the speaker and an assistant and by the speaker's direct behavior toward the subject in the communication situation.

While the subject was completing a preexperimental questionnaire, a female assistant in his presence suddenly appeared to damage a calculator (by dividing by zero, causing the machine to run continuously). The speaker entered the room, ostensibly to pick up some papers, "fixed" the calculator by pressing the stop button, and explained to the assistant how to fix the machine if it gave her trouble again (friendly manner) or told her to fix it herself next time and to learn how to operate it properly (hostile manner).

In the experimental room, the speaker either greeted the subject with a wide smile and a friendly "Hi," introduced himself cordially, and gave the subject a warm handshake, or he paused as he entered, looked silently at the subject, introduced himself gruffly, and gave a limp handshake. He spoke in a warm and friendly manner, or he spoke as if he were disgusted at having to talk to the subject. In an attempt to maintain eye contact at the same level in all conditions, the speaker glanced up briefly at the subject at 25 predetermined points during his talks. The speaker directed his manner toward the subject rather than the content of the message.

Dependent measures. Prequestionnaire and postquestionnaire items, except those dealing with information recall, were answered on 7-point Likert-type scales.

Attitude change. Four attitude items (two for each message topic) appeared on both prequestionnaires and postquestionnaires, asking, for example, whether subjects thought the world would benefit from more emphasis on population planning and control, and whether being open and revealing toward others promoted sound mental health. Four additional items appeared only on the postquestionnaire. Responses were scored so that higher scores indicated more agreement with the speaker's position.

Perception of the speaker. Postquestionnaire measures included rating of liking, status, expertness, style of presentation, and judged persuasiveness, as well as an adjective checklist of the speaker's characteristics. The subject was also asked whether he thought the communicator sat where he did because the experimenter told him to or because he wanted to. A few other items assessed miscellaneous reactions to the speaker.

Information recall. Recall was assessed by having subjects answer specific factual questions about the population speech and complete a schematic outline of that speech. A total of 19 items, weighted according to their correctness, were summed to provide an overall recall score ranging from 0 to 32.

Selective attention. For each message separately, subjects reported the percentage of time they spent thinking about (a) things related to what the speaker was saying, (b) the speaker's manner of presentation, (c) the speaker's physical appearance, (d) other objects in the room, and (e) things outside the experiment. These objects of attention are ordered roughly in terms of their remoteness from the message content.

Social schemata. A social schemata task was completed before and after subjects heard the speaker, under the guise of an aesthetic judgment task. The subject's task was to manipulate three cardboard figures to describe two friends and a mutual enemy. The distance in inches between the heads of the two friends was recorded.

RESULTS AND DISCUSSION

Perception of Distance

Distance was perceived as intended, with the middle distance regarded as the most appropriate one. A postquestionnaire item asked subjects how close the speaker sat while talking with them. Mean scores for the close, medium, and far distances were, respectively, 1.4, 4.7, and 6.3 ($F = 198.02$, $df = 2/84$, $p < .001$), on a response scale where 1 = closer than average, 4 = about average, and 7 = farther than average. The perception of the distance manipulation is not unambiguous, however, since the far distance may have been farther than average, but entirely appropriate for a presentation that was in some ways similar to a lecture.

Perception of Speaker's Characteristics

Subjects reported the friendly speaker as being more friendly (as opposed to unfriendly), warm (as opposed to cold), sensitive (as opposed to insensitive), peaceful (as opposed to aggressive), and outgoing (as opposed to withdrawn) than the hostile speaker. The friendly speaker was rated more sincere, more persuasive, more pleasing in style and manner of presentation, and more of the kind of person people would look up to. He also made a more favorable impression, and subjects were more inclined to say they liked him, wanted to know him better, and wanted to have him as a close friend. All the effects were significant at beyond the .05 level.

Subjects might have reacted differently depending upon whether or not they thought the speaker or experimenter determined the distance. Since subjects were approximately equally divided, half believed the experimenter determined the distance, the other half that the speaker selected the distance; all data were analyzed with a median split on this item as a third way of the design. This analysis produced only minor changes in the results which did not affect the interpretation of the major dependent variables and therefore will not be discussed.

Perception of the speaker was unaffected by the distance at which he sat, with two exceptions. Perceived expertness on the topic of self-disclosure was greatest at the medium distance (F quadratic $= 4.70$, $df = 1/84$, $p < .05$); perceived expertness on population control followed the same pattern, but was not significant. And one of the three liking items was affected by a complex and not readily interpretable interaction between distances and speaker's manner.

Selective Attention

Table 1 shows what subjects were thinking about while the speaker was talking. Entries represent mean percentages of time subjects reported thinking about the different objects and sum to 100 percent at each distance. (Means are for the two messages combined, since the pattern was similar for each message.) The speaker's manner did not affect these data and is not included in the table.

Object of S's attention	Speaker's distance		
	Close	Medium	Far
Message content	39	55	48
Speaker's manner of presentation	28	24	26
Speaker's physical appearance	20	9	12
Other things in room	4	4	4
Things outside experiment	9	8	9

Table 1. *Mean Percentage of Time Subjects Thought about Various Things in Three Distance Conditions*

A subject who attends more to one thing attends less to something else, and an effect of distance in one row of the table will produce complementary effects in other rows. The main row of interest is the top one. More attention was directed toward speech content at the medium distance, less at the close and far distances ($F = 5.95$, $df = 2/84$, $p < .01$). The only other row with a significant distance effect is the third one ($F = 5.51$, $df = 2/84$, $p < .01$), showing that attention is directed more toward the speaker's physi-

Speaker's manner	Speaker's distance		
	Close	Medium	Far
Friendly	39.9	40.8	43.2
Hostile	37.2	40.2	40.7

Table 2. *Mean Attitude Postmeasures Adjusted to Control for Differences in Initial Attitude Scores*

Note: Higher scores indicate more agreement with the speaker.

cal appearance at close and far distances: attention is diverted away from the content of the message and toward the physical appearance of the speaker.

Information Recall

Analysis of variance of the overall recall measure showed no significant effect of the experimental manipulations, although recall was highest at the medium distance $(F = 2.17, df = 2/84, ns.)$. On the possibility that subjects adapted rapidly to the speaker's unusual distances, the data were scored to measure recall of content delivered in the first minute of the message. Even within this subset of data, however, there was no significant effect of distance.

Attitude Change

Since examination of the postquestionnaire attitude data showed similar patterns of response to the two messages, the four attitude items on each topic were summed into an overall score for each subject. In order to control for marginally significant initial differences in attitudes, the sum of the four prequestionnaire items was used as a control variable in an analysis of covariance of the overall postmeasure attitude scores. Mean attitude postmeasures corrected for initial position are shown in Table 2, with a summary of the analysis of covariance in Table 3. Persuasion increased as the speaker moved farther away. As can be seen from Table 1, there was no indication of a quadratic effect. Messages were accepted

Source	df	MS	F
Manner (A)	1	80.84	3.56
Distance (B)	2	87.44	3.85*
A × B	2	9.85	<1.0
Error	83	22.72	

Table 3. *Analysis of Covariance of Attitude Postmeasures*

* $p < .05$.

Speaker's manner	Speaker's distance		
	Close	Medium	Far
Friendly	.2	.3	.5
Hostile	−.4	−.2	.1

Table 4.   *Mean Attitude Change from Before to After Messages*

somewhat more readily from the friendly than from the hostile speaker ($p < .10$), and there was no interaction between speaker's distance and manner.

It is not possible to tell from Table 2 whether there might have been zero or even negative attitude change in some of the conditions. Therefore a prechange to postchange score was computed for each subject based on the mean of four items common to both prequestionnaires and postquestionnaires.

The pattern of the data presented in Table 4 is similar to that in Table 2, although the difference between the friendly and hostile speakers is now significant ($p < .01$), while the distance effect is borderline (p linear trend $< .10$). Significant change toward disagreement with the position of the speaker occurred in the close-hostile conditions ($t = 2.0$, $df = 14$, $p < .10$; or by a sign test, 3 plus and 10 minus changes, $p < .05$).

Resistance to Influence
Since none of the variables which might have plausibly mediated attitude change showed similar linear patterns, the interpretation of the results must be somewhat speculative.

The observation of negative attitude change at the close distance suggests that the speaker may have aroused resistance, or reactance, defined by Brehm (1966, 1968), as a motivational state that operates to resist, reject, or react against any pressure that restricts freedom. The social schemata task provides evidence for this view, since a majority of subjects placed their cutout figures farther apart in the close-hostile condition after encountering the speaker. In the rest of the conditions, most subjects placed the figures closer together ($x^2 = 6.06$, $df = 2$, $p < .05$). If proximity was felt as pressure which constrained or restricted the subject, one way of resisting the pressure was to reject what the speaker had to say.

The experimenters, who went through the procedure as subjects, found interaction at progressively closer distances to be a disquieting experience. As distance decreases, the speaker appears to focus his attention more intently upon the listener and gives the impression of trying to influence him. As a consequence it is difficult for the listener to relax. He must observe the social amenities of paying attention, reciprocating eye contact, and in general avoiding unnecessary movement. When he does engage in expressive behavior, the listener tries to do so as unobtrusively as possible. The attention the speaker directs toward the listener was probably exaggerated in the present experiment because the speaker maintained eye contact at a constant level, although eye contact would normally have decreased when he moved closer (Argyle and Dean, 1965).

Evidence for Spatial Zones
There is some evidence in support of Hall's notion of appropriate spatial zones. Attention to message content was greatest at the medium distance: at the other distances, attention was directed away from message content toward the physical appearance of the speaker. Perceived expertness tended to be greater at the medium distance. Recall was somewhat greater at the medium than at the close or far distances, though not significantly so. The reduction in persuasion that might have been caused by the possible inappropriateness of the far distance was probably masked by the more powerful consequences of a reduction in reactance at that distance.

GENERAL COMMENTS
Except for the social schemata task, no support was provided for the hypothesis that the perceived difference between the friendly and hostile speakers would be exaggerated at close distances. The hypothesis may have been wrong; subjects may have been more concerned with the invasion of personal space per se than with the characteristics of the invader, at least within the range that they were manipulated. It is also possible that the instructions to form an impression of the speaker caused subjects to impute unalterably high importance to speaker characteristics regardless of distance. In addition, other factors may be of overriding importance, such as whether extreme proximity is the result of invitation or is imposed, as in the present experiment.

It is disconcerting to note that the theoretical principles necessary to delineate variables that should be sensitive to variations in distance from those that should remain insensitive still remains elusive. Close proximity, for example, while detrimental to attitude change, did not result in the unselective derogation of the communicator. For example, while his expertness was judged to be lower, the attribution of such traits as bold-shy and peaceful-aggressive were staunchly unaffected.

Finally, a limitation on the generality of the results should be pointed out. Only one speaker was used, and although he did not present both friendly and hostile roles to the same subject, his own expectancies are still of some concern. When questioned after the experiment, the speaker stated that he believed the positive role at the middle distance should have been most persuasive, a result that did not obtain. Further research might employ multiple speakers, as well as record the nonverbal correlates of persuasion associated with different distances (see, e.g., Mehrabian and Williams, 1969).

REFERENCES

M. Argyle and J. Dean, "Eye Contact, Distance, and Affiliation," *Sociometry* 28 (1965): 280, 304.

J. W. Brehm, *A Theory of Psychological Reactance* (New York: Academic Press, 1966).

————, "Attitude Change from Threat to Attitudinal Freedom," in A. G. Greenwald, T. C. Brock, and J. M. Ostrom, eds., *Psychological Foundations of Attitudes* (New York: Academic Press, 1968).

M. A. Dosey and M. Meisels, "Personal Space and Self-Protection," *Journal of Personality and Social Psychology* 11 (1969): 93–97.

N. J. Felipe and R. Sommer, "Invasions of Personal Space," *Social Problems* 14 (1966): 206–14.

H. Garfinkel, "Studies of the Routine Grounds of Everyday Activities," *Social Problems* 11 (1964): 225–50.

E. T. Hall, *The Hidden Dimension* (Garden City, N.Y.: Doubleday, 1966).

W. E. Leipold, "Psychological Distance in a Dyadic Interview," Unpublished doctoral dissertation, University of North Dakota, 1963.

K. B. Little, "Personal Space," *Journal of Experimental Social Psychology* 1 (1965): 237–47.

A. Mehrabian, "Inference of Attitude from the Posture, Orientation, and Distance of a Communicator," *Journal of Consulting and Clinical Psychology* 32 (1968): 296–308. (a)

————, "Relationship of Attitude to Seated Posture, Orientation, and Distance," *Journal of Personality and Social Psychology* 10 (1968): 26–30. (b)

————, "Significance of Posture and Position in the Communication of Attitude and Status Relationships," *Psychological Bulletin* 71 (1969): 359–72.

A. Mehrabian and M. Williams, "Nonverbal Concomitants of Perceived and Intended Persuasiveness," *Journal of Personality and Social Psychology* 13 1969): 37–58.

H. M. Rosenfeld, "Effect of an Approval-Seeking Induction on Interpersonal Proximity," *Psychological Reports* 17 (1965): 120–2.

R. Sommer, *Personal Space: The Behavioral Basis of Design* (Englewood Cliffs, N.J.: Prentice-Hall, 1969).

CHAPTER

Effect of Environmental
Experience on Spatial Ability
in an East African Society

ROBERT L. MUNROE
RUTH H. MUNROE

Reprinted from *The Journal of Social
Psychology* 83, no. 1 (February, 1971):
15–22, by permission of The Journal
Press and the authors. Copyright 1971
by The Journal Press.
  Received in the Editorial Office,
Provincetown, Massachusetts on 29
April 1970, and given special consider-
ation in accordance with their policy
of cross-cultural research.
  The authors are indebted to the
following for aid in various phases of
the research: Printha Berry, Josiah
Embego, Myra Kagasi, Mary Kushner,
Joyce Mmene, Reuben Snipper, Stella
Vlastos, Beatrice Whiting, and John
Whiting. The cooperation of the Kenya
Ministry of Education, the local
officials, and, most of all, the Logoli
people, is gratefully acknowledged.
The research was carried out in 1967
while the authors were members of the
Child Development Research Unit
(John Whiting, general director), University College, Nairobi, supported by
the Carnegie Corporation of New York.
The authors resided in the sample community for one year, collecting ethnographic data and conducting systematic
interviews, observations, and testing
sessions. Data analysis was supported
by a grant from the National Institute
of Mental Health (#MH–15876–01).

This study by the Munroes is a splendid example of how man's environmental experience can influence his psychology. They show how differences in children's familiarity with their physical community and its surroundings are found to correlate with differences in their spatial abilities—those who wandered farther from home in their playtime were those who evidenced the greater skill.

Equally interesting is their finding that these differences in environmental experience and spatial judgment were related to sex. Thus, in general, boys outperformed girls on tests of spatial conceptual ability (although scoring equally on overall intelligence) and it was boys who were found to exercise greater movement through their physical environment.

The Munroes then raise a series of most relevant questions: if the male's greater spatial ability is conceived of as resulting in some way from his greater environmental experience, to what can one attribute that greater experience? Is it that society encourages environmental exploration in boys and inhibits it in girls? Or, is the greater investigativeness in boys an innate sex difference?

The authors consider both possibilities and indeed conclude that it is an interaction between biological givens and social roles that constitutes the current most probable answer. But it is a fascinating piece of data that there *were* two girls who *did* score higher on spatial ability than their male counterparts, and that in both of these exceptional cases, the girls had also been found to have had the greater environmental experience.

A. INTRODUCTION

Evidence indicates that natural experiential differences lead to intellective differences between sexes (Macoby, 1966), social classes
(Jensen, 1968), and ethnic groups (Lesser, Fifer, and Clark, 1965),
among others. Often, however, the experiences are inferred rather
than measured. In the present study, an attempt is made to link a
specific, easily measurable experiential variable with performance
on a similarly structural intellective task.

The study was prompted by a serendipitous finding made in
the course of exploratory experimental work carried out among the
Logoli of western Kenya. Among children in the West, the capacity
to construct a diagonal pattern with checkers on a 5 x 5 checker-
board (after a model was viewed) had been found by Olson (1971)
to require fairly complex conceptual ability, and for comparative
purposes the diagonality task was administered to Logoli children.
Unexpectedly it was found that boys performed significantly better than girls. On a modified form of the Porteus maze test
(Arthur, 1947), male Logoli children also achieved significantly
higher scores than did females. Performance on the mazes was significantly associated with performance on the diagonality task. On
a further test, a conservation task, there was no sex difference and
no association with either maze performance or ability to construct
the diagonal. This appeared to indicate that (a) the diagonality
task and maze test were tapping some specific intellective ability,
and (b) the sex difference reflected male superiority not in overall
intelligence but rather with respect to this specific ability.

Efforts to understand the source of the sex difference led to a
consideration of experiential factors whose components might be
similar to those involved in the tests. The diagonality and maze
tests require in common the capacity to perform a set of behaviors
ordered sequentially in space. One simple way in which practice
would be obtained in spatial sequences would be by extensive movement through the physical environment. It had been noted casually
that young boys were more often to be seen than girls in the neighborhood of the ethnographers' home. Also, in several observations
at a nearby playing field, it was found that the boy-girl ratio was
about 7 to 1. Could the greater environmental experience of the
boys help to account for their greater ability to perform spatial
tasks? In order to obtain at least a partial answer to this question,
it seemed necessary to undertake two separate phases of investigation.

The first phase was designed to investigate the validity of the
supposed sex difference in environmental experience. Selected chil-

dren in a Logoli community were observed systematically in order to see whether young boys did in fact venture farther from home than young girls. The Logoli child spends the majority of his time outdoors. From about the age of three, unless given a task to perform, the child is more or less free to travel away from his immediate home area for brief stretches of time. Although mothers expect that their children will be nearby if needed, wide variations are found both in directions to the child and in efforts to enforce the expectation. Often a mother employs different techniques depending upon her experience with particular children—e.g., a child who wanders may be considered less able to be influenced by mother direction and the mother may attempt few controlling techniques. The children may thus be found anywhere from near home to fairly distant with whereabouts unknown for brief periods.

The second phase undertook to discover whether those persons with greater environmental experience would be superior on intellective tasks requiring spatial ability. That is, if environmental experience were a significant contributor to spatial ability, then this should be demonstrable with the same sample on which measures of experience with the environment were made. Accordingly, in the second phase of the work a set of spatial tasks was administered to the sample of observation children.

B. SEX DIFFERENCES IN ENVIRONMENTAL EXPERIENCE

1. Method

Fifteen boys and 15 girls between the ages of three and seven were sorted into pairs on the basis of age-matching. (Numerous other potential sample members who approximated age-matching less closely were excluded.) Ages were ascertained during genealogical work with the entire community in which the sample children resided. For 20 percent of the sample, the birth dates were recorded by a family member or by a member of the local Quaker church. For the remaining children, the parents' recollected date of birth was checked by the other (extensive) family data available and cross-checked by questioning other members of the community on order of birth of those children close to each other in age. Average error, for the recollected dates, is estimated to be no greater than two months. Education was not associated with either environmental experience or spatial ability within the six pairs in which one or both members were attending school.

Each of the sample members was observed in the natural setting a total of 20 times (except one S who moved away with her mother after 15 observations). A male Logoli observer, who was unaware of the hypothesis, made all observations after a brief period of training. The observer noted several aspects of the S's activity and social environment. For present purposes, however, only the distance of the S from home and the directed or undirected character of his activities are of relevance.

The observer was often unable to locate Ss who were more than several hundred feet away for given observations. Estimates on large distances therefore were in many cases unavailable or unreliable (being based on reports). To circumvent this problem, the distance measure was converted into a five-point rating scale, as follows: (1) 0–99 feet from home; (2) 100–199 feet; (3) 200–299 feet; (4) 300–399 feet; (5) 400 or more feet. Interobserver reliability was obtained on the estimates of distance: For a total of 30 observations, the Spearman rank-order correlation coefficient between the Logoli observer's estimates and those of one of the investigators (RLM) was +.89.

2. Results

For average distance-ratings, there was a nonsignificant tendency for males to be farther from home than their age-matched female counterparts. However, these scores included the observations on which Ss had been instructed by an older person to carry out some assigned task. In the process of carrying out a chore, a child would often follow some route which involved leaving the immediate home area. For example, obtaining water, typically a girl's job, required a trip of several hundred feet from most houses. In such cases the child would indeed be experiencing a different part of the environment than the child who stayed near home, but the nature of tasks and chores meant that a mechanical, unvarying route was being followed. This suggested that observations involving directed activities should be excluded from consideration. More likely to be useful was a measure of the child's distance from home in his free time (1).

When average distances were calculated only for observations in which the S was undirected, it was found that in 13 of the 15 pairings the male was rated as more distant from home on the average than the female ($p < .01$, sign test). This result was in line with the casual observations made earlier.

In addition to the sex difference in free-time distance, it was also possible that males were free for a greater proportion of time. However, this was true in only nine of 13 cases, with two ties ($p < .30$, sign test). (This somewhat unexpected lack of difference was due to the younger members of the sample. Among the nine oldest pairs, the boy was directed in his activities less frequently than the girl in seven cases, and was tied with the girl in another.)

To sum up, the hypothesized difference in the environmental experience of males and females was upheld for free, undirected activities: Male children were farther from home than female children of the same age. Given this finding, comparison could be made between results on the distance measure and the scores on the spatial tasks.

C. ENVIRONMENTAL EXPERIENCE AND SPATIAL ABILITY

1. Method

Twenty-eight of the 30 children who were observed were given a series of experimental tasks. (One child left the community during the observation period, and a second left after the observations but prior to the experimental sessions.) The elimination of one S from each of two pairs reduced the sample to 13 age-matched pairs. A female Logoli university student, who was unaware of the hypothesis, carried out the procedures in the vernacular. The E administered tasks designed to explore several developmental areas; all were chosen or constructed to be appropriate for this non-Western setting. For present purposes, only the tasks with a spatial component are of relevance.

Because of the age range of the Ss, it was difficult to find spatial tasks which could be carried out at least minimally at the varying developmental stages represented in the sample. Of the three spatial tasks administered, only two were successful in eliciting differential performances. Olson's (1971) diagonality task was too difficult for the Ss, only one of the sample members being able to construct the diagonal successfully. The other two tasks proved more workable, and are described below.

a. Copying block patterns. Eighteen increasingly complex block patterns (built vertically) were presented one by one to each S in individual sessions. For each pattern, S was requested to "make one just like this," E indicating by gesture that S should copy E's pattern using blocks laid on the table in front of S. E constructed the model with S watching for the first four patterns. The remaining patterns were built behind a cardboard table screen. The model remained on the table directly in front of S throughout the copying period for each pattern. Unlimited time was allowed. A second trial was given to any S who made an error in the first trial. The original model remained on the table for the second trial. The testing was discontinued when an error was made on both trials for a given pattern.

b. Copying geometric figures. A circle (4.5 em in diameter), a square (3.7 em per side), and a diamond (4.0 em per side) were presented successively on separate 8 x 10 sheets to the *S* in individual sessions. *S* was given a pencil and was told: "Make one just like this. Make it here." *E* indicated the blank space below the model. After *S* had completed trial 1, for the circle, he was asked to copy the circle again, in the blank space remaining on the same sheet of paper. *E* then followed the same procedure with the square and the diamond, obtaining two trials for each figure.

The productions were not scored as pass-fail, as in the Stanford-Binet (Terman and Merrill, 1960) test, although the same criteria for judgment were used. Two raters compared the drawings produced by each pair of age-matched *S*s, and made a judgment regarding which *S* more closely approximated the model for each figure. The criteria used for evaluating the circle were approximation to roundness and degree of closure; for the square, the preservation of the angles and proportions of lengths of lines; for the diamond, positions of sides and angles in relation to each other, and approximation of equality in side length. Raters achieved 85 percent agreement on items. The ratings of the more experienced rater were used for statistical tests. The pair member who was rated as having copied the majority of designs more exactly was assigned a "+" for the purposes of statistical comparison on the sign test.

2. Results

a. Copying block patterns. Of the 13 pairs, the *S* who had been found farther from home in free time during the observations was better in block building in 10 of 11 cases, with two ties ($p < .02$, sign test). The hypothesis is thus supported. Probably the most significant aspect of the results is the fact that both of the girls who had been found farther from home in the observations were superior in block building to their male counterparts, and these were two of only three females who outperformed their age-matched males.

b. Copying geometric figures. The *S* who had been farthest from home in the observations was superior in copying geometric figures in nine of 13 cases ($p < .30$, sign test), a directionally correct but nonsignificant finding. However, most *S*s had had no prior experience with copying figures, and the generally poor reproductions made judgments about superior quality somewhat moot. It is probably fair to say that the task did not adequately measure spatial abilities in the present sample.

D. DISCUSSION

Some evidence is available to support the suggestion of a link between specific natural experiences and intellective abilities. In Mexico, Price-Williams, Gordon, and Ramirez (1969) found that children in pottery-making families achieved better performance on conservation tasks than children in non-pottery-making families. The role of manipulation thus seems to be important for the attainment of conservation. In a comparative study, Berry (1966) argued that a far-ranging hunting and trapping life (as well as other cultural and ecological factors) would lead the Baffin Island Eskimo to develop superior spatial abilities to those of the settled, village dwelling Temne of Sierra Leone. The prediction was strongly borne out in individual testing among members of the two societies.

Distance from home has been conceived as an independent variable contributing in some significant way to spatial ability. However, the factors producing typical distance are themselves worth considering, particularly in view of the fact that boys are regularly farther from home than girls. It may be that the young girl has internalized enough of the domestic aspects of the Logoli female sex role that she is inhibited from venturing as far from home as the young boy (this despite the absence of a significant sex difference in the frequency of chores during the observations). Another possible source of the sex difference is in the basic primate pattern of greater investigativeness and aggressiveness among immature males than immature females (DeVore, 1965; Freedman, Loring, and Martin, 1967). Consonant with this pattern, sex differences in human infant behavior have been found, with male one-year-olds more willing to spend time away from the mother in a strange setting than same-aged females (Goldberg and Lewis, 1969). Further, Mead (1949) implies that boys wander farther from home than girls in all societies. The Logoli data on distance from home therefore may be attributable to an innate sex difference.

Rather than learning or innate predisposition, however, the possibility of interaction between the two should be considered. As D'Andrade has put it:

> . . . because of the genetic biological differences between human males and females, some of the differences on various response measures will be innately determined rather

than learned. . . . these differences compound into complex causal chains, resulting in sets of institutional structures that "act back" on the conditions that created them in the first place, sometimes amplifying the original conditions, sometimes elaborating them in a variety of ways (p. 202).

Thus, to apply such a view to the present discussion, an innate tendency toward greater investigativeness and aggressiveness would lead most males to a higher level of environmental experience than that achieved by most females. For adaptive reasons, child training in most societies would support the innate tendencies and thereby amplify the original sex difference. An unintended and uninstitutionalized but widespread effect of this mutually reinforcing pattern would be the superior male performance found on spatial tasks (Anastasi, 1958; Tyler, 1965). Adult males, buttressed further by supporting sex-role expectations, would be more likely both to attempt and to be successful at skills requiring spatial ability. It is therefore not surprising to find males so disproportionately represented in such fields as the physical sciences, engineering, and architecture, where spatial ability is an important element in successful performance.

E. SUMMARY

In exploratory testing, a finding was made that Logoli male children were more skillful than Logoli female children at certain tests requiring the capacity to perform a set of behaviors ordered sequentially in space. As it had been casually noted that boys seemed to be more away from their immediate home areas than girls, the hypothesis was advanced that extensive movement through the environment might lead to enhanced spatial ability. To test this hypothesis, a two-phase study was carried out. In the first phase, an observational study, it was found that in free time Logoli boys between the ages of three and seven were in fact farther from home on the average than age-matched Logoli girls. In the second phase, consisting of a set of tests, it was found that children who were farther from home on the average than their age-matched counterparts were also more skillful at the spatial task of copying block patterns. The possible contributions of both innate sex differences and sex-role differences to male environmental experience and male spatial abilities were discussed.

NOTE

1. Such a possibility was enhanced by a finding that the development of spatial coordination and perception in young cats was strongly influenced by self-produced movement (Held and Hein, 1963). Although the animal studies have been directed toward initial development, it appears possible that increased voluntary movement, with route-choices nondirected, might aid in forming skills and concepts necessary for some more complex spatial tasks.

REFERENCES

A. Anastasi, *Differential Psychology* (New York: Macmillan, 1958).

G. Arthur, *Point Scale of Performance Tests, Revised Form II* (New York: Psychological Corp., 1947).

J. W. Berry, "Temne and Eskimo Perceptual Skills," *International Journal of Psychology* 1 (1966): 207–29.

R. G. D'Andrade, "Sex Differences and Cultural Institutions," in E. E. Maccoby, ed., *The Development of Sex Differences* (Stanford: Stanford University Press, 1966).

I. DeVore, ed., *Primate Behavior* (New York: Holt, Rinehart and Winston, 1965).

D. G. Freedman, C. B. Loring, and R. M. Martin, "Emotional Behavior and Personality Development," in Y. Brackbill, ed., *Infancy and Early Childhood* (New York: Free Press, 1967).

S. Goldberg and M. Lewis, "Play Behavior in the Year-Old Infant: Early Sex Differences," *Child Development* 40 (1969): 21–31.

R. Held and A. Hein, "Movement-Produced Stimulation in the Development of Visually Guided Behavior," *Journal Comp. and Physiol. Psychology* 56 (1963): 872–76.

A. R. Jensen, "Social Class and Verbal Learning," in M. Deutsch, I. Katz, and A. R. Jensen, eds., *Social Class, Race and Psychological Development* (New York: Holt, Rinehart and Winston, 1968).

G. Lesser, G. Fifer, and D. H. Clark, "Mental Abilities of Children from Different Social-Class and Cultural Groups," *Monog. Soc. Res. Child Devel.* 102 (1965).

E. E. Maccoby, "Sex Differences in Intellectual Functioning," in E. E. Maccoby, ed., *The Development of Sex Differences* (Stanford: Stanford University Press, 1966).

M. Mead, *Male and Female* (New York: New American Library, 1949).

D. R. Olson, *Cognitive Development: The Child's Acquisition of Diagonality* (New York: Academic Press, 1971).

D. Price-Williams, W. Gordon, and M. Ramirez, III, "Skill and Conservation: A Study of Pottery-Making Children," *Devel. Psychol.* 1 (1969): 769.

L. M. Terman and M. A. Merrill, *Revised Stanford-Binet Intelligence Scale: Third Edition* (Boston: Houghton Mifflin, 1960).

L. Tyler, *The Psychology of Human Differences* (New York: Meredith, 1965).

CHAPTER

Water Witching:

Magical Ritual in Contemporary United States

RAY HYMAN
EVON Z. VOGT

Reprinted from *Psychology Today* 1, no. 1 (May, 1967): 35–42, by permission of the publisher and the authors. Copyright © Communications/Research/ Machines, Inc.
    Photographs and artwork in the original article have been deleted for this publication.

Most persons have probably heard of water witching, the technique of locating ground water through the ritual of employing a divining rod. But it is surprising to learn that in the United States, the most scientific, technologically-oriented society in the world, there are an estimated 25,000 water witchers, who profess to find water with their spiritual rods.

Considering the absence of any scientifically controlled studies to support the efficaciousness of water witching, one wonders why such non-scientific beliefs persist in our culture. Applying the anthropologist's Malinowski's theory, Hyman and Vogt suggest that where man *must* make a choice in an area of heightened uncertainty and risk, the need to find an answer is fulfilled by resorting to magic. Hence, we find water witching more frequently practiced in those areas of the country with the greatest problems in locating and procuring ground water.

However, while this general relationship between geographical aridity and water witching is shown, the study at the same time illustrates the variety of man's responses to a particular aspect of his physical environment. Thus, no matter how desperate the search for water, not everybody who decides to sink a well will locate it on the advice of a man and his twig. So, the question remains why do some men seek the services of a water witch while others don't? Are those persons who employ magic less able to tolerate uncertainty, are they more anxious, are they less confident in their own abilities to reason and apply scientific knowledge and technological skill? We can only speculate on these questions, and the final explanation still escapes us as to why the belief and practice of water witching persists amidst a wealth of available scientific information.

This paper also suggests the power of the unconscious. The belief in water witching held by the witch himself is sufficiently strong to cause a muscular response, which turns down the stick. Yet, the witch remains unaware of the relationship between the idea and its execution. Clearly, each of us can ponder the extent to which our own beliefs influence our behavior in ways unknown to us.

Finally, the authors discuss whether the act of utilizing a water witch to locate a well can in any sense be considered rational. If the strategy is to locate a well with a specific amount of water, then clearly it is irrational to resort to a peach twig. However, if the desire is to reduce anxiety and ambiguity, then is it irrational to employ a witch? The authors argue:

> . . . It may be psychologically rational to choose an immediately available solution that provides specific guidance, reduces ambiguity, supplies emotional reassurance, and permits decisive action in a situation of anxiety and stress.

Maybe. But what happens when the hole is dug and there is not a drop to drink? Water witching is certainly psychologically understandable, and when lucky, psychologically functional, but it is never "rational."

For the past half hour Judd Potter has been pacing slowly back and forth over Mark Bond's pasture, a forked peach branch in his hands. Gripping one fork in each hand so tightly that the veins stand out, his head bent forward, his eyes focused on the juncture of the forks, Judd Potter acts like a man in a trance.

Suddenly the branch begins to quiver and dance as though it were alive. As Judd takes a few more steps, the branch is pulled downward toward the ground so powerfully that the bark peels off in his hands. Judd's tense body relaxes and for the first time since beginning the ritual, he looks at Mark Bond, who has been anxiously following behind. "This is the spot," he says. "Sink your well here and you'll get all the water you need."

Judd Potter has just performed the ancient rite of water witching—also known by a variety of other names such as "water divining," "dowsing," "smelling," "witch wriggling"—and his divining rod, the forked peach branch, has shown by its dance where Bond should drill for water.

Until this moment, Bond had regarded the practice of water witching with extreme skepticism. An up-to-date farmer, graduate of an agricultural college, he knew there was no scientific basis for water witching and that scientists view the practice as a relic of the superstitious past. But there had been a severe drought; his well had gone dry and his attempts to drill a new one had produced only dry holes. The county agricultural extension agent, when asked for advice, had nothing better to offer than "Keep trying. Good luck." So in desperation Bond had turned to a neighboring farmer, Judd Potter, an old-timer with a reputation for having successfully witched hundreds of wells. With no other alternative at hand, it seemed sensible to give Potter a chance to see what he could do.

And to Mark Bond's delight and astonishment, when he drilled at the spot where the peach limb had danced and quivered, he found water in abundance. Bond's skepticism was converted into ardent belief in the power of the divining rod, and no wonder.

Mark Bond's plight was of course by no means unique. And neither was his solution. Under similar circumstances, farmers throughout the United States turn today, as they did in the past, to water witches.

Even if water witching were not a fascinating subject for research in its own right, it would be worth studying if only because of its widespread continuing popularity in an advanced technological society, and because it has always been controversial. Ever since the practice began, more than 400 years ago, authorities of church, government, and science have consistently opposed it. Nevertheless, the drama enacted in Mark Bond's pasture may be witnessed in every state in America.

It was the paradoxical persistence of this outcast art within a scientifically and technologically oriented culture that originally aroused our interest in water witching—the fact that today's farmers, who employ the latest findings to help them in selecting seed and fertilizers, and in fighting plant diseases, nevertheless bypass scientific help and turn to ancient divining practices when they seek underground water. We thought that a closer look at water witching might tell us something about the perseverance of non-scientific beliefs within our culture, as an example of a more general phenomenon—the way people try to cope with uncertain and unpredictable environments. The study of water witching might give us clues about why people, under stress and anxiety, turn to unorthodox and pseudoscientific practices in general.

WATER WITCHING AND MAGIC

Many aspects of water witching indicate that its role in our society is similar to that of magical ritual in primitive societies. Water witching, like magic, has an immediate practical aim; like magic, it is carried out only by those who have "the gift"; it is performed according to an unchanging ritual; it is accompanied by a mythology (about the distribution of underground water) ; and its mythology supplies ready rationales for apparent failures.

The study of water witching as a form of magical ritual also offers the opportunity to evaluate a widely accepted but seldom-tested anthropological theory about the function of magic. As stated by the anthropologist, Bronislaw Malinowski, this theory holds that "man resorts to magic only where chance and circumstances are not fully controlled by knowledge." Malinowski believed that people resort to magic when two factors are present in a situation; when there is a gap in knowledge concerning the outcome of an important event in nature, and when an individual must nevertheless act.

In a famous example, Malinowski described the fishing practices of the natives of the Trobriand Archipelago. The villagers living on the inner lagoon could easily and reliably obtain fish by poisoning the waters. Those living on the open coast, however, could obtain fish only under conditions that were hazardous and highly unreliable. "It is most significant," Malinowski wrote, "that in the lagoon fishing, where man can rely completely upon his knowledge and skill, magic does not exist, while in the open-sea fishing, full of danger and uncertainty, there is extensive magical ritual to secure safety and good results."

If Malinowski's theory about the function of magic applies to water witching, we should expect to find a correlation between the prevalence of water witching and the degree of uncertainty and risk that accompanies the locating of underground water. From this we can derive a hypothesis and counter-hypothesis to test Malinowski's theory: We would expect to find that witching is common wherever the outcome of well-digging is highly uncertain; on the other hand, we would *not* expect water witching to be practiced where groundwater conditions and geological knowledge make the outcome highly predictable.

We therefore carried out a large-scale study whose primary objective was to gather information that would confirm or contradict the hypothesis. As by-products of our study, however, we uncovered considerable information about the characteristics of water witches, the types of instruments used, and the folklore which supports the practice in the United States.

THE SURVEY

We needed to obtain two major sets of data: information on the groundwater problems in a representative sample of rural counties throughout the United States, and on the prevalence of witching in these counties. Our first task, that of obtaining a representative sample of counties, was carried out as follows: On the basis of our survey of the 3017 counties in the United States (as of 1956), we divided them into two strata, one of which included all counties in which 50 percent of the population was classified as urban. The other stratum, consisting of rural counties, was subdivided into 10 smaller strata, based on groundwater regions as classified according to the system devised by Harold Thomas of the U.S. Geological Survey. This gave us a total of 11 strata. From the one large urban stratum, and from each of the 10 rural strata, we drew a random sample of counties, giving us a total of 500 counties.

We mailed a questionnaire to the county agricultural extension agent in each of the 500 counties of our sample. The questionnaire contained 26 queries relating to problems of finding groundwater, and to the practice of water witching. In our covering letter we defined a water witch or dowser as one who:

1. uses or has used a forked stick, wire, or pendulum to locate underground water and

2. as a result of whose activity a well has been dug or drilled on the site he indicated.

Our conclusions are based on the 360 usable responses we received, and on the additional information (from census reports and other sources) about precipitation, groundwater conditions, and population characteristics for each of these counties.

THE EXTENT OF WITCHING IN THE UNITED STATES

We used two indices of witching activity: (1) the proportion of wells that are witched; and (2) the proportion of diviners in the population. Of the two, the first index is probably the more direct measure of witching activity, but unfortunately it is harder to obtain and is probably less reliable, for many agents were reluctant to estimate the number of wells that had been witched, and when they did, they indicated that they were not confident of their figures. In our sample, this index ranged all the way from none to 100 percent of wells dug—the latter in a county in southern Nevada.

On the other hand, most of the agents seemed to be reasonably sure that they knew the number of diviners in their counties. Our index of witches was based on the number of reported witches per 100,000 population. In our sample, the index ranged from none to 643, the highest concentration occurring in southwestern Kansas.

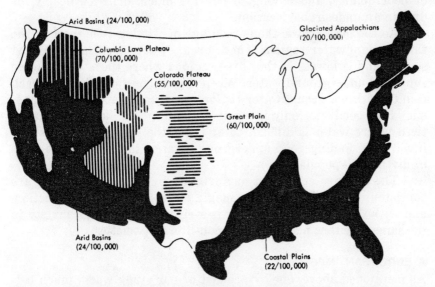

Figure 1.   Results of the survey show that in the three groundwater regions where underground water is difficult to locate (stripes), the number of witches per 100,000 population is highest; in the three regions where water is easy to locate (black), the number of witches is lowest. (Only 6 of the 10 groundwater regions in the United States are shown.)

Since we found that the two indices were very highly correlated with each other, we used the ratio of witches-to-population as our index of witching activity.

If we extrapolate this ratio to the United States as a whole, it appears that there are approximately 18 witches per 100,000 population, or a total of 25,000 water witches in the country. A further breakdown reveals that there are about 35 witches per 100,000 population in predominantly rural areas and only eight witches per 100,000 in urban areas. Of course, these figures are only approximate. Nevertheless, our estimates are sufficiently precise to assure us that the practice of water witching is carried out by a significant portion of the population as a whole, and by a rather large segment of the rural population.

GROUNDWATER PROBLEMS AND WITCHING

We used several indices of the general difficulty and uncertainty of obtaining groundwater: (1) the type of groundwater region in which the county was located; (2) responses of the county agents as to average depth, range of depth, and adequacy of the water supply, and the cost of well drilling; and (3) a "problem score" for each county, based on the agent's estimate of the probability of getting a dry hole, of obtaining sufficient rate of flow, of getting water of poor quality, and having to pay too much, drill too deeply, or drill in an undesirable location.

As the map shows, the percentage of witches is highest in the three groundwater regions where groundwater problems are most severe, and is lowest in the three regions where there is an ample supply of underground water. When we analyzed our data for each county within a groundwater region, we found that the same tendency held good: not only is water witching most likely to be practiced where water is difficult to find, but the greater the problems involved in finding good underground water, the greater the ratio of diviners to population.

The findings confirmed our original hypothesis, and they are consistent with the theory that magic serves an important function, and with the view that witching is a ritual that reduces anxiety in the same way that magic does in non-literate societies.

A EUROPEAN IMPORT

As mentioned above, one by-product of our study was a much better picture of water witching as it is currently practiced in rural America.

On the basis of the evidence available to us, we conclude that water witching is a European practice which was brought to this country, probably in the seventeenth century, by settlers from Germany and from England, especially those from the mining districts of Cornwall. The French and Italians may also have brought it with them, for we now find it among all the European immigrant groups who settled in rural areas, as well as among Negroes who presumably borrowed it from white settlers in the South.

Like almost every other aspect of water witching, its history, too, is controversial. Many claim that the practice goes back 7000 years, and cite the Biblical story in which Moses strikes the rock with his rod and water gushes forth. Indeed, we have been told by several American diviners that Moses was the first water witch. Scythians, Persians, Greeks, and Romans used rods for divination, and Mediterranean idols bearing forked rods have been found, but there is no evidence that these rods were used for divining water, particularly since in the detailed directions for finding water given by many ancient naturalists such as Pliny, there is no mention of anything akin to the divining rod.

The first unambiguous account of water witching occurs in *De Re Metallica*, an account of German mining by Georgius Agricola, published in 1556. His description of the ritual might equally well be used to describe the ritual as currently practiced in America. Water witching is unknown among indigenous populations elsewhere in the world; it seems safe to conclude that we are dealing with a European culture pattern that originated in Germany, spread to the rest of Europe, and thence to other regions as Europeans established colonies and spread their culture to other parts of the world.

The variations from standard practice to be found in America, usually involving the shape of the rod or the material used, are all of European origin, and are described in the earliest accounts. Even "long distance" witching above a map as practiced by the famous American diviner, Henry Gross, is a European importation. The only distinctively American contribution is the term, "water witching." In England it is called "dowsing," in the Latin countries, "divining," and in Germany, "wishing" or "striking." In more than 78 percent of the counties in our sample, the term "water witching" is predominant, while "dowsing" is current only in the New England states, New York, and Pennsylvania. The quasi-scientific terms which are widely used in Europe—"radiesthesia," "dryptesthesia," or "rhabdomancy"— are apparently unknown to the American farmer.

TOOLS OF THE TRADE

From Agricola's time in the sixteenth century until today, the diviner's trademark has been the forked twig or branch. Our data reveal that the forked twig is still by far the most frequently used instrument of American diviners. But even in Agricola's time there were variations. Instead of hazel, ash, or pitch-pine twig, the rod might be of iron or steel; indeed it appears that any rod-like object, forked or not, can serve; walking sticks, surgical scissors, a stalk of grass, and even a German sausage have been pressed into service as divining rods.

We encounter this same diversity in contemporary American practice. Although reports from early colonial days tell us that the witch-hazel twig was the most popular form of rod (indeed, some writers believe that the American term, "witching," originated with the use of the witch-hazel), only two counties in our sample reported hazel of any kind as being commonly used for a divining rod. By far the single most popular tree from which rods are obtained in this country is the peach tree; second in popularity is willow; less popular varieties are cherry, apple (mostly in New England), elm, and in the deep South, persimmon trees. Other trees mentioned only once or twice are hickory, plum, pear, elder, birch, and maple. One informant told us that when nothing else is handy, he has found that poison oak will do!

In arid regions where trees are scarce, wire is used—baling wire, barbed wire from the nearest fence, and coat hangers—or metal tools such as welding rods, tire irons, crow bars, steel files, or pliers. But almost anything will serve in the never-ending quest for water. Our respondents listed horse whips, shovels, pitchforks, and such commercial gadgets as a pair of swiveling rods; the latter is used by the water department of a large New England city to trace leaks in the water mains.

An alternative to the conventional wood or metal rod is the magic pendulum which has a far longer recorded history than has the divining rod. The ancient Romans studied the gyrations of a weight suspended on a thread from their fingers to discover who would win a forthcoming battle or succeed the current emperor. The pendulum was assimilated to water divining, more often to supplement than to replace the information from the forked twig. Today, the American diviner asks the pendulum to tell him how deep he will have to drill before he strikes water. Almost anything can be used as the pendulum: a set of keys suspended from a Bible, a watch attached to a chain or a string, a spool suspended on strands of thread, a penny attached to a wire, or a bottle filled with quicksilver or water suspended on a string.

WHO ARE THE WITCHES?

The folklore of water witching suggests that witches are born, not made. The most frequently-recurring statements contain the belief that the "power" is inherited—"from father to son or daughter," "from mother to daughter," "to one person in a family," or even "to the seventh son of a seventh son." A related belief is that only certain people can be witches; "if you have the gift, you can do it."

Many of our informants assured us that only men have the power. In the Ozarks, for example, this belief is associated with sexual virility. "A feller has got to be a whole man," one old gentleman said, "if he aims to take up witch wrigglin'." But although it is true that the vast majority of witches are men, women diviners are by no means uncommon. Of the counties in our sample in which there were diviners, as many as 42 percent reported that at least one of the diviners is a woman.

Our data indicate that age has little to do with the "power," although about 78 percent of the counties with diviners report that at least one is more than 65 years old, but only two percent reported any knowledge of diviners under the age of 15. As far as we can tell, however, the rod works just as well for children as it does for adults. It is likely that most witches are adult males simply because the opportunity and the need to practice divining is presented much more frequently to this segment of the population.

Among academic skeptics, water witching is apt to be dismissed as being practiced only by the uneducated, and at first sight our data seemed to bear this out, for in about 66 percent of the counties with diviners it was reported that the average diviner has only a grade-school education or less. But the exceptions are impressive. As many as 30 percent of the counties in our sample reported that the average diviner has a high-school education, and no fewer than three percent reported diviners who had received a college education. When we consider that the need for witching occurs mainly in rural areas, and that rural areas as a whole have lower educational levels, it is evident that the witch, by and large, is as well educated as the average man in his community. We know personally many highly educated men, including some with M.D.'s and Ph.D.'s, who both believe in and practice water witching.

Our data on the religious and ethnic background of diviners show that the majority are Protestant; only half as many are Catholic. The most common ethnic designation is "Old American," followed by German, Scandinavian, Negro, and American Indian, in that order. When we compared this information with published census data on the counties in which the diviners practice, we found that the ethnic composition of the water witches almost exactly parallels that of the surrounding population.

In the overwhelming majority of cases, witching is not practiced as a livelihood. Of the approximately 25,000 witches in the United States, probably only a handful try to make a full-time living from divining; for the typical diviner, witching is an avocation —a use of his gift to help a neighbor in need. True, he may charge a certain amount for his services, but it is likely to be a token fee, typically about $25.

"IT DOES MOVE"

We might expect that a practice with so long a history as witching would be accompanied by an elaborate folklore containing "explanations" of how it works, and rationalizations to account for failures. And indeed such a folklore does exist, mostly borrowed from Europe. But while the European folklore is rich and its theories elaborate, much of it has been shed by the practical-minded American.

If we ask an American diviner to explain why the rod moves, he shrugs his shoulders and says "I don't know, it just does." If we press him further or seek out other diviners we do get rationales, ranging from supernatural interpretations (for example, that they derive their power from Moses) to quasi-scientific interpretations (for example, that the muscles of the diviner are affected by electro-magnetic disturbances). An instance of this type of explanation was reported to us by a Harvard colleague. He was observing a diviner in action in northern New Hampshire. The diviner walked back and forth over a patch of land until the rod dipped straight down. The diviner then took one additional long step and said, "Dig here." Our colleague said to the diviner, "I understand what you are trying to do with this procedure, but why did you take that one extra step after the rod dipped?" The diviner replied, "Oh, I was just correctin' for the hypotenuse!"

To explain exactly how and why the rod moves in the diviner's hands would involve a complicated discussion of physics and psychophysics and of the kind of rod used and the way it is gripped. Here we will confine our discussion to the forked twig, held in the standard, palms-up grip—by far the most common mode of witching.

If you grip the forked twig—palms upward, one fork in each hand, the forks pointing forward at an angle of 45 degrees, hands compressed toward each other—you can cause the rod to move by any of four very slight changes of grip.

First, because the rod is so taut, an imperceptible easing of your grip will cause the rod to rotate in your hands.

Second, a slight rotation of your wrists toward each other will cause the rod to dip; rotating them outward will cause the rod to move upward. Depending upon how much the rod is compressed by the initial grip, a very slight rotation of the wrists can impart a considerable "kick" to the rod.

The third and fourth ways to produce movement consist of pulling your hands slightly apart or pushing them slightly together. Either movement creates greater tension in the rod than in the force of the grip. By so upsetting the balance, the rod, acting like a coiled spring, may straighten out with such force that the bark literally comes off in your hands.

In each case the movement occurs because forces and stresses in the rod become greater than the force by which the diviner grips the rod.

So far as we can tell, not one of the diviners with whom we are acquainted consciously makes the rod move. The same mechanical principles hold, however, whether or not the diviner is aware that he has changed his grip. From his point of view, the rod moves of its own accord. Indeed, so convincing is this experience, the diviner will swear the rod was moved by some outside force, and may insist that he was actually trying to keep it from moving. Such involuntary movements imparted to inanimate objects have tempted people throughout history to attribute these effects to supernatural forces. Belief in the Ouija board, the magic pendulum, table tipping, and in a variety of other bizarre manifestations testifies to this. These phenomena were explained more than 100 years ago by William Carpenter, who coined the term "ideo-motor action" to cover all manifestations of behavior that are independent of conscious volition. He observed that "Ideas may become the sources of muscular movement, independently either of volitions or of emotions." Carpenter was particularly referring to situations in which the ideas are suggested to the individual, or are the result of expectant attention, as in hypnosis or in the use of the Ouija board and the divining rod.

William James, the American psychologist, accepted Carpenter's concept of ideo-motor action not as a curious phenomenon, but as an important explanatory principle of all behavior, "simply the normal process stripped of disguise." According to James, the natural course of every idea is to manifest itself in overt action: "Wherever a movement *unhesitatingly and immediately* follows upon the idea of it, we have ideo-motor action. We are then aware of nothing between the conception and the execution. All sorts of neuro-muscular processes come between, of course, but we know absolutely nothing of them. We think the act, and it is done; and that is all that introspection tells us of the matter."

An attempt to apply this principle to water witching in terms of contemporary psychology would involve us in too much technical detail, but perhaps we can convey some idea by presenting a composite picture, pieced together from actual accounts, of an individual's first attempt at water witching.

Let us return to the beginning of this article where we encountered Judd Potter in the act of witching a well. Among the onlookers is Jim Brown. Jim has heard of witching, of course, but he has never tried it. As Jim watches Judd, we can assume that his intense concentration on Judd's movements is accompanied by very minute contractions in his forearms which correspond, on a smaller scale, to Judd's own muscular contractions. Perhaps Jim's neck muscles and general musculature are tense as he leans forward awaiting the outcome of the diviner's effort. Already the idea has been implanted. Suddenly, dramatically, the rod points downward.

Judd looks up and notices Jim's incredulous expression. He walks over to Jim, hands him the rod, and says, "Here, why don't you try it?" He assures Jim that the rod will work for him, too. Our knowledge of ideo-motor action and suggestibility tells us that Judd's suggestion to Jim again produces minute contractions in Jim's forearm muscles. This time, we would guess that the action potentials in the arms are even greater than the first time. Witnessing Judd's performance has enhanced Jim's susceptibility to the direct suggestion.

Jim grasps the rod in imitation of Judd. We see the same tense arms, the same trance-like concentration upon the rod, and we note that Jim becomes oblivious to the onlookers as his attention is completely focused upon the anticipated movement of the rod.

This heightened concentration and the increased tension in his muscles will facilitate the later muscular response; an impulse which under ordinary circumstances would not lead to overt muscular response, might then easily trigger a reaction in Jim's tense muscles. Furthermore, the heightened and prolonged tension is reducing the muscular feedback from his arms and hands; he is not aware that his muscles are "ready."

Now Jim is nearing the site where Judd's rod had dipped. His image of the rod's movement is intensified in the face of his expectation that it will move. The contractions in his forearms spread to adjoining muscle fibers; the minute contractions begin rallying together. Suddenly—in a great wave of unison—they produce a much larger muscular contraction. With an almost imperceptible spasm, his hands come closer together and his wrists turn slightly inward, upsetting the delicate balance of forces existing between his grip and the tensions in the rod. The rod suddenly springs downward with such force that the bark peels off, painfully scratching Jim's hands.

All at once Jim is aware that the rod has dipped—seemingly of its own accord—over the same spot where it had dipped for Judd. At first he is at a loss for words. Then he is overcome with a desire to explain to the onlookers that he did not make the rod move; that indeed, he was conscious only of an attempt to hold it back. He points to the peeled bark and his injured hands as proof. Jim has now entered the ranks of water diviners.

"BUT DOES IT WORK?"

The seemingly automatic, self-propelled motion of the rod is one of the many mysteries surrounding the ritual of water witching. When people ask of witching, "Does it work?" they often mean, "Does the rod move of its own accord?" But equally often they mean: "Are the rod's movements connected with the actual presence of underground water?" Is there something special about witching that makes it a better-than-chance method for finding water?

As you might guess, the evidence is sparse, of varied quality, and highly controversial. Most of it, especially that favorable to the case for divining, is drawn from anecdotes and case histories. Some, however, is derived from field tests which have been deliberately arranged to evaluate the diviner's claims. And although a field test provides better evidence than a case history, in that descriptions of what takes place are more objective, the results are usually inconclusive because there is seldom a base-line against which to evaluate the diviner's performance. In other words, a field test cannot be assessed scientifically unless we know what someone other than the diviner might have accomplished under the same conditions.

The only evidence that can properly be called scientific has been obtained from a handful of laboratory and field experiments which did provide an objective base-line. An excellent example is an experiment performed in Maine under the auspices of the American Society for Psychical Research. It is especially relevant since it was conducted by persons who were sympathetic or at least open-minded about the possibility that the claims of the diviners might be valid.

Twenty-seven diviners (22 men, 4 women, and 1 adolescent girl) were tested separately on a field chosen to be free of surface clues to water. Each used his own mode of witching to select the "best" spot for drilling a well, and was asked to estimate the depth at which water would be found, as well as the amount. Each was subjected to a second test, this time blindfolded to eliminate any visual clues.

As a control, the experimenters systematically selected 16 sites which covered the area in a representative manner. A geologist and an engineer were asked to estimate the depth and amount of water to be found at each of these sites. After the diviners had picked the "best" locations, test wells were sunk at each, and at the 16 sites assessed by the experts, and the depth and amount of water were measured. The experts did a good job of estimating the depth at the 16 specific points, but did poorly at estimating the amount. The diviners, on the other hand, failed completely to estimate either the depth or the amount of water at the locations they had selected.

The experimenters reported that "Not one of our diviners could for a moment be mistaken for an 'expert' . . . we saw nothing to challenge the prevailing view that we are dealing with unconscious muscular activity, or what Frederic Myers called 'motor automatism.' "

There is no need to cite the results of other investigations; indeed, we know of no acceptable laboratory experiment that supports the claims of believers. Both believers and skeptics agree that the most favorable evidence for diviners' claims is to be found in anecdotes and retrospective accounts, and that as we move closer and closer to the controlled experiment and the laboratory, there is less and less evidence that diviners possess any power to detect water.

But this is as far as the agreement goes. The skeptic, of course, interprets this as evidence against the validity of witching; it cannot be justified on the basis of scientific standards. The believer, on the other hand, attributes the failure to the inadequacies of the scientific approach; he claims that the witch produces "when it counts"—in his home environment, unhampered by the artificialities of scientific control and unhindered by skepticism.

THE DIVINER'S DEFENSE

These counterarguments are less a "rationale for failure," essential to the mythology of any magical ritual, than they are a "rationale for belief" that tends to avoid the problem of scientific confirmation. The following are representative of the arguments we encountered.

The "Test of Time" Argument

Solco Tromp, who attempted to justify water witching in terms of physical theory, wrote: "Nonetheless, undeterred by public ridicule, persistent generations of dowsers have upheld their belief for at least 7000 years, almost as long as civilization itself has existed.

This should suggest even to the most critical scientist that there may be some possibility of truth in the stories of diviners." Even if we overlook the fact that Tromp has added 6500 years to the known history of divining, longevity seems to be a poor substitute for scientific confirmation. This argument would call upon us to acknowledge the validity of such ancient practices as astrology, palmistry, and other forms of divination which still survive.

The "Core of Truth" Argument
Almost as frequently offered, and usually coupled with the first, is the proposition that even if individual cases for witching cannot be scientifically confirmed, taken together they must contain "a core of truth." That is, large numbers of positive outcomes, no matter how weak each one, must add up to something. This recalls an old Chinese saying, "If a thousand people say a foolish thing, it is still a foolish thing."

The "Testimonial" Argument
When we refuse to accept the first two arguments, the defense can be relied upon to offer the testimonials of famous men. In a 1962 article in *True* magazine, for example, Dan Mannix quotes the assertion of a Frenchman that divining "has also been endorsed by five Nobel prize winners." Although the five are not named, we know that Charles Richet, a French Nobel laureate, was an outspoken believer in witching. But we do not usually settle questions of scientific truth by a roll call. Even if we did, however, water witching would undoubtedly lose. For every prestigious figure who has endorsed it, there are a sizeable number of equally prestigious persons who have denounced it.

The "It would be a Good Thing for Mankind" Argument
"O.K.! So maybe the evidence at the moment is not scientific but by opposing water witching you may be impeding the development of something that might help mankind" is a typical introduction to this argument. Thus the novelist, Kenneth Roberts, responded to critics of his book on the divining prowess of Henry Gross "When, in *Henry Gross and His Dowsing Rod*, they [scientists who reject water witching] were brought face to face with the evidence of a clearly defined Seventh Sense, and were shown to be so closed-minded that they would sacrifice the welfare of the human race rather than admit they might just possibly be wrong, they grew almost incoherent in their furious contradictions."

In reply the scientist can only reiterate that he does not decide truth and falsity on the basis of desirability. Almost every major scientific boner—and there have been many—can be traced to a zealous desire to see the world as we think it should be rather than as it actually is.

The "Artificiality of the Scientific Conditions" Argument

Many of the arguments amount to a plea for special dispensation from the requirement that judgment be based on ordinary scientific standards. One version asserts that the diviner cannot perform well under scientific scrutiny because the controlled, laboratory-like conditions are artificial. Another version argue that the witching "powers" are so sensitive and delicate that they are adversely affected by the skeptical atmosphere characteristic of experimental inquiry. Tromp claims that "It is often the subconscious wish of many research workers to obtain a negative result." But the essence of scientific inquiry is doubt and questioning. The scientist cannot give his seal of approval to a phenomenon that is said to exist only when he is not looking!

We could list many variants of these arguments. They add up to an impregnable wall of defenses in which neither rational argument nor negative evidence can make a dent. This passionate clinging to conviction recalls the story of the psychiatric patient who believes that he is dead. The psychiatrist employs all the logic and psychological persuasiveness at his command to convince the patient that he is alive. But to no avail. Suddenly, the psychiatrist has an inspiration. "Tell me, do dead men bleed?" he asks. The patient carefully considers the question, then answers, "No, dead men do not bleed." The psychiatrist pricks the patient's finger with a needle. Blood oozes out. "Well, now what do you have to say for yourself?" the psychiatrist asks. The patient thoughtfully considers his bleeding finger for several moments and then says, "Well, by golly! I guess dead men do bleed after all!"

WITCHING AND THE QUESTION OF RATIONAL BEHAVIOR

When we conclude that water witching is a form of magic, we are tempted to conclude, also, that its use is a form of irrational behavior. This temptation should be resisted, for ritualistic and magical behavior is not necessarily irrational. Indeed, it can be argued that under some circumstances the resort to the diviner can be defended as a rational choice among available alternatives.

As current research and theory on choice-behavior and decision-making demonstrate, there is no universally accepted definition of rational behavior. Most models of rational decision-making, however, assume that the individual chooses the alternative that maximizes expected utility—or more colloquially, "gives him the best run for his money."

There are other models which prescribe somewhat different principles for choosing between alternatives. But for each of them it is easy to imagine circumstances in which the rational decision would be to call on the water witch, even though the decision-maker strongly doubts the validity of the practice. In general, such circumstances would involve the following: very inadequate scientific information about where to drill; the fact that, within limits, the diviner is not apt to create too much hardship by locating the well at an inconvenient site; and where there is some basis, no matter how slight, for believing that calling on a diviner may somewhat increase the chances of finding water.

When the farmer needs to find water as quickly as possible, he is likely to look for the most immediately accessible solution to his problem, even if it is of questionable validity, rather than search for a more valid solution that involves long delay and great effort.

Moreover, the valid, rational solutions offered by science—in the person of the geologist—are vague and nonspecific as compared with the clarity and authority emanating from the diviner. The geologist can only supply generalized information about the possibility of striking water; he qualifies his judgment; he cannot guarantee success; and he leaves to the farmer the task of pinpointing the actual spot at which to drill. But the rod's message is decisive and unambiguous. It says, "Dig here." And the diviner goes about his task with the certitude of blind faith.

It must be kept in mind, as well, that witching is most prevalent in areas where water is most difficult to find, where expert advice is unavailable, or where, because of unusual geological factors, the advice is inadequate. The farmer turns to the diviner because whether or not witching is invalid, the witch's judgment cannot be worse than his own. It is, under the circumstances, as rational a decision as any for he has nothing to lose. As an Iowa respondent wrote, "Not too many have faith in witching, but use it in the absence of any other method of locating water." And as another respondent in Nebraska put it, "Farmers drilling an irrigation well feel that the $5 to $25 fee is so small compared to the $3,000 to $15,000 investment that they do it even though they aren't sold on it."

Rarely, if ever, is the choice between witching *or* science. Often the choice must be made between witching or no help at all. Most frequently, though, the choice is to use the best expert advice *plus* witching. Like magical ritual in primitive societies, witching is practiced mainly in circumstances where current scientific and rational procedures are of no avail.

Thus, although water witching may be a type of magic, recourse to it is not only understandable, but is defensible from a psychological standpoint. Because the decision to drill a well is highly important and calls for immediate action, it may be *psychologically* rational to choose an immediately available solution that provides specific guidance, reduces ambiguity, supplies emotional reassurance, and permits decisive action in a situation of anxiety and stress.

From the point of view of the individual who has to make a choice, there can be no rational rule for selecting among alternatives if there is no empirically or scientifically valid information upon which to base a decision. Magic is not always a substitute for or an alternative to science; as Malinowski said, it may be "the outgrowth of a clear recognition that science has its limits and that a human mind and human skill are at times impotent."

CHAPTER

Suicide, Suicide Attempts, and Weather

ALEX D. POKORNY
FRED DAVIS
WAYNE HARBERSON

Reprinted from *The American Journal of Psychiatry* 120, no. 4 (October, 1963): 371–88, by permission of The American Psychiatric Association and the authors. Copyright 1963 by the American Psychiatric Association.

Read at the 119th meeting of The American Psychiatric Association, St. Louis, Missouri, May 6–10, 1963.

A powerfully attractive notion is the apparent relationship between the weather and emotional disturbance, especially suicides. Nearly every facet of our weather has been considered as a factor accounting for the incidence of suicide. The authors of the following paper, however, found the occurrence of both suicide attempts and suicides to be unrelated to cloudiness, temperature, wind speed, wind direction, barometric pressure, relative humidity, visibility, ceiling height, rain, fog, and thunderstorms. Even the increasing use of air conditioners appears to have little effect.

We might ask, if it has been shown that the weather is unrelated to suicide, why is the belief that it is so widespread and persistent? A review of past studies suggests that researchers did not employ the rigorous, appropriate methodology to adequately test for the relationship. This is a good example of a reluctance to shed an illusion, but why? Could it be that in an effort to better understand the phenomenon of suicide we have, once again, continued searching for explanations external to the self rather than exploring the factors within? Is it analogous to the popular belief in astrology?

Special attention should be given to the extended analysis of data, as demonstrated in this study and its consequences. As the reader will note, Pokorny, Davis, and Harberson would have reached quite different conclusions had they merely accepted their initial analysis of selected weather variables for *only* those hours in which a suicide or suicide attempt occurred. It was because they went further and compared the *distribution* of a selected weather characteristic for the year to the *distribution* of a suicide or suicide attempt for the year, that they discovered the *lack* of association between the two patterns.

There is a large body of literature, both technical and popular, which holds that there are causal relationships between weather and affective states, even pathological mood deviations. It is further claimed that weather and physical environment influence suicide rates. Most authorities today appear to view such claims with skepticism, but these statements keep recurring in various contexts. The present study was designed to put such ideas to a definitive test. We felt it should be possible to demonstrate siginificant relationships if they are there, and to refute them clearly if they are absent. Thus at least one distracting factor could be cleared away in the exploration and clarification of this important aspect of human behavior.

Review of Literature

Seasonal variations in suicide rates are mentioned by many observers. Such variations are usually explained as due to weather changes. There is fairly general agreement that rates are highest in late spring or early summer (Curtin, 1909; Durkheim, 1951; Miner, 1922; Petersen, 1934; Sainsbury, 1955; Vidoni, 1925).

Farberow and Shneidman (1961), with far better data than any of the previous authors cited, do not find any *significant* variations in suicidal phenomena by month. Stengel and Cook (1958) report that all but one of their 5 subgroups of suicide attempts show a fairly marked peak—in one of the spring months. (However, when we total their 5 subgroups, the monthly totals even out.)

Durkheim (1951) considers that there is a perfect continuity of the curve (increasing from winter to summer), which would tend to eliminate weather fluctuations as the cause; rather, he considers the important factor to be the *length of the day*, increasing the time during which social factors are at work.

The apparent effect of *latitude* is mentioned by Durkheim (1951), quoting Morselli; the area of Central Europe had the highest rates, shading off in both directions; Durkheim does not accept that climate is the cause of this. Curtin (1909) also states that suicide is more common in temperate climates than in very hot or very cold regions. Mills (1934) says that the higher rates of suicide in the North may be due to "mental exhaustion" in the more rigorous climate.

The effect of *cyclonic storms* and *passage* of fronts in increasing the rates of suicide is discussed by several writers (Curtin, 1909; Tholuck, 1942). Mills (1934) and Petersen (1934) are leading American proponents of this view, Smith (1908), in a subjective report, states that he can predict fronts by onset of his own feelings of depression; he considers this to be related to suicide at such periods.

Barometric pressure has been implicated in our different ways. It is alleged that suicide rates are highest during stable high pressure (Blumer, 1945), or during falling pressure (Mills, 1934), or during low pressure (Dexter, 1900). Finally one study (Tholuck, 1942) finds that there is no significant relationship.

High humidity is linked to high suicide rates by Dexter (1900). Tholuck (1942) does not find any significant relationship.

Rain and *precipitation* are mentioned by several authors. Curtin (1909) says that suicide rates are low when precipitation is the greatest. Miner (1922) finds a small negative correlation between mean precipitation and suicide. Dexter (1900) says that suicide rates are lowest on wet, partly cloudy days. Tholuck (1942) finds no significant relationship to rain.

Cloudiness or sunny conditions are mentioned by Tholuck (1942) as unrelated to suicide, though Dexter (1900) states that rates are lower on cloudy days.

Wind velocity is mentioned by Curtin (1909), who considers that suicide and other violence increases with mild winds but decreases if winds are more intense. Dexter (1900) says that suicides increase with wind speed.

Hot weather increases suicide rates according to Curtin (1909). Mills (1934) also says that suicide rates vary directly with temperature. Miner (1922) does not find that temperature is correlated with suicide rate. Many authors advance temperature as an explanation of their observed seasonal variation. Tholuck (1942) finds no significant relationship to temperature.

Many of the supposed relationships advanced are complex, involving several variables. For example, Curtin (1909) says that in India young females are more suicide prone during highest temperatures! Petersen's (1934) theories are of this nature; he holds that when pyknics are alkaline (as during cold fronts) they are irritable, whereas when leptosomes are acid (during warm fronts) they are morose and blue. It should be apparent that some of these complicated ideas are difficult to put to the test.

A rather different theme mentioned by several authors is that good weather is associated with increased suicide. Durkheim (1951) says, "Neither in winter nor in autumn does suicide reach its maximum, but during the fine season when nature is most smiling and the temperature mildest." Curtin (1909) and Dexter (1900) state similar beliefs.

In general, most of the articles on weather, climate, and suicide are speculative and seem to be based on crude data and coarse time intervals. The authors quote each other's statements, findings, and assertions endlessly, with little attempt to control for other factors. These criticisms are less applicable to the recent articles.

METHODS AND RESULTS

Data

All cases of suicide and suicide attempts reported to the Houston Police Department (1) during 1960 were abstracted. We accepted the decision of the Police Department regarding the ruling of suicide or attempted suicide in all but a very few doubtful cases. Each of the 91 suicides and 400 suicide attempts was then reviewed to establish the time of the act. If this could not be localized within a period of 3 hours or less, the case was excluded. The final list studied consisted of 67 suicides and 373 suicide attempts. In the large majority of cases, the time of the act could be established fairly sharply. The hour which was nearest the midpoint of the probable time of occurrence was then set as the "hour" of the suicide or suicide attempt.

The weather data were obtained from the published hourly U.S. Weather Bureau reports for the Houston Airport Station. These data were also made available on punched cards, one for each hour, or 8784 cards for the (leap) year.

A. Detailed (hourly) study of eleven weather variables. From the large number of weather and climatological items reported for each hour, we selected 11 variables for study. This was done on logical grounds and because these variables had been mentioned in the literature. They were (1) Dry bulb temperature; (2) Windspeed; (3) Wind direction; (4) Barometric pressure; (5) Relative humidity; (6) Visibility; (7) Ceiling height; (8) Rain; (9) Fog; (10) Thunderstorms; and (11) Cloudiness. Each of these was reported in steps along a scale (e.g. percent of humidity, degrees of temperature). We first studied each of these variables for only those hours in which a suicide or, separately, a suicide attempt occurred. This led to some striking and seemingly significant findings. However, it must be recognized that during an entire time interval, such as a year, a particular weather variable will not be evenly distributed over its scale; it will be bunched, skewed, etc. It is likely that the hours during which suicides or suicide attempts occur would, purely by chance, show a similarly bunched or skewed distribution. Therefore one cannot make any valid assertions about relation of suicidal behavior to a weather variable without taking into consideration the actual yearly distribution of that variable.

When this was done with our data, the seeming relationships disappeared. For proper evaluation, we had to "partial out" that portion of the correlation that was due to the fact that there were more hours of the year at certain steps or values of the variable.

The first two columns in Table 1 show the high apparent correlations when the suicides or suicide attempts are simply correlated with the weather variable. The last two columns show how all of these become insignificant when the influence of the uneven hourly distribution for the year was "partialled out."

		APPARENT CORRELATION WITH		TRUE CORRELATION WITH	
		SUICIDE	SUICIDE ATTEMPT	SUICIDE	SUICIDE ATTEMPT
1.	Temperature	.25	.41	.07	.20
2.	Wind speed	—.54	—.63	.22	.20
3.	Wind direction	−.93*	−.78*	−.08*	.41*
4.	Barometric pressure	.11	.16	−.03	−.05
5.	Relative humidity	.51	.63	.10	.06
6.	Visibility	.58	.65	−.01	−.13
7.	Ceiling height	.25	.18	.01	.18
8.	Rain	−.52	−.48	−.12	.02
9.	Fog	−.86	−.88	.17	−.15
10.	Thunderstorms	−1.00**	−.98	0.00	0.02
11.	Cloudiness	−0.39	−0.52	0.33	−0.24

Table 1

* These values may be spurious, in that the complete circle of wind directions was arbitrarily split and converted to a linear scale. For this variable, our chi square was more appropriate; it showed no significant relationship.
** This maximally high correlation was due to the complete absence of thunderstorms during the 67 hours of suicides.

The data were also handled graphically, by plotting the total hourly readings for the year on each weather variable, and then superimposing the readings for those hours in which suicides and suicide attempts occurred. In all cases these three gave very similar curves as is illustrated in Figures 1, 2, and 3.

In each Figure the scale along the baseline represents the steps or intervals of the weather variable. The dot line, with its appropriate scale on the left, represents the distribution of all the hours of the year. The X and O lines, with their scale on the right, represent the suicide and suicide attempt hours' distribution on this weather variable.

In addition to the method of partial correlations, a chi square value was calculated for each weather variable. None of these 22 values showed any significant deviation from chance.

B. Month and season. For this evaluation we used the entire group of 400 suicide attempts and 91 suicides. There was no significant relation of month of year or of season with either suicide or suicide attempts. To check this more fully, we obtained data on the

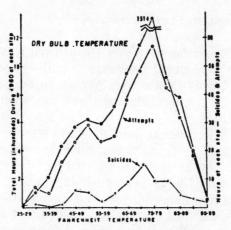

Figure 1. *Temperature Values for Hours of Suicides, of Suicide Attempts, and of Total Hours of Year*

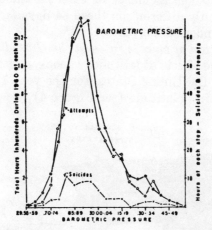

Figure 2. *Barometric Pressure Values for Hours of Suicides, of Suicide Attempts, and of Total Hours of Year*

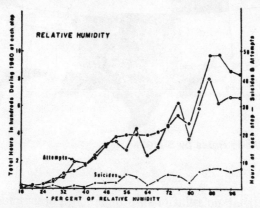

Figure 3. *Relative Humidity Values for Hours of Suicides, of Suicide Attempts, and of Total Hours of Year*

entire State of Texas for the years 1956 through 1961. Each year considered separately would show some month-by-month variation. However, when the five years were plotted on the same graph, the ups and downs did not coincide and there was no clean, repetitive seasonal distribution.

C. *Fronts*. The weather data for 1960 were next studied for passage of fronts. Twenty-eight recognizable northerly cool fronts were identified. The 28 days on which these fronts passed were then compared with the 28 preceding days and the 28 following days, in terms of how many suicides and suicide attempts occurred. The numbers were almost exactly the same (4, 4, 4 suicides; 27, 27, 25 suicide attempts). These days were then lumped together into 84 days of presumably turbulent or changeable weather related to passage of fronts. The incidence of suicides and suicide attempts was not significantly different on these 84 days from the incidence during the remainder of the year.

D. *Distribution of suicide rates in the United States*. In an attempt to check the effects of latitude, we looked at the crude suicide rates for each of the United States, for the year 1959. There is no visible relationship to latitude (see Figure 4).

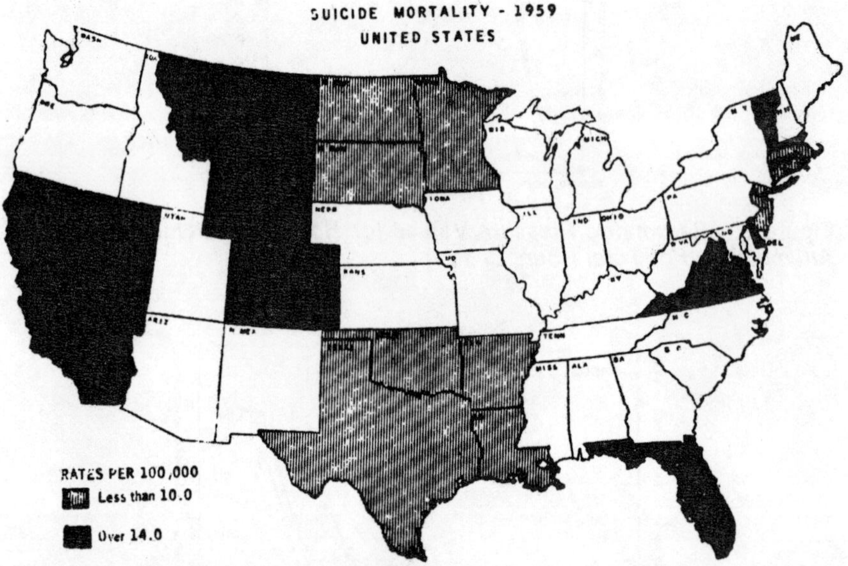

Figure 4.   *Suicide Rates by States*

DISCUSSION

It is evident that no relationship of suicide or suicide attempts to any weather variable was found. It seems likely to us that the many claims and alleged findings in the literature are based on poor, inaccurate data. We have demonstrated that many seeming relationships evaporate when one takes into consideration the very uneven distribution of weather conditions throughout a year; the hours of suicides and suicide attempts turn out to be fairly typical samples of the hours of the year.

It might be claimed that we failed to demonstrate seasonal or monthly changes because of mild weather in Houston. The same might be said of the similar negative findings of Farberow and Shneidman in Los Angeles County. However, any resident of Texas will acknowledge that we have a highly changeable and strenuous climate.

A question might also be raised concerning the possible influence of widespread air conditioning, in lessening the formerly-noted effects of weather. The data for Texas for the years 1949 through 1961 do not show any decrease in adjusted suicide rates (range of 7.5 to 9.4/100,000/yr) (1963). Yet during these 12 years there was a rapid spread in use of air conditioning in the state.

Of course it is a commonplace observation that weather affects how we feel, in the sense of "exhilarating," "gloomy," "oppressive," "bright," "dismal," etc., days. Such mild, "normal" mood responses to weather conditions are a far cry quantitatively from the degree of mental upheaval that is associated with suicide; there may also be a qualitative difference.

SUMMARY

The 67 suicides and 373 suicide attempts occurring in Houston in 1960, in which the time of occurrence could be established, were studied in terms of weather conditions at time of their occurrence. Eleven weather variables (temperature, wind speed, wind direction, barometric pressure, relative humidity, visibility, ceiling height, rain, fog, thunderstorms, and cloudiness) were studied. The distribution of each for all hours of the year was obtained, and this was compared with the distribution during those hours in which a suicide or suicide attempt occurred. No single significant relationship was found. The 28 northerly fronts of 1960 were not found to be associated with any change in rate of suicide or suicide attempts. Month and season likewise showed no significant relationship. It is concluded that suicide and suicide attempts are not significantly related to weather phenomena.

NOTE

1. We are indebted to Inspector Larry W. Fultz, Records Division, Houston Police Department, for his helpfulness and cooperation.

BIBLIOGRAPHY

S. Blumer, *Gesundht. Wohlft.* 25 (1945) : 89.

R. G. Curtin, *Trans. Am. Clin. Climat. Ass.* 25 (1909) : 141.

E. G. Dexter, *Pop. Sci. Mon.* 58 (1900) : 604.

E. Durkheim, *Suicide* (Glencoe, Ill.: Free Press, 1951).

N. L. Farberow and E. S. Shneidman, *The Cry for Help* (New York: McGraw-Hill, 1961).

C. H. Hughes, *Alien Neurol.* 30 (1909) : 634.

C. A. Mills, *Am. J. Psychiat.* 91 (1934) : 669.

J. R. Miner, *Am. J. Hyg. Monogr. Ser. No. 2* (1922) : 1.

Personal Communication, Records and Statistics Section, Texas State Dept. of Health, Austin, Texas, 1963.

W. F. Petersen, *The Patient and the Weather*, Vol. 3 (Ann Arbor, Mich.: Edwards Bros., 1934).

———, *Man, Weather* (Springfield, Ill.: C. C. Thomas, 1947).

W. F. R. Phillips, *Trans. Am. Clin. Climat. Ass.* 25 (1909) : 156.

P. Sainsbury, *Suicide in London* (London: Chapman and Hall, 1955).

F. H. Smith, *Lancet, 2* (1908) : 837.

E. Stengel and N. G. Cook, *Attempted Suicide* (London: Chapman and Hall, 1958).

H. J. Tholuck, *Beitr. Gerichtl. Med.* 16 (1942) : 121.

U.S. Department of Commerce, Weather Bureau, Hourly and Monthly Climatological Data, Houston, Texas, International Airport, 1960.

G. Vidoni, *Manicomio* 38 (1925) : 107.

IUPUI
UNIVERSITY LIBRARIES
COLUMBUS CENTER
COLUMBUS, IN 47201

3 0000 025 310 271

GF 41 .S55
Sims, John H., 1930-
Human behavior and the
 environment